IMAGINE

IMAGINE

WHAT AMERICA COULD BE IN THE 21ST CENTURY

*Visions of a Better Future
from Leading American Thinkers*

EDITED BY

MARIANNE WILLIAMSON

PHOTOGRAPHS BY JOSEPH SOHM

New American Library

NEW AMERICAN LIBRARY
Published by New American Library, a division of
Penguin Putnam Inc., 375 Hudson Street, New York, New York 10014, U.S.A.
Penguin Books Ltd, 80 Strand, London WC2R ORL, England
Penguin Books Australia Ltd, Ringwood, Victoria, Australia
Penguin Books Canada Ltd, 10 Alcorn Avenue, Toronto, Ontario, Canada M4V 3B2
Penguin Books (N.Z.) Ltd, 182–190 Wairau Road, Auckland 10, New Zealand

Penguin Books Ltd, Registered Offices: Harmondsworth, Middlesex, England

Published by New American Library, a division of Penguin Putnam Inc. This is an authorized reprint of the hardcover edition published by Daybreak, an imprint of Rodale Books. For further information, contact Rodale Press, 33 East Minor Street, Emmaus, PA 18098.

First New American Library Printing, November 2001
10 9 8 7 6 5 4 3 2 1

"Reviving Our Passion" by Sarah Ban Breathnach originally appeared in *250 Ways to Make America Better* (from the editors of *George* magazine). Villard Books, 1999.
"Citizenship" by Paul Rogat Loeb is adapted from *Soul of a Citizen: Living with Conviction in a Cynical Time*. St. Martin's Press, 1999.
All other essays in this volume were written expressly for *Imagine*. Grateful acknowledgment is made to each essayist for permission to include his or her work.

New American Library Trade Paperback ISBN: 0-451-20469-7

The hardcover edition of this book has been catalogued by the Library of Congress as follows:
    Imagine : what America could be in the 21st century / edited by Marianne Williamson; photographs by Joseph Sohm.
        p.   cm.
    ISBN 1–57954–302–2 hardcover
    1. United States—Civilization—21st century—Forecasting.   2. United States—Social conditions—21st century—Forecasting.   3. National characteristics, American.
4. Conduct of life.   5. Twenty-first century—Forecasts.   I. Williamson, Marianne, date.
II. Title.
E169.12.I38   2000
303.4973—dc21   00–010547

Cover and Interior designer: Joanna Williams

Printed in the United States of America

Contents

Acknowledgments

Having written several books, I had never had the job of editor before doing this project. I now have a new appreciation of the role. From the beginning, I was blessed with the partnership of Neil Wertheimer and his team at Rodale, who both understood the vision of the book and had the talent and ability to bring it to fruition. Without Neil and his unique brand of talent, this book could not possibly exist. I have never known an editor with greater dedication or skill.

Literary agent Al Lowman donated his services from the beginning of this project, continuing to support it well through publication. I deeply thank him for being there for me one more time.

At the beginning of this project, I did as I often do when I'm at a loss: I called Jean Houston for advice. She suggested the names of many of the people whose essays appear in this book, giving generously of both her time and her contacts. Thank you, Jean.

I'm also very grateful to Betty Appleby for her ideas and efforts early in the process, Thom Mulderick at Rodale for his publicity efforts and genuine enthusiasm, Joanna Williams for the lovely cover and interior design, Chris Potash for the unenviable job of copyediting so many different voices, and James Gallucci for his photo editing.

The concept for this book came from Joseph Sohm, its photographer. His genuine love of this country and his unshakeable faith in both the glory of our history and the possibilities for our future have been a primary thread of inspiration throughout.

My deepest gratitude, of course, goes to the authors who wrote these essays. Each of them gave with a very generous heart, and my greatest desire is that they all feel satisfied with the result. They participated in the creation of a collective vision that gives everyone, I think, more reason to hope.

—*Marianne Williamson*

Foreword

Anne Lamott

Who was it who said that in our acts of goodness and conviction, we are planting shade trees for grandchildren who have not yet been born? I'm not sure, but I remembered the line while reading the book before you. In these essays, I think you'll find ways to help provide shade, rest, fruit, community, and hope—now, and as the new century unfolds.

Whatever your field of interest or accomplishment—education, caregiving, law, ecology, business—there's something in this book that will help you recommit to the work before us, which is to help love the planet back to health: to feed her, care for her, esteem her people, and heal the decades of abuse we've heaped upon her. These essays offer an assessment of the problems, and they also offer solutions, direction, and light. The problem in almost all fields is the same, which is that things seem too far gone, too out of balance. There's a lack of hope; an overwhelming sense that things can't be reversed. It's like our Earth is a formerly beautiful orchard, but one where, through pollution and politics, greed, and laziness, nothing much has grown for years. The soil has been damaged by pesticides and overplanting or neglect. No one who could get the orchard back on its metaphorical feet is speaking to anyone else; and there are so many tangled vines, weeds, debris, and so much rot and infestation, that no one knows where to begin. But there have always been, and always will be, people who don't give up, who see what could be and how to bring that forth. This book offers everyone a place to begin, a section of the orchard where they might push back their sleeves and get to work.

Whenever I travel, the same cabdriver always drives me to the airport, and he has always been reading too many newspapers, so he is always worried. He is worried because the headlines frighten and overwhelm him and everything seems awful and out of control and very foreign and as if it is all deteriorating at an escalated rate in a language he does not understand. He cites the latest stories on random violence, pollution, famine, searing injustice. Yes, I always agree; things can be pretty scary these days. It's not the sleepy pastoral pastel view through a nice hard-sugar Easter egg.

"What do you God people think of all this?"

"We think that there are a lot of people who need a hand."

He mutters, "Yeah yeah yeah." Then he asks what I will be discussing in my next speech, and when I tell him—writing, or faith, or motherhood—he says, "Oh, can't talk about that. Talk about what we should do."

"Do something," I said one time. "Blame no one, and do something."

The problems can mesmerize us, like cobra hypnosis, so people sway, enthralled by the magnitude of what would need to be done or changed if we are to be saved. Many people who have given up trying to help or serve have withdrawn instead into the cocoon of comfort, fixing old buildings or their thighs, for instance, because they can be fixed or improved; pumping up pecs and porches and portfolios.

But this doesn't reduce the underlying fear. It's just distracting. Love and service decrease the fear, and even sometimes change it into joy.

And people are afraid. I'm afraid quite often; my child is afraid. Like the rest of us, he's afraid because he thinks scary thoughts. Late at night, he thinks about the ozone, global warming, worldwide famine.

"It's hopeless," he cries. "What are we supposed to do?"

We're supposed to do what people of conscience and heart and hope have always tried to do. We're supposed to try and save the world. Make the world safer for the children, a little bit sweeter. We're suppose to try and help add some oxygen to the pool of our being and help reduce the grut. You and me and our friends. That's our assignment. "Yeah, right," my bitter little child responds. "Where would we even start?"

We start where we are. And we try to do what Sarah Ban Breathnach suggests in her essay—help return "a portion of the world's lost heart." I think that we're supposed to do what Sam Daley-Harris proposes in his essay, to leave the campsite of Earth cleaner than it was.

I remember Marianne Williamson saying somewhere that Americans are not starving for what they don't have but rather for what they won't give. This book is a collection of essays encouraging and directing us in how to give, how to serve. We all secretly know that giving is the only way to fill up, that it's the only way home. We're not going to be able to buy, rent, lease, or date something or someone who will fill up the Swiss cheesy parts of our souls, or help us deal with what's happened to our beautiful orchard, Earth. We're going to have to get to work. And some days will go better than others. Some days, we will see results, will uncover patches of soil from under the weeds and tangles and garbage, and then add enzymes and nutrients to the rich black earth, and then plant, knowing that something beautiful will grow. Other days, we're just going to feel confused and overwhelmed by how much there is to do, and we'll have lots of false starts and small failures and lose faith and try things that don't work, but that's how everything great gets grown. People like the authors of this book will be there, and they know we can bring the orchard back to health.

The people who've written these essays are some of our most exciting thinkers. They have visions, they have dreams, and they also have schemes and plans for implementing their visions. They are scientists, philosophers, and storytellers, all with a common sense of both urgency and tenderness, and their words contain the potential to help us start moving as a community. I was reminded after finishing this book of something I've seen year after year at the Special Olympics: trainers and friends who are there when the athletes fall or get all turned around; people who step in, reach down, lend a hand, whisper encouragement, help them get to their feet and pointed in the right direction again.

There are pages and thoughts and quotes here that you may want to tape to your wall, to remind you of who and whose you really are; there are pages you'll fax to friends who desperately want to help but are feeling overwhelmed like my cabbie. There are essays on how in the face of such global stress we can find peace and freedom and extend the chance for peace and freedom to others. There are essays on education, on restorative justice, on science. There are lines I came upon that made me laugh, and I tell you, laughter is the most hydrating gift of life. I got spritzed back to presence, too. For instance, Sam Daley-Harris relates an anonymous quote in his piece: "Be outrageous. It's the only place that isn't crowded." I read that line on a plane, and right there, 8 miles up, I got outrageous. I bonded with the right-wing commodities broker in the next seat, and then ministered to the flight attendant. She was very depressed. She got outrageous. Toni Morrison said that the function of freedom is to free someone else, and I would say the same of getting outrageous, getting a second wind, getting committed.

So come on in to the orchard. There is much to do: harrowing, tilling, planting, weeding, watering, reaping. Let not your hearts be troubled; or let them be troubled and then take a deep breath and let someone in the orchard help you figure out how to help and where to begin. There is a lot for everyone to do, and that is the good news and the truth. The truth is not that there are too many people now to feed. The truth is not that that corn and wild berries used to be sweeter, or the ground easier to plow. Hope—that is not the truth. The truth is that loving service will save us and the Earth. Joy is the truth. Peace is the truth. My pastor's mother used to say, "Peace is joy at rest. Joy is peace standing on its feet." So come on in; grow some peace with us. Grow some joy.

★★★

Anne Lamott is the author of many best-selling spirituality books, including *Traveling Mercies*, *Operating Instructions*, and *Crooked Little Heart*.

Introduction

Marianne Williamson

I once sat watching television with a friend while President Clinton exhorted us to build a bridge to the future.

"He's building a bridge to the future," mused my friend, "but are we really so sure we want to go there?"

I laughed when she said that, not only at her quirky humor but at her inimitable way of conveying a deeper truth that so often underlies a less serious one. The future is upon us, that's true. But what it looks like, none of us is all too sure.

I believe, as do most people I know, that beneath the economic giddiness and technological wizardry of America today, there is an underground psychic river of nervous anticipation. The future does not seem as connected to the present as it once did. We feel that something big is about to happen, but none of us knows exactly what it is. Most significant of all, none of us can possibly know if this something is good or bad.

That is because the future is not fixed. The other side of the bridge to the future is not an objective, predetermined, static destination. In reality, it is a moveable object, a set of probabilities, and most important, a karmic consequence of the lives we lived yesterday and the lives we live today. The bridge to the future is a bridge that moves—and the land to which it is connected moves as well—according to how we walk across the bridge and who we are while we are walking.

Our thoughts about the future go far toward creating it; our minds and hearts are like filaments that connect today to tomorrow, they are conduits for either the status quo or the emergence of different, hopefully more loving, possibilities. How we think and how we behave determine where we are going.

Talmudic wisdom proclaims that over every blade of grass there stands an angel whispering, "Grow! Grow! Grow!" I believe that this extends to every moment as well. There are illumined thought forms that emanate from a divine source, guiding us, every moment, away from darkness and into light. The fact that we so often ignore these illuminations does not mean that they are not there. They are our thoughts of wisdom and conscience and love. They are our sense of goodness, the lure of becoming by which we are taken, though often kicking and screaming, in the direction of our healing. It is this illumined presence—in ourselves and others—that inspires us to hope. It carries the miraculous authority to reroute our bridges, individually and collectively, when the ones we have built are leading nowhere. That is because it has the authority to transform the human heart.

Some people are walking without a thought to where they're going; I did not ask them to write essays for this book. Some people are almost immobilized by fear of where we're headed; I hope that they will read this book. Some people imagine great light-filled possibilities ahead and work each day to invoke them; their words are what fill this book. This book is to be read during our collective bridge time. I believe that by illuminating higher possibilities for the future, the essays here have the power to help us create them.

America has no dearth of problems, but neither do we have a dearth of genius. I had a dream once of a long dining table, yards long, at which guests carried on animated, fascinating conversations with one another. I sat in on many of them, wide-eyed like a child, taking in all the exciting ideas flying around the table. People were talking about how the world could be and what it would take to create Heaven on Earth.

That dream, in a way, was the genesis of this book. Every essay was written by someone whose words, upon reading or hearing them, caused my eyes to grow wide with wonder. All of them have aroused in me a big "Yes, that's it! Imagine if we did that!"

We are living in extraordinary times, when old boundaries are melting, assumptions long sanctified are being fearlessly questioned, and mental boxes that had seemingly been made of steel are crumbling all around us. Ask someone in business about their quarterly earnings and they're liable to tell you about emotional factors affecting the workplace. Ask someone about their spiritual awakening, and they're liable to talk about extending their spiritual values into social activism. One simple thought now promises to transform Western civilization: At the deepest level, there is no separation between internal and external. All outer phenomena are mere reflections of consciousness, and there is no changing the external world without addressing internal factors. Knowing that our primary spiritual task is to love, the highest work of consciousness is to not only try to find our love but also extend it into the world.

Thus, in addressing the future of America, we have sought in this book to address issues of both personal, internal transformation as well as institutional, external change. At heart, they are not separate. Writing about our legal system, a law professor speaks of injecting love into the heart of it. Writing about religion, a theologian posits the value of a sacred sensibility in the functioning of our secular institutions. Our deepest understanding of the world today involves our recognition of the creative, yet often fragile, marriage between the inner and outer realms.

No one who has written for this book is naive about America's problems. But each one of these authors has seen at least part of a way past those problems and found a way to articulate the path for others. They have obviously thought and felt deeply about their areas of expertise and responded deeply to their own imaginations. What emerges is a compendium of possibilities for a future whose underpinning is not anxiety but a deep and abiding peace.

My questions to all the authors were the following: In the realm of highest possibilities, what could America look like in 50 years? What kinds of changes would have to occur in order for that to happen? How can an individual or an institution best contribute to such change? What is the deeper story trying to emerge within this nation and the world?

No one who wrote an essay for this book has a lot of time on their hands. They responded to this book project—which raises funds for a nonprofit organization dedicated to imagining and working toward a better world for our children and our children's children—because they are prepared to live by their own bottom-line message: that separately, we face almost inevitable darkness, while together, we face unimaginable light. In their taking the time to contribute their own unique and inspiring visions, they not only describe the bridge to a better future, but they actually walk it and, in so doing, model for all of us what it will take to bring it forth.

These authors gave their essays as a gift. With gratitude on behalf of myself and the Global Renaissance Alliance, I dedicate this book to each of them. I feel honored to call them colleagues and blessed to call them my friends. May the collective vision they have created here inspire each of us in our walk through life.

THE SOUL OF A NATION

POSSIBILITIES

Paul Hawken

We are beginning a mythic period of existence, rather like the age portrayed in the Bhagavad Gita or in other tales of darkness and light such as *The Lord of the Rings*. We live in a time in which every living system on Earth is in decline, and the rate of decline is accelerating as our economy grows. The commercial processes that bring us the kind of lives we supposedly desire are destroying the Earth and the life we cherish. Given current corporate practices, not one wildlife reserve, wilderness, or indigenous culture will survive the global market economy. We are losing our forests, fisheries, coral reefs, topsoil, water, biodiversity, and climatic stability. The land, sea, and air have been functionally transformed from life-supporting systems into repositories for waste.

Feeling the momentum of loss at the beginning of a new century, one wants to close one's eyes. Yet to close one's eyes is to do the very thing that will bring forth the fruits of ignorance. I believe in rain, in odd miracles, in the intelligence that allows terns and swallows to find their way across the Earth. And I believe that we are capable of creating a remarkable future for humankind. Although each American is causing damage to places and people we don't even know, each person also contains the basis for hope, because none of us individually wants what we are doing collectively. As Gandalf, the wise magician in *The Lord of the Rings*, said, although the storm is coming, the tide is turning. Just as there can be no courage without fear, hope arises in the face of hopelessness.

3

The possibility I imagine for America is that we will be able to see again. If you cannot read, books look like fuel for cooking. You may see a bird as gossamer and feathers, but it is also an extraordinarily powerful creator of forests and meadows, flying as it does with its small sac of undigested seeds. We can see the world as doomed and fatally flawed, or we can see every trend and statistic as a possibility of transformation. We can see ourselves as fortunate and separate from the suffering of others, or we can see that our bounty rests heavily on the shoulders of others. Concomitant with our good fortune is the responsibility to create a world of equals, not just a nation of equals.

If we were to do a quick inventory of where we are at the threshold of this new century, it would read something like this:

◆ Since 1950, we have lost one-third of all forests, one-fourth of our topsoil, and one-fifth of our farmland.
◆ Over the past 100 years, we have lost one-fourth of all species of plants and animals; at present rates, by the end of this century one-half of all species that live on Earth will be gone forever.
◆ In our oceans, two-thirds of the world's fisheries are overfished.
◆ In the past 150 years, we have raised carbon levels in the atmosphere by 30 percent.
◆ We usurp and divert 55 percent of all fresh-water flows.
◆ Two billion people live on less then $2 a day.
◆ Two billion people have no electricity and use firewood to cook.
◆ Two billion people lack sanitation, and 1.3 billion have no clean water.
◆ Nearly a billion people are severely malnourished or starving.

By the time we reach 2050, we will need to feed, clothe, house, and employ nearly twice the number of people that are on Earth today. We will need to provide for a new world.

We know that in America, 36 million live in poverty, including 14 million children; 27 million Americans are functionally illiterate; 40 million have no health insurance; and 300,000 are homeless. We have the highest rates of teen pregnancy, abortion, drug use, violence, and release of toxic materials of any industrial nation. Further, we have the world's largest prison population, exceeding both China's and the former Soviet Union's Gulag.

We need not turn away from such difficult information. It is a gift. Like birds carrying seeds, we can't necessarily digest this information. It is large and unfeeling and fearsome. But we can carry it with us in our quotidian ways, committed to making the small things in our lives different than they are today.

In his book *The Clock of the Long Now*, Stewart Brand discusses what makes a civilization resilient and adaptive. Scientists have studied the same question about ecosystems. How does a system—whether cultural, global, or natural—manage change, absorb shocks, and survive, especially when change is rapid? The answer has much to do with our use of time and our respect for it. Biological diversity in ecosystems buffers against sudden shifts because different organisms and elements fluctuate on different time scales—flowers, fungi, spiders, trees, and foxes all have different rates of change and response. Some respond quickly, others slowly, so that the system, when subjected to stress, can sway, give, and then return and be restored.

What we are witnessing in the world is a clash of chronologies or time frames. The dominant time frame today is commercial. Businesses are quick; they welcome innovation in general and have a bias for change. They are growing faster than ever before—or face punishment in the market if they are not. With worldwide capital mobility, companies and investments are rewarded or penalized instantly by a network of technocrats and money managers who move a couple of trillion dollars a day seeking the highest return on capital. The Internet, global communications, and high-speed transportation are all making businesses move quicker than ever before.

The second time frame is that of culture. It moves more slowly. Cultural revolutions are resisted by deeper historical beliefs. The first institution to blossom under perestroika was the Russian Orthodox Church. I walked into a church near the Russian writer Boris Pasternak's dacha in 1989 and heard priests and babushkas reciting the litany with perfect recall, as if 72 years of repression had never happened. Culture provides the slow template of change within which family, community, and religion prosper. Culture provides identity. In a fast-changing world it becomes especially important.

The third time frame is that of governance, which is faster than culture but slower than commerce.

The fourth time frame is that of Earth, nature, the web of life. As ephemeral as it may seem, it is the slowest clock, responding to deep evolutionary cycles. Today, we live as if we have discarded that clock, have decided it wasn't necessary, and have attempted to bypass slow time.

What makes life worthy and allows civilizations to endure are all the things that have negative financial returns under commercial rules of quick time: universities, temples, choirs, literature, museums, terraced fields, long marriages, slow walks, line dancing, and art. Almost everything we hold dear is slow to develop and slow to change.

Commerce requires the governance of politics, art, culture, and nature to slow it down, to make it heedful, to make it pay attention to people and places. Commerce has never done these things on its own. The destruction of languages, cultures, forests, and fisheries is occurring worldwide in the name of speeding up business. Yet even business itself is stressed by rapid change. The rate of change is unnerving to all, even to those who are benefiting. To those who are not benefiting, it is devastating. It will not continue because physically it cannot. Slow time always reasserts itself.

In the United States, more than 30,000 nongovernmental organizations, foundations, and citizens' groups are addressing the issue of social and ecological sustainability in the most complete sense of the word. Worldwide, their number exceeds 100,000. Together they address a broad array of issues, including environmental justice, ecological literacy, public policy, conservation, women's rights and health, population growth, renewable energy, corporate reform, labor rights, climate change, trade rules, ethical investing, ecological tax reform, water conservation, and much more. These groups follow Gandhi's imperatives: Some resist, others create new structures, patterns, and means. The groups tend to be local, marginal, poorly funded, and overworked. It is hard for most groups not to feel anxiety that they could perish in a twinkling. At the same time, a deeper pattern is emerging that is extraordinary.

If you ask each of these groups for their principles, frameworks, conventions, models, or declarations, you will find that they do not conflict. Never before in history has this happened. In the past, movements that became powerful started with a unified or centralized set of ideas (Marxism, Christianity, Freudianism) and disseminated them, creating power struggles over time as the core mental model or dogma was changed, diluted, or revised. The sustainability movement did not start this way. Its supporters do not agree on everything—nor should they—but remarkably, they share a set of fundamental understandings about the Earth, how it functions, and the necessity of fairness for all people in partaking of the Earth's life-giving systems.

These groups believe that self-sufficiency is a human right. They imagine a future where the means to kill people is not a business but a crime, where families do not starve, where fathers can work, where children are never sold, where women cannot be impoverished because they choose to be mothers. They believe that water and air belong to us all, not just to the rich. They believe that seeds and life itself cannot be owned or patented by corporations. They believe that nature is the basis of true prosperity and must be honored.

This shared understanding is arising spontaneously from different economic sectors, cultures, regions, and cohorts. And it is growing and spreading, without exception, throughout this country and worldwide. No one started this worldview, no one is in charge of it, no orthodoxy is restraining it. It is the fastest and most powerful movement in the world today, unrecognizable to the American media because it is not centralized, based on power, or led by charismatic white male vertebrates. As external conditions continue to worsen socially, environmentally, and politically, organizations working toward sustainability multiply and gain increasing numbers of supporters.

There is a difference between blind, heady optimism and the deep conviction that no force can counter the truths we share and hold so deeply. This is the work of peace, and it is rapidly becoming the work of many. As Václav Havel, president of the Czech Republic, has said, we are at the brink of a new world because the old world is no longer valid. It is no longer valid to have one billion people dis- or unemployed in the world; this means that in 50 years we will no longer be the species without full employment. There will be more meaningful, dignified, living-wage jobs than there are people who can fill them. It is no longer valid for America, with 4.5 percent of the world's population, to consume 30 percent of the world's resources. If we are losing our legacy forests, a valid world means that we will begin anew and create primary forests of the future. If the population is too large and growing, a valid world will be one in which every child is cared for and made welcome. The way to reduce overpopulation is for all people to feel honored.

We will not be able to bring back all that we have lost. It would take five million years to restore the diversity of lost species. Nevertheless, within 50 years we can begin to undertake the very necessary work of restoration. We will have begun to reduce carbon in the atmosphere; recharge aquifers; bring back lands that have been taken by deserts; create habitat corridors for buffalo, panthers, and gray wolves; and thicken our paper-thin topsoil.

Our children, who will look back 50 years from now in amazement at what they accomplished, are avidly reading Harry Potter books. What they know from these books is that there are too many Muggles in the world. As the environmental writer Bill McKibben wrote in his articles on the protests at the November 1999 World Trade Organization meeting in Seattle, one kept seeing signs reading WAKE UP, MUGGLES. If the Muggles stand for a hyperrational world of economic analysis, no magic, and hypergrowth at all costs, then what we are beginning to see is the reemergence of a celebratory resistance to what visionary author Caroline Casey calls the reality police—the George Wills and Paul Krugmans, the angry columnists, the vacant politicians, the incensed economists, the people who cannot see that what is emerging now is the possibility of being fully human.

In Seattle, people dressed as clowns, butterflies, undertakers, and turtles danced to drums around the Muggle hotel, with the Muggle delegates agape at the loss of order. What is possible in 50 years is a world that is wonderfully messy and deliriously creative. It doesn't fit a single scenario written anywhere by anyone. It is not an America defined by technologies, tools, and toys; an America that can be measured in money; or an America that can be summarized by demographics. It will be, perforce, a country in a world defined by the acts of restoring life on Earth—dancing, donning costumes, singing, performing rituals, enjoying magic, praying, worshiping, playing—and thus carefully reconstituting what has been lost.

In 50 years, America will be a culture where no materials used in industry cause damage to anyone now or later; it will be a society that emulates the design brilliance of nature, which we have never fully appreciated; it will be a time of work that is extraordinary because it is the work not of a decade or a century but of millennia. It will be a people who have thrown off the tyranny of compressive time, coercive work, and erosive competition. It will be a country still rent by massive discontinuities as the momentum of today's world extends far into the future, but it will be a country that is connected, aware, and committed to the future. It will be an America that can see, and it will see that it knows all it needs to know to sustain and honor life on Earth. That alone will distinguish it from where we are today.

★★★

Paul Hawken is the coauthor of *Natural Capitalism: Creating the Next Industrial Revolution* and the author of *The Ecology of Commerce: A Declaration of Sustainability.* Hawken focuses his time on working with governments, commerce, and nonprofit organizations on issues of cultural and ecological restoration.

OUR COLLECTIVE SOUL

Caroline Myss

For years now, I have been involved in the study of the soul and its intimate relationship to our bodies, our minds, and our emotions. When I first studied theology, the soul was discussed by my teachers in passive language: an external force that absorbs our negativity and thrives on our faith. Never was the soul represented as having a primary voice in our biology. Nor was thought given to the possibility that our individual souls were active fragments of a *global* soul that formed the aura of all planetary life. This paradigm had yet to be born during my academic years.

But this profound shift in reality was given birth amid the emergence of the human consciousness movement. And with this awakening, we were given free license to explore the spiritual domain that exists in the world *behind* our eyes, and not just in front of our eyes. This excavation began to reveal to us the depth of the bond that exists between body and soul. We learned that we cannot make a movement with our bodies that our soul does not record, and we cannot have one dialogue with our soul that our bodies do not absorb. There are no boundaries to this conscious partnership of body, mind, and soul.

As the souls of many began to consume the spiritual fire of the world's many sacred teachings, the tightly controlled, centuries-old borders between different religious traditions melted like snow. The time had come; we were ready to receive the spiritual impulse directing us to forge a foundation strong enough to support the new truths that we now hold:

◆ The interconnectedness of the human psyche that we were discovering on the microcosmic level about ourselves is equally true on the macrocosmic level.
◆ Our souls are conscious entities that exist in full and unrestricted partnership with our bodies and our minds.
◆ What we think is what we create.
◆ All is one, from the microcosm to the macrocosm.
◆ There is no manifestation of life that is without a soul.
◆ The health of our bodies relies upon the health of our souls.

These perceptions must be understood as the Sacred Truths of our emerging new era of consciousness. There are two related truths, but they are the most difficult for the world population to grasp, much less to represent through its politics. They are:

◆ Each nation on this planet is an organ of one body, and the health of this body rests upon each organ receiving the same care and respect.
◆ Each nation has a soul of its own that is as real as the soul within every human being.

Just as people united form the global soul of this planet, so also do the souls of each nation participate in the maintenance of the life force of our global soul. Nations therefore must learn the laws and the truth that govern body, mind, and soul awareness from the perspective of macrocosm politics. For example, if a nation harms another nation, it is harming itself. It is consuming a poison in the hope that it will destroy its opponent.

These spiritual laws must be incorporated into the practical laws governing the people of the nation. The leaders of nations should be understood as representatives of the collective soul of that nation. And we should be encouraged to understand that the judgments we direct at our leaders, be those thoughts positive or negative, become a part of the collective political psyche of our nation. Indeed, we need to realize and then live by a code of spiritual discipline that recognizes that an abundance of negativity generated by us citizens provides a type of homeopathic permission for our leaders to take action and make decisions based upon the quality of that energy. A personal negative reaction, a criticism said in private instead of a prayer, is no different than the negativity being released by a political decision made at the ground level of life. It is merely one's micro-contribution to the creation of a macro event.

I knew that to be true, but I had never experienced that truth until I was part of a conversation a few years ago that changed my life forever in less than 5 minutes. While I was having coffee with two friends, a heated conversation began based upon the controversies surrounding Bill Clinton. One negative comment was expressed, followed by another and then another. But one man remained silent. Finally, I asked him if he had any opinions at all regarding the dramas taking place at the White House. He replied, "I have no right to an opinion because I did not pray for him. Therefore, I owe him an apology. He doesn't owe me one."

He was already living what I was learning, and in that learning I realized that becoming aware of these truths is merely the first step. As I have discovered in my work with countless individuals in the field of health and human consciousness, what we know is of minimal use to our healing—both as individuals and as part of the soul of life— without action.

From a practical and grounded perspective, then, how do we identify the souls of nations? Can their charism be recognized as unique voices? My own research into human consciousness leads me to believe that just as each person has his or her own Sacred Contract with life, so also does each nation carry an individual charism, a grace force unto itself that speaks of its purpose and its role within the whole of the global soul. As we move forward in the structuring of this new paradigm of one Earth, one soul, one people, it might well be that an essential part of this plan includes a merger of the charism of the soul of each nation, uniting the fragments of Divinity that are maintained within the psyches of the population of each nation.

What then is the charism of the United States? What is the grace that this nation carries into the global soul that represents its contribution? We must look toward the founding principles of our nation for that answer; we must return to our beginnings, to the document that first articulated our charism, the Bill of Rights.

The majority of the nations on this planet have been birthed out of the ashes of war, either as a result of a nation conquering a nation, or defeating an aggressing nation, or providing a people with a nation by those more powerful. The souls of so many nations carry within them scar tissue that spans hundreds or, in some cases, thousands of years. This country was also born out of a war, a revolution fought by a handful of rebels determined to birth a nation unlike any that had existed on this Earth before. And they succeeded. This country is unlike any other, and it is its distinguishing charism that needs to be reborn and renewed as we make our way into this new millennium.

What makes the charism of this nation so profound, so powerful, so inspiring? What current of Divine electricity is it that flows through Americans that makes our spirit crave liberty as if it were equal to the breath of life itself? I have asked so many people this question so many times, and understandably the most popular answer I am given is that liberty equals economic freedom, and that equals power. Oh so true, but economic power and the leadership that a rich economy gives a nation is a *result* of the manifestation of our charism, not the cause.

The United States of America is the only nation on this planet that was founded on the rights of the human spirit as the priority rights of life. Our Constitution, specifically the Bill of Rights, forms our charism with each amendment, beginning with the first—and doubly impressive because it is the first—guaranteeing us freedom of religion, freedom of speech, freedom of the press, and freedom to assemble and express our grievances. This nation placed the freedom of its collective soul as the most important freedom required for its existence. No other nation had made such a claim, that the rights and privileges of the human soul surpassed those of the human body and also the rights of the government to control that human body. The people of this nation were promised the right to believe whatever their soul required, to express whatever thoughts they had, to write and communicate the content of their minds and hearts, to come together in public and openly speak of their visions. Prior to this precious document, such freedoms were feared and repressed. But once the soul had its freedom written within the parameters of a political document, true liberty was born upon the Earth.

Of equal spiritual significance is the most noted legend of the many known about this nation's first leader, George Washington. For all of his many victories—from Valley Forge to the extraordinary escape he led of his rebels across the Hudson River through the night, hidden by a mysterious fog, while the British waited for morning to fight what they thought would be the final victory of their war—the most famous is Washington and the cherry tree. Did he eat the cherry? "I cannot tell a lie," he replied. He did eat the fruit. A brief story in the telling, a forever story in its impact. The children of this nation were once fed on the cherries from this mythic tree, inspiring them with the principle that speaking the truth and having integrity and honor were the virtues to which a human being should aspire. For how can the human soul thrive without honor, without truth, and without integrity? At the very beginning of this nation, we were provided with a legend that spoke of the characteristics required for us to build a strong and healthy soul, a soul that was guaranteed a nation in which it could thrive by its very charism.

I believe that it is time to resurrect the significance of the charism of this nation, perhaps now more than ever. As we work to cultivate this new paradigm of a conscious global soul, it is of the greatest importance that we bear in mind that we have a responsibility to represent and maintain the charism of this nation's soul, to give that charism room to thrive within our own souls. We must consciously appreciate the power that is contained within this nation, recognizing that the spirit that flows over her shores is the most inspiring source of liberty that exists in our global community. The souls of millions of people are lifted in hope because of the Divine vision that formed this nation. It is important for us now to reframe the Bill of Rights of this nation, transcending its physical boundaries. We need to consider this profound script as an archetypal document that belongs to the global soul.

If we are to think of ourselves as one soul, one planet, one people, one Divinity, then we must hold in our individual souls permission for all peoples to thrive off of the electricity of liberty and honor that is our charism. We ourselves must embody a code of honor and integrity, for it is our souls that elect our leaders far more than our votes. If we wish to live consciously, then we cannot separate ourselves from that which happens in Washington. We are a part of the governing body and soul of this nation, and thus the quality of who we are as people, from our most private thoughts to our personal honor code, casts a vote in the energy field of our politics.

And we must welcome as equals the charism that every other nation offers our planetary soul. This is our patriot duty, and our Divine one.

★★★

A former journalist turned medical intuitive, Caroline Myss fuses Hindu, Christian, and Judaic thought in her many best-selling books on healing and wellness. Books she has authored include *Why People Don't Heal and How They Can*, *The Creation of Health*, *Spiritual Madness*, and *Three Levels of Power and How to Use Them*.

LEGACIES

Fred Branfman

PEOPLE PLACE THEMSELVES FIRST, FAMILY SECOND, TRIBE THIRD, AND
THE REST OF THE WORLD A DISTANT FOURTH. THEIR GENES ALSO
PREDISPOSE THEM TO PLAN AHEAD FOR AT MOST ONE OR TWO
GENERATIONS. SO TODAY THE HUMAN MIND STILL WORKS
COMFORTABLY BACKWARD AND FORWARD ONLY A FEW YEARS,
SPANNING A PERIOD NOT EXCEEDING ONE OR TWO GENERATIONS.

—*E. O. Wilson, "Is Humanity Suicidal?" (1996)*

We are the first generation of humans, through our newfound ability to manipulate the biosphere without and the gene within, to pose a greater threat to people who will live centuries from now than to ourselves. As six billion human beings pursue a U.S. standard of living at the turn of the millennium, humanity has reached a critical mass in material consumption. We are heating our climate, decimating plant and animal species, fouling our oceans and rivers, poisoning our fish, and depleting our water aquifers, forests, soil, and ozone layer. We are introducing thousands of chemicals into our air, water, and bodies, and we're using biotechnology in ways that amount to a dangerous and uncontrolled experiment on the lives of billions who will live in the centuries to come.

17

This behavior has occurred so quickly and is so unprecedented in human experience that its implications have barely begun to sink in. You and I are alive at the first moment in history when one generation's material comfort threatened the well-being of later generations—an inversion of the universal assumption underlying all human cultures that elders smooth the way for those who follow. We cannot yet see that we have become the greatest threat facing future generations.

If America and the world are to thrive in the year 2050, therefore, we must become the first generation in human history to love our more distant descendants in the same way that we love our children and grandchildren. We will neither see the faces nor hear the voices of those who will follow us in the centuries to come, and they will remember us no more than we can remember our own ancestors. But learning to love future generations is crucial to the quality of our own lives nonetheless. We can feel truly alive and at peace in the present only if we know that we are contributing to the future. Our lives can have no meaning now if we diminish those of our descendants later. We care for our descendants not only for their sakes, but for our own.

Learning to care for future generations will not be easy. As E. O. Wilson's "dour scenario" quoted in the epigraph suggests, it may well require reversing an evolutionary heritage stretching back thousands of years. Although Wilson believes that such a reversal is possible, he suggests that it will require an unprecedented redirection in our science, technology, and ethical systems. It seems clear that making the required shifts in our economics and politics will require psychological and spiritual transformations on a scale reached before only during periods of great religious awakenings.

Ours is a terrible responsibility. None of us now alive need fear a crippling disease because of human-caused global warming or misuse of biotechnology that began 200 years ago. We need not fear that we will die of thirst because long-dead ancestors depleted our water aquifers. But all of those born after us will live with those fears—and will owe the quality of their lives to our wisdom and mercy.

If we continue to misuse this power, we will be cursed by our descendants and we will rob our own lives of meaning and dignity. But our power over the future is also a potential blessing. Human beings have struggled through the millennia to find some meaning in this brief candle of life. We are the first who can know that if we use our powers wisely, we can enhance the quality of life of tens of billions of people who will follow us.

Never before has one generation been given so great an opportunity to live lives of transcendent meaning, to take action that can be of such great benefit to so many over such a long period of time. If we can preserve and protect the biosphere and conduct the genetic revolution in a way that extends and improves life far into the future, then our lives can gain a deepness and significance unavailable to those who came before us.

We are far closer to our descendants than we often realize. When our grandchildren speak to their grandchildren of their memories of us, we will directly enter the living memories of people who will be alive more than a century from now. Our lives could gain added meaning if we knew that these memories would be fond ones, that our grandchildren would remember us with gratitude for caring how they would live.

OUR SPIRITUAL TRANSFORMATION

Realizing this potential will require transforming the fabric of our society. We will need to shift massive sums of money from our present consumption of fossil fuels and from our present military expenditures to generate the investment needed to create a hydrogen age. Automobiles will run on, and electricity will be generated by, solar photovoltaic cells and hydrogen. We will save and expand the great rain forests upon which the world's biodiversity depends. We will cleanse the oceans, coral reefs, and seas, replenish water aquifers, and find safe substitutes for dangerous chemicals.

Doing all this will require institutionalizing a concern for future generations in our legal, political, and economic systems. Unborn generations will have standing in our courts of law and will have legal representation by public advocates. We will have a new politics that unites people around the great cause of saving humanity over the long term rather than dividing them in a fight over short-term spoils. Special interests—mostly corporations seeking short-term advantage— will no longer dominate politics. Politicians will be rewarded rather than penalized for raising fuel efficiency standards or promoting massive buys of photovoltaic cells. Our economics will favor long-term investment over short-term consumption. Prices will reflect not only the social but also the generational costs of products. New sustainable energy and energy conservation industries will come into being and will generate millions of jobs and substantial economic growth.

Our culture will transform itself as well. Our children will learn that contributing to their descendants is the most important measure of how well they live their lives. We will place a lower value on fame and wealth, and a far higher value on psychological and spiritual experiences, such as interacting with people and nature, or sensory stimulation through food and music.

Given the present short-term orientation of our law, politics, economics, and culture, however, it is clear that such institutional changes cannot occur unless they have been preceded by a psychological and spiritual transformation, built upon individual experiences of transcendence through connecting with the future.

On an individual level, the experience of feeling connected to future generations is one of the most painful and sublime known to humankind. It hurts because it reminds us not only that we will die, but that our entire life span is but the blink of an eye in human—not to mention cosmic—time. But facing this pain can propel us to a far more exalted place in which we are filled with a sense of awe and humility that we have been granted a precious opportunity to be part of the Great Chain of Being, and filled with a feeling of transcendent meaning and purpose that energizes our lives. We can be transformed by the experience of living on through our very real contributions to all those who will follow us—knowing that although we must die, others will not only live but learn and remember our experience, just as we have stood on the shoulders of those who preceded us.

Spiritual experience, closely tied to a desire to transcend personal death, has long been central to civilized life. Religions have built whole cultures around the promise that their gods will protect the faithful from death; Buddhists meditate to move beyond the individual self and experience a consciousness that cannot die; humanistic psychologists speak of peak and flow experiences in which conventional bonds of time and space disappear; people turn to ideology, ethnic kinship, nationalism, cultural identity, or "making history" to achieve a sense of meaning beyond their own life spans; and, of course, we raise children and grandchildren largely in order to transcend our personal deaths.

What is needed now is to augment these religious and secular experiences with a new human-based spirituality that allows us to transcend death through feeling a deep connection to our more distant descendants.

Concern for the flesh-and-blood human beings who will carry our hopes and contributions into the future and who will remember that we have lived is perhaps the only psychic motivation strong enough to cause us to make the massive investments in new technologies and the voluntary cuts in consumption needed to protect the biosphere.

WHY WE MUST CHANGE

Concern for future generations is not presently institutionalized because it has not been necessary. The old adage "Care for the present; the future will take care of itself" has largely held true. Despite all the horrors of the past century, human life—at least as measured by the number of humans alive and their average life span—is flourishing. And even most qualitative measures—women's rights, democracy, freedom from slavery, reduction in the need for manual labor—are up. Until now, we could live meaningful lives simply by assuming that future generations would be better off than ourselves.

But now, the experts who study such matters have reached a consensus that the earth's biosphere is seriously threatened by the combination of global warming, biodiversity loss, chemical contamination, ocean pollution, nuclear and toxic waste, and depletion of water aquifers, forests, soil, and the ozone layer. There is also growing concern about endocrine disruption and unintended consequences of biotechnology, nanotechnology, and artificial intelligence.

These phenomena jointly pose an unprecedented threat to the future. It's as if our generation had suddenly decided to treat ourselves as laboratory rats, conducting experiments upon ourselves without the slightest concern about or knowledge of how our grandchildren and their grandchildren would be affected.

This crisis has three unprecedented features:

♦ It threatens future generations far more than ourselves—unlike nuclear war, which we have an immediate self-interest in avoiding. Although we are living through the greatest mass extinction of species in 36 million years, for example, it is future generations, not we, who will suffer its effects.

♦ It constitutes a threat to the entire biosphere, not just to local regions. Many before us have destroyed their local regions through overgrazing or depleting their soil. We are the first to threaten the entire planet through our abuse of natural resources.

♦ It will require reversing behaviors that have long been rewarded by evolution—the abilities to procreate, wage war, and transform raw materials into finished products. Only if we value co-creation over procreation, conflict prevention over war-making, and investment over consumption will humanity flourish in the millennium to come.

War and peace were the great issues of the past millennium; meeting these three challenges and saving the biosphere for future generations have become the great imperatives of the next.

The Road from Here to There

What is both maddening and encouraging about the effort to save future generations is that we know how to do it. Our problem is thus not primarily economic or political but psychological: creating the will to take the actions we already know are necessary. There is more hope that we can do so than is readily apparent. Four basic psychological and political trends already in place must and can be extended.

Extending Our Concern

Human beings have encoded within them a considerable degree of concern for future generations.

We can see this concern at work in the average family. Parents do not maximize their financial resources at the expense of their children and grandchildren, for example, by putting them on half-rations, making them go to work at age 10, or buying them secondhand clothing. They instead make huge investments of money, time, and energy, at the expense of their own short-term material gratification, for the future well-being of their children.

There is also much evidence that humanity has evolved far beyond a short-term hunter-gatherer consciousness. The international community is increasingly involved in global projects that go far beyond family, tribe, or nation. The United States spends vast sums annually on the health and education of children, spending that will continue indefinitely. Those who can afford to do so often leave bequests to charitable organizations that far exceed what they leave to their own children. Professionals in all walks of life devote considerable energy to contributing to posterity, not merely to the next generation or two.

As more of us come to understand the biospheric crisis facing our grandchildren's grandchildren, we may well be motivated to extend our concern for our descendants out in time.

Taking Environmental Responsibility

The debate about reducing the budget deficit and the national debt indicates that the human need to contribute to future generations can be translated into the political arena.

It was widely believed in the 1980s, as the Reagan administration joined Keynesian-oriented Democrats in expanding budget deficits, that seeking to reduce the deficit—let alone our national debt—was fruitless. This conventional wisdom was proven wrong, however. Although politics and the booming economy played large roles, deficit reduction was primarily driven by a moral belief—shared by conservatives and liberals—that burdening our children with debt was wrong.

The task now is to achieve similar political success in saving the biosphere. This will require that the mainstream environmental movement extend its present focus on largely technical issues to touch deep psychic and emotional concerns for our descendants.

Shifting to a Future-Generations Movement

The environmental movement has done extremely important work in beginning action to end global warming, preserve biodiversity, save the oceans, and the like. Unfortunately, the movement's current focus on technical, legal, and short-term political strategies is not enough to save the biosphere. By the movement's own admission, the biosphere is growing worse despite the tens of millions of dollars the movement spends annually. Its current strategy implicitly relies on the hope that the weather will get bad enough to awaken the public.

The movement also has a tendency to believe that the biospheric crisis will solve itself as corporations shift to renewable energy sources on their own because they are more cost-effective. But although this is devoutly to be wished, there is little evidence that it will occur soon enough to save a biosphere that is degrading daily. And arguing for this solution becomes a non-self-fulfilling prophecy, as it diminishes the nation's political will to take the tough actions necessary to create a renewable energy future.

Many environmentalists themselves are motivated by a concern for future generations. If they are to succeed, they will need to extend their concern for their descendants into new strategies that touch people's deep psychic concerns to pass on a better world to their grandchildren than they inherited from their parents.

Embracing Our Mortality

Although worsening weather and a redirected environmental movement will help, more is needed. Americans probably will act on a scale sufficient to save the biosphere only if they undergo psychological and spiritual transformations on an individual level.

How 77 million American baby boomers—who now largely control the world's culture and economy—respond to their growing awareness that they will die may well be key to how future generations will live. The baby boom generation's first confrontation with death, in Vietnam, spawned a cultural explosion. If the prospect of personal death now creates a new explosion that propels large numbers of boomers to seek transcendent meaning, there will be hope of saving the biosphere.

America's once-proud baby boom generation—a huge, self-aware cohort that began their lives with great promise, idealism, and commitment—is now in the afternoon of their lives. Vietnam, materialism, and the responsibilities of adulthood have taken their toll on this generation's idealism.

But if the sun is low in the sky, it is also a richer and deeper orange than ever before. In its descent, this richer sun may illuminate portions of our generational psyche of which we were unaware. If we can discover the part deep within each of us that cares about our grandchildren and our grandchildren's grandchildren, future generations can still be saved. If we are the single biggest threat facing our descendants, we are also their potential salvation.

We baby boomers always knew we were special, but it is only now that we can understand how. We are distinguished not by our size, wealth, or colorful past, but because we are the first humans in history who have had to answer this simple question: How much do I care about future generations?

Much is riding on the answer to this question—not only the quality of life of tens of billions of our descendants, who have no less right to decent lives than we do, but also our own quality of life in the short time we have left. There is, it turns out, something worse than dying. It is to die knowing that we have failed all who will follow us.

As individuals, there is both little and much we can do. We cannot hope to reverse the course of evolution on our own. But we can, each of us, transform ourselves. We can stop our present way of life and begin instead, on our own, to live for future generations. Our individual acts, by themselves, will change nothing. But if enough follow, our cumulative actions will transform everything, in the only way that fundamental change has ever occurred: person by person, life by life, dream by dream.

We can perhaps begin this process by summoning to our imagination a single face from among the tens of billions who will follow us—perhaps someone who will resemble us, perhaps a child, perhaps our grandchild's great-grandchild. And we can give her or him a name, a smell, a voice, a laugh, a personality. We can reflect or meditate upon this person who now exists only in our imaginations as we once existed only in the dreams of our ancestors. How will she think and feel? What will be his fears, loves, and hopes? How will she feel within? How important is it to us that he live well and remember us fondly?

Such reflections can transport us to undiscovered regions of thought and feeling that can redeem our lives. As we approach our final hours, our memories of our past will fade and our desire to connect to coming life will grow. This desire to tend the garden of the future can give birth to an impulse that will save not only the biosphere but ourselves. We will be able to take satisfaction from how we have lived because we will know that we will survive in future generations' grateful memories—the only true measure of how we have lived. And the pain of accepting our deaths will be eased by a deep love, the love we feel for them and the love that we know they will feel for us.

★★★

Fred Branfman spent 25 years in state and national politics, serving as a speechwriter and advisor to several governors and presidential candidates. In 1990, he left the political scene to go on a 5-year spiritual journey. Today, Branfman focuses on the issues of living more fully in the face of death and developing concern for future generations. He is the director of the For Generations to Come and the Gifts of Death Awareness projects. He is the author of *Voices from the Plain of Jars* and has written for *Salon, Harper's, Playboy, The New Republic, Washington Monthly,* and *The Nation* magazines, the *New York Times,* the *Washington Post,* and many other publications. He lives in Santa Barbara, where he is working with Dr. Robert Firestone on the forthcoming book *The Good Life.*

REVIVING OUR PASSION

Sarah Ban Breathnach

Have you ever watched the sun rise? To do so is to bear witness to the re-creation of the world. But apart from getting a jump start on the day, early rising has another gift. It reminds you what you're supposed to be doing during the day. Living. Loving. Learning. Leading. Letting go of everything that holds you back from returning, through your authentic gifts, "a portion of the world's lost heart," as the poet Louise Bogan so beautifully puts it.

To sit silently in the shadows as the Earth is seduced into being, coaxed into becoming, and slowly roused from her slumber by a lover—at once ancient and new—is to succumb to passion's embrace at a safe distance. You need not turn your gaze away in fear, as you do when strangely familiar but new eyes begin to recognize your face. You need not begin reciting the mind's pernicious litany of reason when risk invites you for a cup of coffee. All you need to do at dawn, in the dark, all you must do, is pray. Pray that you may know once, or once again, passion before you die.

Passion. When you think about "passion," what immediately comes to mind besides clandestine bodice-ripping clichés that have given romancing the soul a bad rap? Wild. Chaotic. Emotional. Selfish. Indulgent. Permissive. Excessive. Obsessive. Swept away. Out of control. Bad to the bone. Beyond redemption. Fatal attraction. Unpredictable. Unrestrained.

Un-American activities.

Precisely. Which is why I believe that if, like our founding mothers and fathers, we want to restore America to its rightful place—as our spiritual home as well as our primary place of residence—we need to give ourselves permission to revel in our passions. Notice that I do not suggest merely the occasional indulging in passionate impulses but reveling in them, as in revelation. And what will be revealed as you carouse and celebrate your good fortune to carry an American passport, which bestows upon you the unalienable right to pursue your passions and not deny them? How about the truth that will not only set you free but change the rest of our lives for the better, as well as this country's destiny?

Passion is embodied prayer or embodied despair. We are conceived in passion and die in passion; everything in between is our choice. Passion is holy—a profound Mystery that transcends and transforms through rapture or rage, renaissance or revolution. A sacred fire burns within each soul and humanity, whether we're comfortable with this truth or not. Passion is what the Sun feels for the Earth. Heat and light. And just as the Earth cannot exist without either, neither can Americans, no matter how self-reliant or arrogant we may be, and as a nation we are both. Pick up a newspaper in any city or town in this country or turn on the evening news. Forget the headlines. Read between the lines. Listen with your heart. The tectonic plates are shifting beneath us, and below this thin, cool crust is a molten core of transformative energy. But every day the same force that in the beginning created this magnificent country destroys it, as passion erupts in cruelty, brutality, and violence. Why? How can this be?

Could it be that the same sacred pulse meant to keep us alive turns on us with a vengeance? A rogue cell enraged, determined to bring the collective body down because it was excluded, left out in the cold, left to wither away and die? Could it be that Divine Providence disapproves of our smug, savvy, and sophisticated attempts to defy the laws of Heaven and Earth by keeping a lid not only on our own passions but also on those of others? Could it be that if we do not give outward expression to our passions, we will experience self-immolation as individuals and a nation: the spontaneous combustion of our souls? Violence may be random, but it is not senseless. Violence is calculated and cunning because it catapults us through horror into an exile of existence, the realm of the unspeakable. If the eyes of a hungry child, homeless family, abused woman, or abandoned man dying of AIDS do not grab our attention, then violence, the vigilante of the vanquished, will. We think we're just getting up in the morning to do whatever it is we believe we should be doing to "make it" in America, when what we're really doing in every conversation, encounter, argument, or decision is searching for that flicker of flame to guide us through the darkness that surrounds us. The darkness of complicated need. The darkness of indifference. The darkness of ignorance. The darkness of pride. The darkness of prejudice. The darkness of our own second guesses.

Passion is the muse of meaning. It lights up our lives and the lives of others while leading us to the Promised Land. It casts away the shadows of self-sabotage and regret. Passion is the primordial, pulsating energy that infuses all of life, the numinous presence made known with every beat of our hearts. The gift of each day on this Earth offers us another opportunity to live passionate lives rather than passive ones, if we will bear witness not only to the sun's rising, but also to passion's immutable presence in the prosaic, in poetry, and in politics.

★★★

Sarah Ban Breathnach is the author of *Simple Abundance*, the publisher of the Simple Abundance Press (an imprint of Scribner), and the founder of the Simple Abundance Charitable Fund.

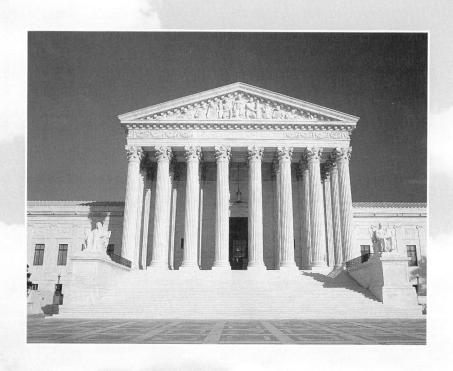

JUSTICE

Denise Breton, Christopher Largent, and Stephen Lehman

We can't imagine a new world, a new America, without imagining justice anew. Justice isn't only about law, courts, police, and prisons. It's about how all of us live, every day. Justice shapes how we think and feel about ourselves in the world because it touches everything we do—every expectation we have, every decision we make, and every action we choose. Justice has this all-pervasive quality because it forms our sense of meaning and self-worth: What are we here to be and do? Where is it worthwhile to channel our energies?

Because justice is so pervasive, we ask much of it. Immediately, we need its help in balancing our relationship with ourselves, since this most intimate relationship is fraught with injustices for all sorts of past-experience reasons. What does it mean to regard and then treat ourselves fairly? Which internalized self-messages do us justice, and which don't? Whatever model of justice we apply to ourselves shapes our relations with others. Ideally, we ask justice to harmonize and protect all of our relationships—with loved ones, communities, businesses, animals, nature, and the Earth—so that justice serves as the backbone of personal, social, and planetary well-being.

When we see hurts inflicted, we ask justice to work as a correcting, reforming power. We want wrongs righted. But even more than that, we want justice to keep us alive to the possibilities of who we can be together—how diverse beings can share a house or planet happily and peacefully.

We ask all these things of justice, and rightly so, but we're not getting our requests answered. The current model simply doesn't work. For one thing, it's depressing. It's all about judgments, punishments, guilt, and fear. For another, we're not even sure justice exists. How many times have we heard the lament, "Justice? There is no justice!"—not economically, politically, or legally, nor even in families and love relationships. The lack of justice plagues us so much that we resign ourselves to injustice as the inevitable way of things.

Contemplating justice, the three of us have come to believe that the current model presents a counterfeit justice, and it's the job of a new century to replace it with the genuine article. A new vision of America calls us to do justice greater justice by evolving models that come closer to fulfilling our ideals of what true justice can be.

THE CURRENT PARADIGM OF JUSTICE

Before we explore what justice can be, let's look at the current model, the counterfeit that we've all accepted. In courts, families, schools, religions, and workplaces, justice has meant getting our just deserts—the rewards and punishments coming to us. Tests, grades, praise, disapproval, merit programs, promises of heaven, and threats of hell all teach a model focused on externals: Who gets which reward or punishment? Accordingly, we come to think about our lives in external terms. What's in it for me if I do X? What punishment will I suffer if I do Y? When harms occur, retribution is used to right them: pain for pain, hurt for hurt.

As much as this model is ingrained in us, it makes a mockery of justice and a mess of our lives. First, the standards for meting out rewards and punishments can be unfair. For millennia, race and gender have decided who gets what, as have favoritism, money, and clout. Second, externals can be manipulated, so that the most aggressive and cunning get the rewards and avoid the punishments. Those who hold power over others define justice in ways that serve their interests. For example, economic powers claim land from indigenous peoples and enslave them—a Darwinian, survival-of-the-fittest justice. Corporate culture has its own version: CEOs give themselves stellar salaries and golden parachutes while laying off workers by the tens and even hundreds of thousands. Third, many factors go into human thought, feeling, and action. For a fair reward-punishment system, all factors should be taken into account. Yet they aren't, nor could they be. We'd have to be omniscient to do so. Every judgment is inevitably based on incomplete knowledge. Finally, is justice reducible to who gets what? In the end, do externals satisfy us, living as we do for meaning, purpose, transformation, and healing—stuff that transcends externals?

Whereas true justice—harmonizing, healing, transforming justice—deepens our philosophy of life, supporting all that's good and true about us, counterfeit justice—judging, punishing, pain-extending justice—plays havoc with our philosophy of life. It dismisses our uniquely personal meaning, superficializes our values with the common coin of the marketplace, and then installs a view of existence that's harsh, impersonal, meaningless, and unforgiving. How?

Simple: An externally focused justice makes us think of ourselves in outwardly measured terms. We judge ourselves on the basis of externals (grades, incomes, possessions, visible achievements), and the quest to maximize externals—What will most advance my outer interests?—becomes our criterion for making decisions.

How we conceive of ourselves is directly affected by the current paradigm of justice. Because we gain externals through competitive struggles, we come to think of our interests as not only separate but also in conflict with others' interests. If we want rewards for ourselves, then we must beat someone else to get them. Or if we want to avoid punishments, then we learn to deflect blame, direct it elsewhere. Instead of asking, "What are the problems we face, and how can we work together to solve them?" we fight over such questions as "Whose fault is it?" and "How can I spin things to my advantage, and what's the penalty if I don't?"

In other words, with counterfeit justice comes a philosophy of what it is to be an individual in the world. Counterfeit justice makes us see ourselves as isolated beings, put on this earth to compete for external rewards. We think about ourselves in narrow, ungenerous, scared, and reactive ways. How we're connected doesn't enter our minds. It is not that we wish to conceive of ourselves this way; rather, externalized justice creates these self-perceptions. One of our university students said, "I feel terrible about it, but I can't help feeling relieved when a fellow students fails, because then I have a better chance of getting a higher grade." This is justice? This harmonizes our relationships?

Reward-punishment justice takes an equally heavy toll on our emotions. We feel as if we're constantly being judged, which we are. In schools and businesses, in sports and at home, every action carries a reward-punishment tag. Because we internalize the model early in life, we soon become to ourselves the critical judge that parents and teachers were to us. The judge lives on in our own feelings and reactions as the external standards of counterfeit justice take up residence within.

With judgment comes fear. Will we make the grade? If we slip up, how badly will we be punished? From this model of justice, we inherit a life of stress and anxiety. No amount of rewards satisfies, since punishments may well hit us ahead. We become insatiable about winning, gaining. Not only are we entirely occupied with externals, over which we often have little control, but also we're chronically afraid of being judged negatively.

Author Alfie Kohn goes further, arguing that even praise works against us. It reminds us that we're being judged and that next time the judgment on us could be the reverse. When we react to praise, we step out of our authentic activity and focus on how we're being judged, even if it's positively. Not the activity itself but the judgment on how we're doing it predominates—and takes all the fun out of it.

Indeed, our inner life becomes the greatest casualty of counterfeit justice. Reward-punishment justice forces a shift in our motivation structure. Instead of being inwardly guided, we become outwardly motivated. We don't learn because learning is fun and we're drawn to a subject; we learn because we'll be graded or paid. We stop listening to what's within as a reliable guide. We do things for external reasons; not because we find joy in the doing, but for what we'll gain outwardly by doing so. We do what's expected from without.

By dismissing inner experiences, the external model of justice disconnects us from our souls' leadings. It teaches us not to listen to the ways our souls speak to us, not to honor the messages we get from our feelings, intuitions, longings, joys, dreams, excitements, bodies, or, above all, our loves. With a model of justice that disregards inner values, all the rich inner resources we possess to create a meaningful life get dismissed at one stroke.

That's why we call this model counterfeit; true justice doesn't work this way. Far from reducing or fragmenting us, true justice defends our wholeness. It protects what's most essentially us—our whole being, inner and outer.

A New Model: Justice from the Inside Out

Can we envision an alternative? A justice that rings true to who we are and to what we ask of justice? Absolutely. An alternative model of justice has been sitting around, begging to be noticed in Western culture, for 2,500 years and in indigenous cultures long before that. In *The Republic*, Plato and Socrates take a dim view of the reward-punishment model of justice. It's not justice, they suggest, but a distorted shadow of it. In fact, reading *The Republic* was what spurred us to rethink justice from the ground up. In place of the external model, Plato and Socrates suggested a justice that operates from the inside out, from our whole being to our life's expression. Instead of imposing social order on people from family, law, and culture, they envisioned justice as us cultivating the gifts that we bring to the world. We make our contributions to society not because we're forced to conform or stay in rigid roles, but because our entire beings move us to do what's ours, what feels right and good, what has meaning and makes life worthwhile.

That's true justice—satisfying because it embraces all of who we are and affirms what matters to us. The 13th-century Sufi poet Rumi expressed this way of living from the inside out:

> *When you do things from your soul,*
> *you feel a river moving in you, a joy.*
> *When actions come from another section,*
> *the feeling disappears.*

Nor is this inner orientation unique to a few esoteric thinkers. Some indigenous cultures have practiced their own versions for millennia. Observing the Pawnee during the early 1930s, Gene Weltfish wrote:

> [The Pawnee] were a well-disciplined people, maintaining public order under many trying circumstances. Yet they had none of the power mechanisms that we consider essential to a well-ordered life. No orders were ever issued. No assignments for work were ever made nor were over-all plans discussed. There was no code of rules of conduct nor punishment for infraction. There were no commandments nor moralizing proverbs. The only instigator of action was the consenting person. . . . Whatever social forms existed were carried within the consciousness of the people, not by others who were in a position to make demands. . . .
>
> Time after time I tried to find a case of orders given, and there was none. Gradually I began to realize that democracy is a very personal thing which, like charity, begins at home. Basically it means not being coerced and having no need to coerce anyone else.

But what is ours to do? To answer that, we have to know who we are. We need to get in touch with our souls, our inner beings. As we do, we may at first encounter question marks and gaping silences, since we're not accustomed to poking around inside our essences. On the other hand, we may find our souls bursting to tell us what gives us joy, what inspires meaning. For justice to honor us and our relations with one another, we have to be there, all there, not just in body and possessions but in soul and meaning. We have to first honor ourselves by finding out who we really are and what's ours to do. What calls us in life?

Without this foundation of self-awareness, justice becomes an external matter, an empty shell fiddling with which stuff belongs to whom. As justice, this is unsatisfying, because there's not enough of us in it. We're more than our stuff, and true justice means more than shuffling property. We feel justly treated when we've been seen for who we are, when our life stories have been heard and our sense of meaning understood. Then we feel that we've found our fair place in a relationship, family, or community.

All the Platonic dialogues suggest a radical shift from an outer to an inner orientation, and the dialogue on justice is no different. To have justice live for us and fulfill our ideals of what justice can be, we cannot reduce it to external terms. The inner must have a place, and if Plato is right, the inner must lead. Being true to what's within us reveals the path of justice.

But won't each of us doing what's ours to do lead to chaos? It all depends on which philosophy we accept about the nature of things and about human nature in particular. If we assume that we're all greedy so-and-so's competing for the biggest piece of the pie, then no way would an inner model of justice work. Our inner lives under that paradigm get so traumatized and soul-disconnected that we lose our compass and behave at our worst. As long as we're externally oriented and dismiss our souls, we'll have trouble.

But then, that's what we have now. The chaos and suffering that we see every day is not because we're all following our souls or living the model that Plato, Rumi, or the Pawnee understood. It's because we've factored our souls out of our officially regulated lives.

An inner approach to justice calls our souls back in, front and center. Following our souls is the key to real social order, mystics believe, because they assume that reality is one. At the deepest levels of our being, who we are is connected to who everyone else is, and through that core connection, our soul-guided actions are synchronized. We don't think it out from our heads, because we don't have access to that level of whole-knowing. Rather, in being true to ourselves, we tap into our link to the whole. Through our souls, we're whole-guided, which means that we're led into harmony with one another. Our actions are coordinated from beyond us.

Granted, it's not ours to see how. Rather, it's ours to follow what's within, for that's how the symphony of being speaks to us and guides us. Rumi says that God speaks to us through our loves, our most powerful inner feelings:

> *Love is the way messengers*
> *from the mystery tell us things.*

In following our loves, we follow the "messengers from the mystery," and this mystery-connectedness unites us with the true loves—the souls and authentic expressions—of everyone else.

RESTORATIVE JUSTICE

Not only can an inner-oriented model of justice work, it is already working, and far more powerfully than the one-sided, external-only approach. We're referring to the paradigm shift in justice practices that falls loosely under the name of restorative justice. This new vision of justice, birthed somewhat independently around the world over the last few decades, seeks not to punish but to heal, not to extend hurt by adding more pain but by restoring broken relations and righting whatever wrongs have occurred.

To do this healing work, everyone must be involved: victims, offenders, families, and communities. We hurt one another when we don't feel connected, either to ourselves or to others. From isolation, we act connectedness-blind, and that's when harms happen.

Restorative justice helps us rediscover our soulful connectedness. In the "healing and sentencing circles" of the Hollow Water community in Canada, of which Canadian prosecutor Rupert Ross writes, everyone comes together and listens to one another's stories. People talk not only about immediate circumstances but also about what happened in the course of experiences that led them to behave one way rather than another. Through this open, inner-revealing exchange, transformations occur. Those who have harmed others feel genuine remorse as they hear victims speak. Victims, in turn, understand what led offenders to act as they did, which often inspires compassion and heartfelt forgiveness. The trauma that plagues victims diminishes and sometimes dissolves entirely.

Whereas punishment sends offenders to years of crime school, restorative justice strives to break the cycle of crime and so achieve prevention. By inviting everyone involved to interact person to person, soul to soul, restorative justice restores the balance between inner and outer. We come to experience one another not only through the outer "what" of our lives but more through the inner "how" and "why."

The healing impact is powerful. In *Yes!* magazine, Tag Evers tells the story of Thomas Ann Hines, a mother whose 21-year-old son, Paul Hines, was murdered by a 17-year-old car thief named Charles. Her immediate response, which persisted for 13 years, was the desire for punishment. Yet a life driven by revenge is no joy, she discovered. After years of support groups with other parents of murdered children, as well as 3 years of preparation in a victim-offender mediation program, Thomas Ann Hines was ready to meet her son's killer. The effect of their first, emotional, 6-hour meeting was profound. The mother saw a boy, now 30, abandoned on the street at 13, left to fend for himself, never having received the mothering her son enjoyed all his life. Charles, on the other hand, experienced from his victim's mother, now herself transformed, an understanding and compassion that he'd never known.

> *"I wanted him to look in the eyes of the mother of the boy he had killed," says Hines. "I wanted him to know there is love in the world. . . ."*
>
> *"The intensity and depth of emotion ran the whole gamut—from hopelessness and sheer despair to hope and a sense of faith," says Dave Doerfler, who mediated the session. "Charles was locked in his pain, saying there was nothing he could do to bring back Paul's life. But Thomas Ann was relentless—she broke through—and insisted while Charles couldn't do anything about her son's life, he could do something about his own. . . ."*
>
> *[Charles] agreed to work on his GED and pursue vocational training. Additionally, with Thomas Ann's support, Charles listed personal and spiritual goals that might strengthen him as he prepared for his eventual release from prison.*
>
> *Up to that point, Charles had amassed 148 disciplinary violations, losing up to 10 years of possible "good time." But he now had something he did not have before: hope and the knowledge that someone loved him. . . .*
>
> *"The criminal justice system operates on the principle that if someone is down, you kick 'em," says Hines. "Until we start*

looking at the roots of crime instead of the results, it's not going to change. . . ."

"At the close of our session, I said to Charles: 'I had a choice—I could spend the rest of my life hating you. But I don't hate you. I just want you to move forward with your life.'

"As we parted, Charles reached out and wrapped his arms around me. I've had lots of hugs in my life, but besides Paul, I can't think of a person in the world I'd rather have hug me."

Amazing as this story is, it is not uncommon in restorative justice. It demonstrates the healing power of justice, not as a judging, condemning force in our lives, but as a powerful advocate for who we are, honoring our innate worth and urging us to find and fulfill our life's callings. By shifting the focus from outer to inner and working to heal our lives from the inside out, we imagine not only a new justice for America but that more of us can live it right where we are. Starting with ourselves, our relationships, and how we deal with hurts, we can invite a new and truer justice to be born among us.

As this happens, we together create a revolution in justice that can't be stopped—a revolution that will transform, heal, and lighten every aspect of our lives. That's powerful stuff. That's true justice.

★★★

Philosophers Denise Breton, Christopher Largent, and Stephen Lehman have worked together on several books, including *The Paradigm Conspiracy: Why Our Social Systems Violate Human Potential—And How We Can Change Them* and *Love, Soul, and Freedom: Dancing with Rumi on the Mystic Path*, Denise and Chris as coauthors, Steve as their editor. They are currently writing *The Mystic Heart of Justice*, on which this essay is based.

PILLARS

HEALTH

Dean Ornish

In the next 50 years, more and more people will begin to realize that the psychosocial, the emotional, and the spiritual dimensions are important determinants of health, and that they all interrelate. Traditionally in American medicine, health has been defined as the absence of disease. Beginning about 25 years ago, some pioneering physicians began talking about wellness—not just the absence of disease but a higher level of functioning and well-being.

So, the doctor of the future will be one who integrates all of these dimensions with more traditional approaches. Hospitals will integrate the best of high tech and high touch, using all therapeutic modalities that work, including drugs and surgery when needed but also drawing from a wide variety of systems of healing. Fifty years from now, there will be a much broader body of scientific studies showing which approaches are most effective, under what circumstances, and for whom. When you walk into a hospital, it will feel warm and comfortable rather than cold and toxic.

When I was a medical student and first started going on the hospital wards to learn clinical medicine, I would begin to feel sick just walking inside. Hospitals are dangerous places; a recent report by the Institute of Medicine reported that between 44,000 and 98,000 people die in U.S. hospitals annually as a result of medical errors. I hope that we can keep the best of scientific medicine and apply it across different disciplines to create healing environments.

The general public needs to understand the power it has in effecting these changes. Birthing centers are a good example. Thirty-five years ago, women made it clear to their doctors that childbirth is not a disease and they didn't want to give birth in what they felt was a hostile environment. Some decided to deliver children at home, but many others legitimately were concerned about the risks. So, birthing centers were . . . well, born. They integrate a healthy healing environment; the best of traditional scientific medicine; the nurturing, listening role of a natural practitioner (a doula or midwife); and an overall approach that is natural and holistic.

I have been interested for many years in finding and understanding leverage points of how change occurs. When there is suffering, there is an opportunity for new approaches—both individually and socially. In our program, we help people use suffering as a catalyst for transformation.

Change is often difficult. Part of the value of pain is to get our attention, and part of it is to make it easier to change: "Well, it may be hard to change, but I'm in so much pain that I'm ready to try just about anything." And when people make comprehensive lifestyle changes, they usually feel so much better so quickly that they sometimes look at their earlier suffering as a blessing in disguise.

Many have told me, "Having a heart attack was the best thing that happened to me."

"Are you crazy?"

"No, but that's what it took to get my attention. My life is so much more joyful and meaningful now, because I made so many changes in my life that I probably never would have made otherwise."

Of course, I would never say to someone who is suffering, Hey, what a great wake-up call, what a great opportunity. The proper response would be a punch in the nose. We don't look for suffering, but there it is. Suffering can provide meaning if we use it as a catalyst for transforming our lives for the better.

Suffering also occurs beyond the individual, creating opportunity for social transformation. Social networks have shifted radically in the past 50 years. There has been an increasing breakdown of community. Most people don't have an extended family or even a nuclear family that they see regularly; they don't have a strong sense of community in their neighborhood, they don't have a church or synagogue they attend regularly, they don't have a stable job. While the Internet has brought great progress, studies show that as people spend more time online, away from friends and family, social isolation, depression, and loneliness all increase.

These are more than just touchy-feely concepts; these are ideas that science is beginning to validate, many of which are described in my most recent book, *Love and Survival*. People tend to think of my work as being primarily about diet. Clearly, diet is important, exercise is important, avoiding smoking is important, and managing stress is important, but there's more. Study after study has shown that people who feel lonely, depressed, and isolated are 3 to 7 times more likely to get sick and die prematurely than those who have a sense of love, connection, and community in their lives. And yet, these are factors that we tend not to learn about in our medical training and tend not to value in our culture.

Awareness is the first step in healing. In the 1960s, when research clarified the relationship between smoking and illness, many people quit smoking. In the 1970s, research on the benefits of exercise caused many people to start jogging. In the 1980s and 1990s, scientific studies on the importance of controlling stress and monitoring diet caused many people to meditate and eat differently.

When we realize that the time we spend with our loved ones, the quality of our relationships, the strength of our communities, and the openness of our hearts are major determinants not only of the *quality* of our lives but also the *quantity*—our survival—then this awareness of the importance of love and intimacy may help people make different choices in their lives, both individually and socially.

These factors affect our behavior. People are more likely to smoke, overeat, drink too much, abuse drugs, or work too hard when they are lonely, depressed, and isolated, because it helps them numb, cope with, be distracted from, and bypass the emotional pain that they feel. Because of this, providing people with health information is important but not often sufficient to motivate lasting changes in behavior. If it were, nobody would smoke, because everybody knows that smoking isn't good for you. The Surgeon General's warning is on every package of cigarettes, yet 30 percent of Americans and 80 percent of people in some Asian countries smoke.

I think the real epidemic is not just physical heart disease but also emotional and spiritual heart disease. Many people are in a lot of pain, both individually and socially. Telling somebody who feels lonely and depressed that they are going to live longer if they just quit smoking or change their diet may not be that meaningful or motivating. We often assume that people want to live longer, but many people are just trying to get through the day. A woman who was in one of our studies said, "I've got 20 friends in this package of cigarettes, and they're always there for me, and nobody else is. If you're going to take away my 20 friends, what are you going to give me instead?" Someone else might use alcohol or another drug to numb the pain, or they may use food to fill the void.

One well-known food writer told me, "You know, when I get depressed, I eat a lot of fat, because fat coats my nerves and numbs my pain." We may work too hard, spend too much time on the Internet, or watch too much television—all socially acceptable ways of distracting ourselves from pain. But the pain is not the problem. Pain is the messenger, saying, Hey, listen up! Pay attention! You're not doing something that's in your best interests!

If we just numb or bypass the pain without also listening to it, then it's a little like clipping the wires to a fire alarm or going back to sleep while your house is burning. We've just killed the messenger without addressing the underlying causes.

While genetics plays a factor, much more important are the diet and lifestyle choices that we make each day. The decoding of the human genome makes exciting new therapies possible, but diet and lifestyle still remain the most important factors in determining health and illness. For example, a recent study published in the *New England Journal of Medicine* followed identical twins (who have the same genes) for many years and found that the twin of a person with cancer had only a moderate risk of developing cancer at that same site. The researchers concluded that environment—diet, lifestyle, social factors— is the principal cause of most cancers.

Paradoxically, many people find that it is often easier to make big changes in diet and lifestyle than to make small, gradual ones, even though that goes against conventional wisdom. When people make comprehensive lifestyle changes, they often feel better and have more energy. Blood flow to the brain improves, so they think more clearly. Blood flow to the heart improves, so chest pain (angina) usually decreases dramatically. (In our studies, we found a 91 percent reduction in the frequency of angina.) Blood flow to sexual organs improves, so potency often increases. These changes often occur within days or weeks. On a deeper level, many people report that their relationships improve, and they often rediscover inner sources of peace, joy, and well-being.

When we change our diet, meditate, exercise, quit smoking, and increase our intimacy with other people all at the same time, we may find that we feel so much better so quickly, that it reframes the reason for changing diet and lifestyle: from prevention, risk-factor reduction, or living a few months longer, which most people think are really boring, to something much more meaningful—in short, from fear of dying to joy of living.

Love and intimacy are basic human needs, as fundamental as eating and breathing. We can measure cholesterol levels and blood pressure more easily than love and intimacy, but it is an indication of how powerful these needs are that the relatively crude measures that we do have are so powerfully predictive of survival years later. The social factors that we have a harder time measuring are often the ones that are most meaningful to people. As Dr. Denis Burkit once wrote, "Not everything that counts can be counted." Not everything meaningful is measurable.

For example, one study looked at men and women who were about to undergo open-heart surgery. The researchers asked two questions: "Do you draw strength from your religious faith?" (the faith didn't matter) and, "Are you a member of a group of people who get together on a regular basis?" It could be a bridge club, a bowling league, or a bingo game. The study found that 21 percent of those who said no to both questions were dead within 6 months, compared to only 3 percent of those who said yes to both questions. That's a sevenfold difference in mortality. Those who said yes to only one of the questions had about a fourfold difference in mortality. I don't know of any other factor so powerfully predictive of mortality just 6 months after open-heart surgery. We're not talking about warm and fuzzy; we're talking about premature death, the hardest endpoint measure.

While loneliness and isolation increase the likelihood of self-destructive behaviors, they also affect our health through mechanisms that we don't fully understand. Even when we take into account all of these behaviors and control for all of the known risk factors, studies show that people are many times more likely to get sick and die prematurely when they are lonely, depressed, and isolated, for reasons that we don't fully understand. The history of science is such that we often can document phenomena before we understand the mechanisms that cause them.

There is pain that comes from not getting the things that we think are going to bring lasting happiness, but there's an even deeper pain that comes from getting those things that we thought were supposed to make us happy only to find that they don't. Before, at least, we had the illusion or myth to keep us motivated. Because of the prosperity in our culture, many people are coming to the end of this myth. While this realization can be painful, it also can be liberating if it motivates us to start looking in different places for our happiness and well-being.

50

We present stress-management techniques such as yoga, meditation, and prayer as powerful tools for helping to quiet down the mind and body, thereby allowing a person to experience a greater sense of inner peace and well-being. These techniques often provide the experience of interconnectedness and oneness, which is where healing often begins.

For the past 23 years, my colleagues and I at the nonprofit Preventive Medicine Research Institute have demonstrated that the progression of even severe heart disease often can begin to be reversed by making intensive changes in diet and lifestyle. We showed this in randomized controlled trials published in major peer-reviewed medial journals. We are now conducting a trial to determine if the progression of prostate cancer can be similarly affected.

I once thought that if we just do good science and the evidence becomes accepted, then that will help change medical practice. But I was naive. It's not enough to have good science; we also have to change reimbursement. We doctors tend to do what we get paid to do, and we get trained to do what we get paid to do. Changing reimbursement would help change medical practice and medical education.

Thus, we went to insurance companies. At first they said, "No, we don't pay for diet and lifestyle—that's prevention. About 30 percent of people change insurance companies every year, and it may take 5 years or more to see the benefit, so why should we spend our money today for some future benefit that, even if it occurs, chances are some other company's going to receive?"

My reply is that such factors are not just preventive but can act as alternative treatments. For example, every man and woman who can avoid coronary bypass surgery by changing diet and lifestyle saves $30,000 immediately—real dollars today, not theoretical dollars years later. Also, there may be additional savings because one-half of coronary bypasses reocclude or clog up again within just a few years, and 30 to 50 percent of angioplastied arteries restenose or clog up again within 4 to 6 months. Last year, more than $23 billion was spent in

51

the United States on these two operations alone. So, there is a lot of money to be saved.

The insurance companies said, "Well, that sounds great in theory, but your program is too hard for most people to follow. If we pay for your program and they don't follow it, then we'll end up paying for their bypass anyway, and now our costs have gone up because we're paying for both." I replied, "Well, look at our studies. We already showed that most people can follow the program. They showed some reversal of heart disease after only a month; they showed more improvement after a year, and still more improvement after 5 years. They not only *felt* better, but in most cases they actually *were* better in ways that we could measure. Paradoxically, we used expensive high-tech, state-of-the-art, 21st-century diagnostic technologies like cardiac positron emission tomography and computer-analyzed quantitative coronary arteriograms to prove how powerful these low-tech, inexpensive, and ancient interventions can be." And they said, "Yes, but you live in California—it's an altered state, they'll do anything there, but this will never play in Peoria, no one else can do it." I said, "Well, let's find out."

In 1993, my colleagues and I at the Preventive Medicine Research Institute began training hospitals and other sites around the country. Mutual of Omaha was the first major insurance company to cover our program; now more than 40 are reimbursing it.

We followed several hundred people for 3 years, all of whom were told that they needed a bypass operation or angioplasty but chose instead our 1-year lifestyle program as a direct alternative to surgery. Nearly 80 percent of the people involved were able to safely avoid the operation for at least 3 years. Insurance companies found that they saved almost $30,000 per patient immediately, plus additional costs in the longer run. One of the companies, Highmark Blue Cross Blue Shield, has been covering and providing our program. Of the first 300 people with severe heart disease who went through the program, 299 were able to avoid bypass surgery or angioplasty.

Because of these findings, Medicare recently agreed to pay for

1,800 patients to go through our program at the sites that we've trained as a demonstration project. If they decide to make this a defined benefit for all Medicare beneficiaries, most insurance companies will likely follow their example. Then the people who most need these kinds of approaches will have access to them. (The program is now available worldwide on the Internet at much lower cost. Visit WebMD.com.)

During the next 50 years, an increasing number of people may learn that getting older doesn't necessarily mean slowly deteriorating. The mortality rate is still 100 percent, but there are many traditions of healing that say you don't have to die of a chronic disease. By analogy, an alkaline battery tends to deteriorate slowly over time, whereas a nickel cadmium battery works at the same level until its last few percentage points of power, then it rapidly declines. Many people may find themselves leading vigorous and joyful lives right up to the last few months.

In a way, all of our work can be summarized in a very simple idea: If we don't treat the underlying causes of a problem such as heart disease, but rather bypass them literally with surgery or figuratively with angioplasty or lifelong medication, then the same problem often comes back again, or you get a new set of problems or side effects, or, on a social level, you have painful choices. For example, more than 47 million Americans don't have health insurance. When we offer them only drugs and surgery, health care costs go up exponentially.

Efforts to contain medical costs that do not address the more fundamental lifestyle choices that determine *why* people become sick inevitably result in painful choices: Should we ration health care? Raise taxes? Increase the deficit? Force doctors to see more and more patients in less and less time? Exclude 47 million Americans from medical care? Instead, if we treat the underlying causes, then we find that we have new hope and new options. In the next 50 years, we can help create a new model of medicine that is more caring and compassionate *and* more cost effective.

If I went to a major insurance company and said, "We want to teach people how to open their hearts to one another, create communities, and reduce suffering," they might show me the door. But if we show them scientific evidence that heart disease is often reversible, and cost-benefit analyses showing that insurance companies and employers are saving, on average, almost $30,000 per patient, then this opens the door to begin working at a deeper level. It's a conspiracy of love.

★★★

Dean Ornish, M.D., is the founder of the nonprofit Preventive Medicine Research Institute and a clinical professor of medicine at the University of California, San Francisco. He was the first to prove that heart disease is reversible by changing diet and lifestyle, groundbreaking work that has made him one of the best-known and most respected doctors in America. He is a member of the White House Commission on Complementary and Alternative Medicine Policy, and he's on the board of directors of the United Nations High Commission on Refugees. Dr. Ornish was recognized by *Life* magazine as one of the 50 most influential members of his generation. He is the author of five best-selling books, including *Dr. Dean Ornish's Program for Reversing Heart Disease*; *Eat More, Weigh Less*; and *Love and Survival*.

FOOD

John Robbins

It's the year 2030. A meal is served. It was quick to prepare—just a few seconds in the food enhancer (actually an irradiation chamber based upon the old microwave ovens) was all it took. Of course, there was the time that Mom spent driving, parking, reading labels, and standing in line in fluorescent-lit grocery stores listening to canned music, then driving again, getting stuck in traffic, opening packages, and disposing of the trash. But she hardly noticed. She also didn't notice the thousands of BUY NOW messages to which she was exposed, or the chemical-laden air that she breathed. Her mind was elsewhere, spinning a mile a minute, but the behavior- and mood-altering drugs she takes keep her from being too unhappy.

The food is flavored and enhanced by an array of artificial chemicals, produced in factories located in those parts of the world where labor costs are lowest and environmental regulations are most lax. The foodstuffs involved were grown in assembly-line conditions on monocrop and factory farms in nations where there are no limits whatsoever on the use of toxic pesticides or hormones, and they have been so heavily refined and processed that it is impossible to tell from what plant or animal they might have originated. All seeds and food animals, like most of the people who work in the fields and animal factories, are now bio-safe, the term used for seeds, animals, and people that have been genetically engineered to tolerate huge doses of herbicides, insecticides, and other toxic chemicals.

Once in a while, Mom wonders what's in these foods and how much fat or salt or sugar they might contain and whether the many chemicals she and her family are eating might cause cancer. But no one has seemed to care much about such things ever since food labeling of ingredients was banned as an unfair barrier to trade.

The televisions are on throughout the meal. Advertisements no longer exist, since commercial messages are now fully incorporated into the programs. Each person is tuned to his or her own channel. Mom is trying to create a semblance of family life and sometimes thinks perhaps they should once in a while watch the same TV show together, but it never works.

And it's an impossible struggle to get anyone to help with the dishes. Maybe they should just eat out all the time. Identical McDonald's restaurants are now found in every neighborhood. The food is cheap, especially if you don't count the cost of the gas to drive there or the health consequences of eating what they sell. Occasionally, a TV show will say something about the rain forests that are now almost gone, or the ever-worsening climate conditions, but with everyone who can afford to living in totally controlled conditions, it's easy not to think about it much.

Eventually, Mom gives up trying, gives in to social pressure, and her family becomes even more normal. If anyone gets hungry, they just fend for themselves, grabbing whatever is around and convenient to appease whatever sensation they are experiencing. Stores are full of colorfully packaged, artificially flavored ready-to-eat items with indefinite shelf lives. It takes only the push of a single button to order, via the Internet, the food pellets, injections, and implants that increasingly take the place of meals.

Scientists are busy looking for a drug to handle the eating disorders, cravings, and addictions that are so common now. The children are obese, the teenagers are fixated on body-image obsessions, and people of all ages are walled off in their own worlds.

"It could be worse," Mom tells herself, remembering for a moment the billions of children in the world who have nothing to eat at all. But human hunger isn't talked about much anymore, with everyone taking happiness medications. Plus, people have been extremely reluctant to discuss such things ever since the National Cattlemen's Beef Association sued a prominent author for food disparagement. She had dared to expose the fact that if Americans ate 10 percent less meat, enough grain would become available to feed 60 million people.

A Different Scenario

It's the year 2030. A meal is served. The old wooden table has been in the family for several generations. Sturdy and simple, it carries something of meaning from all the life it has witnessed and made possible. Around it sit people who communicate freely and easily. Each person is honored for the unique gifts and talents he brings. Each person is supported to fully express her powers. People eat in comfort and safety, knowing that, thanks to the changes that have taken place, no one anywhere, anymore, goes hungry.

The food this family eats, like the food now eaten by most families in the nation, is wholesome and natural. Much of it comes from nearby. Throughout the land, families and communities of every race and ethnic background gather together to enjoy healthy foods that represent their unique cultural heritage. Families gather around steaming bowls of fresh soup and meals made from delicious natural ingredients. Large and colorful salads contain fresh leaves, not only of lettuce and other vegetables picked from family and local gardens but also of several wild plants that grow nearby. Children are always excited to find these plants, as they are to find the wild edible mushrooms that are frequently served with rice and a delicious sauce of seeds and homemade vinegar. Grandma made the vinegar last year from apples that had fallen fully ripe from the tree.

Children from different families play together and help in the family and community gardens, where they learn to cooperate with youngsters from different backgrounds. Small fingers in every hue— black, brown, yellow, white, and red—play around in the fertile soil, pulling weeds, playing with water and mud and worms. Worms abound in the deep, rich soil, for it is teeming with organic life and a vast mix of nutrients for the plants. For the children, it's a game to harvest vegetables and carry them to the kitchen, where adults wash and chop. Some of the vegetables they planted themselves.

As the children plant seeds, then watch the seeds turn into small seedlings that will in turn grow into healthy plants, they know that they, too, are part of the Earth community and they, too, can grow strong and steady into people who can contribute to the lives of others. Understanding that they, too, have roots and stems, leaves and seeds, they relish the harmonious development of all their powers and potentials. Seeing how plants depend upon the health of the soil, they learn the importance of caring for the environment we all share.

Most families shop at the local farmers' market, where community farmers gather to sell direct to consumers. They don't have to charge as much when there aren't huge distribution, transportation, and marketing costs to pay, and when there aren't corporate entities taking a share of everything. At the market, people meet the people who grew their food and learn what's in season and what's ripe today. The market is a pageant, extraordinarily alive with the vivid colors of countless varieties of fruits, vegetables, seeds, beans, nuts, and grains. Much of the food is grown organically. People come together here to talk about local issues and topics of importance, and rally around those concerns and people needing support.

At home, in a kitchen, a mother and daughter are shelling peas. Other family members are peacefully sorting beans and making a soup. Everyone in the house is smelling the fragrances of the simmering soup, savoring the sensual pleasures and the creativity of it all.

People still go out to eat, but it is usually to sample new ways of preparing wholesome foods and a variety of ethnic cuisines, not because they have no place else to eat and not because they don't have time to prepare a decent meal. For most families, the time spent preparing meals is sweet, as is the time afterward, cleaning up together. There is chatting, laughing, and joking. Even the teenagers love it because there is time for them to talk about what is going on in their lives and be heard.

WHICH WAY WILL WE GO?

We could go either way.

We could go toward ever more chemicalized food and ever less real human contact. We could go toward agribusiness-dominated factory farms, where animals and workers are treated with disdain for their needs, where water is poisoned and topsoil lost. We could go toward ever more artificial ready-to-eat foods, instant everything, where convenience and saving time are the only values. We could feed ever more of our grain to livestock while ever more of humanity is malnourished.

Or we could go toward real contact with ourselves and one another and the natural world that makes our lives possible in the first place. We could go toward farming systems based on respect for the lives of the people and animals involved. We could eat food grown on living soil, with respect for the vast ecological web that underlies all that has ever been human. We could eat a plant-based diet that is healthier for us, for the Earth, and for the millions of people who then could, because we ate simply, simply eat.

I am very clear about which way I'd prefer us to go. If I had my way, we'd eat healthier food that was delicious not because it had been processed and refined and loaded with artificial chemicals, but due to its natural wholesome goodness and because our ability to taste was heightened by the vitality and quality of the lives we lived. If I had my way, our agriculture wouldn't be single-mindedly devoted to profit at any cost, but would be sustainable and friendly to the Earth and its creatures. If I had my way, we wouldn't depend on genetic engineering to feed the world, but on sound agricultural practices undertaken in harmony with the laws of natural systems. No one would go hungry, because basic human needs would be given priority over wasteful human greed. If I had my way, we'd see that our relationship to food has much to teach us about our relationship to life.

I remember once appearing on *Town Meeting*, the most popular regional TV talk show in the Pacific Northwest. Filmed in Seattle, the show features a debate type of format, where representatives of opposing points of view have at each other. On this occasion, I was one guest, while the other guest represented the National Cattlemen's Association. He didn't particularly appreciate my views. When I expressed my vision of an ecologically sane agriculture that produced healthy food, he puckered up his face and scoffed, "It's just some ex-hippie's dream."

Is he right? Is it just a dream? I don't think so—not if it's actually possible, not if it's a realistic alternative. Is it just an idealistic fantasy? I don't think so—not if we can actually get there from here.

Getting There from Here

It's the year 2030. We can look back now, from this perspective, and see how we actually came to bring our food production and consumption practices into alignment with the well-being of not only ourselves and our health but the whole Earth community.

In the late 1990s, you may remember, the USDA proposed organic standards that would have severely watered down the definition of the word *organic*. Had the proposed standards been implemented, food that was genetically engineered, irradiated, and grown with toxic and heavy-metal-laden sewage sludge could have been called organic. Consumers would have lost all trust in the organic label.

The Department of Agriculture had every intention of putting the proposed standards into practice. But then consumers made their voices heard. They sent in postcards, they commented directly on the USDA's Web page, they wrote long and specific letters, they called their congressional representatives and asked for their support, and they wrote to President Clinton. Meanwhile, natural-foods companies and representatives were creating flyers, posters, advertisements, Web sites, and letters; putting messages on cartons; and educating people in a host of other ways. By the time the smoke cleared, the USDA had received more than 275,000 comments, virtually all of

them vehemently opposing the agency's plan. As a direct consequence, the proposed standards with the watered-down definition of
organic were scuttled.

People prevailed over agribusiness again a few years later. In the
first few years of the 21st century, there was a tremendous push by the
agribusiness/chemical conglomerates toward genetically engineered
food. With the chemical companies so intent on profiting from the
genetic engineering of foods, it seemed inevitable that they would get
their way. But as had happened a few years before with the organic
standards, enormous consumer outcry, once again coupled with sound
ecological and health considerations, shifted the direction of the culture. Monsanto said "Trust us," but weren't these the same people
who had brought us Agent Orange and PCBs? When human and
planetary health are at stake, it was recognized, arduous testing must
be undertaken to be sure new innovations are safe.

Agribusiness's plan to monopolize the world's food supplies took
another hit a few years later when a new series of diseases linked directly to the factory farming of livestock prompted enormous public
outcry. The livestock industry had long pushed food irradiation as the
answer to the outbreaks of *E. coli*, salmonella, *Listeria*, and other path-
ogenic bacteria carried by meats, dairy products, and eggs. But the
emergence and widespread incidence of new disease agents and the
overwhelming evidence that these purveyors of death and disease
stemmed from animal-factory-confinement operations had a striking
influence on public opinion.

Meanwhile, in the first dozen years of the 21st century, extreme
weather events were striking major population centers head-on, and
the cataclysmic results were waking increasing numbers of people up
to the unmistakable reality that human actions were causing severe
damage to the biosphere. It's a shame that it took so much suffering.
But perhaps, looking back, we can say now that the enormous hurri-
canes that struck Miami and other coastal cities, the floods that inun-
dated heavily populated river basins, and the fires that raged out of
control in the drought-stricken Great Plains served a needed purpose.

They provoked an undeniable recognition that the greatest threats to human security were not from military invasion but from environmental degradation.

It was an electrical storm of unprecedented proportions that fouled up computers worldwide and thwarted TV reception for months in 2007 that turned out to be pivotal. The worldwide outpouring of sentiment for saving the environment was enormous. Finally, a critical mass of public perception was achieved, and elected officials were willing to take substantive action.

Looking back, it is fair to say that the one event that was most crucial in turning the tide toward a food and agriculture system that sustained life rather than exploited it was the tax shift of 2008. Taxes, of course, had always been supposed to raise money for the common good. But now it was recognized that a good tax system could also help us reconcile our needs for a prosperous economy with our needs for a healthy environment. When it was first proposed that products which harmed the environment and human well-being should be taxed far more than those that contributed to the public welfare, the oil, cattle, and chemical industries were hysterical, calling such a plan un-American. But commentators had a field day pointing out that the Boston Tea Party, after all, had been not about tea but about taxes.

It was such a simple idea, and it had such profound consequences. After the tax shift of 2008, we stopped taxing things that add to the general welfare, such as paychecks and enterprise, and started taxing things that cause harm, such as toxic waste and resource depletion. Many existing taxes were reduced or eliminated. The lower and middle classes were delighted to see the end of regressive property, payroll, and sales taxes. The wealthy were overjoyed to see the end of business taxes, and just about everyone was glad to see the end of the personal income tax. Instead, public revenue was raised by taxing actions and products that damage the public good.

It started innocently enough, when the sales tax on gas-guzzling cars and trucks was raised. Soon, taxes were implemented on emissions of deadly fine particles, greenhouse gases, and other air pollutants. Not long after, other taxes were instituted on discharges of toxic heavy metals and other water pollutants. Enough revenue was pouring in from polluting industries that income taxes began to be scaled back and eventually were eliminated.

It was all very creative. Traffic jams began to be taxed out of existence when drivers were taxed for use of major routes at rush hour. Natural ecosystems were protected by taxing the pumping of fresh water, the damming of rivers, and the felling of virgin timber. As polluters paid more, and those who tread more lightly on the Earth paid less, incentives were created for people to do the right thing.

The industries whose products were responsible for polluting the environment and endangering public health fought against the tax shift tooth and nail. Calling anyone who opposed them overwrought extremists, they brought forth experts and scientists who were willing to speak in their defense, and they spent huge sums claiming that things were too confusing to justify decisive action.

But even within these industries, there were those who saw the writing on the wall, understood that change was inevitable and found a way to make a profit from it. Oil companies began to see themselves as energy suppliers and became heavily involved in photovoltaic solar panels and hydrogen. Car companies started pouring their research and marketing dollars into vehicles that provided transportation without harming the biosphere.

The cattlemen started investing in windmills, converting much of the vast acreages of the western states to wind farms. McDonald's led the way among the fast-food companies, first going to all-organic meat and dairy products and then eventually phasing out most of their animal products entirely, becoming the world's leading supplier of organic soy burgers.

The reason was simple. The old practices that had caused so much damage were no longer profitable. The tax shift of 2008 harnessed the profit motive for environmental and health ends. The phenomenal engine of market capitalism no longer drove us toward disease and eco-catastrophe but toward the fulfillment of the human potential and a healthy relationship with life.

Whereas before, restaurants that offered vegetarian fare had signs emphasizing that fact, it was now accepted that all restaurants featured primarily vegetarian offerings. By 2012, restaurants that offered meat advertised that in their signs. Otherwise, people assumed they didn't.

One of the unexpected results of the tax shift of 2008 was a steady drop in heart disease, cancer, and other disease rates. By 2012, the reduced demands on the medical system were so dramatic that universal health care became an affordable reality, and no American ever went again without coverage for basic health care needs.

Of course, by then organic agriculture had become the norm rather than the exception. There had been worry that what the chemical companies claimed might be true—that if taxes on pesticides were increased, there wouldn't be enough food to go around. But that's far from what actually happened. Instead, higher taxes on pesticides stimulated farmers, researchers, and government agencies to devote far more attention to low-chemical cultivation. With the highest taxes imposed on those compounds that presented the greatest danger to people and the environment, the revenue was used to fund research and education programs to develop nontoxic alternatives. Gone were the perverse incentives that led farmers to poison themselves, their families, and their surroundings in order to survive. Communities became not only less polluted but more prosperous, with the USDA now supporting family farms and natural methods of cultivation as fully as they had once subsidized chemical-based factory farms.

Then there was Project 2020, the remarkable plan first conceived 5 years earlier, in the year 2015. Recognizing that 20-20 vision had long been the standard of perfect eyesight, the idea was that by the year 2020, we would see the virtual end of malnutrition and hunger. The idea moved toward fruition as taxes on junk food not only decreased their consumption but also provided the revenue to subsidize the production and widespread distribution of many varieties of whole grains, legumes, and fresh vegetables.

We look back today and shake our heads at how bleak the future might have looked to people at the beginning of the New Millennium. At the surface level, the economy was booming. But even as

Internet stocks were rising to staggering new heights, most of the Earth's environmental systems and resources were deteriorating under the impact of human economic activities. The Nasdaq was skyrocketing, but shrinking forests, eroding soils, falling water tables, rising temperatures, dying coral reefs, melting glaciers, and disappearing plant and animal species bespoke a frightening future.

Today, when we have faced up to the fact that we depend entirely on the Earth's natural resources and systems to feed and sustain us, we have much cause for gratitude. Now that we eat well, breathe clean air, and listen to one another, it is stunning how much creativity has been released for the realization of humanity's needs, both physical and spiritual. The Pope, of course, played a crucial part in this Global Renaissance, when in 2023, moved by the unbearable burden that ever-growing populations were placing on the biosphere, he called for an end to the Catholic Church's historic opposition to contraception. God wanted us, he told the world, to limit our numbers and cherish Creation as stewards, not destroy it as polluters.

Now, when every day it seems we discover new opportunities to live in greater harmony with one another and the Earth, we honor and appreciate all those who played a part over the years in the Global Renaissance. Humbly, we bow our heads in gratitude to those far-sighted people whose actions and choices helped to create the world of prosperity and peace that we now accept as our birthright. They persisted even when the future seemed bleak.

We thank them with all our hearts.

★★★

John Robbins is the author of the international best-sellers *Diet for a New America: How Your Food Choices Affect Your Health, Happiness, and the Future of Life on Earth* and *Reclaiming Our Health: Exploding the Medical Myth and Embracing the Source of True Healing.* He is the founder of EarthSave International, a nonprofit organization that supports healthier food, environmental preservation, and a more compassionate world.

THE ARTS

Peter Coyote

Art is the creative play of the human mind." The Pulitzer Prize–winning poet Gary Snyder offered that definition in 1975 when we were discussing our mandate as members of the California Arts Council, a government agency. We adopted his definition as the starting point for our deliberations. It was a good insight then, and it continues to be useful.

When we peel away all of the constructs that society has accreted around the core truth of "art"—the business of art, the status of art, the cultural importance of art—we are left with nothing more than a playful, curious human impulse, an impulse that knows neither its ultimate destination nor how it may finally arrive. This impulse explores the opening before it intuitively, orienting itself and constructing its map as it travels, solving problems and mastering skills, step by step, for the same inexpressible reason that the grain dances in a piece of wood and plum trees blossom exuberantly in spring.

At the ceremony at which council members were formally introduced to the public, one of the new members, the African-American sculptor Noah Purifoy, read remarks that changed my life. During his speech, he surprised me by substituting the phrase "creative process" where I expected him to use the word "art." He defined this process as "a problem-solving mechanism" unique in its ability to coordinate and integrate both hemispheres of the brain into an optimally functioning state.

To oversimplify a bit, the left brain is the apparent locus of orderly, sequential thinking and the right brain is the site of feelings and sensibilities. A simple example of how art integrates both types of cerebral activity is to imagine the practice of scales on the piano as a predominantly left-brain activity, primarily involving digital, sequential thinking. The *playing* of music, however, is predominantly a right-brain activity, involving feelings and a multiplicity of expression. This integration of complementarily opposed capabilities is what creates an optimal mode of brain function. Indeed, heightened communication between the brain hemispheres when creative work is being performed has been empirically observed and measured.

Purifoy reminded us that the process all artists employ is essentially the same. They begin with an idea, an impulse, a question, a hypothesis, and then they act upon it—create a line, a movement, a sentence, a splash of color. They step back and observe what they have done, then, receiving their instruction intuitively or logically from the thing itself, commit the next line, movement, sound, and so on. In this way, a map is constructed that leads artists to where they have never been before. They arrive at the finished piece in these self-reflective fits and starts that define the creative process.

The Power of Creative Thought

The other council members must have been as impressed as I was with Purifoy's speech, because the council decided to create its programs according to the principles of this process. If I ever entertained any doubts about the utility of Purifoy's hypothesis, they had completely disappeared by the end of my 8-year tenure on the council. By that time, the council had posted many victories:

◆ Winning the social and political support to raise its budget from $1 million to $14 million annually
◆ Creating relationships with more than a dozen state agencies that employed artists to help those agencies solve intractable problems for the taxpayer

◆ Creating state-local partnerships (minicouncils) in every California county that planned local cultural policies in cooperation with the state council (collectively, these minicouncils have raised more than $50 million in new monies for cultural programs)

◆ Creating artist-in-the-community programs that organized community murals, taught new skills to prisoners, used dancers to help senior citizens learn how to move more nimbly, and commissioned painters to create posters for state parks and other agencies; local musicians and institutions created community music ensembles and offered lessons to the disadvantaged; hundreds of artists annually offered programs that were eagerly sought by the public and paid for in partnership with the state government

◆ Making staunch allies of formerly adversarial legislators who had previously tried to abolish the council

California's senators and representatives were incredulous when I first appeared before them as chairman and admitted, "The program you gave us money to implement last year failed. However, we learned X, Y, and Z from the failure and would like to continue the program, refocusing and refining it with what we've learned." The legislators said that they had never heard such a candid admission of failure before and were curious. They became engaged in the process with us and refinanced the program (an experimental education program) that year and for 7 more, eventually becoming fascinated by the council's work and respectful of its successes. This was a real-world victory for some very airy conceits. How and why they worked and what they might mean for our nation's future is worth a little space and time.

Even the hardest-boiled legislators I ever encountered during my Arts Council experience understood that one can only be so good and so successful operating on technique and logic alone. They understood the edge that intuition offers the best lawyer, doctor, plumber, or politician. Through the success of the council's programs, they became aware that artists are an extraordinary reservoir of creative problem solvers for society and that even a rather mediocre artist can be extremely effective at training and inspiring others in the use of creative problem-solving techniques. They understood that we were not supporting the arts to create future audiences or to "civilize" wild young men and women (the traditional, nebulous justifications for most government arts subsidies) but rather to unleash the creative potential of our future citizenry.

ART AS A SOCIETAL TOOL

And yet this knowledge is not widely embraced. At the historical moment in which our nation is deluged by intractable problems, the freest, most creative minds who could contribute radical new conceptions, insights, and skills toward solutions are prevented from participating. One of the primary reasons for this is the enduring assault on the nation's arts agency, the National Endowment for the Arts.

I realize that some legislators have an ideological fixation against government as a source of anything other than military protection and economic stabilization, but beleaguered citizens cannot afford this ideological fixation. The response to mental and physical rigidities needs to be fluidity and creative responsiveness. Not ideology but rather the creative process holds the best hope of affording us peace, prosperity, and national security.

Art is the research and development arm of culture. No high-tech firm could hope to thrive and remain competitive without massive expenditures on R&D. Why should we assume that a culture can? If the support of art is left solely to the marketplace, the only arts we will have are those that can be bought and sold, those that glorify the market or the sponsor.

Such a restricted arts world represents a critically dangerous reduction of the one winning constant in every evolutionary history: diversity. Where in that diminished model is the common celebrated? Where are the overarching visions of an integrated, diverse culture? How will we ever create public visions, monuments, music, and expressions of common citizenship if all funding is left to the private sector and all public arenas are dominated by private concerns?

If, for instance, we want to see movies and television that mirror realities other than the most shocking, sexually stimulating, and violent, as a culture we need to make the tools for making and distributing them more widely available. Technology is on our side. Digital video equipment can produce movies for one-hundredth of the commercial cost. Just as important as the creation of these films and programs are the channels of distribution through which the distinctly noncommercial can be disseminated. Digital technology makes the short film an easily available subject for high school curricula and the notion of interschool film competitions a viable reality. With 500 channels a near reality, dedicating a number of them to emergent filmmakers could promote filmmaking to the popularity of sports.

Imagine movie studios spending some of the money dedicated to long-shot development deals to underwriting the budgets of small theaters. This would create an untold number of apprenticeships and loyalties and would afford training to screenwriters, actors, directors, costumers, and technicians. Further, the studios would be germinating new talent instead of merely harvesting the finest blossoms from each annual crop and giving nothing back to the soil.

Moreover, if the creative process were understood as a cheap, renewable, problem-solving resource, it would be demanded as a dominant part of public school curricula. Every pupil would be studying music, sculpture, dance, acting, drawing, poetry, and writing—not to create more artists, but to nurture people in whom senses and skills operate at peak efficiency. This is how we will train the integrated and organized minds to appreciate nuance and detail and to make the creative leaps necessary to keep culture and industry vital. This is where we will find the renewable resources to produce more beautiful products, architecture, and cultural expression.

Design sense and keen aesthetics, after all, are not merely right-brain "creative" activities—they are forms of intelligence. Look at the patterns on a computer chip. It is impossible to separate their function from their design. In fact, part of the intelligence imbedded in them is design. The same is true for a honeycomb. The repetitive octagon of the honeycomb is the most efficient design for maximizing storage capacity in a given space. A chambered nautilus, the valves of the heart, a coral reef, a kimono, and a lacquered bowl all represent a fusion of form and function that is a kind of heightened problem-solving intelligence. This intelligence, which can be studied, learned, replicated, and reproduced, needs to be integrated into our schools' curricula if we want to reap the public rewards inherent in a highly skilled, educated citizenry and labor force.

Imagine turning the powerful engine of the creative process on America itself, giving imagination free reign to re-vision what each of our institutions and economies might be like if they were reevaluated through the lens of a playful, problem-solving intelligence.

Why should culture be accepted as carved in stone? It has evolved, like fashion, over two centuries. Why not make its evolution conscious rather than accidental, driven by the desire to honor grander orders than the purely economic? In such a remodeled and rethought America, definitions of art would be expanded to embrace much that is now abandoned to the minimal standards of popular culture: malls, miniparks, retaining walls, buses, trucks, parking lots, and lobbies. Conversation might sparkle again as it once did in the age of refined and educated wits as poetry slams, Chattauquas, debates, and rhetorical competitions inject elevated standards into public discourse. Popular music might begin to express affection for things other than sexual objects, might expand its scope to include love of place, parents, friends, other species, and water. (I once had the good fortune to live for several weeks with the Hopi snake priest David Monogye. Well into his nineties when I knew him, he was a wry and sophisticated observer of mainstream culture. He used to tease me by observing, "We Hopis have lots of songs about water because it's so rare and precious in the desert. I notice that your people sing about love all the time. Is that because it's so rare for your people?")

Popular music, driven by joy, curiosity, and intuition rather than the lowest common denominator of marketing, would scarcely resemble what we hear thumping and bumping next to us at the stoplight. When every park sports a band shell for community music programs featuring local talent, school competitions, and major artists who happen to be visiting local classical, folk, and jazz venues, we may once again hear the full range of musical voices representing the varied cultures and heritages we live with on a daily basis. Who knows what operas American Finns, Africans, Irish, Poles, Native Americans, Indonesians, Hawaiians, Micronesians, Polynesians, and Latinos might produce? All have ancient and vibrant musical traditions that need to be admitted to full aural citizenship and represented in public life.

When carbon-fiber technology supplants most steel in automobiles and the reality is that quick, responsive, clean-burning, 1,000-pound cars can be constructed in local workshops, imagine what an evolution of personal transportation will take place. Imagine the curriculum of an entire school organized around the creative processes necessary to build such a vehicle: math and science classes calculating the physics of wind resistance, friction, and power trains; history classes researching the car and the federal highway system; political science and environmental classes studying the extraction of copper, tin, zinc, and rubber to make different types of cars, and the relationship of such activities to foreign policy and environmental degradation. Shop classes might deal with the problems of construction, molding forms, welding, sound-proofing, and upholstering, and as a by-product, students who do not intend to pursue higher education might develop usable, marketable skills.

When the school-designed and -constructed car is finally completed, imagine the competitions for beauty, performance, outrageousness, and speed attended by proud parents and communities celebrating the achievements of their students—and the competitions between the schools to sell the tastiest, most exotic foods and beverages from their traditions to support their teams.

The California Arts Council programs were minitrials for such ideas. Through them we learned that pedagogical information (the three Rs) is absorbed along with aesthetic information. When children are engaged and amused, math and science are ancillary problems, mastered quickly so that they do not impede the pursuit of fun.

Imagine what heightened standards of public architecture and monuments a sensitized and aestheticized populace might demand.

What would be the incentive for energized and switched-on people to accept the boxy, unimaginative storefronts and strip malls mushrooming in their neighborhoods? Why would people who are alive to color, design, form, sound, and movement settle on the cube as the organizing principle of most architecture?

CREATIVITY DIRECTED

The reconfiguring of our cultural institutions based upon an openly creative society is much too important to be politicized and left to the puff and venality of Congress and eventual usurpation by corporate largesse. The tasks are endless, challenging, and fun:

◆ The reshaping of cities in which residents could be bound by commonalities of citizenship rather than divided by class and race
◆ The discovery of alternatives to the rapidly disappearing old-school corporate employment model for participating in the national economy
◆ The dedication of government power to the rebuilding of national wealth—clean, fresh air and water, replanted forests
◆ The revivification of stable communities
◆ The revitalization of fisheries and their attendant industries

Such issues must be rescued from the thrall of corporate dominance and allowed to enter real public discussion and debate, where the creative process may flourish.

Great Britain, for instance, funds the BBC from a tax on the sale of televisions and radios, and those funds, independent of political interference, have created the greatest public television in the world. The budget of the National Endowment for the Arts should be multiplied tenfold by a mandated contribution from each department of the federal government as an extension of its work. Each agency should have a research and development wing that explores creative solutions specific to its mandated area of focus, using artists as the technicians of the imagination.

Research and development will, by its nature, be wasteful, messy, and difficult to monitor. This should not deter us any more than the explosion of a multi-billion-dollar rocket should cause us to cancel the space program. We need to adopt a generous and patient attitude toward cultural R&D and judge its contribution not by the annual but by the decade's returns.

If we consider the mind as the ultimate wilderness—a self-organizing, interdependent system—we have ample evidence from those who have explored it most diligently (our artists) that it is not a savage place to be feared and conquered. It is, in fact, like the rain forests, a mother lode of resources for exploration, healing, and inspiration. Only people completely ignorant of artistic history could make movies and television shows like those that fill our airwaves. Only people whose feelings and receptivity have been blunted and who are blind to natural splendor could create the wasteland of shopping malls and characterless condo communities plopped down on our landscapes and deadening our expectations for beauty and surprise. Only people who rely exclusively on left-brain functions could reduce the nuances and shadings of daily life to the reductionist pap of the morning paper or the nightly news.

We have the right to expect more of ourselves, our institutions, and our cultural life. The resources to make the transformation from our present-day acceptance of the mediocre to future realization of our expectations resides in skillful play with the wildness of our own minds. It is free, and readily available. The energy and discipline to transform that wildness into a glorious imagining of the present moment is the discipline and joy of the creative process.

★★★

Peter Coyote has performed as an actor for some of the world's most distinguished filmmakers, including Barry Levinson, Roman Polanski, Pedro Almodovar, Steven Spielberg, and Sidney Pollack. He is the author of *Sleeping Where I Fall*, a memoir of his adventures in the 1960s. A chapter from that book, "Carla's Story," won a Pushcart Prize for excellence in nonfiction. A successful screenplay author, he is also well-known for his voice-over work. He has done numerous documentaries and television specials, including the 9-hour PBS special *The West*. In 1992, he won an Emmy as the host of *The Pacific Century*, a 9-hour television series.

THE MEDIA

Eric Utne

Imagine what life would be like if every magazine, every newspaper, and every radio and television station the world over made community a high priority. Imagine if Rosie O'Donnell, Sally Jessy Raphael, and even Jerry Springer did what Oprah does. Like Oprah, the greatest salon-keeper of our time, they could make community one of their top priorities. Rosie could encourage her viewers to get together, like Oprah's book groups do, in one another's homes to watch her show. Perhaps once a week, Sally would introduce a discussion topic such as "What does it mean to be human?" or "What are your concerns for your neighborhood?" or "Where do you turn for inspiration?" Imagine if Jerry Springer encouraged everyone on his show as well as those watching from home to speak and listen from the heart, just like Oprah does so beautifully and skillfully. These hosts could start a conversation among Americans all over the country. They could build on the movement Oprah has already started, a movement that could revive the endangered art of conversation and start a new era of community-building in America.

By community I mean the feeling of connection that we have to a place, to other people, to ourselves, and to our spiritual source. I believe that the popular media have been the principal destroyers of community around the planet over the last 100 years. I also believe, with highly qualified optimism, that these same media can become the connective tissue we need to restore community to our lives.

One Vision of the Media of the Future

The current buzzword among media types is *convergence*, as in the emerging convergence of television and the Internet. Recently, a leading television executive told an audience of television professionals, "Our challenge is to understand that we are in the business of serving the needs, interests, and desires of individuals. We need to forget everything we know about mass media. It is not our business anymore. Now viewers have the ultimate ability to tailor-make their own programs, consuming environments, and marketing and merchandising options."

On the face of it, this vision looks terrific. But then the television executive went on. The future, he said, is in consumer-driven media, which "dramatically shifts us from a share-of-market business to a share-of-customer business. Every moment in a buyer's life, every point of media they consume, every message they interpret, every transaction they conduct, is a marketing moment."

A marketing moment, he explained, is "that instant in time when sellers can connect with buyers' needs and wants, when and where these needs and wants occur. The really smart new marketers . . . the survivors in the new marketing information age . . . will be able to leverage [this moment]. Our new task is to increase usage and revenue and profit-per-customer, across all media, across all platforms, wherever our customers are: at home, at work, at play, in-car, onboard, by phone, by wire, or wireless."

What troubles me most about this vision is that it views people as passive consumers rather than as active participants and co-creators of information. It's all about marketing to individuals rather than increasing people's ability to express themselves creatively or to communicate and assemble with others. I'm concerned that this commercial vision of our media future is atomizing, alienating, and ultimately destructive of community.

I'm not arguing that we should abandon the market economy. But for their long-term survival, the media would do well to reconceive their roles. The media need to see their audiences not just as consumers or markets, but as constituents. If they hope to carve out a vital and sustainable role for themselves, they must re-create themselves as conveners of community.

COMMUNITY: A MOST HUMAN NEED

Human beings are social animals. According to the anthropologist Margaret Mead, for 99 percent of the time that humans have lived on this planet, we've lived in what she called tribes or bands; that is, groups of 12 to 36 people. It's only during times of war, or what we have now, which she called the psychological equivalent of war, that the nuclear family prevails as the dominant or primary social unit, because it's the most mobile unit and is therefore more likely to ensure the survival of the species. "But for the full flowering of the human spirit," Mead said, "we need groups, tribes." Community.

The desire for stronger, cleaner, safer, and more cohesive communities is a principal concern of people these days. We yearn for a sense of connection and meaning in our lives. There's a tremendous unserved market for community, but unless the media begin to address the interests of communities rather than the interests of a few private individuals and corporations, people will reject them, as they are now doing by creating their own community-access television programs, desktop publications, online computer conferences, and the like.

WHAT WE'RE MISSING

Most of the people on this planet live in real communities, while a majority of North American college-educated people arrange themselves in networks. We work with, live with, and hang out with people like ourselves, with similar educational levels and similar media habits. This has tended to isolate and alienate us from others. We've come to mistrust people who are differently educated and informed. We don't know them. We're distant from them. We've turned them into just that: the Other.

Jeffersonian democracy is based on the belief that the greatest wisdom lies in the majority of the people, not in the few "best and brightest" who would plan for the rest of us. The social critic Christopher Lasch wrote that true democratic community requires an educated, informed citizenry. But people only become informed, he wrote, if they actively seek out information.

Today, most people have stopped using the media to seek out essential information, and it's easy to see why. The mass media barrage us with an unrelenting cascade of mindless entertainment and commercial drivel. This information washes over us daily, and we absorb it passively if we take it in at all. This sea of information we're all swimming in is completely congested. Each medium is competing for our overtaxed attention, trying to deliver its messages through the clutter. People quite naturally, as a survival mechanism, tune it out.

Television gets most of the blame. It has rightly been called the plug-in drug. But all the media can have a similar mind-numbing, eye-glazing, soporific effect if consumed indiscriminately. As the author Neil Postman said, we're "amusing ourselves to death." We're not just tuning out the media; we're tuning out one another. We may be losing our capacity to listen. That, of course, is not good for community.

Community is an activity, a process. It is based on people's experiences, relationships, and common learning. The only way to have a truly informed citizenry, an active and motivated citizenry, Lasch pointed out, is through live, personal discussion and debate. "We come to know our own minds only by explaining ourselves to others," he wrote.

The information that we need, the knowledge and the wisdom, comes by word of mouth as well as through contemplation and inspiration. Think of what life was like before the advent of commercial media. People got their news from one another, through storytelling and small talk and shared observation. You'd learn when to plant, what the weather meant, and the gossip about what was happening in the community. There was little interest in the notion of celebrity; outside the circles of political leadership, there were few nationally famous people.

In startling contrast, today the media focus our attention intensely on entertainment, trying to convince us that what's happening to celebrities someplace else is more interesting and important than what's going on with us right here. What the media are really doing is undermining community by distracting us with amusing but irrelevant information that ultimately separates us from our neighbors.

So how do we get from where we are now, with commerce-driven media that tend to separate us, to community-oriented media that bring us together?

First, we must recognize what we're missing. When we realize how much richer and soul-satisfying life could be with community-oriented media, we won't settle for anything less. Then, we must create and support media that give us news, entertainment, and other forms of information that truly connect us to one another, to the world, and to our selves.

Turn Off, Tune Out, Drop In

One of the most liberating things that you can do for yourself is to go on a media fast: Turn off the television and radio, cancel your newspaper subscription, and drop back in to life. Several years ago, when I began a sabbatical from my job at the magazine *Utne Reader*, my wife and I did exactly that. We canceled our subscriptions to the national edition of the *New York Times* as well as our local daily, and we cut back on our already meager amount of television watching.

The effects were surprising and almost immediate. I started having conversations, real conversations, with people I ran into in the grocery store. Instead of the old, "Hi, how are you?" asked without even listening for a response, now I was 15 minutes into the conversation before I'd realize, and savor, how novel the experience was. I started reading more books. And I began to rely on my neighbors for important local, national, and international news. It's amazing how much time and energy gets freed up, how rarely you or your kids actually feel bored, and how informed you can stay simply by keeping in touch with your neighbors.

ANOTHER VISION OF THE MEDIA

Fifty years from now, when the media are imbued with goals and values that support community, the content of print and electronic media will look very different than it does today. There will be less sex and violence, more inspiring and positive examples. There will be less so-called objectivity and more passion, quirkiness, and straightforward, honest, unapologetic subjectivity. Less national news and more local and international coverage. Less head and more heart. Less observation and entertainment, more interaction and participation. Less hand-wringing and blaming and problem orientation—more shouldering of responsibility and solution orientation. Fewer false choices and more true alternatives. More discussion and debate. More context. More spirit. More wisdom.

Instead of shows like Ted Koppel's *Nightline*, in which Tweedledum and Tweedledee debate the pros and cons of policy inside the Beltway, we'll have our greatest spiritual thinkers hosting shows that bring diverse perspectives to the subjects at hand. When there's a school shooting, a spike in the Nasdaq, or conflict in the Balkans, people like Clarissa Pinkola Estés, Robert Bly, Christiane Northrup, and James Hillman will be invited to help us explore what the events mean to our own lives.

Media could bring us together if they would make it their purpose to become the matchmakers, the conveners, the community salon-keepers. The dictionary defines *media* as "an intervening agency, means, or instrument"; *to mediate* means "to bring about (an agreement, accord, peace, truce, etc.) as an intermediary between parties by compromise, reconciliation, removal of misunderstanding, etc." Most media represent a one-way broadcast model, with the information coming from the center and radiating out to the periphery. Editors and station managers feel happy and successful if they get feedback in the form of phone calls and letters to the editor. But what they're not doing is introducing their audiences—their constituents—to one another. That's where community begins. And that's what the media of the future can do.

MEDIA CAN BE THE CONNECTIVE TISSUE

Utne Reader staged a conference some time ago with the theme "Media and the Environment." At this conference, we introduced several hundred of our subscribers to one another and invited them to speak from the heart about the things they cared about and believed in. The result: Genuine, new relationships were formed. We quickly realized that we should try to do this for all of our subscribers. So we ran an ad in the magazine inviting them to let us know if they'd like to meet other *Utne Reader* subscribers in their area. In other words, we played the role of salon-keeper.

Nearly 10,000 people responded, and soon more than 20,000 people all over North America were meeting monthly in one another's living rooms and often doing things together. Some married; others started businesses, schools, or cooperative housing projects. All kinds of good things have come out of these salons. They have convinced me that Americans have an enormous craving for human interaction and true community.

Since our early initiative, hundreds of newspapers around the country have gotten involved in what has come to be known as public journalism. This kind of journalism is not only a service to the community, it's also good for business, because people who are connected to their communities tend to read their local newspapers.

TRUE COMMUNITY

Too often, the popular media have effectively distanced people from their genuine, flesh-and-blood community and linked them to anonymous others who share their special interests. Such self-selected groups of people who share common belief systems, lifestyles, interests, and worldviews are called media communes by the Yankelovich Monitor, a service that tracks marketing and social trends. Because the members of these media communes circle the wagons around a particular set of cultural norms, they risk falling out of touch with anyone who has a different way of looking at things.

Some people are calling these media communes "networks" and

confusing them with true community. The Internet is not a real community; it is simply a medium that allows users to network. In networks, people arrange themselves according to common interests and by choice. You can choose to be in or you can opt out. In true communities, however, diverse people are required to deal with one another, to "mix it up" face-to-face and work through their differences. Living in community is not easy, but for the "full flowering of the human spirit" we need one another.

Utne Reader discussion groups might seem similar to media communes. Their members are highly educated, active in their communities, and generally like-minded. The groups may begin as the kind of self-selected networks I'm criticizing, but soon the members start looking to bring people who are different from them into their conversations. We think that the next stage of the salon movement is to work with media organizations of very different political, social, and cultural points of view to encourage more inclusive communities.

Imagine if your favorite magazine, your daily newspaper, and your local radio and television stations made community a top priority. They might help you get to know your neighbors, and yourself, in ways you never imagined. Your neighborhood might start feeling more neighborly, with people feeling connected to and responsible for their communities. Participation in all sorts of activities would increase. We might even see a revival of direct democracy.

Your life might be very different from how it is today. Imagine that.

★★★

Eric Utne is the founder of *Utne Reader*, a bimonthly "preview of the emerging culture." As of September 2000, he is the seventh-grade teacher at the City of Lakes Waldorf School in Minneapolis.

LOWER EDUCATION

Dee Dickinson

When I imagine the best ways to educate children, I am always drawn to a vision of communities built around the concept of learning at its very heart. It is a costly vision, rich with ideals. But as caring for our youth—as well as the need for lifelong learning—moves higher on our social agendas, I know it can become a reality in the decades ahead.

I know this because my vision is based on seeds being planted today at schools throughout the world, seeds that are already bearing some fruit. In this vision, education begins in the home, supported by early childhood/parenting centers. These programs might be inspired by the pioneering Family and Intelligence projects in Venezuela, the remarkable early childhood schools of Reggio Emilia in Italy, or Parents as Teachers and other fine parent education and preschool programs in the United States. Future community learning centers with supportive child/family services might replace today's schools, and Lighthouses of Knowledge, inspired by those now existing in Curitiba, Brazil, might evolve from existing public libraries. New, low-cost educational technologies are already becoming more available throughout the world.

What follows, then, is my vision of the places, teachers, and technologies that will educate our children—and ourselves—some 50 years from now. I'll start my tour with the newer educational structures for adults and parents and then move on to the child's classroom of the future.

LIGHTHOUSES OF KNOWLEDGE

Welcome first to a Lighthouse of Knowledge, a large, modern facility once known as the local library but that has transformed into a community focal point. It is made of transparent, shatterproof material. Like glasses that darken in the sunlight, the windows here cut glare when the sun is shining but otherwise let light pour in. As you can imagine, when the Lighthouses in all neighborhoods are lit up at night, the view is inspiring.

Open 24 hours a day year-round, Lighthouses are accessible to everyone, and many of the resources are free: a library of real books (some people still like the feel and smell), databases of electronic books, access to the Internet, satellite-broadcast studios and receivers, multicast facilities, rooms for shared virtual realities, and other resources related to finding information and turning it into knowledge throughout life.

Each Lighthouse-keeper is in charge of maintaining a comprehensive database of all the educational resources in the community as well as booking uses of the facility. Businesses and individual entrepreneurs rent space for telework and electronic meetings, or use the technologies for specialty training and distance learning. Those fees support the facility and provide space for nonprofits at low cost.

There are also special classrooms used by the Global University—the name that has emerged for adult learning programs—that have become a part of almost every worker's life. Even though much of the learning is now electronic and connects students to experts throughout the world, there is still a need and desire for learners to collaborate with one another. They frequently meet in small learning teams, but they also use Lighthouses for meeting virtually with students from other parts of the country or from anywhere in the world. Simultaneous translation is available for those who do not share a common language. The facilities include rooms with interactive video walls so that distant students can see one another as they share information, collaborate on projects, and learn together.

EARLY CHILDHOOD/PARENTING CENTERS

In every neighborhood, early childhood/parenting centers have been created that are free and easily accessible. The first years of life are critically important to healthy physical, emotional, and mental development, as it is during these years that the foundation of successful learning is laid. Because of this understanding, these centers have become an essential part of the educational system and have resulted in more children coming into school with the skills they need to learn successfully.

Prospective parents are urged through all the media to take free parent-prep classes in the centers, usually in the evenings. Neonatal and early childhood specialists offer information and practice on the importance of nutrition, love, sensitive sensory stimulation, exercise, and social interaction. In essence, parents and other caregivers learn how to create optimal conditions for their children's healthy, happy development. During the day, parents may visit the centers to observe children at various stages of development as well as to participate in programs with their own children. Day care is also provided, and for parents who have not been able to attend classes, there are daily programs on interactive digital television that also provide access to databases of relevant information and links to appropriate World Wide Web sites that offer on-demand guidance.

Parents and other caregivers bring babies and toddlers to the centers periodically, to learn the best ways to nurture them and help them develop. Children with physical, cognitive, or emotional challenges are identified early and helped through well-integrated social and health services on-site. There are early childhood programs that prepare children aged 3 to 5 to be successful academic learners, mostly through play and exploration.

Many of the centers are located near retirement homes, and that's a great source of joy for both the children and the elderly. There is much loving care, active play both inside and outdoors, dancing, music, storytelling, and other human interactions in stimulating, multisensory environments. But because they might pose risks to rapidly developing neurological systems, no screen technologies are used with the very young. These will be introduced later.

COMMUNITY LEARNING CENTERS

Over the years, there has been increasing demand by parents for more choice in the kinds of schools available to their children. In our future scenario, this goal has been achieved. Most children from age 6 to 16 attend community learning centers that take many different forms. For example, some may be located in museums; others may be connected to farms or greenhouses that produce healthful fruits and vegetables for the centers. Some may be located in workplaces or near theaters or hospitals, or connected to churches. Some look like malls in the center of the community, to connect more directly with its resources.

What is certain is that few look like the large factory-model schools of today. Each community learning center has been designed in response to the needs, interests, and preferences of the community that it serves. The centers are part of a public, decentralized educational system operated by neighborhood councils, with a coordinator for each. Standards for all the centers, however, are set nationally, and most students meet or exceed them. There are elementary programs for 6- to 12-year-olds as well as a broad variety of educational programs for teenagers, and children with special interests may be accommodated even though they live outside the district.

As in the early childhood/parenting centers, there are support services on-site to identify problems early and provide intervention. Unlike today's fragmented support services, health, social service, and welfare agencies have integrated their efforts through collaborative, continually updated databases and Web sites, assuring continuity and continuation of help as needed.

The centers are open 18 hours a day year-round and have extended-day programs for both students and adults. Parenting groups meet regularly to learn about and discuss the rapidly developing minds, emotions, and bodies of children age 6 through adolescence, and how best to help them develop to their fullest potential. The centers include job exploration and training programs, branches of social service agencies and health clinics, and recreational facilities that may include theaters, galleries, art studios, gyms, swimming pools, and ball courts. Income from adult or family use in the evening and on weekends and holidays helps to support the facilities.

At the turn of the millennium, some people thought that in the future there would be no need for schools as a result of new technologies that would be developed. If people of all ages could learn anything on any subject through interactive digital TV, videos, teleputers, the Internet, or virtual reality systems, why have schools with walls at all? Most parents, however, whether they are working outside the home or not, wish to have their children with other youngsters in caring educational environments. Also, most human beings are by nature social and learn best with human interaction, although new technologies offer additional opportunities for individualized learning.

By midcentury, there are electronic personal tutors, or EPTs, that are so sensitive to the user that they can interpret facial expressions and sense mood, confidence, or anxiety level and offer appropriate help. Students will learn at their own pace, and as they do the work or answer questions, the EPTs offer new material that is close enough to the students' levels so that they can succeed, but just a bit beyond so that they are constantly challenged. With these technologies in the learning rooms, learning specialists—who used to be called teachers—are able to work closely with small groups of students.

Consider a community learning center that is adjacent to a visual and performing arts facility. Here, students concentrate on acquiring knowledge and skills individually with a variety of electronic devices or in groups facilitated by learning specialists or older students. There is also a virtual library of experts available to both students and specialists. Math and science skills may be applied to home or community projects, business enterprises, or environmental conservation. Writing and speaking skills may be applied to projects such as news broadcasts to the community, communicating with learning partners locally or abroad, or writing books for younger children. Working with visual arts, music, dance, drama, and a great variety of materials and manipulatives helps make abstract ideas more easily understandable.

There is much emphasis on developing interpersonal skills, as students learn to work collaboratively, and attention is paid to creating an environment that facilitates the development of ethical, moral, and responsible behavior. Because students with different abilities and disabilities learn together, they have rich opportunities to learn empathy and compassion. Challenges are often given that require wise and responsible decision making in such activities as student government.

A Classroom of the Future

Imagine a group of elementary-aged youngsters in one of the center's interactive learning rooms. Each room can be adapted to a current theme, which in this case is the study of marine environments. Do you hear Debussy's *La Mer* playing softly in the background? On one wall is a digital video image of the ocean, including sound and smell, as well as linked databases and Web sites accessible on the students' computers. In front of the video, the children have hung their mobiles of various kinds of sea life, and overhead are their mobiles of seabirds. On the opposite wall are projections of famous sea paintings from different periods of history.

Some of the children are painting a mural of undersea life, and others are working at their teleputers, researching and producing multimedia reports on various marine topics. Some are working with augmented reality programs, studying ocean currents with flow patterns superimposed over the images of waves. And there is a stage on which this evening there will be a community performance of *Dance of the Tectonic Plates*, choreographed, costumed, and with sets by the students. As an introduction to the performance, four students will present a multimedia explanation of the tectonic system with images and current data from different parts of the world. By the window is a small group of students reviewing their work and planning their next project with a learning specialist.

For the last hour of class today, the video sea wall will link to Neptune IV for a virtual visit to the deep-sea floor observatory off the northwestern coast of the United States. This research project was created in the early 21st century to study newly discovered forms of life in volcanic vents. Part of a search for the earliest life on Earth, the project has now gone far beyond that. The students and scientists will compare what they know about the microorganisms called archaea, or "ancient ones," with new data coming in about organisms in the sea on Europa, one of Jupiter's moons. The youngsters are learning about how scientists merge research from our oceans with that from outer space, a topic that will tie in to the next theme 6 weeks hence. At that time, the students and learning specialists will work together to transform the interactive learning room into a planetarium, with mobiles of the planets and projections of the solar system on the walls and overhead. Can you imagine Holst's *The Planets* playing in the background?

Learning specialists are held in high esteem in the community and are paid accordingly. No longer the primary sources and purveyors of information, their role in educating has expanded and become even more creative and interesting. In addition to having degrees in specific subjects, their training includes studies in the neurosciences, human development, and the most advanced educational strategies from around the world. Because the learning centers operate year-round, there is time to take one day a week for the specialists to learn, to plan, and to share ideas and materials. During that day, the students go on field trips, do special projects, work on remedial or advanced studies, or do community service projects.

The specialists play an important role in inspiring, guiding, and facilitating learning, but as students learn to use the infinite resources available to them through new technologies, they become increasingly independent. They also learn the importance of interdependence—in meeting rooms or on the Internet, in real laboratories or in virtual labs, in art studios or in museums, in gyms or in gardens, in the wilderness or in exploratoriums, and in the community itself. Students clearly have enormous freedom and choice, but they also learn to take responsibility for their own progress.

The students may be at different levels in different subjects, and they are often with students of different ages, including adults, who are welcome. The students move through levels of expertise, from beginner to accomplished, and at any age, when they are ready, they can advance. There are also exchange programs with other countries, and most centers have foreign students subsidized by foundations and businesses.

There are ongoing assessments that offer timely feedback to guide learners as well as the specialists' instructional practice. The assessments, usually active demonstrations of achievement, go far beyond assessing memorization and recall to reveal whether students have understood and can apply what they have learned. For example, a learning experience might culminate in a presentation for the community, a multimedia report, a dramatic performance, or teaching other students, even adults, as is often the case in introducing new technologies.

There are still children with learning problems, but they can be helped by diagnosticians skilled at observation, who may use such new technologies as advanced, low-cost magnetic resonance imaging devices that make it possible to observe the brain while it is in the process of thinking. These tools assist the diagnostician in making recommendations for appropriate help with tutors, remedial techniques in the learning room, or innovative learning technologies. A great variety of intuitive, adaptive technologies are also available for the physically challenged, including the sight- or hearing-impaired. All community centers depend on trained community volunteers who assist in remediation and help the learning specialists in many ways. Students have mentors or advisors with whom they meet weekly.

Students of all ages maintain personal Web sites that include information on their learning styles; their strengths and areas that need improvement; academic progress and projects; portfolios of representative work; video interviews with learning facilitators, peers, and parents; and goals for the future. The Web sites also provide another means for assessing academic achievement, and they are updated throughout the years until students are ready to go into the adult world.

All secondary students do volunteer work while they are learning. In the process, they have opportunities to apply what they have learned as well as to develop other practical skills. As part of a teen transition program, students do a research project in the community or beyond to see what resources are available and what needs may be unmet. Then, with fellow students—or even peers in other countries—who have common interests, they design a project that may become a new resource for the community, or even a small business. These projects and the products or services they produce must be approved as contributing to the health and well-being of the communities they serve. There have been programs like these for many years, but new technologies open fresh fields and make it easier to keep records of accomplishment.

From Now to the Future

This vision is not based on my own idle daydreams. For the past 20 years, through an international education network called New Horizons for Learning, we have been seeking out the most effective ways of helping people to learn at all ages and ability levels. We have gathered information from educators, researchers, parents, and policymakers in our own country and around the world. What we have discovered is that educators everywhere face similar problems—and are reaching similar conclusions about potential solutions. For example:

◆ Students who come from impoverished environments find it difficult to achieve academically without expanded, integrated support services. Schools alone cannot meet the needs of these students.

- When children of normal intelligence enter school without the ability to learn successfully, it appears that parent and early childhood education have become critically important.
- Students of different social, cultural, economic, and educational backgrounds have different ways of learning, so educators must expand their array of teaching methods to reach all students effectively.
- In this time when rapid change affects every kind of work and every social institution, education must become a lifelong process.
- As new technologies continue to connect our increasingly interdependent world, it is critically important for students to develop technological know-how and to have steady access to the technologies.

Although many teachers are dealing successfully with these challenges, too many educators and policymakers are spending fruitless time and energy debating details of educational practice, such as whether phonics or whole language is the superior method and whether pure math skills are more or less important than problem-solving skills. (Might it not be both instead of either/or?) Meanwhile, students are dropping out or graduating without literacy, the skills to be self-sufficient, or the ability to work with others. Private charter schools may well cause the public system of education to become further segregated by race, ethnicity, socioeconomic status, and student performance, as has happened over time in New Zealand and other countries that have similar ratios of minority populations as the United States.

Anxious to improve the system, policymakers and educational planners have created new academic standards and tests that are simplistic solutions to a complex problem. Educators are feeling intense pressure from policymakers, parents, businesspeople, and other stakeholders in this high-accountability environment. It is important, however, to recognize that educational systems are not the only solution to problems that spring largely from social, economic, and environmental changes.

Numerous crises have raised the level of urgency: violence in the schools, disconnected communities, growing economic disparity, a pervading sense of helplessness over our futures. Moreover, new technologies are emerging at a speed that is surpassing our ability to understand how best to use them wisely and responsibly. This newest challenge has resulted in intense, meaningful discussions of what it means to be human—how to develop altruism and compassion, and how to foresee the consequences of our actions.

All of these challenges bear directly on how best to educate and prepare young people to become responsible, contributing members of society. There is now a call not just for restructuring but for a real transformation of education.

We have all the knowledge and tools we need to create an effective system that can help meet the needs of today's and tomorrow's students. In some ways, the community learning centers that we imagine are not so different from some of the innovative educational systems emerging today. We have already seen many new, interactive technologies, along with a renaissance of the arts in education, hands-on projects, inquiry-based learning, cooperative learning, internships, and community service projects that deeply engage students and result in academic achievement.

Throughout this country and the world, there are exemplary classrooms and schools that incorporate the most effective educational practices. But there must be a collective will to bring about the transformation of whole systems based on new understandings of the brain/mind/body system and how it learns; new technologies; more choices in educational facilities; and the integration of child/family services.

Educators are beginning to pay attention to the importance of the first 3 years of life, new research from the neurosciences, and studies in human development. An Institute for Mind, Brain, and Learning is being developed to train educators. Instruction is becoming more individualized as teachers learn how to meet the needs of a broader spectrum of individual differences through recognizing different ways of learning or different intelligences. These include not only verbal and logical-mathematical intelligence, but also visual-spatial, bodily-kinesthetic, musical, naturalist, interpersonal, and intrapersonal intelligences, as identified in Howard Gardner's *Theory of Multiple Intelligences.*

More educators are beginning to understand as well that emotional intelligence is even more important to success in school and in life than IQ, and they are not only discussing but learning how to include the spiritual in education. In essence, they are beginning to focus on how to create a system that engages students emotionally, cognitively, physically, socially, and spiritually in a humane environment.

Finally, our world now has a telecommunications infrastructure that can support a quantum leap in learning and collective intelligence, and more of us have learned that we can work together as a global community of learners.

How we use these powerful new tools will determine the course of the future. Now more than ever, parents and communities must work together with educational systems to create the vision and means for present and future generations to live in a healthier, more peaceful, wiser world. "And at the end of all our exploring," wrote T. S. Eliot, "will be to arrive where we started and know the place for the first time."

★★★

Dee Dickinson is the founder and chief executive of New Horizons for Learning, an international education network based in Seattle and in a virtual building on the Internet at www.newhorizons.org. She has taught at all levels—elementary through university—and has produced several series for educational television as well as created nine international conferences on education. She is an internationally recognized speaker, author, and consultant to educational systems, policymaking groups, and corporations. Her publications include *Positive Trends in Learning*, commissioned by IBM, and *Creating the Future*. She also is the coauthor of *Teaching and Learning Through Multiple Intelligences*.

HIGHER EDUCATION

Judith A. Sturnick

M y Swedish immigrant grandparents viewed education through the eyes of imagination and promise. Coming as they did from a hardscrabble background where piety, suspicion, and superstition often ruled human lives, they looked to higher education as the limitless gift offered by America. Education was the horn of plenty, the great equalizer and liberator, the empowering force that granted choices in life and freedom from class constraints.

When my grandparents spun sagas about family dreams and sacred myths, they included the commanding attraction of learning. Part of the story of Grandmother's journey in the strange land of Michigan's Upper Peninsula centered on her hunger for education. Forced to leave school at the end of the sixth grade, she tried to bargain and cajole her father to continue her learning "in town." In response, he gave her a set of nearly impossible physical tasks to perform. If she could accomplish these, he would allow her to go to school. After weeks of inspired labor fed by her dream, she showed him her accomplishments. His eyes filled with tears. "Oh, Hannie," he said. "I never thought you could do this. We need you at home. You can't go to town."

She grieved, of course—deeply enough that she could painstakingly describe the event some 50 years later. But pragmatic as she needed to be, she then went about the business of life. As I was growing up, she filled my head with her rich fantasies about the realms of learning, which to her were realms of gold. Her stories were reinforced as I watched my father struggling to work, study, and care for our family on the GI Bill. If education had not been so precious, he would not have sacrificed so much for it.

These vignettes are a kind of parable for me as I compose this chapter. They reflect the faith many immigrants had at the turn of the century that education was transforming, that it was accessible, that it was a key to a better life, and that it was worth whatever necessary price must be paid to attain the greater good.

As my grandparents' story illustrates, the history of American higher education is a complex fusion of idealism and pragmatism. Part and parcel of its making is the story of the establishment of Land Grant institutions in the mid-19th century as well as the opening of our colleges and universities through the GI Bill following World War II. Perhaps more than any other single element, the latter legislation democratized our system of higher education while it strengthened the vocational/professional components.

This contradictory mix of vision and practicality is a product of American culture. The combination of intellectual challenge, liberal learning, and research heritage with nuts-and-bolts professional preparation serves simultaneously to energize and fragment contemporary higher education. At its best, these colliding values endow our system with the capacity to produce splendid philosopher-practitioners, those individuals who not only think about enacted learning but implement it in the greater world. At its worst, it manifests an unshakable schizophrenia about what education should be and do.

THE QUESTIONS OF FUTURE EDUCATION

It is no wonder that as we enter a time of radical cultural and technological change, we are once again encountering a crisis of identity and purpose in higher education. We continue to wrestle with fundamental questions.

◆ To what extent should the marketplace drive the modern curriculum?

◆ What is the value of liberal learning in the workplace?

◆ Does the concept of lifelong learning draw us away from "core education" to focus instead on discrete skills tailored to professional and vocational requirements of the marketplace?

◆ How can we halt the exodus of young males from high school, thereby closing doors on educational opportunities, and what are we clearly not comprehending about pedagogy, learning styles, and human/intellectual maturation?

◆ How deep will be the impact of technology on how and what we learn as well as who learns—and who controls what is learned?

◆ Does education any longer have a role in bettering human society, or are we now so focused on the economic, entrepreneurial aspects of learning that we have severed the connections between education and social responsibility'?

◆ Who will be able to afford advanced education in the coming decades, and how should that education be financed?

Pressing as these queries are, there remains an even larger question which as a society we dare not ignore: What forces, values, and rewards will shape the American Mind in this century and this millennium?

This was a question posed eloquently by Henry Steele Commager and other American intellectuals more than 70 years ago, and we hear its resounding call once again. The query demands a new response for our contemporary world. A compelling aspect of this inquiry is that it still anticipates the role of American higher education as a creator of legacies. It still envisions higher education as a vital component of the answer.

THE THREE ACTIONS OF HIGHER EDUCATION

All of these comments build a bridge to my vision for higher education in this century and this millennium. That vision is distinguished by three practical components and four intrinsic values. The three practical components that provide the infrastructure for the future are differentiated mission, accessibility, and responsiveness. The four values, which I will discuss later, are service, community, the heroic spirit in learning, and stewardship.

Differentiated Mission

As we explore the shape-shifting quality of modern education, we have to keep returning to the importance of institutional mission. Differentiated mission—that is, the creation of a unique campus identity for each institution of higher learning—serves to lessen the confusion about educational purpose.

Due to competition for enrollment numbers, too many campuses try to be all things to all learners. That unnecessary duplication of educational services and waste of resources has brought many colleges and universities to the brink of crisis, with large physical plants and budgets that cannot be sustained without a critical mass of students—at a time when the numbers of traditional-aged students are declining. Equally to the point, when an institutional mission is all-encompassing, accountability is obscured. We cannot know what is being done well, and by which educational institutions, if we do not know to what purpose they hold themselves accountable.

There is a clearly defined and special niche, for example, for research institutions, the Ivy League campuses, elite women's colleges, and community colleges. Harvard is not Keene State College, and Keene State College is not Berkeley, and so on. We should not expect them to be otherwise.

At the same time, the advancement of many new, for-profit higher education organizations as well as the offering of more corporate degrees (Kodak University was just the beginning) will be an expanding reality, adding more dimensions of competition. At the same time, the growing number of adult learners is rapidly forcing new pedagogical theories into being while demanding the same flexibility and nimbleness in the classrooms (virtual and real) that the corporate world is demanding of its organizational components.

Although competition sometimes breeds contempt, it can also

generate more creative processes. Add to this mix the power of a still unknown quantity—global higher education for an even more diverse population and for an even greater variety of complex missions and purposes—and the volatility and unpredictability of higher education's future becomes even more apparent. This is a splendid time for new visions to be defined and tested, as continuous change reshapes visionary substance and parameters. In light of these changes, we already are reinventing American higher education, including the redefinition of what we mean by academic "degrees."

Accessibility

As American higher education becomes more expensive (and the advent of new technologies is making it even pricier), the question of who is allowed into academic circles continues to be an urgent one. Middle-class learners are now graduating with enormous financial debts, and that affects their choice of professions (who can afford to carry $60,000 worth of debt with a teaching job that begins, for example, with an annual salary of $24,000?) as well as their disposable income for years to come.

Moreover, society has legitimate concern about how a "digital divide" between economic classes can affect children's skill development, comfort levels with technology, and interest in technological careers. Issues of academic accessibility, then, are driven by class, race, economic realities, and cultural values. We are only beginning to derive an educational system that is genuinely accessible to all who seek to learn—truly an explosive force in our future vision of higher education and social transformation—and we must reinforce the infrastructures (and the values) that maintain that accessibility.

Responsiveness

Issues of institutional mission and access are complicated even further by concern about education's inability to respond rapidly to change. The workforce is inventing and reinventing itself at an amazing pace. New job fields emerge overnight in technology areas, and even the less volatile emerging professions (such as personal and professional coaching) have only brief histories thus far in the marketplace.

In this environment, all of us who work and plan for higher education must constantly be scanning the landscape, assessing the newest applications of technology, the growth of new professions, and the emerging needs for specialized training in a vast number of fields. New competencies are being defined and old ones redefined in rapidly shifting contexts. That corporations have created their own universities is a strong indicator that higher education still lacks a nimble response to the changing marketplace as well as the capacity to help define new professions and specialized jobs. We are thus wagged by the dog more often than we should be.

In our vision of reshaped American higher education, we can begin to translate an understanding of technological and economic trends into redesigned academic programs, majors, and specializations. We can use Internet marketing strategies and course delivery to implement new concepts and skills. We can pursue research through the Web and other technologies, research which in turn allows us to measure swiftly and more comprehensively the effectiveness of what we are doing.

This should be a time when research and the scholarly missions of some institutions are reaffirmed; when regional colleges and universities validate their responsiveness to their regional marketplaces and deepen their roots in those communities; when elite schools open their doors even more freely to diverse groups. Some of our campuses, marginal in size or too slow to adapt, will disappear, to be replaced by new, less cumbersome institutions.

THE UNSHAKABLE VALUES OF LEARNING

Let me connect these three practical components to four intrinsic core values that I view as essential to the ideals of teaching and learning. These values affirm the fundamental power of education not only to transform individual lives, the quality of leadership, and human society, but also continuously to transform itself.

Service

In the 1890s, when Frederick Jackson Turner espoused his Frontier Theory, he stressed the individualistic, fierce, independent spirit of the American character. He noted that pragmatic anti-intellectualism accompanied the ruggedness fostered by the vastness of that frontier (think Daniel Boone and Kit Carson). One of the outcomes of such national character formation is that our educational systems often reinforce individualistic self-interest. We are more interested with statistics indicating the lifetime increase in earning power afforded by a college degree than by the life-quality differences it provides. Too often, our achievements are measured in dollars rather than in intellectual capital. As is true of so many anomalies in our society, this pragmatism perpetuates tension between the practical and the theoretical, the doer and the thinker.

In my worldview (certainly influenced by those Swedish grandparents), an enduring value in education is that we learn in order to serve. We learn in order to strengthen moral order and to accept our obligations to society. We learn in order to become more creative and inventive in finding solutions to social problems, and we understand that addressing those problems is part of repayment for the inestimable gift of education. We learn in order to live out our ethics and to instill more mindfulness and humanity in our institutions. We learn in order to draw forth the spirit in our organizations, and then to serve the greater good.

To place service as a concept and reality at the core of our educational missions would be to shift the tone, function, and greater outcomes of teaching and learning. By crafting new models and paradigms, the concepts of service learning, servant leadership, and societal transformation could be woven throughout our educational processes. If nothing else, this educational approach would offer another perspective on viewing the role of Self in the greater world, and it would also raise salient questions about the purpose of one's education and the ends that it can serve.

The theologian Matthew Fox has called work "a Eucharist." Education too is a Eucharist, a sacrament that draws us close to divine purpose and allows us to enact sacred ritual in our daily lives. To think of education in this way is not to place it within rigid structure but to embrace the in-spiriting of intellect and mind. An aspect of the Eucharistic nature of education is that it is rooted in service.

Community

The vitality of educational vision in this century and millennium is also anchored in the importance of community. From that center, energetic filaments extend to every community in which we exist. The learning community, working community, family community, divine-celebrating community, reflective and contemplative community, and all the other circles in which we take our place—these all influence, are influenced by, and define our being.

The connection between learning and our roots in the community takes us back to Emerson again, but also forward into the future. As thinkers and learners have always done, we can still envision "the good society," and it is still possible to think it into creation through our actions. "Do the work that lies nearest thee," the Scottish philosopher Thomas Carlyle exhorted us. Lead, serve, and transform wherever you are; embrace and serve your community. The exhortation is not rhetorical; it is a moral action.

Through new technologies, our actions—far more than ever before—can affect, or have the potential to affect, a critical mass of other human beings. People whom we do not know and will never meet can be impacted upon by our conduct in cyberspace. The role of education in providing an ethical framework around the uses of learning, the morality of the Internet, and our mutual responsibility within this both vast and small human community must continue to be defined, reflected upon, debated, and probed. Every second of every day, we are reminded that each of us is part of the human community. The web that vibrates as we move resonates through an entire social pattern.

The Heroic Spirit in Learning

Connecting a contemporary vision of education to service and community leads to a very Emersonian third point: the Heroic Spirit in learning. Education is the path of the Hero's Journey—the path that joins wisdom and experience, opens our individual lives to universal meaning, and allows for initiation and return to the community with a new life template and mission.

There is empowering boldness in reminding ourselves as both learners and teachers that cycles and circles are part of the rhythms of learning as well as of the universe. Education lets us map the journey, to an extent at least, and also allows the journey to shape us. If we are encouraged to see the educational journey itself as heroic—even spiritual—then we can also see ourselves as the heroes of our own lives, as worthy individuals who carry sagas, live out our poetry, and create meaning in our individual lives and the lives of our communities. Thus universal archetypes are validated, as is the discovery of our own presence within those archetypes. The sacred nature of learning is affirmed.

Why shouldn't something so significant and life-changing as the process of learning and teaching be viewed as heroic? Our world and worldviews are transformed, and we are granted roles to play that might not otherwise be given to us. As we place heroic language around our articulation of education's purpose and function, we also express the intrinsic value, not merely the extrinsic worth, of this mighty enterprise. In this context, education is not about dollars and cents and career advancement, but about change, transformation, and human promise. It is also about the nurturing of individual social conscience.

In the same breath, we can speak of education providing a healing environment—a place where healing leadership can be taught and modeled, where learners are healed rather than wounded, where the creation of healthy and healing organizational structures is explored. Linking educational principles to community and the heroic

105

spirit, we can consciously aspire to compassionate leadership styles that are reflective, open, renewing, and effective. Such leadership models affect not only higher education and social institutions but corporate and business cultures as well.

Stewardship

The interweaving of these contiguous values brings us to the fourth quality of visionary higher education: stewardship. Of course, this encompasses the obvious activities of wise allocation of human and fiscal resources through planning and accountable management. However, stewardship also directly reconnects our thinking back to service and community. In the words of Peter Block, an expert on organizational transformation, stewardship embodies "choosing service over self-interest."

Stewardship, in addition, provides the framework within which a series of ethical choices are made about changing the nature of leadership and realigning the spines of our organizations. "Stewardship depends on a willingness to be accountable for results," Block states, "without using control or caretaking as the means to reach them." Even as we steward, then, we create a better entity for that stewardship to embrace. In this way, we can acknowledge the role of education as both a conservatorship and a construct for radical expressions of new thought.

For this is what stewardship allows us to seek in higher education—the colliding energies of conserving what deserves to be held in trust, and reshaping or creating new patterns of thought for what still needs to be born.

WHERE WE COULD GO

It is not enough merely to pose questions and lay foundation. Let us imagine what higher education could be 50 years from now. Recently, with a group of valued colleagues at lunch, I said, "Vision with me for a while. What will higher education look like in a few decades?" I was surprised to find that they reacted cautiously rather than enthusiastically. One of them said, "I can't begin to imagine it. Things are changing too fast, there are too many variables." He threw his hands up in a gesture of frustration and shook his head. "Even the technology that was hot 4 months ago is obsolete today!"

Two hours later, however, one of them brought to me two papers he had collected at recent conferences on higher education. Then one of the group dropped by to talk about multiculturalism and peace studies. And then another colleague handed me three handwritten pages with the heading "This Is My Vision." I was heartened; beneath the feelings of fatigue and confusion, many of us still have optimism, visionary dreams, and the power to imagine.

Imagine, then: a no-boundary world of education that invites a completely new description of what learning is, how it occurs, and who benefits from it. We are no longer circumscribed by site, environment, or geography. Learning is available 24/7, to virtually everyone. There is no longer an educated elite that defines social class and caste by limiting the aspirations, professions, jobs, and life possibilities of those who are excluded.

In fact, all learning, all information, is available through cyberspace. We have access to that technology everywhere, easily and inexpensively; more of us have portable work and learning environments, and we take them with us wherever we go through handheld devices and other amazing inventions. We are instantly on the cutting edge of new discoveries in science-math creativity.

Culture is instantaneous and accessible. We write and disseminate poetry and literature, in addition to other art forms, on the Internet (or whatever we will be calling it 50 years from now). More than this, we learn methods of creativity from great artists and teachers, all of whom are available to us at our fingertips. We can hear it, read about it, experience it through touch (as virtual realities become more sophisticated). Creativity is less of a mystery practiced by specialized groups and more a part of our own artistry as we are encouraged to explore our talents.

The capacity of the human brain to learn has expanded, like an ink spill spreading across blotting paper. New parts of our brain are being used and we are able to perform—imaginatively, intellectually, and creatively—in ways no one in 2001 could envision. At the edges of our minds, we explore new ways of thinking and being that, in turn, lead us to greater spiritual possibilities. Because we know (even from quantum physics) that expanded intellectual energy expands other aspects of our energetic bodies, we have come to understand and use astral projection, psychic power, and ESP in ways that no longer seem eccentric, strange, or downright weird. These elements are simply perceived as other legitimate ways of knowing.

Access to new and continuously renewing human potential, possibility, and awareness moves us into the frontiers of inner space, as we begin to explore states of consciousness in new ways, aided both by technology and by expanded emotional and intuitive insights. The question "What does it mean to be human?" gets posed in new ways that morph into still undreamed of transformations of mind, body, spirit.

Imagine. All boundaries are in a state of flux and change, as learning opens up every aspect of our lives. Degrees and titles take on a different meaning; baccalaureate, associate, doctoral degrees do not designate superior professional and social class so much as they represent a chosen course of self-discipline. For example, the M.D. whose assistance we seek has become a co-creator of our health care, but we participate in the process by owning our lives, bodies, and decision making. Indeed, perhaps all of these degree-related titles will disappear entirely from the lexicon. They are, after all, degrees of separation that are becoming increasingly meaningless.

In education, we have created learning circles and learning communities. Rather than referring to "professor," "faculty," and "student," we speak of "learning consultants," "learning resources," and "learners." We give up the authority of the title/status in order to create an open learning environment without fear, coercion, or robotic expectations. Learning is genuinely a shared endeavor and a shared creation in which all of us continue to teach and to learn. At the same time—imagine—there are no restrictions on the topics that we study and around which we learn. Forty years ago, who would have thought that Gay Studies, for example, would take its place as an academic discipline?

Within multiple-learning contexts, "circles" are both a metaphor and structure for the building of communities and for the models of leadership within those communities. Hard-edged and selfish individualism authentically can be replaced by celebration of communities, which gather diverse groups of people around a shared purpose or purposes as well as a shared intention. The power of the Internet to call forth communities is beginning to be recognized as I write this. Isolated rural communities can connect to other rural villages and towns to discuss similar problems and engage in problem solving; communities become naturally multicultural as folks in Alexandria, Minnesota, connect with economic resources in Cairo, Egypt, around both local and global matters (such as water conservation and tourism). Imagine!

The learning and shared knowledge here cannot be compartmentalized into courses, academic disciplines, or degrees, yet it taps into vast learning resources and capabilities that would once have been controlled by the academy, with or without corporate alliances. Social capital, a term now in common usage, has many layers of meaning and practical applications for individuals who would never have had a cent of this in their cultural bank accounts. Imagine how dramatically this has revised national and global social structures!

As we come to know each other around the globe—a South African grandmother, for example, who through technology shares her environmental activism with a 10-year-old boy in India and a corporate vice president in Silicon Valley—new possibilities for world peace, environmental conservation, academic disciplines, research, and global parliaments emerge. And the learning pool, so accessible through technology, expands by the minute, ripple upon ripple moving across the oceans of cyberspace. Education and learning now are without limits of class, ethnicity, geography, time, or other artificial barriers.

From these circles and communities of learning and problem solving, we will create new ways of leading in all arenas; the study of leadership will focus more inclusively on partnership, stewardship, and the individual, in addition to group empowerment. We will be able to refine and develop our conversations around contemplative leadership, the dynamics of morphic fields and leadership for life (Meg Wheatley's process), leaders as social artists (Jean Houston's term), and new forms of team spirit (the work of Barry Heermann). As we learn and teach in the circles of empowerment, we explore the obligations each of us has to serve in partnership and stewardship within our institutions and with other people. We also explore the importance of balanced lives that derive equilibrium from contemplative space, and the infinite significance of mindfulness, intent, and connectedness to community and to spirit.

Such future imaginings provide us a richer context for understanding this moment in the new century and millennium. Higher education will continue to evolve, change, adapt, and embody many purposes in this century. But the wisest and most dramatic transformation will be created by moving the weaving shuttle back and forth in designs that interlace the values of service, community, the heroic spirit, and stewardship. In the decades to come, we will redefine and re-create these concepts as we redesign our patterns of learning and education. The more imaginative we are, the more richly complex in their simplicity will be those new creations. We are the loom, we are the threads, we are the weavers. Imagine.

★★★

Judith A. Sturnick, Ph.D., is president of the Union Institute, a national university offering accredited degrees to working adults. Previously, she served as a national vice president for the American Council on Education in Washington, D.C. She has served as president of two universities—Keene State College in New Hampshire and the University of Maine at Farmington—and has successfully run her own consulting and executive coaching business for 5 years in the San Francisco Bay area. She is the author of two books.

THE CORPORATION

David C. Korten

On November 30, 1999, world television broadcast dramatic scenes of Seattle police clothed in Darth Vader riot gear brutally wielding clubs, tear gas, pepper spray, and plastic bullets against thousands of people who had come from around the world to protest the destruction of democracy by a secretive and previously obscure body known as the World Trade Organization (WTO). The 70,000 protesters were of all ages and colors and identified with a bewildering array of organizations and causes. They came from churches, labor unions, universities, peace groups, environmental groups, and many other organizations. They came to defend democracy from the tyranny of the new corporate world order.

Seattle 1999 made visible the awakening of America and the world to the reality behind the constantly repeated mantra of the financial press that there is no alternative to the new corporate global order. Those who took to the streets in Seattle were among the millions who looked ahead to the future this new order is creating and concluded that the turn of the millennium marks a critical moment of choice for humanity. We can resign ourselves to an American-imposed world corporate order that is recklessly destroying the life of society and the planet to enrich a small ruling elite. Or we can take on one of the greatest creative challenges in history: consciously and intentionally to reinvent ourselves and our institutions to create a planetary system of radically democratic, self-organizing societies grounded in a love of life and a respect for all beings. They lead to two sharply contrasting futures.

America's Corporate World Order

At the conclusion of World War II, the U.S. government set about establishing America's economic hegemony in the world. U.S. State Department Policy Planning Study 23, a top-secret document written in 1948 by George Kennan, a leading architect of the U.S. role in the post–World War II era, lays out the case starkly.

> We have about 50 percent of the world's wealth, but only 6.3 percent of its population. . . . In this situation we cannot fail to be the object of envy and resentment. Our real task in the coming period is to devise a pattern of relationships which will permit us to maintain this position of disparity. . . . To do so, we will have to dispense with all sentimentality and daydreaming; and our intention will have to be concentrated everywhere on our immediate national objectives. . . . We should cease to talk about vague . . . unreal objectives such as human rights, the raising of living standards, and democratization. The day is not far off when we are going to have to deal in straight power concepts.

Inequality and injustice are not accidental outcomes of the corporate world order (otherwise known as global capitalism); they are its defining characteristics. As demonstrated throughout its history, the corporation is a legal instrument designed to facilitate the massive concentration of private political and economic power freed from public accountability for the consequences of its use.

The processes of corporate globalization remove economic borders and weaken the regulatory powers of government so that the largest corporations have ever greater freedom to consolidate their hold over the world's resources and markets. The World Bank, the International Monetary Fund (IMF), and the WTO—together known as the Bretton Woods institutions—have been its most visible architects. The U.S. government, however, pulls most of the strings. The U.S. Treasury Department, which itself marches to the tune of Wall Street banks and investment houses, largely calls the shots for the IMF and World Bank. The U.S. Trade Representative's Office, which functions as an extension of the U.S. Business Roundtable, has had the lead role in the WTO.

One might conclude from the U.S. government–sanctioned policies of the Bretton Woods institutions that our goals are threefold: to assure that the world's productive assets are owned by transnational corporations and are used to produce for export; to assure that all education, health, communications, and public utilities services are owned and operated by transnational corporations on a for-profit, fee-for-service basis; and to guarantee that everything people consume is imported by transnational corporations from somewhere else. It's the vision of a world in which life exists only to serve the corporate bottom line, a world in which money is the ultimate value and life simply a means.

The dark history of U.S. military intervention—both overt and covert—in Latin America, Africa, and elsewhere is well known. Its most consistent purpose has been to overturn governments—many of them democratic—that threaten U.S. corporate interests. The *New York Times* foreign correspondent Thomas Friedman, a tireless cheerleader for corporate globalization, puts it clearly. "The hidden hand of the market will never work without a hidden fist. McDonald's cannot flourish without McDonald Douglas, the designer of the U.S. Air Force F-15. And the hidden fist that keeps the world safe for Silicon Valley's technologies to flourish is called the U.S. Army, Air Force, Navy, and Marine Corps. . . . With all due respect to Silicon Valley, ideas and technology don't just win and spread on their own."

The year is 2050. The world's political divisions and sense of national identity have been largely erased. The world is divided into 12 global megacorporations, which control virtually all the world's economic activity, and four distinct social classes.

The world is ruled by a small superelite that controls the ownership of these corporations. Governmental functions—including military, police, and prisons—have been wholly privatized and operate as corporate subsidiaries. Members of the superelite, who measure their wealth in the trillions of dollars, live above the global pollution line in highly fortified mountain fortresses from which they travel by helicopter to their corporate headquarters. They convene each year in Davos, Switzerland, as the secretive world-ruling council.

Next in line are the well-paid managers, scientists, technicians, celebrities, and sports stars, who live and work in gated communities and corporate campuses with walls, guard towers, and electrified fences.

The marginalized laboring classes work for bare subsistence wages in service jobs in factory compounds, mines, and agricultural fields. Most live in crime-infested ghettos near highly polluted industrial complexes.

The excluded billions, the human refuse at the bottom of the pile, live on the streets or in shantytowns constructed of packing boxes and other discarded materials. They survive on what they can scavenge or pilfer.

Average temperatures are now 5 degrees higher than at the turn of the 21st century. The world's oceans have risen by an average of nearly 2 feet, many islands have disappeared, along with vast coastal areas, and severe weather events kill millions each year. The last wilderness areas disappeared years ago. Those lands and waters not rendered permanently unproductive by toxic wastes and mismanagement are devoted to vast industrial-agricultural estates producing food, timber, fish, and livestock under corporate ownership and management. A group of scientists risks their careers by secretly circulating an unauthorized report presenting evidence that the Earth is dying. The corporate press denounces them as fanatic alarmists whose wild claims lack scientific proof and whose recommendations would bankrupt the economy.

A HUMAN AND PLANETARY ORDER

Those who argue that there is no alternative to the corporate world order reveal their lack of imagination, insult our intelligence, and demean our humanity. The alternatives are both obvious and deeply imbedded in American values. Why not, for example, create an America in which life—not money—is the measure of value, and democracy, responsible citizenship, and markets are the organizing principles?

The year is 2050. America has come a long way in the last 50 years. When I turned on the morning news today, there was a report on America's social health index followed by a panel discussion of local, national, and global initiatives intended to improve the indicators, and how people could get involved. Yesterday, a similar report covered the living planet index.

It now seems incredible that 50 years ago, this airtime was devoted to reporting on the day's stock market performance. The social fabric and the planetary life-support systems were collapsing—but all the media seemed concerned with was corporate profits and stock prices. Of course, those were the days when most of America's media were controlled by four massive corporate conglomerates: General Electric, Time Warner, Disney, and Westinghouse.

Seattle 1999—when protesters shut down a meeting of the WTO—was a turning point. People still refer to it. People were waking up to the fact that the more rights and freedoms corporations have, the fewer rights and freedoms real people have. Following the protests in Seattle, more and more people took to the streets in protest. Eventually, the corporate elites found that they could meet only behind police barricades. This turned the abstraction of an elite-ruled corporate police state into a powerful visual image. Public pressures built to the point that the World Bank, the IMF, and the WTO were all dismantled, third-world debts were repudiated or canceled, and rule-making responsibility for the global economy was assigned to the United Nations.

The real breakthrough for the United States was a radical campaign finance reform bill—the result of possibly the most dramatic citizen protest ever held. Two million people descended on Washington,

D.C., surrounded the Capital building, and refused to leave until Congress passed a sweeping campaign reform bill that prohibited individual political contributions larger than $100, barred corporate political involvement of any kind, provided public funding for election campaigns, and required media using the public airwaves to provide ample free time for qualified candidates. This set the stage for a string of legislative victories ending corporate welfare, withdrawing special corporate rights and privileges, breaking up concentrations of corporate power, guaranteeing every person the right to a means of livelihood, giving workers control over their own pension funds, and implementing ownership reforms to help workers obtain ownership stakes in the productive assets on which their livelihoods depend. Labor unions began to organize worker and community buyouts, in part with workers' pension funds.

At the same time, a deep cultural shift was taking place. Voluntary simplicity was in, conspicuous consumption was out. People realized that advertisers were manipulating their values and self-images so that they would feel compelled to devote their energies to earning money in order to buy expensive merchandise that gave them no real satisfaction. It is as if society acquired a collective immunity to advertising. Many people turned off their televisions and became more mindful consumers, buying only what they really needed, seeking good value, and giving preference to goods and services provided by local, independent businesses. Now, most people find that they need to work only 20 to 25 hours a week to meet their financial needs. The rest of the time, they devote themselves to things that give them real satisfaction, such as gardening, family, and community service.

As people recognized that most advertising is socially pernicious, they passed legislation to place strict limits on the advertising expenditures corporations are allowed to deduct as business expenses. The pollution of both private and public spaces with advertising has largely been eliminated.

Nearly all businesses are now human-scale, which in practical terms means that they have no more than 500 workers each, and nearly all are owned by persons who have an immediate nonfinancial stake in them—employees, customers, suppliers, or members of the communities in which the businesses are located. The giant corporations that sparked Seattle 1999 have gone the way of the dinosaurs and smallpox.

Typical of our time is the business where I work. The No Waste Resource Management Corporation is a waste recycling business that employs 150 workers. Since landfills have been prohibited by law, we have been responsible for seeing that 100 percent of the waste from our community is recycled. Forty percent of shares are owned by employees like me, 30 percent by the local households and businesses whose waste we process, and 30 percent by the farms and manufacturing firms—mostly located within a 100-mile radius of our processing facilities—that depend on us for compost and raw materials. Of course, there are many other forms of stakeholder-owned enterprise, including family firms, cooperatives, and partnerships.

In our company, management reports to a board elected by all the shareholders. Our shareholders, all of whom are local, take their ownership responsibilities very seriously. Board meetings are well attended and often lively. At our last meeting, shareholders were up in arms about the mishandling of some toxic material that nearly contaminated the municipal water supply. These are folks who drink that water. They told the CEO in no uncertain terms that his job will be on the line if this happens again.

My job at No Waste is to oversee the shipment of materials that we are unable to process in our own facilities to a regional recycling center with more sophisticated equipment. The center is jointly owned by the 120 stakeholder-owned municipal recycling corporations in our region. We call this bottom-up ownership, which assures that accountability is clearly rooted in local communities.

These days, it is difficult to imagine that only 50 years ago there were corporations with internal economies larger than those of most states—and their only accountability was to owners, who bought and sold their shares as if they were placing bets in a gambling casino, with no concern or liability for the consequences of corporate behavior.

What an invitation for abuse! I understand that so long as a corporate CEO kept his share prices rising, he was largely insulated from accountability to anyone. If share prices fell, he needed only to fire a few thousand people and the speculators would push the price back up again. I read somewhere that in 1999, corporate managers were paying themselves an average of $12.4 million a year, 475 times the salary of the average worker.

They say that economists called this the triumph of the market economy. What kind of economists did they have back then? Apparently, they didn't even know the difference between a corporate-ruled capitalist economy and a market economy. No wonder things were such a mess.

Now, most firms cut back on everyone's paid working hours before laying off worker-owners. It is rare for even the highest-paid executive in a firm to earn more than five times the pay of the lowest-paid worker.

When the idea was first proposed back in 2000 that individual enterprises should be no larger than 500 employees, a lot of people were skeptical and started coming up with lists of things a small firm would be unable to do. Frankly, it has been amazing to see what can be done locally in human-scale firms once society decides that this is what it wants. Start with the basics of food, clothing, housing, education, and health care: Most of these needs can easily be met locally by human-scale firms that provide local employment and care for the local environment. Of course, we still import coffee and tea and some exotic fruits. A combination of greenhouses and hydroponics even allows us to grow many fresh vegetables in the winter season.

For larger projects, such as the manufacture of high-speed trains, we have learned to make very effective use of manufacturing networks, a concept pioneered in the 20th century in Italy and Denmark. Dozens of smaller firms form network alliances within which they divide up the tasks involved according to their respective skills. The late-20th-century practice of large corporations contracting out most of their manufacturing work to smaller producers helped prepare the way for the move to manufacturing networks. People discovered that most production tasks had already been broken down and distributed among many firms, most of which were being squeezed dry by the big firms that monopolized control of technology, markets, and finance. As the big guys were stripped of their monopoly powers, the formerly captive contractors decided to organize themselves into cooperative networks. These networks have developed such sophisticated management methods that there is now scarcely any product or project that cannot be handled by networks of firms, none of which exceed the 500-employee limit. This approach allows for extraordinary flexibility with a high degree of employment stability and security.

America's economy has been fundamentally transformed in the past 50 years. In the end, what we have created looks remarkably like a classical market economy of small buyers and small sellers. We call our version a mindful market economy, because we recognize the importance of mindfulness in all our economic choices—from the choice of our own employment to the nature of our production processes to the products we produce and buy—mindfulness not only of our own needs but also of the impact of our choices on society and the planet.

The results of the transformation have been striking. The breakup of corporate conglomerates and the selling off of local branches and subsidiaries restored the practice of community banking—local community banks and credit unions dedicated to financing local homes and businesses. Most communities now also have locally owned newspapers and radio and TV stations. Many community-based media outlets depend on a mixture of advertising revenues and public contributions and in turn offer a mix of commercial, national public, and local broadcast offerings appropriate to community needs and the funding mix. Local family farms are flourishing using predominantly organic methods. Previously depressed communities, including inner cities and small rural villages, have come alive with thriving local economies. Unemployment is largely unknown. Community currencies are commonplace. The combination of economic security, low unemployment, and strong community ties has virtually eliminated crime, mental illness, and welfare expenditures.

In our economic relations with the rest of the world, we take seriously the principles set forth by the revered British economist John Maynard Keynes, who said, "I sympathize, therefore, with those who would minimize, rather than with those who would maximize, economic entanglement between nations. Ideas, knowledge, art, hospitality, travel—these are the things which should of their nature be international. But let goods be homespun whenever it is reasonably and conveniently possible, and above all, let finance be primarily national."

Once freed from their international debts and the dictates of the U.S.-dominated Bretton Woods institutions, other countries began to reshape their domestic economies along the same lines as those we followed in America. As countries reoriented their economies toward local production using local resources to meet local needs, the total value of world trade fell significantly. Countries and communities now mostly trade their surplus production for things they cannot reasonably produce themselves. It is now the recognized right of each community and nation to decide what and how much it will trade, with whom, and under what circumstances.

As economies have localized and people have reestablished a sense of connection with community and place, travel has declined significantly, but it has also become far less frenetic and more interesting. Most travel now centers on learning and international exchange. A 1- to 2-year around-the-world journey is a rite of passage for young people approaching adulthood. An extended journey at midlife is also common, used as a time to reflect and gain inspiration for the next stage of one's life. With cheap oil reserves exhausted, there is little air travel. As a result, many are rediscovering the joy of the journey itself—taking time to make new friends and stay over with a family to better experience other ways of life. International friendships are sustained over the years by electronic communication. Cross-oceanic travel by sun- and wind-powered ships is quite popular. Land travel is by hiking, biking, and train. Many young people travel as members of performing arts groups, sharing their own cultures with others along their route in return for local hospitality. With global corporations removed from the scene, there has been a much-heralded rebirth of cultural diversity that greatly enriches the travel experience.

Personal economic security and deep international friendships have turned international competition into cooperation—especially in the sharing of information, experience, technology, and culture. Because human-scale firms are primarily involved in local markets, they have relatively little interest in creating monopolies on intellectual property rights. Most people take pride in having created something others find of value—especially beneficial technologies—and are inclined to share their innovations freely.

As Americans realized that our lives became richer as we consumed less, our dependence on the labor and resources of the rest of the world declined dramatically. With no further need to maintain a global corporate economic empire and no enemies on our borders, the U.S. military has been trimmed back to a small force whose primary mission is to participate in United Nations peacekeeping missions. Enjoying free access to beneficial technologies from around the world, and freed from the burdens of foreign debt and other forms of foreign control and extraction, living standards in what were formerly known as third-world countries have improved dramatically.

Which America do we want for our children? Which world? The choice is ours and the time to make it is now.

★★★

David C. Korten is the author of *The Post-Corporate World: Life after Capitalism* and the international best-seller *When Corporations Rule the World*. He is a cofounder and the chairman of the board of the Positive Futures Network, publishers of *Yes! A Journal of Positive Futures*, and the founder and president of the People-Centered Development Forum. He holds M.B.A. and Ph.D. degrees from the Stanford Graduate School of Business and is a former faculty member of the Harvard Graduate School of Business. He has 30 years of third-world development experience, including resident assignments in Ethiopia, Nicaragua, Indonesia, and the Philippines.

THE SPIRIT OF WORK

Lance Secretan

The last 200 years have been the centuries of the personality. Our interest in the personality began with the industrial revolution and intensified as a result of the work of Freud and Jung. We have been on a 200-year quest to deepen our understanding, perfect our skills, and strengthen our abilities to manipulate the personality. As we became more successful at this, we have also succeeded in banishing the soul from the workplace.

But a shape-shift is underway. The focus on metrics and personality has created a paradox for employees—a feeling of being empty and sad even as they become rich. This has caused a spiritual hunger and thus given birth to a huge spiritual awakening in the workplace that is stirring within our society for the first time since the industrial revolution. A tsunami, unnoticed by many "old story" leaders, bigger than *excellence* in the 1980s or *reengineering* in the 1990s, is advancing upon us. It promises to redefine what we know about leadership and change the world. It is called *spirit in the workplace*—the "new story." We are entering the Century of Spirit.

While old-story leaders tend to dismiss the concept of the soul at work, the antennae of new-story leaders are tuned in to this rapidly advancing phenomenon. Signs of the new story are sprouting everywhere: the Business and Consciousness Conference, held each December in Mexico, is one of the fastest growing and largest events in North America; books about the spirit in the workplace (*Spirit at*

Work, Reawakening the Spirit at Work, Care Packages for the Workplace, Chicken Soup for the Soul at Work, The Goddess in the Office, Jesus, CEO) are hot; people are returning to their faith or spiritual roots in numbers unmatched since the 1950s; the top five consulting firms are investing millions, creating alliances and developing task forces to study this emerging trend. These developments will first challenge and eventually overwhelm old-story leadership practices. The leader of the future is in a brave new world.

The next two decades will be the years of crossover, from reliance on personality alone as the determinant of human behavior at work, to the embrace of spirit as an equal part of the human experience at work. This transition will be the single most significant factor in workplace practices and will transform the concept of leadership as we have known it. Here are 11 harbingers of the new story of leadership in business that will redefine the landscape that we call work.

LEADERSHIP

Leadership will change in two ways. First, inspired leaders have become aware that the global network of organizations, especially commercial corporations, has become the most powerful force on Earth. Half of the world's largest "economies" are corporations, not nations. No other institutions—not the great religions or the world's political systems—have as much reach, intellect, power, talent, money, and therefore the opportunity to influence the world. This influence can be positive or negative—the choice is ours. New-story leaders see business as the greatest instrument of positive social change known to man and have reframed their role as leaders accordingly. The success of future corporate leaders will not be measured by market share, profit, and increased shareholder wealth alone, but by their effectiveness as missionaries, stewards, and custodians of the human spirit.

Second, most leaders have achieved their corporate success through their finely developed skills in decision making and rational thinking. But followers are looking for leaders who are more, who are deeper than this; they are looking for leaders who understand the *feelings* of others. Old-story leaders got to the top by using their heads;

followers are looking for new-story leaders who lead from the heart. Old-story leaders emulate warriors, but we are all yearning for human intimacy and sensitivity—for servant-leaders. We are tired of fear and competition; we are all searching for a new style of corporate leadership, one in which workplaces are characterized by love and truth, meaning and fulfillment—qualities of the spirit. The new-story leader will change the world by subjecting organizations to a more demanding criterion: whether it feeds the soul as well as the pocketbook.

VALUES

We are passing from the old-story era of morally deficient and redundant management philosophies to a new story; from rampant materialism, consumption, and rationalism to a new, humanistic approach rooted in values. As we have observed the weaknesses of our political, religious, or business leaders with increasing horror, people have realized that we must each contribute to the moral renaissance for which we all yearn. Followers, like customers and suppliers, know that we can achieve something different, something nobler; and slowly but surely we are concluding that, to quote Gandhi, "We must be the change we seek in the world."

Corporate leaders have the potential to heal the wounds that ail us, and the new-story corporate leader is ready to renounce the old story and rise to this formidable challenge, using the modern organization not only as the most potent means of creating wealth, but also as the greatest instrument of positive social change in history. Values dictate strategy, not the other way around.

THE END OF COMPETITION

The word *compete* is derived from the Latin *com*, which means "together," and *petere*, which means "to seek"; hence, *compete* means "to strive together." The more colloquial dictionary definition is "rivalry; seeking or striving for something in opposition to others." Usually, the term carries lethal force, literally or metaphorically, implying enmity, unfriendliness, even hostility. Competition creates personal stress, weakens physical and mental health, causes low self-esteem, demotivates, toxifies organizations, and damages personal relationships. Moreover, competition is an ineffective way to build teams. It focuses on the negative energy of destroying an opponent instead of on the positive energy of enhancing value for customers, employees, and suppliers by meeting their needs. Competition plays to the base aspects of the personality instead of the strongest and humblest force in the universe—the love within our souls.

The controversy over genetically modified foods teaches us that corporations cannot unilaterally compete with nature. The cola wars show us that marketing campaigns based on competition produce two losers, not a winner and a loser. The "battle in Seattle" trade protests represent only one of many recent concerted efforts to articulate a need for a new story. Respecting our interdependence will create greater opportunities than we have ever known.

THE CAUSE

For example, here is a mission statement from a large public company: "Our mission is to grow consistently as a mature and stable enterprise known for: being the most customer-sensitive and responsive specialty retail organization in the markets within which we operate; having a people-oriented work environment where our people are allowed the greatest possible freedom to carry out their responsibilities, take ownership of what they do, have fun, learn, and earn fair financial rewards; and providing a superior financial return to investors as a result of being customer-driven and people-oriented."

This is a grand statement that, if lived up to, would make for a remarkable company. The problem is that very few people will remember it, much less articulate or live it; and if we replaced "specialty retail" with any other descriptor, it could be yours. In other words, it has come from the same generic, consulting firm/MBA lexicon that has supplied the text of most contemporary mission statements.

People today are yearning for a merciful release from the monotony and institutionalization of old-story mission, vision, and values statements. They want to work for a Cause that inspires the soul. A Cause ignites passion and lifts the spirit. A mission statement is "sold" to the personality; a Cause doesn't have to be sold because it is a magnet for passion—a call to the soul. A mission statement describes the metrics; a Cause articulates the higher purpose of an organization. A mission statement describes our needs; a Cause describes how we serve. Old-story leaders organize a "shared buy-in" to the mission, but a Cause is so inherently powerful that it draws people to it from afar—hungry spirits yearning to be connected with and contribute to the Cause.

THE NEW CUSTOMER

Brand image used to be externally managed. Loyalty to the product or service was achieved by creating strong product image and brand awareness through the manipulation of the relationship between the customer and the organization. Expenditures on advertising in the United States nearly quadrupled, from $80 billion to $300 billion, during the 1980s and 1990s. This created the impetus for the extraordinary technical expertise developed over the last 40 years, during which we became experts at identifying even the subtlest needs of customers. In our old-story thinking, we have been remarkably successful this way, which has, until now, been necessary and sufficient to motivate customers to buy our services or products. We have perfected the arts of marketing, selling, customer service, and quality. We have fine-tuned our skills in motivating customers and identifying their needs. We did this in an era when too many suppliers chased too few customers.

But this has been all about "me." We have been talking about ourselves for years and, as in every other aspect of our lives, it has become tedious for the listener. The egocentric old story of leadership results in chopping down one and a half trees per person each year to create junk mail, 44 percent of it then being thrown unread into the garbage. People are tired of self-promotion. We are realizing that the time has come to honor "you," to shift away from our egos and toward meeting the needs of *your* soul.

Furthermore, it is now the employee's turn to stand in the limelight formerly occupied by the customer alone. During the last 30 years, the U.S. economy has doubled while the birthrate has declined by 24 percent. The number of headhunters has grown by 45 percent to 9,000 during the last two decades, in response to the lowest unemployment rate in 30 years. Annual economic growth is forecast at 2.4 percent, barring any major shocks to the system, while employment grows at a glacial 1.2 percent.

This focuses attention on the new marketing: to employees. The new-story leader honors employees as much as—and often more than—external customers, not just with innovative perks, creative working conditions, and compensation systems but through behaviors, practices, values, and beliefs that lift their hearts and stir their passions and thus lift the hearts and stir the passions of external customers too. This is the beginning of a remarkable shift caused by the intense search for internal customers—employees. The old story, the this-is-the-job-take-it-or-leave-it approach, has become our old-story baggage. Ninety percent of the market value of Coca-Cola is in the brand name, yet during the 1990s, Coke first added 6,000 new employees and then "downsized" them all again in 2000. This damaged the brand and dramatically lowered Coca-Cola's market value. New-story leaders recognize that employees and suppliers are partners who are just as critical to success as customers. The trail is being blazed by the new-story leaders of organizations like Herman Miller, Home Depot, Medtronic, Nordstrom, Patagonia, SAS Institute, ServiceMaster, W. L. Gore, and Southwest Airlines, which have built their brand leadership through their people-friendly cultures more than through old-story marketing—through the heart, not the head. Last year, Southwest Airlines received 136,371 applications for 1,689 vacancies—80.7 for every job opening. The brand no longer emanates from a billboard but from the values practiced internally and experienced by customers, and this determines whether relationships, and therefore fortunes, grow or decline in the marketplace.

INTEGRATION

People want it all. They feel, quite understandably, that this is their birthright. They want the fast life of converging technology, global roaming, rising opportunities, adrenaline-pumping challenges, and life at Web speed—and they want to spend time with their families and friends, meditate, keep fit, relax, and play. It's not about a work/life balance; it's about the complete integration of work and life, a holistic, seamless fit between these two and every other aspect of life. The new-story leader encourages employees to engage their creative juices about their work when they are walking along a beach, or to shop for their groceries online while they are at work and not be self-conscious—indeed, to be unaware of the difference. Life is whole, not separated into two solitudes called "work" and "life."

The new-story leader recognizes that integration is leading in real time. SAS Institute, the largest independent software company in the world, reached that status by, among other things, shutting their offices daily at 5:00 P.M., providing on-site day care to 700 children, and recognizing that people have lives outside of work. Their staff turnover is 3 percent in an industry that averages 20 percent, and in one recent year they received 27,000 applications for 945 job openings. The bottom line? SAS Institute saves an estimated $50 million each year in recruitment and training costs alone. We are entering the age of living fast *and* slow.

THE CALLING

More people than ever before are resolving to find joy in their work, rather than just having a job. A calling or vocation (from the Latin *vocare*, "to call") depends on the relationship between our souls and our work—the degree to which our work engages and nourishes our souls. People have recently discovered that the point of life is not to slave away for years until the age of 65 and then say, "Phew! Glad that's over!" Rather, it is to make sure that we do not die with our music still inside us.

The leader's job is to enable each follower to find, grow, and excel in his or her calling. This goes beyond career counseling, employability, or job enrichment programs—it seeks to honor the most profound, even the most secret, vocational dreams deep inside everyone, finding the right assignment and place that will inspire their creative brilliance so that their music within can be heard.

SOULSPACE

People are yearning for sacred workplaces. For thousands of years, cultures around the world have honored the concept of sacred space—the Eastern concept of feng shui being just one of many examples. When we discount the importance of the physical environment to human performance by focusing on the cold efficiencies and economics of workspace allocation, we create a paradox—we are asking people to perform to the highest standards of which they are capable, to dig as deeply as possible into their creative genius, while situating them in some of the least creative and most dreary environments in their lives—workplaces.

We will witness extraordinary increases in productivity and creativity through the liberating impact of sacred workplaces designed to inspire the soul. Designing workplaces with the soul in mind will transform factories, offices, and distribution facilities. By revering our work facilities, we will come to love and respect them. Because we will create beautiful workplaces—which I call soulspaces—we will love them, and this will transform human performance. We will rediscover the creative genius that lies within us all but that has been repressed by the old story of leadership and work setting. The yearning for integration in our lives will bring about the wholesale migration of work from downtown Dilbert-style cubicle farms to the wired and connected home office, and it will take just 10 short years.

TECHNOLOGY

Visit AvantGo.com to see how the Web is reaching people's souls. Here you can download personalized data from 350 different Web sites directly to your personal digital assistant (PDA) or mobile computing device, including up-to-date stock quotes, flight schedules, movie listings, restaurant reviews, maps, weather reports and forecasts, and excerpts from headline news stories from the *New York Times*, *USA Today*, *Industry Week*, TheStreet.com, TRIP.com, Hollywood.com, Restaurant Row, MapQuest.com, and The Weather Channel—all automatically tailored to your needs when you hotsync your PDA.

The company I used to run, Manpower Limited—which, for

the time being, is the largest employer in the world—is about to be reinvented: Today, temporary help can be purchased online through free-market auctions or exchanges. In my day, I moved gross profit margins from the low 20s up to the 40s. Since I left nearly 20 years ago, competition has eroded those margins to the high teens, and free-market auctions are about to eliminate them.

Seattle-based Onvia.com has created a Web site for small business, linking tens of thousands of suppliers. Present your request for a proposal on, say, your office insurance, specify how many bids you would like to receive, and hit the submit button—your quotes will be ready in less than an hour. Ford, General Motors, and Daimler-Chrysler have formed an online exchange linking tens of thousands of suppliers from whom they purchase $250 billion worth of supplies and whom in turn purchase upwards of $500 billion. These formerly hostile adversaries are sweeping away the concept of competition as we have known it as they embrace a new, converging, and interactive world. The price and demand for electricity in the Mid-Atlantic States, which can fluctuate wildly, used to be posted every 15 minutes. Now it is posted every 3 seconds on the Web. It took Cisco Systems, born in 1984, just 16 years to become the world's most valuable company. This is a company that functions at Web speed: 500 managers are worth between $10 and $40 million; Larry Carter, Cisco's CFO, has achieved the incredible feat of closing the books at the end of every single working day; the company acquired 25 companies in one recent 12-month period. And Cisco is ranked by *Fortune* as the third-best company to work for in America, with a staff turnover of only 7 percent in an industry averaging 20 percent.

Technology will form the sinews of our soul, and new-story leaders will not shrink from the opportunities to work virtually, leverage the latest breakthroughs, pay attention to shifts, experiment, and be brave in order to work and engage the soul at Web speed. We have at last been presented with the most powerful tool in human history—the Internet. It took 37 years for radio to reach 50 million homes, and it took the Web 4 years to do the same. With Internet traffic doubling every 100 days, we will now achieve what we have been dreaming about for so long—the integration of our lives. This will create the time we need to live fast *and* slow.

We need to understand and embrace the potential of the Internet to create a real web for the first time in human history: the web of human consciousness. Think of it as the noosphere—the envelope of consciousness surrounding the globe—a concept made famous by French philosopher Pierre Teilhard de Chardin. We are entering the time when universal consciousness manifests itself through the Internet, an omnipresent oneness. The Internet is the last piece of a human jigsaw puzzle in which we, at last, link the souls of humanity into one. This is a concept that is larger by far than the pedestrian and utilitarian limits we have currently placed on the potential of the Internet. New-story leaders will reinvent their organizations within this context, not in response to it but by riding and initiating it.

LEARNING

The most important "fringe benefit" is no longer health care or a pension. It is the right to learn, which is an inoculation against irrelevance. Our challenge is not just to learn in order that our skills may remain relevant to our careers, but to learn fast enough to keep pace with change at warp speed. Research shows that more than half of those surveyed believe that they are unable to keep pace with change, not just in technology or work but throughout their lives. Those who commit to a practice of lifelong learning—intellectual maintenance, you might call it—can rest easy knowing that they will stay relevant and young. What's more, it's good for the soul. Learning leads to regeneration; it is the fuel of the soul. Without learning, we cannot grow, and without growth, the soul withers.

INSPIRATION

We have been confusing motivation with inspiration. The dictionary tells us that to motivate is "to provide a motive; to induce, incite, impel"—it is something that we *do* to people. It is a self-focused practice; when we attempt to motivate others, we intend to cause behavior in them that achieves something we want. When we attempt to motivate, we are not usually intending to serve others in their best interests. At its best, motivation is an attempt to serve others in *our* best self-interests. It is this transparently selfish intent that has caused much of the widespread cynicism among so many followers today.

Inspiration is strikingly different from motivation. The word is derived from the Latin root *spirare*, meaning "spirit, to breathe, to give life, the breath of God." The dictionary defines inspiration as "breathing in, as in air to the lungs; to infuse with an encouraging or exalting influence; to animate; stimulation by a divinity, a genius, an idea, or a passion; a divine influence upon human beings." It is not difficult to see the difference between being motivated and the blissful experience of inspiration. Motivation is a relationship between personalities; inspiration is a relationship between souls. Motivation is based on greed; inspiration is an act of love. The old-story leader motivates; the new-story leader inspires. The role of the inspirational leader is to inspire others—all the time.

America during the last 200 years has been defined by corporate America—the American dream as measured by the individual material success achieved through corporate success. Thus, being the world's leading nation has meant being the world's leading economy. America will continue to lead and define success, but we will add new measures to this definition. The personality will continue to be an important arbiter of success, but the spirit will gain an equal voice.

★★★

Lance Secretan built Manpower Limited into an international organization with 72,000 full- and part-time employees. Manpower Inc. has since become the largest employer in the world. He left Manpower at age 40; since then, he has been a professor of entrepreneurialism at two universities and has founded the Secretan Center Inc., a worldwide consulting organization. He serves as a trustee of the International Heart Foundation Trust and is the founder of the Higher Ground Community, a worldwide network dedicated to reawakening spirit and values in the workplace. He has been voted one of the nation's top 10 speakers, and one in four of *Industry Week*'s Best Managed Companies is his client. He is the author of 10 books, including *Managerial Moxie, Living the Moment, The Way of the Tiger, Reclaiming Higher Ground*, and *Inspirational Leadership: Destiny, Calling and Cause.*

THE REWOVEN FABRIC

TRANSFORMATION

Vicki Robin

Tiffa watched her daughter Peri laughing and talking with several friends over by the old boathouse at Green Lake. She recognized Peri's arched neck, tilted head, and cocked hip. Yes, Peri's in heat, Tiffa thought, recognizing body moves a woman never forgets. Do all mothers hold their breath in these years, unable to protect, direct, and . . . well, mother?

At Peri's age—17—Tiffa was still Tiffany (she'd disabused herself of that Barbie name when she turned 50 and gray). It was 2000. She had just graduated from Seattle's Garfield High. Forty years ago. Tiffa had been part of the "environmental disaster" generation, the one brought up on horror, on the thought that there might not be a world to grow up or grow old in. The one that named their children after dying species like the peregrine falcon (Peri). How odd to think of all that had changed—and in ways they'd never imagined.

Green Lake. In most ways, it looked the same as it did in the year 2000. People bicycling and roller-blading and power walking the 3-mile course around the lake. Pairs of friends engrossed in deep conversation. There were clearly differences . . . but what?

Facile with multiple ways of knowing (as most people were these days), Tiffa allowed herself to sink into a reverie that drew on her meditation practice, her scientific training, and her keen Web columnist's eye for the current and the quirky.

Her mind swam upstream like a spawning salmon, attracted to

the headwaters where true explanations arise. The change, as always, happened first in the invisible and mysterious, in tiny shifts in thinking and feeling that alter the whole watercourse of history. At some point, the lonely majority of closet meditators and weary activists reached critical mass and came out in force, wearing their love for life on their sleeves. Before the tipping point, we all answered the question "What do you do?" by describing our jobs. After the shift, we'd reply to the same question by mentioning what we do to serve one another. Spirit was out of the box called church. It was everywhere and everywhen.

Who or whatever is running this show is a great "just in time" manager, Tiffa thought with the wryness of her columnist self. We needed that base of shared communion to deal with the shared time of Sorrow. Who could avoid being a mystic, thinking about the many arks that were sent to us to ride those rough waters? What a time . . .

People seemed different now, too—and not just because of Afro-Asian fashion or the features of the young people, who carried more and more races in their blood. Strangers talked openly with one another. People hugged a lot. And they were forever whipping out their pocket communicators (PCs) to exchange useful information or arrange S-n-S (service-and-swap) barters, enriching their lives without spending a dime. The self-proclaimed Nosy Neighbors were out in force, using their PCs to match people in need with offers for beds and meals in private homes. Great outdoor volunteerism for folks over 80!

There was also the Green Lake community café. That was different, too. As with so many of the changes, it had come about out of recognizing the obvious—in this case, that all the boating and walking and fishing was really an excuse for conversation. So now there was an open-air conversation pavilion with tables and fresh-food stands. Anyone could announce on the Web or the ubiquitous electronic kiosks a topic and a table number and get a conversation group together. Several clumps were congregated now, probably talking philosophy or poetry or astronomy or politics (with six political parties and election debates free on the Net, there was no shortage of things to talk about) or who knows what.

Neighborhood conflicts also got aired in the "con-res" circle. Now that everyone was trained from kindergarten on to use the whole range of awareness and conflict-resolution tools, grievances had gone from private hell to public pageants. People loved the basically good-natured verbal brawls where you proclaimed your bitch as eloquently as possible, listened fully and accurately to your "opponent's" version of the same predicament, and together found a creative solution. "Mention the tension and resolve the dissension" was the motto for these public "con-res" sessions. Crowds gathered, cheered for elegant innovations, and often reenacted the conflicts with hilarious skits. At best, there would be some musicians who'd get everyone dancing and people would go home in a happy mood to some juicy private celebrations of good feeling. Strange, Tiffa thought. In the old days, we watched music and sports.—now we *play* music and sports. We stuffed our feelings and our faces and went to the movies. Now we *are* the movies. It's so different.

The other difference (and it was hard to remember how it had been) was silence—there wasn't even the whisper of an internal combustion engine. Small electric cars and buses glided along the street, all filled to the brim. It was so easy with a communicator to pick up hitchers: Just punch in your destination and route and the names of everyone needing a lift popped up. A quick series of e-mails and barters and you'd have a full car and parking credits. Thank Gaia that the Chinese got smart and decided to leapfrog over the fossil fuel economy. They sure cornered the market on alternative-energy technology, Tiffa mused. Talk about a survivor civilization . . .

Peri had pulled out her communicator to make a date with one of her friends; she talked to another on the celly and then punched in OFF-LINE TILL 3:00 P.M. and put it back in its holster. She came over to Tiffa and went from standing to bench-sprawling in one gangly plop. "So I have to write something about modern history for my Webzine group and I thought you could help."

"Help . . . or do it for you?"

Tiffa got the look that said she had damaged the delicate trust a mother needs to rebuild as her child becomes an adult. Backing off, she inquired, "And that topic is . . ."

"Money and stuff. Like I know when you were growing up there were so many people starving and that the rich didn't seem to care. Some people had it all and wanted more. Some had barely anything. That's like totally gonzo. I need to interview three old-timers"—Watch your language, lady! Tiffa thought—"about why and how they think things turned around."

"Funny, I was just thinking about the changes. But why did they happen? That's a great question. Tomorrow I might give a different answer, but today what occurs to me are three big trends: the Great Sorrow"—Peri rolled her eyes; why does everything start with Great Sorrow stories?—"the Simplicity Pioneers, and the strange way e-commerce actually transformed the economy from a market for things to a market for needs.

"I saw your eyes, honey. I know you've heard about the Great Sorrow years. But if there's anything we learned, it's that wisdom comes from keeping our stories alive. That, and the Journey of the 18th Year."

"Do you think I'm not up to it?" Peri suddenly looked like a young colt, nostrils flared, a bit of wildness in her eyes. Tiffa knew bravado when she saw it. The Journey of the 18th Year was devastating for so many young people brought up since the Sorrow. As they visited the global sites of past ecocide and war, they pondered our blindness as a species and the darkness that could filter again into our midst.

"No, Pumpkin . . . I mean, Peri. I think you will come through it a wise woman. You will understand the Sorrow from inside. You know, anyone could have predicted it, and many did, even in the 20th century, but we didn't really know it was upon us until we were years into it. Everyone knows that the Great Sorrow came from the synergy of the crash of the global financial markets, the terrible die-off from AIDS and other antibiotic-resistant diseases, the flooding of coastal regions around the Earth, and the end of the fossil fuel era.

"My generation—into whose childhood was woven mourning

for the loss of nature and culture—was so much more able to handle this era than our parents were. They'd grown up in the 1950s and 1960s and believed in the economic boom, like previous generations had believed in a flat Earth. They kept thinking there was going to be a rally. We understood ecology and cycles and limits to growth. We knew that the economy existed within the natural world; they thought they'd transcended the laws of nature. They were like children, really. They just couldn't cope with it. It was so sad. They'd developed so many medicines for life extension but they just didn't want to live in a world that looked so diminished.

"So while the old-timers were partying themselves to death in Hawaii and OD'ing on everything they could find, we were prepared to hospice the death of the old mindset and midwife the new world that was being born. Within a decade, our numbers were decimated and a third of the species were destroyed."

Against the will of the savvy adult she was cultivating, Peri had sunk into that quiet space of storytelling.

"Yet we survived, and for good reason. Your grandparents' generation also had some shining lights. Like the Simplicity Pioneers. These were 'my people.' We started having congresses in 1999, I think. Give or take a few years. The whole movement was a loose-jointed, grassroots-y affair. People everywhere were hitting the same cultural lie: that more is better and it's never enough. They were bone-tired, from overwork, overstimulation, overspending, and overconsumption of stuff they didn't need. It's like 50 million lonely, spent consumption junkies hit bottom in one decade and started seeking solutions. With some kind of ancient homing instinct for health, we turned from competitive consumption to the shelter of community. Study circles, conferences, chat rooms, church groups, books, journals, barter nets—you name it, we flocked to it. At first we only wanted to heal ourselves, but soon we saw that we couldn't be healed inside a sick system and on a dying world. We organized and got active, developing trade associations and activist pods and policy and research institutes and, of course, the PopEcon Pranksters, with our wicked street theater. There were some great leaders at that time—a whole group of them that seemed to instinctively know that they would all be stronger if they worked and played together. They were like a moral compass, pastors of the whole culture. I think that was the beginning of the end of the old days of the lone charismatic leader."

"Why would any one person *want* to be a lone leader? That's like *so* not natural."

"Surely they've taught you Western history, Peri! The whole saga is the story of just that struggle for dominance."

"Get fluid, Mom. The guys who played that game wrote your books. My books tell the story of the universe, not that penis-dueling junk. Maybe you think humans have changed since you were born. I just think the rule makers, the process guides, and the storytellers have changed, and"—Peri's eyes sparkled—"they tend to have vaginas."

Peri was right again. Tiffa felt old and rejuvenated both at once. Will the young people celebrate the die-off of her generation as holders of the old way of thinking, just as her cohorts secretly prayed for the boomers to be gone? Yet sitting with Peri and her many friends always gave Tiffa the tingle of youth, the desire to live forever and keep participating in the great unfolding mystery.

"To continue with my oh-so-antiquated interpretation of history . . ." Tiffa said, feigning indignation. "With all that talk, action was bound to happen. Buy Nothing Day got bigger than Earth Day. A Million Meek March on Washington was planned for the 2005 BND. The theme was "The tide is turning" and the motto was "We want less." But none of the organizers anticipated how big it would ultimately be. It was like Woodstock meets Seattle WTO." Do they still teach about those events? Tiffa wondered. "The message was risky, sophisticated. There were signs that read, IN THE LAND OF MORE, LESS IS RADICAL. People with bullhorns led chants: 'What do we want less of?' they'd bellow. 'Pollution!' or 'Greed!' or 'Overwork!' we'd reply. 'What do we want more of?' 'Species!' or 'Time!' or 'Justice!' we'd shout. And then, even louder: 'What do we want enough of?' and we'd say, 'Enough for all!'" Tiffa hadn't realized that her hand had gone to her throat, a gesture the scientist in her often used to smooth emotion out when Tiffa the teacher was weaving the tale of a great historical moment.

"Why doesn't anything trans like that happen anymore?" Peri moaned.

"I thought the same thing about the 1960s when I was growing up in the 1990s. Like I'd missed all the action. Your generation has big challenges ahead, Peri. I can see them coming. Despite the Journey of the 18th Year, people will forget the Sorrow. They will decide the World Wisdom Council is a bunch of reactionaries. Every generation has its revolution. Just watch the horizon. And maybe watch those young guys a little less . . ." Gaia, I sound like my mother, Tiffa thought. Age—who knew it would creep into my radical life? . . .

"Keep telling, Tiffa," Peri demanded, mesmerized by the story and willing to overlook Tiffa's slide into mothering.

"Two million people . . . thirty cities simultaneously . . . never before . . . never since. So many people and concerns that had been pushed to the margins in the quest for the material 'more' were pushing back together for a new set of values. We were speaking with one voice about the world we wanted and were creating, not just protesting the world that was being forced on us by large institutions. The labor movement joined, realizing that they could fight for shorter work time rather than higher wages. The tax shift folks joined, promoting their consumption tax/guaranteed minimum income/no subsidies for extractive industries package. Youth was there, with their message of 'We want a world to grow up in.' Kids. Toddlers. Heartbreaking . . . and very media-genic. And, best of all, the poor were there in droves. They were marching for more libraries, computer centers, swimming pools, and free public transport in their neighborhoods. And right alongside the poor and homeless, the Millionaires for Justice marched. They were mostly in their twenties and thirties, people who'd made out like bandits on Wall Street—and knew how true that term really was. Call it guilt, call it giving back, they were advocating an end to corporate welfare and a voluntary lowering of CEO compensation.

"Representatives of NGOs from the two-thirds world came too, protesting the domination of commercial interests abroad. From that BND on, money as the sole measure of value had lost its stranglehold on the public psyche.

"The third fascinating occurrence was the surprising social renewal that evolved from e-commerce. It's all so obvious to you, I'm sure, but it really was a revolution equal to, well, alt-fuel. It took hold just after women discovered that e-mail was a cheap, easy way to keep the family connected. Everyone and her grandma were online then, and e-commerce was an obvious next step. Cutting out several middlemen between producer and consumer lowered transportation costs and perhaps had something to do with the decrease in carbon emissions and global warming."

"I cannot believe those old stories about doing errands in a car," Peri chimed in, rolling her eyes with what she thought was a sophisticated flourish indicating disgust.

"Nor I, frankly! I think the next step was when somebody coined the term 'be-commerce'—that whole service industry of coaches/salespeople. I love the way they not only help you figure out what product to buy and how to use the damn thing once you have it, but ask you whether there might be nonmaterial ways to fill your needs better than getting more stuff. Once be-commerce caught on— and it wasn't cheap back then, but the triple savings of buying less, buying cheaper, and liberating shopping time offset the cost—other specialized types of transactions surfaced.

"'We-commerce' became the new name for public spending. People thought afresh about what they wanted to own personally and what they wanted to borrow from a community source."

"Like transportation," Peri offered. "I can't imagine everyone wanting a private car, when a little intelligence and a few taxes so easily created the mobility system that we have today. I mean, how could people be so solid, so, like, 2020?"

Tiffa silently voiced the mother's prayer of hope: May she have a daughter just like her. But what she said was, "It *is* strange what a name will do. The ideas had been around for years, but calling it we-commerce captured the entrepreneurial spirit of the times. Libraries became we-commerce in books; the vidi-wall became we-commerce in entertainment, and fees for cable television disappeared. Suddenly we were thinking about the kind of world we wanted for everyone and looking for we-commerce solutions rather than government regulation or private consumption. It was easy—once we could see it. And cheaper. So American.

"Then there were the Simplicity Pioneers, who started pushing nonmonetary 'you-and-me-commerce'—the barter nets that became the S-n-S system of today. It was such a no-brainer to realize that none of us use all our possessions all the time. Sharing brought our costs of living down dramatically—and brought back good old-fashioned neighborliness. The you-and-me-commerce folks eventually grew beyond barter to all sorts of consumer-owned buying clubs. Neighborhoods organized and partnered with organic farms. A group of my girlfriends designed a kind of tunic that we thought would be cool to wear and partnered with an immigrant women's sewing club to produce them."

"What I love, though," Peri said, "is the see-commerce. I'm glad someone figured out that getting out is fun. For me, see-commerce in mall showrooms is more about seeing my friends than seeing stuff I might want to buy on the Web. I mean, once I've played with the latest techno toys at the mall, I just don't want to spend my e-script on them."

"I guess mall showrooms are like window-shopping down on old-time Main Street," Tiffa replied. "I like being able to visit my purchases with no pressure to buy. Well, except for the 'flea-commerce' areas. I remember when we ran flea-commerce like squatters in the parking lots of the old malls. Once shopping centers became showrooms where no money changed hands, though, I think us ragtag tag-salers were no threat, so they just let us move inside.

"I just realized that e-commerce used to only mean 'electronic.' My oh my, times really have changed. You take enviro-commerce for granted, but back in the beginning, there were no ecological screens for products. People had no way to know the cost to the Earth of what they were buying. So much has changed!

"Gaia, we were so worried in the early days that the Internet was going to be one more tool of the commercial devil, but look how inventive and playful we became. For all our activism, for all our protest, I don't think we ever thought that commerce itself could be a force for healing.

"Peri, I think it all comes down to good people living in elegant human systems that enhance the big system—the living system that includes us all. Frankly, I'm damn proud of this little species we have here. We've gone through such a terrible time, but look what we've learned and invented. Look how we've grown."

Peri started going solid, braced for a lecture about the bad old days—but it didn't come.

"In a way, honey, you are a celebration for me of all that is good about being human and being alive in the universe. During the Great Sorrow, no one wanted children. After the Sorrow, those of us who made it through knew we had to reproduce very carefully to survive in a world where ten million other very precious species shared the world's natural wealth. Having you was my way of saying, 'The tide has turned.'"

Peri had gotten more than a Webzine story. She'd gotten to bask in the attention and intelligence of the woman who, truth be told, she most admired. Tiffa, normally not very demonstrative, hugged Peri and cried. Peri, normally not very tolerant of mushy emotions, cried too. Then her communicator beeped. It was 3 o'clock—time for her online chat with her three best fillies. Not that Tiffa wasn't like a filly too, but after all, she was kind of prehistoric.

★★★

Vicki Robin is a speaker, writer, and activist on sustainable consumption and cultural transformation. She is coauthor, with Joe Dominguez, of the best-selling book *Your Money or Your Life*. She is president of the New Road Map Foundation, a nonprofit organization dedicated to helping people lead more sustainable, simple lives. She is also cofounder of Financial Integrity Associates, an international outreach network that teaches the nine-step program laid out in *Your Money or Your Life*.

IDENTITY

Stanley Crouch

Since the emergence of an "identity politics" in America, we have had a number of battles over what amounts to the question of whether or not assimilation is even vaguely a good thing. It used to be argued that America was destined to become this big melting pot that would produce an alloy of largely indistinguishable particulars. With the rise of identity politics in the 1960s, that idea was shunted aside and defined as some order of cultural and psychological totalitarianism.

By 1970, the leaders of different movements were telling their followers what the recipe for authenticity was. Black people who didn't fit the bill were called "oreos," which meant black on the outside, white on the inside; Hispanics used the term "coconuts," for brown on the outside, Anglo on the inside; and we eventually heard about "the woman who thinks like a man." All of these people were seen as victims and, potentially, enemies of their movements because their allegiance was to those who oppressed them, who set the standards, who imposed definitions on them, who let them know when they were good and when they were bad. Such people were considered descendants of mission Indians and Uncle Toms—individuals so brainwashed by the oppressors that they had no love for their culture, for themselves, for their people. If the word came down from the white folks or the menfolks, well, it had to be right. No argument; that was close enough to the voice of God.

Consequently, many people believed that new directions had to be brought into the American struggle for freedom from stereotypes and unfair treatment. But, as it turned out, if one didn't adhere to the proclamations that purported to be radical, if one didn't buy what very quickly hardened into the new stereotypes, he or she could be, essentially, ostracized.

Since that period of emerging Balkanization, I have written many times on what is now called multiculturalism, one of the dumber terms produced by our fumbling discourse on group identity. *Notes of a Hanging Judge* (1990), *The All-American Skin Game* (1995), and *Always in Pursuit* (1998) are books of essays that, among many other things, take on the dilemmas and decoys of separatist politics. Those books express my sense of our collective Americaness. But I did not get there by being Boy Scout honorable all the way. I came to myself after having been vociferously involved in the separatist movements that emerged from the declaration of Black Power in 1966.

But by the start of the 1970s, I was on my way out of the separatist movements. By then, Black Power had destroyed the civil rights movement. Its exponents had called for throwing whites out of organizations that had provided integrated teams of workers against discrimination. They had rejected King's march-on-Washington vision in favor of a politics based on skin tone, an international black unity, a hatred of European and American culture, and a remarkably naive conception of Africa as some kind of a paradise lost. So Black Power, as I wrote in the introduction to *Notes of a Hanging Judge*, "sent not only black America but this nation itself into an intellectual tailspin on the subjects of race, of culture, of heritage."

We have yet to come out of that tailspin. One of the most tragic examples of what those limited ideas on ethnic authenticity have done over the years is made clear in the performances of black schoolchildren, some from blue-collar backgrounds, others from well-to-do suburban families. In studies done in Washington, D.C., 10 years ago and in Shaker Heights, Ohio, in 1998, it has been observed that too many of these kids think themselves out of step with the "real" members of their ethnic group (at this time, we need to set aside the unscientific term *race*). The kids fear doing well in school because they might be accused of trying to be white, as if high-quality work were outside the province of Negro American engagement.

This is remarkable because, in the past, Negroes protested against minstrelsy and the stereotypes of innate intellectual inadequacy by struggling up through the barriers of illiteracy and doing the very best jobs that they could. They knew that excellence is one of the highest forms of protest against charges of inferiority. It was also formerly understood that learning itself provided one with interior experiences that could not be taken away, regardless of how unfair the external world might be. So now, for all our social progress as a nation, these kids are self-victimizers perpetuating inner group stereotypes that deny the constantly expanding presence of women and so-called minorities into positions of power and influence. There can be no other explanation if we remember the way America was in, say, 1960, that Kennedy era when everything of importance was done by white men in dark suits, white shirts, and slender ties.

What we can say about one aspect of our moment is that we don't like to look very closely at shortcomings across the board, or from the bottom to the top, the top to the bottom. That is because we don't want to believe that any group other than those guys at the top can influence the nation. Power is only supposed to arrive from one place. But, as the Mexican novelist Carlos Fuentes once observed, it is difficult to understand the nature of power in the United States because it is so diffuse. In other words, power arrives from many places and it is that fact which makes us, as Americans, what we are. We are touched by many, many things, and it is what we do with them that defines us not only in terms of our supposed groups but in terms of how we have formed our individual lives. We need to realize the complexity and reverberations of those touches as we move deeper into the time that is ours. We might then come to understand more about the nature of our freedom as well as our refusal to assert it.

The question of the nature of that freedom and the diffusion of inspiration and influence came together for me in *Don't the Moon Look*

Lonesome (2000), a novel that allowed for another angle from which to address what has happened to us as a nation over the last 40 years. What I was after was a chance to look at the complexity of the human sides of the things that I have written about in nonfiction, examining our history, our arts, our politics, and our conflicts in the arena of color. I wanted to give narrative and dramatic power to what I see as the realities of American cultural life. Beyond that, there is no richer subject or set of subjects in the history of our nation than race, sex, class, identity, and art. Every one of those areas gives so much tragic and comic and heroic substance to our cultural tale; into them, I wanted to send a highly intelligent character, one whose experience would raise questions about authenticity, purported self-hatred, media brainwashing, confusions of identity, and so on. I started with what I thought would be a short story but it got out of its cell, made it across the yard, went up and over the wall, and by the time I brought it back, the simple little 15- or 20-page story of an interracial romance under attack from within and without had become a 546-page tale swallowing American life at will.

Much of the work arrived as a protest against the kind of segregated fiction that denies just how well Americans are doing when it comes to incorporating the humanity of others different from themselves into their own conception of living. In *Don't the Moon Look Lonesome*, Carla Hamsun, the heroine and a white woman, moves into the Negro world and through a good number of others as her story unfolds. Her story, essentially a tale about her development into a jazz singer, is set against the problem of maintaining a romance that is under siege. Her black lover of 5 years is being told by more and more black people that he shouldn't be with a white woman. He, Maxwell Davis, a tenor saxophonist and budding celebrity in the jazz world, is beginning to yield to the pressure, some of the strongest from black women who say to him, "You brothers need to come home." In essence, the question is: What constitutes home to an American? Is it something stationary or something that one improvises based on career, sensibility, and environment? Or, more accurately, is it what one makes of where one comes from and where one chooses to go?

Carla is from South Dakota, where the Indian wars ended with the massacre at Wounded Knee in 1890. She has the pioneer woman's willingness to take the hard knocks that fully living demands. That means she is up to the game of learning how to accept the multi-leveled elements of her American identity. As a woman in a troubled relationship, her tale brings us up to date on what was once called the battle of the sexes. As she travels to Chicago, to New York, through the South, and to the Southwest, Carla sees Americana hummed in many different keys, all of them in some way uplifting and hurtful, illuminating and befuddling. Along the way, she learns that there are plenty of expected and unexpected types of people out there in this land and that they are united by the variations that they make, both good and bad and in between, on the national ethos.

Carla is a jazz musician because jazz is a uniquely American music, an original mixing of European melodic and harmonic roots with African-derived rhythms. After all, we Americans are improvisers, and we play a remarkably complicated set of cultural themes rooted in our political structure, our religious beliefs, our common history of what the writer Albert Murray calls "kinship and aginship." Goading and inspiring us is the great dream of this land, which says that social background does not preclude the human essence at the center of individuality. So the American is always trying to find just who he or she is, according to a number of things, none of them the result of one lane of influence.

That is what Carla Hamsun has to come to terms with as she learns that what we love and devote ourselves to in the modern world always has something to do with the human heritage that is available to all. We add to what we choose from that human heritage the things we also choose from our familial and immediate cultural backgrounds, no matter our color, our sex, or any of the other things that make us each what we are. She is stubbornly American in her courage, and open to the humanity of what she encounters. That does not mean that she likes everything she comes to know, which is part of recognizing the commonality of our human traits. No group or division escapes the "pressure of life," as literary scholar George Steiner calls it.

But to be an American is to be the product of many, many things. Seventy years ago, the great scholar of American culture Constance Rourke observed that the American was part Yankee, part frontiersman, part Indian, and part Negro. This was the four-ingredient basic blend. We can now, stepping back a bit, add to the mix the Mexicans of the Southwest, who were central to what one writer called cowboy culture, supplying the basic tools that allowed those distinctly American kinds of people to come into existence. We would also have to add the Asians, who have so influenced our national cuisine and our sense of physical fitness and exercise through the martial arts, and who also brought many converts to different kinds of meditation through various schools of Buddhism.

Carla Hamsun, who is 38 years old when the novel opens and the daughter of a college professor of history and classics, has to grapple with all of that, both in her own thoughts and in her conversations with other Americans who are trying to find out what it means to be authentic. Few of them would use the word "authentic," but the question is still there. That is because we are always being asked to add something new to the mix that might redefine us. This question of renewing or diluting the mix is the fundamental challenge at the heart of our democracy.

That is why Carla covers so much of this country in her travels. She is vain and somewhat provincial when she leaves South Dakota, but the world changes all of that. I wanted her to be sort of a female Odysseus—someone who goes away and has many adventures before returning home, matured by the wounds, the self-revelations, and the range of experience that scrapes away all small-mindedness but makes home that much more humanly important. Along the way, as she tries to hold on to her love with her black man, Carla remembers growing up with Lakota Indian kids; working as a waitress in New York and overhearing white college girls complaining to their mothers about Asian women taking the white guys on the campuses in northern California; studying music at Chicago conservatory during the day and dancing to blues bands on the South Side at night; exploring that South Side culture with a tenor saxophonist and card partner; coming to New York and running around with a wealthy Anglo-Irish stockbroker and yachtsman; learning from a doomed black drummer who tells her shocking tales of Vietnam; becoming best friends with a topflight black fashion model; singing country and western music before deciding finally to become a jazz singer; working the rough-and-tumble world of high-class restaurants where women are not welcome; adjusting to the shifting social classes and careers and backgrounds that make Manhattan, which becomes her home of choice, the imposing urban thing that it is.

Like all of us, Carla realizes that she is "a sponge, not a sieve," but she is ever more herself, not a person so at a loss for an identity that she keeps disappearing under new influences. What she experiences and hears and argues about is what makes an American. What Carla discovers is what I laid down as a credo in a section on writing in *Always in Pursuit*: In our own country, contrary to certain opinions, writing that focuses on color needn't be less good than any other. The challenge staring down at any writer who uses color conflict in our American context is how close he or she can get to the standards set by writers such as Homer and Shakespeare, two champions who were never unwilling to narrate a fight, blow by blow, nuance by nuance.

Whether or not the novel succeeds in doing what I wanted it to do, it was an attempt to bring to the surface many of the things that I see missing from American fiction at large. The book exemplifies what I call tragic optimism, which is something I see at the improvising center of the conception that brought us the Constitution. Our form of society is built upon a paranoia about both the abuse of power and the limitations of vision as made public by policy. Our system of checks and balances is set up so that people have to deal with one another, compromise—improvise—as they put together laws. We also have in place the tools to nonviolently change short-sighted, prejudicial, or downright stupid policies. When we conclude that something those before us thought right is far from correct, we change, we improvise our policies to try and keep up with what we come to believe about the nature of human beings. So, our tragic sense of human limitations is countered by our optimistic idea that we can keep improvising our way into a more civilized and fair society. That is why Carla's tale is subtitled *A Novel in Blues and Swing*. One side of the blues faces the troubles of our human condition, while swing is the unsentimental affirmation. Swing is the beat that underlies whistling through the graveyard, not in disrespect but in recognition of the fact that all of these people in these graves are dead, some having died comfortably, others not—but, right now, I'm alive and breathing and life itself must be celebrated as the force through which we come to know all that we know. Blues and swing constitute tragic optimism.

We tend to understand others through the common feelings that transcend the decoys of cultural specifics. We remember so much of what has happened to us when we listen closely to others, waiting for those human tones that boom forward the reality of our interconnections. These interconnections have not been missed in our popular media, in our films and the best of our television dramas, even in our soap operas. Throughout, we see men and women of all colors telling us about the news of the day, hosting talk shows, sitting in judgment in courts, giving their opinions on the stock market, the law, international politics, and so on. For better or for worse, or—as usual—for both, we see a certain kind of trans-ethnic pop culture in place on MTV.

As our digital economy expands itself, we will continue to learn that what used to be a barrier to success—sex, color, religion, class, sexual preferences—will mean nothing in the e-mail world of high-velocity international business. All the person on the other end is concerned about is whether or not the one to whom he or she is talking has the goods. Cecelia, one of the characters whom Carla greatly admires, is a black woman who has started a school in one of the worst sections of Washington, D.C. She is fully aware that education can well prepare one to fight the very demons that remake themselves for every generation. But, in this era, those demons are most successful when stereotypes and fear overshadow all of the scientific information that makes ideas of innate alienation laughable.

IDENTITY • *Stanley Crouch*

We should be made quite optimistic by the fact that the most high-minded ideas about our human commonality have now been proven out by science; in fact, this proof is perhaps the most important thing to have happened on the front of objective understanding of our species since the Enlightenment. If we had a better sense of just whom we happen to be, our public education would make that part of the common pool of human knowledge. Further, as Americans, we need to realize that our society has most truly realized the finest ideas of the Enlightenment, and that one of the reasons why is that we are always educating ourselves about one another. Therefore, if we rebuild our public schools and keep an unsentimental eye on where we are and where we are going, we will continue to move forward. We will continue to add chairs to the cultural and political table. The grand dance of our society will see the floor scuffed by new feet and new shoes, from sea to shining sea—those patterns on the floor are the autographs of an ongoing democratic rhythm. At that dance, different kinds of people will fall in love, crossing the lines of ethnic artifice, just as those within certain groups will hug up with those from their own backgrounds.

Even given the inevitable moments of backsliding, we will keep moving closer and closer to a purer understanding of our commonality. As written above, we already have a much larger variety of human presence in the positions of power, entertainment, sports, art, and media. If you look at advertising today, one thing is apparent: Company after company is hiring models and actors to make it clear that you—no matter your color, the shape of your eyelids, your sex, and just about whatever else—should have some of this. Welcome—this product is for you. When the advertising world catches on, you know that the ongoing integration of our society is a pretty sure thing.

★★★

Stanley Crouch, one of America's foremost essayists and columnists, writes on government, race, and citizenship. He is also well-known for his writings on jazz music. *Always in Pursuit* is a collection of his columns written for the New York *Daily News*. He is also the author of *The All-American Skin Game; or, The Decoy of Race: The Long and Short of It*.

RACE RELATIONS

Kokomon Clottey and Aeeshah Ababio-Clottey

What is our vision for America in the year 2050? As we pondered and prayed over this question, we became filled with the spirit and hope of what could be. What we see is almost unimaginable—the ultimate fruition of the words "The holiest of all spots on Earth is where an ancient hatred has become a present love."

We are at a wedding. Our friend Tunisia, an African-American beauty and direct descendant of the founder of the Nation of Islam (a separatist organization based on the superiority of black people), is marrying John Paul, a white man and a descendant of the Grand Wizard of the First Era of the Ku Klux Klan (a white-separatist supremacist group). They are getting married on a sunny Saturday in Shreveport, Louisiana. Tunisia was named after the country Tunisia in North Africa. At 5 feet 8 inches, she walks like an African princess. Her skin is a delicate dark-chocolate brown, her eyes beautiful brown, her face blissful. John is 6 feet tall, pastel pink skin, blue eyes, blond hair, and very handsome. He stands tall and courageous like a Viking prince. Their friends come from many cultures and ethnic groups. Tunisia and John met at Louisiana State University and fell in love.

We are walking into a room of diverse people filled with love and happiness. Some are Tunisia's family, but many of the guests are Caucasians, John's relatives. And yet everyone sees one another's humanity and the beauty in the colors of our skin. We also see other human beings from different ethnic groups and cultures whose physical coverings accent their beauty. We honor and respect one another. The ambiance of acceptance and love is intoxicating. The focus of the conversation at the wedding is the excitement of their honeymoon in Africa. They will begin their sacred time in Victoria Falls and will end it on the west coast of Africa, relaxing on the white, sandy, palm-tree-lined beaches of Ghana for at least a month.

Also, people are talking about the miracle of America acknowledging the importance of economic justice. Charity has become a way of life for the wealthy. They practice wholeheartedly the belief that charity is a process by which those who temporarily have more give to those who temporarily have less. They have found joy in endless giving. Also, one can hear stories being shared about the positive impact of numerous young men and women participating in community projects, planting gardens, mentoring younger children in the local parks—a deep sense of community fills the air.

Apparently, on Louisiana State University's campus, all the various student organizations have monthly circles in which they all dialogue and share cultural stories. Visiting the campus is like walking through a world in which there are no boundaries. One can see a collage of multiethnic and multicultural students all communing and interacting together. There are no racial categorizations on the admittance forms, and diverse student populations immediately welcome new students. Ethnic student unions are still very important on campus. They serve as a means for students to network and learn the process of giving and receiving support. One can join the mixed-race student union, the white student union, the black student union, the Asian-American student union, the Native American student union, the Mexican-American or whatever union with which one wants to identify. Each union rotates its memberships throughout the year, so that by the end of the educational process, every student will have experienced all of the unions on campus. The students love this process, and all will graduate as fully developed human beings.

In a nearby neighborhood community center, children between the ages of 6 and 13 are playing, unafraid. The children are working on a project called Me and My World, an after-school program for early childhood soul development. For the sole purpose of personal growth and respect, the volunteers—young people, along with elderly from diverse cultures—are creating life-size paintings of themselves, building and creating workstations where the old as well as the young interact and dialogue together as though equals. The elders are sharing their wisdom, and the young reciprocate with laughter and innocence.

The concept of race and color is evidently not important, because many of the children are of mixed race. Black/white parents, Japanese/white parents, Chinese/white parents, Mexican/white parents as well as other ethnic groups are experiencing this phenomenon. Every child in this community has an adult who is committed to their welfare and well-being. This attention and affection cut the number of children who receive psychotropic medication.

The elementary school, which is opposite the community center, receives $25,000 per year for each child under age 13. The consensus of the community is that by giving attention and time to children at this early age, before they turn 13, the chances of the society having to give them penal time will be almost zero. Walking on the school campus, one can see groups of children giggling and screaming on the playground. They are holding hands, many different colors standing side by side, looking into each other eyes and proudly singing, "We are many different colors, but we are one, we are one." For every seven children, there is an adult mentor standing with them, showing how to listen to and support one another in all their learning. Senior citizens play a major role in school environments. They are the storytellers and the keepers of the wisdom in the community.

This devotion to the children enormously has reduced the population of young black men in the prison system. The industrial prison system has disappeared like the dinosaurs. Prisons have shifted their focus to treatment and education and have changed their names to Soul Development Treatment Centers. The programs there help individuals develop their souls as well understand what it means to be truly human. The residents in these facilities also receive employment training in fields such as computer technology, education, carpentry, welding, plumbing, electrical work, painting. True and lasting rehabilitation is happening in these settings; recidivism is zero. They, too, are experiencing the birth of authentic racial harmony that is now prevalent in the wider society.

Upon close examination of their investments in new prisons, people realized that it was not the highest and best use of their resources. Citizens operate from the notion that ideas, when shared, grow—and so the more we share fear, the more fearful their daily lives become. This realization opened the door to holding public conversations on forgiveness. Citizens asked that a national apology be extended to the indigenous people of this continent. South Dakota led the way in officiating the first ceremony at Wounded Knee, with an official apology to Native Americans for the crimes perpetuated against the Lakota people. Wounded Knee healed its wounds and is now known officially as Lakota Land.

Most impressive was the decision by Congress to pay reparations to indigenous people and African-Americans for the hundreds of years that they gave free labor and the years that they were denied the right to an education. Descendants of people who were enslaved in the United States receive free education from kindergarten through college and free health care as compensatory settlement for the physical, economic, emotional, and psychological suffering that African-Americans and Native Americans have endured in the United States.

History books began to tell our story, a multicultural history of America. All Americans are respected and honored for their contributions and are given an opportunity to create a safe community.

On July 4, 2050, the entire nation turned out for the National Day of Apology and Forgiveness. At least five million celebrated and marched in Washington, D.C. And in every major city in America, there were huge crowds holding peaceful, joyful celebrations, singing and holding signs representing the struggle of our ancestor Dr. Martin Luther King Jr. "Free at last! Free at last! Thank God almighty, we are free at last!" The freedom that the people sang about was for the release of the soul of America.

A recent documentary on inner-city America showed the benefits of reparations in the form of revitalization and increased employment to individuals of African and Native American descent. Walking through an urban neighborhood like Harlem is most inspiring. Harlem is experiencing a cultural renaissance that is unparalleled in history; the people of a darker hue are joyful as they share the wealth of beauty in Harlem with the world. There are learning centers on every corner, supporting the young and old alike in personal growth and development. International shops from the continent of Africa open wide their doors, selling beautiful garments. Colorful customers of every ethnicity are enjoying the finest of fashions. One can see as one walks through the city beautifully restored buildings, tree-lined streets, community gardens, day care centers for every 30 children, small community stores with fresh vegetables and fruits that are grown in farms in upstate New York. There are shops and restaurants that are being run by a variety of ethnic groups who live harmoniously together. There is a sense of safety that encourages anyone to have a nice walk through the city at night.

Organizations that used to espouse hate and separation are working together for the benefit of all. All fear-based organizations have new missions and objectives to be more inclusive, caring, and loving to all people in America. These organizations are dialoguing with other groups in safe settings, with clear intentions of healing past hurt feelings. It is profound to see members of transformed separatist groups as well as various religious and sexual-preference groups sharing their stories in a circle and listening deeply to one another. The fruits of these types of meetings include opening people's hearts and creating peace, love, and understanding. These new opportunities are making it possible for these organizations to take practical steps to reconcile past misunderstandings so that each organization can invest financially in all children. Their intentions to make the American dream accessible to everyone are remarkable and commendable.

WHAT NEEDS TO BE DONE

The road to this noble vision is unfolding. However, there is much heart work to be done. To resolve America's racial pain and separation, we have to do what President Clinton suggested in a speech made in October 1995 in Austin, Texas:

"I ask every governor, every mayor, every business leader, every church leader, every civic leader, every union steward, every student leader—most important, every citizen in every workplace and learning place and meeting place all across America to take personal responsibility for reaching out to people of different races, for taking time to sit down and talk through this issue, to have the courage to speak honestly and frankly, and then to have the discipline to listen quietly with an open mind and an open heart, as others do the same."

Long before President Clinton made this bold and profound statement, we launched in Oakland, California, a process of dialoguing and sharing in safe groups called Racial Healing Circles. The underlying philosophy of these circles is that "the concept of race has no validity in the human species." In this perspective, we see racism as a life-threatening disease from which we all are dying. We recognized that our primary work in these Circles was the work of healing our hearts of the disease of fear, ignorance, and hatred. These Circles give us the opportunity to start the heart work that is necessary to create a world of racial harmony.

How will we live out this multicultural world that is unfolding before us? We believe the answer lies in the inner work—opening the hearts and souls of mankind to complete racial acceptance. We have already passed laws for which our hearts were not ready. How would we make ready our hearts to accept the children of tomorrow? How would we classify human beings? Would we have just one race, the human race? What would the United States Census Bureau do with its racial-categorization policies? Would we do away with redlining communities along racial lines? Would we rewrite our dictionaries that give emotional and psychological definitions to colors and relate these behaviors and feelings to human beings? How would our institutions reflect this change? Would there still be more people of color in prisons than in colleges? Truly, what would America look like? These questions and many others are arising in the Racial Healing Circles we conduct.

162

If we do not do this inner work, will we become what the pundits predict—a nation made up of distinct racial regions: the American Asia on the West Coast, the American Mexico in the Southwest, the American Caribbean in Florida, the American Africa in the Midwest, the American Europe in the East? This old paradigm is based in fear and will lead inevitably to racial conflict. Moreover, a conglomerate of racial regions will create monocultures, which will spark and espouse an "us or them" environment. This can be cancerous and detrimental to all of America.

STARTING THE INNER WORK

One cold evening at the Racial Healing Circle in Oakland, a woman we will call Priscilla sobbed while she spoke. She was raised in Mississippi, and although she and her family moved from the hate and bigotry, she said that her brother is still racist. She explained that his youngest daughter has a beautiful biracial child. Her brother is refusing to accept his grandchild and his African-American son-in-law. Priscilla's niece wants her father's blessings for her life as well as for her dark-chocolate husband and her olive-looking angel baby called Imani, which means "faith."

"There is something special about Imani," Priscilla said. As she poured out her heart in the Circle, one could sense Priscilla's pain. She spoke of how her heart ached for her entire family. She especially ached for her Imani because her love and affection for this new member of the family was enormous. She was deeply concerned for her brother, who was denying the natural love that flows from a grandfather to a granddaughter. She was concerned that his fear of the "other" was destroying the entire family.

Her intention in participating in a Racial Healing Circle was to look deeply into her heart and to do her part to bridge the gap of racial divide, to help free Imani from inheriting the pain of rejection and fear. If she worked on her heart, she hoped that her brother would somehow receive support through her spiritual growth.

Priscilla was showing her brother true charity. Seeing him as if he had already opened his heart and mind to love, she hoped to increase her growth by doing the inner work:

- Understanding that admitting that racism is a problem is the first step toward recovery and healing
- Acknowledging her attitudes and beliefs that are based in racial prejudice and bigotry
- Learning more about cultures and ethnic groups that she considers to be the "other"
- Striving to be open-minded by practicing the art of nonjudgmental acceptance of racial and ethnic differences
- Coming from a place of compassion to speak up whenever someone makes a racist remark
- Focusing on the wholeness of life rather than on the fragments, and becoming a love finder rather than a fault finder
- Making new friends amongst groups whom she had seen as somehow different or the "other"

This work must be done by all. Many times, when we are on a spiritual path, we do not see our blind spots. The inner work is grounded in working to uncover any stone that may, unbeknownst to us, harden our hearts and keep us blind to our racial biases.

We must uncover our denial. We must heal our shame, guilt, and blame and begin the process of open dialogue. Each individual, each mother, son, daughter, husband, priest, nun, doctor, lawyer, farmer, teacher—all of us must be willing to look into our own hearts and rid our minds of the fear that keeps us separate.

If we are to live the vision that we have shared with you, we must reeducate ourselves to the urgency of what we must do to save our souls. We must create classrooms where young and old alike learn truth together in a horizontal process, as equal teachers with respect and love for one another. We must bring to life the joy of what it means to work for the good of the whole; that is, we must serve the community. Then and only then will we be able to create a society that works for everyone. Then and only then will we be able to make corrections of our past crimes, because we will understand that we cannot lose because there is no "us or them."

The Path to Forgiveness

The great spiritual book *A Course in Miracles* says, "Forgiveness is an empty gesture unless it entails correction." It is a truth we must face as we move to an America in which race is irrelevant.

Let us have the courage to make the necessary corrections. For example, we can start simply, with the dictionary. The color black as interpreted in the dictionary is "wicked, disgraceful, and without hope," whereas the color white is interpreted is being "pure, innocent, free from evil intent, and harmless." It is disingenuous and misleading, especially to children, to remotely equate emotional and negative behavior with color. This misinformation keeps America in bondage, separate and in fear of one another, and acts as the matrix that supports a white-supremacy society.

We can create a world that works for everyone and supports all human beings, regardless of color, religion, ethnicity, or sexual orientation. However, this re-creation will require us to make some corrections. There has been a great deal of resistance to an official apology and reparations for Americans of African ancestry who were descendants of a people enslaved for almost four centuries in the American society. We see that as we move closer to creating a society that works for everyone, opposition to this idea diminishes, and Americans of every descent will begin to see value in releasing themselves from this historical baggage.

In our Ancestral Healing/Racial Healing Workshops, many Americans who attend—regardless of what country their forefathers came from—speak of feeling that the issue of racism is a yoke around their necks, even though they are recent immigrants to this society. They have not escaped its cancerous hold. They realize that the American society is an entity, and that as they are inheriting the wonderful things about our society, they are also inheriting its skeletons. Many people are eager now to let go of these inherited ancestral wounds.

The only way that we can let go is by doing our heart work: reconciling, healing, and forgiving.

Thich Nhat Hanh, the renowned Vietnamese Buddhist monk, said, "It is possible that the next Buddha will not take the form of an individual. The next Buddha may take the form of a community—a community practicing understanding and loving kindness, a community practicing mindful living. This may be the most important thing that we can do for the survival of the Earth." This will be our task for the next millennium: to build an America that works for everyone.

In Ghana, West Africa, where I, Kokomon, grew up as a member of the Ga tribe, we were taught to always share and to know that *nee ni-ah bu no kolo ye-ah*—"in my defenselessness, my safety lies." A village needs no protection because all the individuals that make up the village are working together for the good of the whole. Imagine a village that rears all its children and keeps the elderly in the ranks of the family and looks to the elderly for wisdom and support rather than isolating them in what is called old-folks' homes. Imagine a village, no matter how large, in which each individual will hold caring and sharing as core values by which to live.

Our tasks as individuals will be to bring to life each day the village concept and make it the matrix of the society at large. The village concept holds as its core values trust, acceptance, gentleness, joy, defenselessness, generosity, patience, and hope. Imagine a world without fear. Imagine this world—then take the action that will be necessary to create such a world.

★★★

Kokomon Clottey and Aeeshah Ababio-Clottey are founders and leaders of the Attitudinal Healing Connection, a nonprofit organization dedicated to the eradication of fear and violence in America. They are the authors of *Beyond Fear: Twelve Spiritual Keys to Racial Healing* and are currently working on their forthcoming book, *Fetch and Cleanse It: The Power of Ancestral Healing.*

SYSTEMS

Peter Senge

We live in a time of paradox. Arguably, at no time have humans had greater power in the sense of greater ability to shape the world around us. Yet we experience utter and complete powerlessness to shape the course of change.

Recently, I was part of a small 3-day meeting that included many highly successful entrepreneurs, authors, and similar "thought leaders," as the meeting organizers had dubbed us. Many of the participants had founded companies, created new technologies, or contributed to important intellectual movements. Needless to say, this was not a group lacking in self-confidence. Yet, as the meeting progressed, I sensed a deep undercurrent of unease. All had much to say about the future, our ostensible subject, yet all seemed to me to express a common fatalism. Finally, I drew a simple curve on the board during one of our conversations. "Is this not the future that all of us assume, that none of us believe can be influenced?" I asked. Everyone agreed. "Does this future not raise deep, perhaps troubling questions for us all?" Again, there was common assent. "What does this say about our plight?" No one seemed to know how to respond.

The simple picture I drew was an exponentially rising curve, one of those curves that continually bends upwards, ever accelerating. I labeled it TECHNOLOGICAL ADVANCE. But I think I could have just as easily labeled it ANXIETY or UNCERTAINTY or POWERLESSNESS. It is, I believe, the icon of our age. It is the background that we all assume and yet rarely talk about directly.

The irony of this curve is that it is a human artifact. It is created by us. *Relentless technological progress is not written into the cosmos.* It is not one of the laws of physics. It is a product of the way our present modern society is organized and functions. It brings new wondrous devices. But it also brings incessant frenzy, disorientation, and dependence—or at least it has throughout the Industrial Age.

The Industrial Age has been an epoch of harvesting natural and social capital to produce productive and financial capital. We have destroyed forests, topsoil, and farmland, and with those the habitat for many species. The loss of biological diversity has been matched by the loss of cultural diversity. Not only have one-quarter of all species vanished in the past century, so too have more than half of the 2,000 or more human language systems, and with them the diversity of thought and expression that humans have developed over tens of thousands of years. The waste of natural capital (about a ton per American per week) is matched by waste of human capital: vast numbers of underemployed and over a billion of us, today, severely malnourished, many starving.

And the real changes may be just around the corner.

Writing in *Wired* magazine, Bill Joy, chief scientist and cofounder of Sun Microsystems, recently described "Why the Future Doesn't Need Us." He speculated in harrowing terms about a convergence of robotics, genetic engineering, and nanotechnology (making things smaller and smaller—especially the onset of "molecular" electronics and computing) that is making self-replicating "sentient machines" no longer a science fiction fantasy. "The age of spiritual machines," in the words of inventor Ray Kurzweil, is upon us. Joy quoted several technology leaders who not only think about this but also accept it as virtually inevitable. Some find the prospect of humans merging with robots unthreatening. Joy paraphrased one famous inventor: "The changes will happen gradually, and we will get used to them."

Others are less sanguine, including several who see sentient robots succeeding humans as the Earth's dominant species. Just when we thought that ecological disaster might be the ultimate unintended consequence of technological advance, welcome to the Matrix. Indeed, the two—ecological deterioration and the age of living machines—may go hand in hand. If we continue to foul the environmental conditions required for many previously successful species and perhaps our own biology, might we be setting the table for a species more symbiotic with such a fouled environment?

So it is not as if technological advance had been an undiluted benefit. This, of course, is not news. Such concerns run through a large number of the essays in this volume. Yet we continue to act as if there were no possibility of exerting any influence over it, as if uncontrolled technological advance of the sort that characterized the past 200 years (and appears to be accelerating still) is some immutable law of nature.

I think this suggests a rather different problem and perhaps a different key to a future that we would be proud to leave for our grandchildren. The problem is not technology per se. The problem lies with the creators of technology, that is, us. The problem is that we have lost our capacity to make choices, especially on a scale commensurate with the scope of our impact. What sort of future lies ahead may hinge on discovering that capacity.

THE AGE OF MACHINE SYSTEMS

Ironically, individual technologists rarely feel that they have no control over their own efforts. Indeed, many exhibit a kind of technological hubris. Yet these very same individuals feel that they have little or no influence over the larger patterns of technological advance—for example, whether or not genetic engineering, or even particular applications of genetic engineering, is good. The reason for this larger fatalism lies in the systems that control these patterns, or appear to.

What do I mean by "the systems"? I mean what most of us mean when we use this term. For example, there is the system of global financial markets, which interacts with the system of capital ownership, which interacts with the system of corporate management and, in particular, the system of executive management, including the system of developing, guiding, and rewarding corporate executives. Taken together, these multiple interacting systems—in concert with labor markets, consumer demand patterns, and governmental legislation and regulation—compose what people often call global capitalism or the global corporate order or whatever current term is in favor to point toward that which we cannot control but which controls us. Often, such terms are actually a mask for a type of conspiracy theory, that some small group of people behind the curtain is really in control. But having been behind many of these curtains, I have not found any such people. I have only found more people who feel that they too must keep running like crazy, that someone or something else is in control.

Donella Meadows, a noted environmental researcher and writer, put it eloquently many years ago: "No one wants or works to generate hunger, poverty, pollution, or the elimination of species. Very few people favor arms races or terrorism or alcoholism. . . . Yet these results are consistently produced by the system-as-a-whole, despite many policies and much effort directed against them."

This is what I mean by *the* system.

In fact, most of us have a particular understanding of *system*, which is rooted in the Industrial Age, the age of machine systems. From 1750 to 1820, labor productivity in England increased 200-fold! Thus was born the era of the assembly line, in many ways the paragon of the Industrial Age machine system. The assembly line was such a transformative social construct that it became the model for school as well as work. The modern urban school system, a product of the mid–19th century, was overtly copied from the assembly lines that educators so admired, complete with discrete stages, rigid time schedules, and bells on the walls. It is no surprise that this machine-age systems thinking eventually produced the modern corporation, which while more organizationally complex than a single assembly line, still exists in our collective social consciousness as a machine for making money.

The irony is that *we* created the machines and the machine systems. We then convinced ourselves that someone else was the culprit. This is how powerful the image of the machine has become in this age of technological advance. We have learned to see everything in our world as if it were a machine. Biologists contrast living systems from machine systems by the terms *autopoetic* versus *alopoetic*—literally, self-created versus other-created. Machine-age thinking has led us, logically and relentlessly, to see more and more of our world, including ourselves and the larger systems we create in the image of the machine, as if they were created by someone else.

So, it really is no surprise that we experience powerlessness despite our technological prowess. The powerlessness is a by-product of the same thinking that produced the prowess. Unless this changes, I hold little hope for fundamental change.

THE AGE OF LIVING SYSTEMS

Our machine-age way of seeing is just that—a way of seeing. There is an alternative. We can see "the system" as patterns of interdependency we enact in our daily ways of living. While this may sound abstract, it is actually quite concrete.

Imagine a group of people working together to create a new product. Imagine that they are struggling, not achieving the targets for quality and timeliness to which they have committed themselves. The first question they ask is, Who set these aims? They realize that they set them themselves, out of their excitement at creating a product that is truly unique. As soon as they step back, they discover anew the excitement of creating a totally new product that serves real needs and demonstrates a new possibility for environmental stewardship. The product will be 100 percent remanufacturable. Not only has this never been done before, but no firm has ever reaped the financial rewards of both vastly reduced production costs and a different commitment from customers, who will now share in the emotional and financial rewards of purchasing a product that will never go into a landfill.

But despite these inspiring aims, now the team is in trouble. The product is late and everyone is blaming one another. The design engineers believe that the manufacturing engineers are causing delays by adding last-minute requirements for ease of assembly and disassembly. The engineers responsible for the electronics have also added new functionality that they believe will excite customers. Other engineers responsible for other engineering subsystems have done likewise. So they have come together to have it out. First come the complaints, and along with them, frustration. There is little point in disguising the feelings of victimization each engineering group feels vis-à-vis the others, or pretending that each group is on top of their situation and is only waiting for the others to get their acts together. Everyone senses the frustration and soon realizes that they are all feeling more or less the same.

One of the engineers says, "There's only one boat here, and we're all in it. We can either keep acting as if the hole were in the other group's end or figure out how to sail together." Everyone recognizes the truth of the analogy.

A young woman engineer asks, "Aren't we creating a tragedy of the commons here?" She proceeds to draw a diagram (the sort that engineers love) that many recognize right away—it reveals a recurring pattern first identified many years ago by biologist Garrett Hardin, who observed that people often get trapped in a pattern where each individual or group, pursuing their own self-interest, expands their activities to the point where some commons upon which they all depend is destroyed, and all lose. "We are like the sheepherders," she continues, "who each want to expand their own flock, until they overgraze the commons and all end up losing. Our 'flock' is our engineering subsystem, and our goal is to make it the hottest, most mind-blowing thing we can imagine. This gets us the praise of our peers and perhaps a promotion as well."

"Yes," adds another engineer, "and the commons we are destroying is our goodwill toward one another."

"And," adds another, "our ability to work together to come up with really creative solutions that actually help one another, not just our own specialization."

Suddenly, everyone seems to see the same pattern. "My gosh," whispers another, "look what we are doing to ourselves." From that point, the frustration begins to dissolve, and a new collective creative capacity emerges. They finish the product several months prior to the scheduled release, and at record levels of quality.

Actually, we are all born as natural systems thinkers. Few children by the age of 4 have not discovered that if they do not clean their rooms, their mother or father will. They understand perfectly well the pattern of interdependency around keeping their rooms clean, just as they understand many of the other social systems enacted within their families and networks of friends. Then, unfortunately, they go to school.

But imagine a different kind of school, where our natural love of understanding the world around us and our desire to make a difference are continually nurtured. Children continue to pursue their innate curiosities about why things happen the way they do. Rather than being instructed in received wisdom dispensed by all-knowing authority figures, they are guided in becoming more aware of how they make sense of things, how they construct their world. They learn through doing rather than listening. They learn in the many ways that suit who they are as unique people. Rather than rebel against adults seeking their obedience, they seek out the adults who can mentor them, who represent role models they respect, who have life experiences they value. And they find these adults everywhere in their lives.

Andrea and Paolo are middle school students in a science class—although not really like any science class you would recognize. First, their entire yearlong science curricula revolves around understanding the ecological, cultural, and economic impacts of a new national park being created north of their town. They are consultants in designing the park. They have worked with local farmers to better understand land-use consequences, and with American Indian groups whose land abuts the park. Now, Andrea and Paolo are back in their classroom to sort out different options for trail systems in the park. This is important because, next week, they will go back to the farmers and American Indians with their recommendations. If everyone can agree, they will jointly present their proposals at the formal Park Service planning meeting next month.

But now they have a problem because even the two of them

can't agree. Andrea favors a trail plan that takes advantage of especially beautiful overlooks, but when she simulated this choice using the system model they had developed with their teacher, she was surprised to see the erosion caused in a delicate wetlands. Paolo had warned her that this was a fragile nesting area and they should completely avoid it. But, his preferred route crossed near an old burial ground, which she was convinced would offend the American Indians. Moreover, the simulations alerted them to the possibility that while Paolo's trail system could accommodate more visitors and generate more revenues, the possible political backlash might lead to economic disaster.

After vigorous debates with the other students, they agree on a plan of attack. They will stop worrying about coming up with the answer—in fact, there is no one answer, just different options and trade-offs that require thoughtful choices. The key, they decide, is to get everyone thinking together about these options. Working with the small group of local farmers and American Indians, they will try to develop a range of scenarios that embrace the options. They will transform the formal planning meeting next month into a learning laboratory, just like their classroom. In fact, they even think of a way to do a dry run of the whole plan: They will create a mock-up at next week's Community Day.

This is no extracurricular project for the science students. This is the way they learn science—incidentally, about twice as fast as in the old classroom instruction mode. In fact, it is also the way they learn English, history, and foreign languages. Their school is now a staging ground for young people working in their community. After all, they are teenagers, not little children. Just like most of the world's peoples have long recognized, they are becoming adults and need to be engaged in making their world a better place. How else can this be done except by turning the school inside out?

Community Day, where they will try out their ideas, is a monthly gathering when everyone throughout the community who is involved in the students' hundreds of joint learning activities gets together at the school to talk about how their projects are going. As a researcher from the local university puts it, "On Community Day, the social network that is the school looks at how it is functioning." For Andrea, Paolo, and all the other students, school is no longer a system created by someone else and imposed on students and teachers alike. It is hundreds of co-learners throughout their community continually creating a living curriculum—"lifelong kindergarten," as MIT media-laboratory researcher Mitch Resnick puts it.

Actually, neither of these is an imaginary story. Both are based on ways that people are working and learning together today. They do not characterize an ideal Utopia. They simply illustrate how feasible it is to approach any setting in a way in which we can continually learn how we are enacting the systems that shape our daily lives. Such learning is not easy. Indeed, it is full of natural conflicts that arise because we enact systems with competing objectives, and because we are unique human beings with unique ways of making sense of things. If anything, when people become more and more who they are, their differences are amplified. And so are their similarities. Both are necessary to live together with respect and dignity, and in greater harmony with nature.

I have seen hundreds of such stories, many of which have been instigated and studied through the collaborative efforts of members of the global network called the Society for Organizational Learning (SoLonline.org). Yet they are only small beginnings. They can, at best, intimate what it would be like if our daily ways of living continually deepened our appreciation of the world we create together.

THREE WAYS OF THINKING ABOUT THE FUTURE

There are three fundamentally distinct ways to think about the future. The easiest is extrapolation—to conceive of a future that is an extension of the present and recent past. The second is to imagine what might be, independent of what is, or as free of influence from the present as one can become. The third is to cultivate awareness and reflectiveness—to become open to what is arising in the world and in us and continually ponder what matters most deeply to us.

The first is the easiest and by far the most common. It is also the most dangerous in a time of deep change. If indeed there are many as-

175

pects of our present ways of living that are not sustainable, such as the destruction of living systems upon which social systems depend, then there are few things more certain about the future than that it will *not* arise as a mere extrapolation of the past.

The second way of thinking about the future is the ostensible aim of this collection of essays. But I believe that it, too, holds hidden dangers. It is easy to engage in "reactive imagination," focusing on some facet of the present situation that we dislike and imagining a world that is very different from this. However, this "negative image" actually offers only a disguised version of the present. It can appear imaginative when in fact it is not. It can be an unintended projection of ego, rather than a true expression of the course of nature.

"All great things are created for their own sake," wrote Robert Frost. In these simple words, Frost expressed the timeless sensibility of the artist, who looks deeply within and without, who takes responsibility for her or his creation while simultaneously experiencing an overwhelming sense of humility as a mere agent for what is seeking to emerge. This is the fundamental distinction between machine-age planning and the creative process. The former seeks to manifest human intentions. The latter seeks to align human intentions and actions with the course of nature.

Paradoxically, in this aligning lies real freedom and choice. "The free man [mensch] is the one who wills without arbitrary self-will," wrote Martin Buber. "He must sacrifice his puny, unfree will that is controlled by things and instincts for his grand will, which quits defined for destined being. Then . . . He listens to what is emerging from himself, to the course of being in the world . . . in order to bring it to reality as it desires."

This third way of thinking about the future is also a way of thinking about the present. In fact, the two are inseparable. We become agents of creating a future that is seeking to emerge, by becoming more aware of the present. This third way requires deep thinking about not only what exists today but also how it came to be this way. This third way replaces blind trust in human ingenuity with trust in life. Imagination, rather than becoming more limited, is actually freed and becomes the servant of awareness, which in turn requires a life's work to cultivate.

In this third way, human and nature become integrated spontaneously. We become nature's agent. There is no nature outside ourselves, nor ourselves outside of nature. In fact, the very word *nature*, pointing to something outside ourselves, becomes unnecessary, as it is for many indigenous people.

Several writers in this volume cite modern quantum physics as evidence of a deep change in understanding the universe that holds promise for creating a more sane way of living. We would do well to heed the admonishment of noted quantum theorist David Bohm: "What folly to think that we can correct the fragmentation of the world via processes that re-create that fragmentation." This fragmentation starts when we see a world of corporations, institutions, and systems outside of and separate from ourselves. Ironically, only by recognizing that these are continually created by our daily acts of living will we start to see that they are also expressions of our own choices.

None of this should be taken to imply that an isolated individual can reshape a living human system or can rehabilitate our collective capacity to choose. But it does imply a guiding principle: We produce what we do not intend because we enact systems that we do not see. And, learning to see is a life's work. Rudolf Steiner, echoing a sentiment of Goethe's, beautifully articulated the twofold nature of this work: "In searching for your self, look for it in the world; in searching for the world, look for it in your self."

★★★

Peter Senge is the founder of the Center for Organizational Learning at MIT's Sloan School of Management. His 1990 book, *The Fifth Discipline: The Art and Practice of the Learning Organization*, was named by *Harvard Business Review* as one of the "seminal" management books of the past 75 years. His 1999 book, *The Dance of Change*, builds on the concept of the learning organization and systems thinking, and *Schools That Learn* (2000) extends these ideas to rethinking Industrial Age education.

COMMUNITY

Thom Hartmann

During the time you spend reading this chapter, 500 people—300 of them children—will die of starvation. Two or three species will vanish forever. A quarter million pounds of toxic and cancer-causing waste from corporate polluters will pour into our air, soil, and water. More than 2,000 acres of rain forest will be burned, cut, or bulldozed. In America alone, guns will kill two or three people, and at least one teenager will commit suicide.

It doesn't have to be this way.

Imagine a future America where these problems are part of a bitter past. Imagine an America where people care for one another and life is rich and meaningful, where we actually know the names of our neighbors because we talk, eat, and laugh with them regularly. Imagine America a generation from now—if we make the right choices today.

The resurgence of community imagined in this essay would be brought about by an oil crisis. Nonetheless, it would improve the quality of Americans' lives.

In the ideal America of the future, neighborhoods are again places where people live as neighbors. When one family is in need, it becomes the business of the entire community to fill that need. If one family has a sick child, everybody says a prayer for her or baby-sits or brings over soup or medicine—often a mixture made from herbs grown in the garden. If one person's house burns down, everyone else opens their homes to that person and the community mobilizes to erect a new home.

Nearly every neighborhood has a community building, often part of the power station or the place of worship, where people gather during the day to converse and during the evening to share potluck dinners and entertain one another with music, storytelling, dancing, games, and reading aloud. Some communities have saunas or sweat lodges attached to their community buildings, or hallowed groves, stone circles, labyrinths, public crucifixes, or other sacred sites. These are important for prayer and meditation, and for the rites of passage that communities conduct as children grow up and adults grow older.

Families tend to stay in the area where they were living at the time of the Crash, so cousins now play together and children are raised with their grandparents' help.

People walk everywhere, for exercise as well as for social interaction. Extensive systems of hiking trails are set up in the forests. In the cities, historic and other interesting sites are well marked, and residents who would enjoy hosting visitors leave their front doors open. People spend evenings on their porches, simply rocking in chairs or chatting with family and neighbors and offering tea, snacks, or music.

Most goods and resources are locally produced and locally consumed. Lawns—anachronistic 20th-century imitations of the greenswards of the medieval British aristocracy—are long forgotten; people now grow vegetables and grains in the soil around their homes. Fruit and nut trees are popular both for decoration and for shade. Families grow much of their own food, while the community garden supplies most of the rest.

Electricity and heat are produced by small local stations the size of garages, each one serving its own local community of 12 to 50 homes. The fuel sources vary, depending on the climate, from solar to wind to biomass to trash. The community stations supplement home power stations—rooftop photovoltaic collectors and basement fuel cells—which supply most of the power needed by families. Each central station also purifies water for the community and processes its liquid and solid wastes.

Even though resources are primarily produced and used locally, there is considerable trade among neighborhoods. Some communities specialize in growing particular types of food or in making unique clothing. One may have a healer with special talents. Others might have brilliant technical specialists who help maintain the power plants or who mentor youngsters in the upkeep of homes and gardens. Trade is almost always done by means of barter; goods may be exchanged for labor, and vice versa. Food, however, is considered sacred and is never traded for anything except other food. The free giving of food is one of the highest social obligations, and one of the fastest ways to achieve status in the community. So much so that the practice of potlatch was resurrected—competitive food generosity.

Laws and cultural norms are mostly determined locally. Neighborhoods have names and can seem a bit tribal: Residents of a particular neighborhood are often related by blood and usually share lifestyles and religious values. Although most are racially homogenous, some communities have chosen to go the full tribal route, particularly those who still have historic tribal roots.

Tribalism is no longer considered racist—as it was before the Crash—because "other" no longer means "inferior," "competitor," or "to be conquered." Physical and cultural differences are respected and even celebrated. People living in a community understand that their neighborhood is theirs, that they are who they were born to be, and that every other neighborhood has an equal right to be itself.

Each community administers its own justice. The concepts of sin and punishment, which grew out of the king-based religions of ancient Sumeria, with their idea that human nature is evil, have been rejected. People have returned to the concepts of harmony and disharmony, balance and imbalance, reflecting how humans had lived for millions of years before the Younger Culture Eruption from 6000 B.C.E. to 2012 C.E. The assumption is that people are essentially good and their misbehavior is an aberration, not the converse.

When a person's behavior steps outside the standards of the community, everybody feels it as a ripple of imbalance within the neighborhood. People gather in the community center to discuss with the out-of-balance person and those he may have harmed ideas about how to come back into harmony and restore balance. When Americans figured out that having the world's fastest-growing prison population was a sign of cultural failure and noticed that tribal people had never had police or prisons, we relearned the ancient ways of valuing every member of the community and working as a group to restore harmony. Only rarely is a person so far out of balance that he must travel to a refuge or an outside community of healers.

Teaching is done by groups of families, who take turns hosting schools of 5 to 10 children. The goal is to make sure that all children grow up with strong self-esteem, a sense of personal power, and certainty about their options and passions. Each teenager chooses a career based on his own passions; then an appropriate mentor in that trade or profession teaches the teenager during an apprenticeship, whether in power-plant maintenance, sewing, or surgery.

Negative labels such as "attention deficit disordered" and "learning disabled" are recognized as vestiges of the Bad Old Days, also known as the Era of the Corporate Kingdoms, when schools were run like factories with children as standardized products on a conveyor belt. These negative labels simply described children whose gifts weren't useful to corporations, children who wouldn't work well in factories or cubicles. (People woke up when they noticed that there were no diagnostic categories, therapies, or medications being developed or sold by the big drug companies for "art disabled" or "creativity disordered" or "music deficient" children because these were disorders of talents that the corporations did not care about.) Instead of trying to determine what's wrong with children, the goal of education now is to determine their individual gifts and help them develop these into both vocations and avocations.

There are still universities, but they're no longer beholden to corporate interests to fund their research or determine their curricula. Americans awakened to realize that "government of, by, and for the people" meant that the government wasn't the enemy and its function was, first and foremost, to make sure that basic human needs were met and human rights respected. When multinational corporations tried to usurp this function, attempting to control human needs such as those for health care and food and to limit human rights by placing themselves above living, breathing people in the legal hierarchy, the laws that Thomas Jefferson first put into place to restrain corporations were restored. Corporate charters now must be renewed annually, and the first obligation of a corporation is to its community; the profit it makes for its shareholders comes second, as was the case for the first 100 years of American history.

Even if this image of a future America sounds unrealistic or idealistic, it's not. It's simply a practical way to live. Americans have used all aspects of it at various times over the past 300 years. Even if it sounds nostalgic, it's not. It's based on the way most stable human cultures have functioned for 200,000 years or more, the way most Native American cultures have functioned for 10,000 years, and the way a dwindling number of tribal, intentional, and remote small-town communities function in America today.

It's quite different, however, from the way typical Americans experience daily life at the dawn of the 21st century. Instead of a life filled with family and friends, in the past 30 years we've entered a time of hypercompetition, fear of HMOs and insurance companies, and the frenetic struggle to earn more, more, more and buy more, more, more. We wake up to nightmares of downsizing and stock market crashes, and we try not to wonder what will happen when the world's oil runs dry sometime in the 21st century. We pretend that it's normal that suicide is the second leading cause of death among schoolchildren, and that it is merely unfortunate that the majority of America's lakes, streams, and coastal areas are measurably polluted with toxic waste and human pathogens.

The same industry that brought us DDT now brings us bioengineered foods that may well usher in the silent spring Rachel Carson warned us about, but we consider it impolite to discuss in the media the millions of dollars that chemical companies and agribusiness give our politicians, the employment revolving door between these corporations and the governmental agencies that regulate them, and the growing stranglehold that corporations have on the funding and publication of university research.

What happened?

Somewhere along the way—many would say between the development of the advertising industry in the 1920s and the time in the 1960s when, for the first time, more than half of all American households owned televisions—we lost our bearings. We became confused and disoriented, shifting our attention from our communities, neighbors, and families to an electronic neurological drug delivered hourly by multinational corporations.

In our collective mythic identity, we moved from the truly middle-class life of Jackie Gleason's and Lucille Ball's 1950s apartments to Frasier's multimillion-dollar penthouse, complete with a beautiful maid and expensive furniture. The Joneses with whom we tried to keep up shifted from the neighbors we actually knew to those we watched on television, where the average home cost more than a million dollars.

A national explosion of upscaling brought us a country studded with child care facilities for our preschoolers and TV sets waiting in every bedroom for school-age children. Fully half of all American children at the beginning of the 21st century come home to a house silent but for the television.

Within two generations we have become the most voracious consumers on Earth, using 30 times the planetary resources per capita consumed by a typical resident of India. As we slid from an American culture based on community into one based on consumerism, we turned this nation from a rich garden into a giant mall.

Although feel-good evangelists for a consumer culture preach that there's enough for everybody, the fact is that if every human on

Earth adopted the lifestyle of a poverty-level American, we would need the natural resources of at least four Earths to sustain that level of consumption. We turned the poor of the world into our slaves: Peasants in China work for a dollar a day so that we can buy cheap jeans, faux Tiffany lamps, and inexpensive area rugs. We didn't end slavery; we simply exported it.

This wasn't lost on the rest of the world. Planetwide, people watching American television began to demand the standard of living they saw on *Beverly Hills 90210* and *Baywatch*, a standard of living their governments could never deliver because the planet simply doesn't have the resources for six billion people to live that way.

Some of the world's poor believed in the American Dream that if they worked hard and long enough in sweatshops, they could lift themselves out of poverty. A few did reach a local version of the middle-class life in countries such as Korea and Thailand. But when labor became expensive in these places because of this upward mobility, post-GATT multinational corporations simply moved their factories from one nation to another, leaving economic and environmental disasters in their wakes.

As a result, the third world began to revolt. From Chiapas, Mexico, to Nicaragua to Indonesia to the Congo, people rebelled against governments aligned with multinational corporate interests that used the people of these countries as cheap labor to supply America's stores. From the outback of Australia to the tribal lands of North America, indigenous people protested the strip-mining and destruction of their environments to provide cheap metals for a throw-away American culture. From the rain forests of Borneo to the jungles of Colombia to the forests of California, local residents protested with increasing noise and violence the theft of their trees to feed the junk mail avalanche and the furniture fads of Americans, Japanese, and Western Europeans.

Throughout the 1980s and 1990s, the more loudly people protested, the more repressive governments became. Intelligence agencies were omnipresent, and America trained the armies of the third world's governments in the subtle and coarse arts of brainwashing and torture, the tools for which were provided by multinational weapons companies. By the year 2000, the world's food supplies were so poisoned that Inuit people were told not to eat seal blubber, their traditional delicacy, because of dioxins; fishermen from California to Michigan to Georgia were warned about mercury contamination of fish; and red-tide algal, bacterial, and viral contamination was wiping out shellfish and coral around the planet.

Then things got really bad in the first two decades of the 21st century.

We Americans first realized that change was necessary when poor countries began to withhold their oil from us. Some, such as Burma, were down to just 2- or 3-year oil reserves. They couldn't pump cheap oil to sell to us any longer even if they wanted to. We could no longer just send in the Marines to protect our "vital national interest" in $1-per-gallon gasoline; we had to change the way we lived.

But we were facing this problem in the 21st century, the age of the automobile and the airplane. The shock of skyrocketing gasoline prices came first, and it toppled our stock markets, collapsing a worldwide economic house of cards. But we had to recover: There were simply too many humans on the planet to ignore.

It took from the time of the earliest fossils of fully modern humans, 200,000 years ago, until the year 1800 for us to produce the first one billion members of the species *Homo sapiens*. That 200,000-year-long feat was then repeated in only 130 years, as we hit a population of two billion in 1930. Our population grew to three billion in only 30 years (1960). We added the fourth billion in 14 years (1974), the fifth billion in 13 years (1987), and the sixth billion in 12 years (1999).

By the year 2000, humans outnumbered rats as the most numerous mammalian species on Earth and had gone from consuming about 3 percent of the planet's total resources and 5 percent of its fresh water in 1800 (when there were one billion of us) to more than 50 percent of each. This left all other plants and animals to fight among themselves for the remaining half of the planet's resources, and they didn't do it particularly well: In the year 2000, species were becoming extinct at a rate of more than 120 a day.

We entered what Richard Leaky called the Sixth Extinction about the same time that the climate became violently unstable and butterflies nearly vanished from North America. Droughts and floods swept the land; tornadoes, frosts, and killer heat waves occurred in places that had never seen them before; insect and rodent populations exploded in some areas and wildlife and forests died off on a massive scale in others. We realized that not only was plant and animal life on the planet in crisis, but, for the first time in history, so was human life.

At first, we told ourselves that this was a predictable result of human nature. We believed that we were created defective, accursed sinners and that it was human nature to murder, ignore the environment, and stockpile personal wealth while ignoring other people's poverty. We thought that this was how it had always been, and we even guessed that it was because of a stupid mistake a woman had made millennia ago, a deal with a snake that justified 6,000 years of the oppression of women worldwide.

And then we noticed that there were other peoples who were not this way. We'd always called them primitive and stupid because we found it easy to kill them, to steal their lands, and to take their people as slaves. Our technological superiority was, in our minds, the proof of our cultural superiority. Some of us had even organized groups to evangelize them and convert them to our way of living because we were so certain that we represented the pinnacle of human evolution.

But they lived sustainably. Their populations were stable. Many didn't even have words for war in their vocabularies, and genocide was a totally alien concept to them. They didn't build prisons, and withholding health care or food from people was unthinkable to them. Their children didn't commit suicide.

What we found when we boiled it down was that our ways of acting and living were not as destructive to the world's ecosystems and our own future as our way of thinking was. Our behavior over the long term always derives from our beliefs, and the toxic beliefs we held in our culture—that people are inherently evil, that humans are meant to live hierarchically, that women are responsible for the "fall" of humankind, that happiness comes from having more toys, that nature is something different and separate from us, and that God or divinity or spirit is distant and is to be put in a box or building and visited only once a week—these toxic beliefs are what brought us to the brink of destruction. Even our initial attempted solutions were grounded in the belief that the world is a machine and that we need only find the right levers—salvation through action.

So the difficult reality of the end of the era of cheap oil and fabulous American wealth in the midst of a poverty-struck world caused us, in the first decades of the 21st century, to begin systematically to reinvent our culture by changing our core assumptions about what is real and true and meaningful.

At first it seemed impossible; the bad news was that it is exceedingly difficult for a culture to change its foundational beliefs. But we made it happen. The good news was that we'd already made several very radical belief-shifts in just the past few generations (resulting in the enfranchisement of women, the abolition of slavery, and the outlawing of segregation) and that we didn't need to invent new stories from scratch—we only needed to borrow them from the older cultures that still inhabited our planet.

The voluntary simplicity movement had already gained a number of adherents by 2000, but by 2020, 8 years after the Crash, it was a national way of life. Americans awakened from their drugged stupor and disconnected their cable TVs, preferring only local news and programming. It became fashionable to wear clothes until they were threadbare, to live in smaller and simpler houses, to use things until they were totally worn out. *New* meant "to replace something that is no longer useable," instead of "to make you happy just because of the novelty"; it ceased to be a useful word for advertising. People recycled not because it was fashionable or even because it was mandated; there just weren't very many disposable things around anymore. Folks saved jars and string and wire, and they handed down or passed around clothes their children had outgrown. A way of life that had once seemed quite normal, but then was derided by the corporate-driven consumerism religion of the late 20th century, returned. It fit Americans comfortably, like an old shoe.

As we reconnected with family, community, nature, and spirit, we discovered the deepest meanings of life in ways that were often startling to those who had been raised on a diet of shock television, dysfunctional schools, and violent movies. Those who believed that the fastest route to happiness was to go shopping discovered the shallowness of their previous lives and the richness of family, friends, and personal communication. In the late 20th century, only those who worked with the dying and heard their final regrets knew that at the ends of their lives, people never wished they had bought more things or worked more hours. By the mid–21st century, it was common knowledge that true happiness and a meaningful day-to-day life comes through creative work, gentle play, and connection with others.

Out of this new way of life, we naturally began to take better care of our environment, to live more lightly on the Earth, and to reverse the toxic slide that seemed so irreversible during the Era of the Corporate Kings.

Can you imagine this new America? Will you help us build it? I know you can.

★★★

Thom Hartmann has written best-selling books on spirituality, the environment, and health, including *The Last Hours of Ancient Sunlight*, *The Prophet's Way*, and *Healing ADD: Simple Exercises That Will Change Your Daily Life*. His most recent book is *The Greatest Spiritual Secret of the Century*, a novel.

THE ENVIRONMENT

Ed Ayres

In 1962, when Rachel Carson published *Silent Spring*, the book that first raised the alarm about widespread toxic chemicals in our water, she unwittingly launched the American environmental movement on a dangerous course. There is no way she could have known what would happen, but people didn't like to be told that their country was threatened from within. Americans had won World War II, repelling a terrible threat from abroad, and were keeping the Soviets at bay. They liked the new industrial economy that was bringing rising affluence, suburbs, and cars, and many didn't like to hear it disparaged.

The chemical industry took quick advantage, vilifying Carson. A pattern was established, one that would increasingly brand those who issued environmental warnings as troublemakers or spoilsports— or as anti-American. Even as environmental decline accelerated, the industries whose products were contributing most heavily to the decline were booming, enriching their managers and shareholders.

So it was that American kids of the late 20th century, taught by a generation that had enjoyed unprecedented income growth and material wealth, never got a chance to learn an essential truth about life: that the environment is not just a world of remote rain forests or endangered species unrelated to their interests in the latest music or clothes, but rather is the basis of all the material well-being with which they were growing up. In high school, very few got to learn that the hydrological cycle and carbon cycle are global processes without which there could be no soccer, sex, or rock and roll . . . or great books or friendships or plans. A survey taken at the end of the century found that the average American could identify more than 1,000 corporate logos or brands, but knew only 10 species of plants. Kids grew up in the 1980s and 1990s far more knowledgeable about products than about life.

During those years, leading scientists tried to get the public's attention, but their message—that something had gone dangerously wrong with the American dream—went unheard. Like Rachel Carson before them, they grew increasingly concerned about what they perceived to be a massive denial.

In 1992, a gathering of 1,670 of the world's most accomplished scientists issued an extraordinary document, the *World Scientists' Warning to Humanity*. It summarized the ways in which the fast-growing human population and its expanding industries are destabilizing the Earth's life systems, and it concluded, "Human beings and the natural world are on a collision course." The warning was signed by 104 Nobel Prize winners in the sciences—a majority of all those living. Yet most Americans never heard about it.

Three years later, climate scientists from around the globe issued a warning that greenhouse gases generated by the growing number of cars, furnaces, forest fires, and coal-fired power plants appeared to be causing a rise in the Earth's temperature that could act like a planetary fever—melting polar ice, bringing more frequent and more destructive weather disasters, precipitating massive flooding of coastal cities, causing crop-killing droughts, and disrupting ecosystems everywhere. These warnings, too, were vilified by business and political leaders and largely ignored by the media, which, by then, were not only caught up in the economic euphoria of the time but were financially dependent on the commercial advertising of the very industries whose products the scientists implicated in global climate change.

By the late 1990s, environmental organizations were aware of a disturbing truth: The harder they worked at warning the public, the more persistent the destructive trends seemed to be. By the end of the century, the number of environmental organizations in the country had climbed into the thousands, and they had achieved thousands of legislative and regulatory victories. Yet the membership of these organizations constituted only a small minority of the American population, and meanwhile, all the major environmental trends—habitat destruction, global warming, biodiversity loss, and groundwater pollution—were continuing to run in the wrong direction. While the U.S. Clean Air Act succeeded in reducing smog over cities like Los Angeles, for example, the most destructive air pollution problem—the concentration of climate-altering carbon dioxide and other greenhouse gases in the atmosphere—got steadily worse. Denis Hayes, who organized the first Earth Day in 1970, asked at one point, "How can we have won so many battles, yet be so close to losing the war?"

BRINGING CONCERNS HOME

As the 20th century came to an end, those of us who have been laboring for environmental causes began to understand that we would have to find a very different way to reach the hearts of our fellow citizens. It was painful to admit that our efforts had failed. Those of us who had tried to warn that continued ecological decline could dangerously destabilize the world were labeled as prophets of gloom and doom, and the label stuck. We could not get rid of it. But then we began to realize what, in retrospect, we should have seen much earlier. Like many epiphanies, it is a simple truth: In a world that has been wracked by fear—of nuclear war, AIDS, anarchy, gunfire in schools— the way to move people to action is not to give them something more to fear, but to give them something to embrace.

As the new century dawns, there are unmistakable signs that this has begun to happen. Suddenly, we have the makings of a powerful new strategy for transforming public consciousness. The new strategy begins with a focus on where people live—their homes. This, in itself, is a departure, because to the extent that environmentalists have tried to appeal to people's positive impulses in the past, they have talked of pristine rain forests, coral reefs, and wild rivers—places far

193

outside most people's day-to-day experience. Anyone who is immersed in the stressful routines of domestic arguments, screaming kids, demanding supervisors, defective products, computer viruses, road rage, and too much TV violence might well wonder: What does a threatened rain forest or coral reef have to do with me? Why should I make sacrifices for those, when I have to deal with all this?

What environmental educators will eventually need to emphasize is that the deteriorating condition of the living planet has everything to do with the rising stress of everyday life, because they're both being driven by the same phalanx of forces. The growing dominance of large global corporations that drives the deforestation of Malaysia to provide export income for Malaysia's ruling class while supplying cheap lumber for Japan's consumer class, for example, also provides the cheap gasoline from Venezuela or Nigeria that drives the expansion of U.S. suburbs and the rising stress caused by traffic congestion and lost time. But this is all terribly, fatiguingly complicated.

So it makes sense, for now, to expend less effort on warning of those distant phenomena, even if in the past few years they have driven half a billion people from their homes in far-off places. Those phenomena may account for much of the anxiety we feel in our homes, but the connections are too circuitous to be explained in any way that can compete with the nightly news flashes about the latest celebrity scandals and plane crashes. Instead, the goal should be simply to show, by example, how satisfyingly different everyday life can be when it is reconnected to the life of the planet from which our homes, not to mention our families and ourselves, are made.

To begin, we can show that a good home is not just a box, and a good neighborhood is not just rows of boxes connected by strips of pavement. A good home is an extension of the people who live in it. If it is identical to all the others on its street, glutted with mass-produced furnishings and wired to consume large amounts of electricity without the occupants having a clue about how that electricity was made—well, then that house is quite a lot like a person who consumes large amounts of junk food without having the slightest curiosity about the ingredients. If the house is built according to a developer's plan that makes no accommodation for local topography, flora, soil, sunlight, climate, and culture, it reflects an apparent willingness by the inhabitants to exist disconnected from whatever lies outside their door.

Around the country, however, there are now scattered enclaves of homes that have been built with great attentiveness to their relationships with the world around them. Many use the energy of their immediate environment—wind or sun—to provide heat, cooling, and light, with as little dependence as possible on fuels that have been extracted by some environmentally invasive oil-drilling or coal-digging operation. These houses are built largely of local materials such as stone, adobe, or sustainably harvested wood. They are free of toxic glues, paints, and carpet fabrics. They make ample use of natural shade from trees or low-powered fans rather than energy-intensive air-conditioning. They are equipped to conserve water and recycle waste. They are architecturally pleasing, often individually designed to suit the personalities and lift the spirits of their occupants.

Relatively few Americans live in such places today, but those who do have generally found their lives changed. Living in a place that allows its occupants to be more conscious of the functions of rain, sunlight, and photosynthesis—of the great hydrological and carbon cycles of which both the house and the people who live in it are part—has a far more uplifting effect on environmental resolve than reading about new amendments to the Clean Water Act.

As more ecologically distinctive homes are built, they will generate ripple effects in public consciousness in a way the hardest-won legislative changes rarely do. It is those ripples, spreading across the economy, that will create a sea change in our patterns of behavior and thought. As homes change, so will neighborhoods. Those changes in turn will start a cascade of changes in the industries that build and fuel the American infrastructure, and as that happens, new kinds of employment and a new sense of purpose and spirit will emerge. Here is how it can work.

A New Form of Community

The first ripple effects of the new ecological houses or apartment buildings are their effects on the surrounding neighborhoods. People who want their homes to be in harmony with their surroundings tend to build or renovate in places where others of similar inclinations are doing the same. As clusters of such homes are established, whole neighborhoods appear and more are planned.

Implicit in this clustering is an understanding that ecology cannot exist without community because no person or thing can live long in isolation. In Littleton, Colorado, for example, there is a neighborhood quite different from the one that was home to the two teenagers who massacred their high school classmates in 1999.

The area where the two alienated boys resided was described by Lakis Polycarpou, a graduate of Columbine High School (where the killings occurred), in the *Washington Post*. What impelled him to write, he said, was hearing all the news reports about how the massacre had devastated "the community," and how "the community" would pull together in its grief. He was struck, he wrote, because this was not his idea of a real community. It was a place where expensive new houses had been built on the prairie and then occupied by people who had come from other places and knew nothing about either the prairie or the people who lived next to them.

Yet, not far from that neighborhood is the neighborhood of Highline Crossing, where houses are not isolated from each other but gathered in congenial clusters around common parklike areas (in lieu of separate front yards) and a common house for periodic shared meals and other community events. That kind of interactive arrangement offers a much greater opportunity for social and environmental connection than the tract of isolated houses where the two teenagers lived—and then ended—their lives of quiet desperation.

Ecologically designed neighborhoods are typically arranged in such space-efficient clusters, sharing communal playgrounds, gardens, ponds, toolsheds, and meeting places as well as green space. Moreover, the land use has been carefully planned so that motor vehicles have only limited access and are never allowed to dominate. In some of these communities, homes, workplaces, schools, parks, and stores are all within walking or bicycling distance or within easy reach by public transit. For the growing number of Americans who will live in such places in the coming years, auto commuting will be unnecessary or infrequent. For the occasional times cars are needed, car-sharing systems will be available. Instead of one car for every two people (the U.S. ratio in 2000), we will be able to get along quite happily with one car—most likely a silent electric one—for every 10 households or so.

Imagine the reactions of the growing numbers of Americans who will have occasion to visit such neighborhoods in the coming years. They will notice that homes built with natural materials are quite pleasing, in a way that structures made of synthetic materials rarely are. If electricity is provided by solar or wind power and in-village transportation is provided mainly by human legs, it will be surprisingly quiet in the neighborhood—no heat-pump motors disturbing the peace, no whining leaf blowers or revving SUVs. The air in the houses will be surprisingly fresh because there will be no particle-board floors or petrochemical carpets emitting toxic fumes into the rooms. Because shade trees will be abundant, windows will be left open whenever the weather is temperate. No tailpipe fumes will drift in.

Because ecologically efficient neighborhoods are designed to minimize travel distances, people will do more walking or bicycling than they did where they lived before, and therefore they will be more physically fit. With more people moving between home, work, and school on foot, more spontaneous exchanges will take place and more people will strike up friendships with neighbors. As a result, there will be more sharing of tasks—watching the kids, running errands, fixing things, dealing with crises. Less will be done by service people, more by the people next door. And less money will be spent on stuff that just sits in the garage or closet. In one of these new communities, 10 houses may share one push lawnmower. It won't be needed much, because most of the neighborhood will be landscaped with native plants and some of the land will be left wild.

Visitors will be impressed with how relaxed life is in this place. That's not to say that it will be utopian or without tension and conflicts. Globally, the 21st century will likely be a time of enormous tensions. But here, with much of the noise, pollution, clutter, hazard, haste, and road rage removed, life will be noticeably different than elsewhere. People will be less numb. They will be more conscious of their bodies, their houses, and their physical and social surroundings.

So, the first step in transforming consciousness is accomplished in a very simple way. It's not necessary for people to be hooked by a passion for exotic rain forests, tigers, or whales. If you simply care about whether you feel in harmony with your home, the essential connection has been made.

The psychological effect of this strategy is to activate a latent yearning for community. The economic effect is to create a market for the satisfaction of that yearning. Visitors will realize that they, too, want to live in a place like this. Suddenly, they will see a way out of their alienation. It's an alienation that has been variously attributed to the blights of suburban homogeneity, media violence, parental permissiveness, broken homes, or the spread of big-box stores. But what all these add up to is a loss of community. And what that almost always entails is a loss of connection with the living environment—a sense of place—on which all community depends. As the word spreads about places like this, their real estate values will rise and the whole economy will begin a tectonic shift.

NEW FORMS OF POWER

The second ripple effect takes place in the energy and transportation economy. As the value of compact, green, car-free neighborhoods increases, the value of more highway-dominated, chain-store-riddled areas will decline. The demand for oil—for asphalt, gasoline, lawn chemicals, cosmetics—will also decline. The great oil companies of the 20th century will face a momentous choice in the 21st: either slide into decline or metamorphose into renewable-energy companies. Car makers, after decades of stubborn resistance, will finally retire the internal combustion engine in favor of fume-free, silent electric cars and scooters made entirely of recyclable parts, and many people will stop driving cars altogether or drive only for occasional outings. Most parks and wilderness areas will be closed to motor vehicles.

New Sources of Food

The third ripple will transform the great industries of agriculture and food. The demand for oil as an input to agriculture, too, will decline as the market for organic, non-genetically engineered produce takes over and the use of pesticides and petroleum-based fertilizer wanes. Farmland, experiencing a renaissance, will no longer be marginalized in the American mind as physically dusty, socially backward, biologically homogenous, and monotonous. A farm will become a place of rich diversity—of vegetables, fruits, grains, small herds of sheep or goats, fishponds, patches of forest and wetland and meadow that provide habitat for wild pollinators, soil microbes, and songbirds. This transformation will come about in part because agricultural experts will find that vast expanses of a single crop are too vulnerable to disease in a world where genetic and species diversity are in free fall. But it also will come about because on farms, as in urban communities, people will find variety more attractive than sameness.

So farms will shuck their hayseed stigma and lose the deadly sameness that impelled so many of their restless young to drift off to the cities. Farms come to be seen as exciting new frontiers of discovery about the coexistence of Earth's wild and cultivated life—a coexistence at the root of civilization and critical to human survival. Farmers will no longer just produce food or fiber; they will conduct botanical and biodiversity studies, set up seed banks, and raise their children in places where kids can listen to bullfrogs and catch lightning bugs. On farms, as in towns, it is the pleasures of a variegated and unpolluted environment, rather than the fears of a ruined one, that get people to embrace life rather than shut it out.

New Attitudes about Consumption

Perhaps the most important ripple is the one that affects personal consumption, which ultimately determines what kinds of industries we will have and what their impact on the environment will be. The new communities will help people achieve a heightened sense of their biological origins and interdependencies by providing a less compartmentalized and mediated kind of daily routine. There will be less need to live your life in vinyl-lined or wallboard boxes, moving from box to box—from apartment to car, car to elevator, and so on.

This liberation, in turn, will help break down the artificial mental compartmentalization of modern life, in which the car salesman knows nothing about the effects of greenhouse gases on climate, even though his product is a major producer of those gases, because his department is sales, not climate. (In a contemporary cartoon strip, America's favorite lower-middle manager, Dilbert, complains to a colleague, "This product would melt the polar ice caps and doom humanity." She replies, "That's okay." He says, "You're part of humanity." She replies, "No, I'm in marketing.")

With people getting more oxygen into their brains and clearer light to see by, life becomes less fragmented and discouraging, more hopeful and whole. As preoccupation with shopping and consuming recedes, the American mind will open to other values. By the second or third decade of the century, we will fully embrace the idea that the environment is our greatest earthly asset—and is indispensable to all our other assets.

Making the Ripples Real

For those who have watched the relentless bulldozing, burning, paving, and polluting of our planet with growing distress, it is reasonable to question whether this ripple-effect strategy is anything more than an idealist's dream. In fact, those ripples are already well underway—in the United States and in many of the other countries that have long looked to us as a country of great innovation and imagination. More than 200 ecologically designed cohousing communities have been built or are under construction in the United States. They are just one manifestation of a much larger emerging "new urbanism" movement, which has brought renewed emphasis to designing neighborhoods that are responsive to the needs of local people and their living environment rather than to the escalating demands of global commerce. In the energy field, the wind turbine industry is now growing even faster than the personal computer industry. In agriculture, writers such as Wendell Berry and Gary Snyder are leading a vigorous movement to turn back the ecological ravages of multinational industrial agriculture and bring new vitality to the culture of locally managed, ecologically conscious stewardship—and they are succeeding. Organic produce has become the fastest-growing agricultural sector in the world. Green building is booming. The ripples are increasing and the signs are now unmistakable: A sea change is coming.

★★★

Ed Ayres is editor of *World Watch* magazine and author of *God's Last Offer: Negotiating for a Sustainable Future.*

TO WHOM WE BELONG

FAMILY

John Bradshaw

Before making any suggestions about the family of the future, I would like to present how I think many people today would define the "traditional" family: a God-fearing man and woman of sound mind and body, the same age, race, and religion, who marry—as virgins—in their middle twenties and are sexually faithful for life. The couple raises their children with loving discipline that includes corporeal punishment, and the children grow up to follow their parents' example. The parents retire and die; if one parent dies first, the other is free to remarry.

Up until about 50 years ago, religious and/or social stigma was attached to any variance from these norms. Divorce was looked upon as failure, and those who divorced were often branded by the religious as sinners if they remarried. A child born out of wedlock was called illegitimate. Any two people of the same sex who lived together past college age were suspected of being gay. Gays and lesbians were seen as sinners and social outcasts. People who married several times were labeled unstable and neurotic; the same was true of those in biracial marriages. Any kind of group marriage was considered a cover-up for wife swapping.

Some people believe that the violence, moral depravity, chaos, and uncertainty that society is experiencing today is due to the collapse of the traditional family. But in her profound and scholarly book titled *The Way We Never Were: American Families and the Nostalgia Trap*,

Stephanie Coontz, a faculty member at Evergreen State College in Olympia, Washington, argues that those who want to go back to the "traditional" family—whenever they think that was—must accept the circumstances that go with the chosen model.

For example, if you favor the idea of the colonial family, with its strict patriarchal discipline and lack of divorce, then you should consider the resulting lack of individualism and the high mortality rates that made the length of most marriages less than a dozen years. Disobedience by women or children was punished harshly, and children were exposed to frank and detailed sexuality at an early age. Or perhaps you'd prefer the traditional family of the 1950s, the age of *Leave It to Beaver* and *Ozzie and Harriet*. Rates of divorce and illegitimacy were half what they are today, and there was impressive economic prosperity. But a full 25 percent of Americans were poor, and a majority of the elderly lacked medical insurance. The Cleaver and Nelson sitcom casts were all white—even the Hispanic gardener in *Father Knows Best* went by the name of Frank Smith—and African-Americans in the South faced systemic, legally sanctioned segregation and brutality. Beneath the polished facades of many ideal families of the 1950s there was battering of children and rampant wife beating, which was not considered a real crime by many people, including the law.

In short, the image of an idealized traditional family is a myth. As Stephanie Coontz says, "Families have always been in flux and often in crisis; they have never lived up to nostalgic notions about the way things used to be."

THE FAMILY TODAY—AND TOMORROW

Realizing that the past was not all it was cracked up to be doesn't mean that all is well today and for the future. More than 20 percent of American children live in poverty; on any given night, almost 100,000 souls are homeless; every day, 135,000 children take a gun to school; every 14 hours, a child younger than 5 is murdered. In a recent national poll, one in seven Americans claimed to have been sexually abused as a child, and one in six claimed they were physically abused. Women and children have always borne the brunt of poverty in two-parent so-called traditional families. The U.S. Surgeon General noted that "the home is actually a more dangerous place for American women than the city streets."

The fact that there are no easy answers to such problems, and that there never were, should not cut off the discussion but rather open it up. If we are to project new solutions onto the future, we must stop trying to recapture traditions that either never existed or existed in a totally different context.

The common reaction to discordance between myth and reality is guilt. I have had several hundred clients tell me that they feel guilty because their families do not measure up, and I have come to see that my own work on PBS television and in the book *Bradshaw On: The Family* overly deified and vilified what I called dysfunctional families. In the 16 years since I made that series, I have revised my book because I have come to believe that what I described as a dysfunctional family is closer to what takes place in a *majority* of families, at least some of the time.

In spite of pronouncements about the disintegration of the American family, the truth is that there are today, taken as a whole, probably more healthy, highly functioning families than in the recent past.

In a nationwide study by the Search Institute, when youngsters from 12 to 18 were asked to name the three people they most looked up to, more than 55 percent identified one or both parents. When asked whom they would consult if they had a serious problem, parents topped the list for more than 50 percent.

So what about the future? My belief is that our adherence to the mystical image of a good traditional family is part of the reason we are having so many problems now, and why the problems might be exacerbated in the future. We would do well to recall the list of sins posted by the most influential men in Boston after the Synod of 1679. Among them were substance abuse, teenage pregnancy and illegitimacy, frivolous lawsuits, economic greed, unjust profit-taking, and, worst of all, the breakdown of the family, especially permissiveness and the loss of discipline. Could our current crisis be in part a case of the solution becoming the problem?

In systems thinking, we know that when an inadequate solution is given to a problem, *the problem remains the same or worsens.* The more we apply the inadequate solution, the more the solution becomes the problem. The strict colonial families were having many of the same problems that top our list today. Sri Aurobindo, the Indian sage, Pierre Teilhard de Chardin, the Christian evolutionist, and Stanley Kripper, the psychologist who has researched states of higher consciousness, all agree: "Evolution is an assent toward consciousness" (Teilhard de Chardin), and "evolution of consciousness is the central motive of terrestrial existence" (Sri Aurobindo).

THE ROOTS OF THE MODERN FAMILY

Knowing that there has never been a single typical family type opens the door to examining how the 20th century changed our consciousness, our entire way of life, and how those changes will affect the family of the future.

From the past century, I see four dominant events or thought shifts that have most influenced our notions of family and authority.

The World Wars

The First World War ended four major aristocratic empires: the Russian, the German, the Ottoman, and the Austro-Hungarian. The aristocracies of these empires were overthrown and their riches divided. Germany was set up for the rise of Hitler, Russia for Stalin.

The Second World War exposed the most heinous darkness of the human shadow. We saw some of the greatest brutality the world has ever known. At the Nuremberg trial, blind obedience, the shining star in the crown of patriarchy, was crushed. Individual conscience was acknowledged as a higher morality than obediential morality—the unchallenged following of some other human's moral decree, in this case Hitler's Nazism.

The Loss of Certainty

Einstein presented his theory of relativity, and within 41 years we were incinerating cities in an instant. The Wright brothers flew a few hundred yards, and 66 years later we walked on the moon. Heisenberg's principle of uncertainty changed the tidy Newtonian world in a radical way. All of this occurred in the 20th century. The coupling of the collapse of obediential morality with this new scientific uncertainty left us in a state of raw vulnerability, not knowing to whom or where to look for moral assurance and guidance.

Multiple Intelligence

Howard Gardner's theory of multiple intelligences (MI) challenged IQ tests and expanded our beliefs, positing that musical, spatial, kinesthetic, interpersonal, and intra-psychic intelligences are as important as literary or mathematical intelligence. Interpersonal and intra-psychic intelligence came to be called emotional intelligence, which is seen as more important for marriage and family life than literary and mathematical IQ. As a result of these concepts, our awareness has expanded in terms of the physiological and psychological make-up of human love and intimate connectedness.

The Information Age

Finally, we have awakened to find ourselves smack in the middle of a new and almost incomprehensible information revolution, what Heidi and Alvin Toffler called the third wave of human history's great economic epochs.

I believe that if the Tofflers' economic wave theory is accepted, the family of the future will embody the best that we have had in the past, plus something new and exciting.

Briefly, the wave theory sees three great economic periods in recorded history. The first begins about 8000 B.C., when people settled down, built communities, and lived off the land. That was the agricultural revolution. In this period, extended families lived together and much activity was focused around the home. Schooling, medical treatment, and caring for the aged all took place at home.

The second economic wave began with the cotton gin, steam engine, printing press, and smokestack factories. This second wave, the industrial revolution, had a dramatic impact on the family. The home was no longer the center of family life. Schools, hospitals, and nursing homes were created, and children were put to work at an early age. Father left home each day to go to work at a new form of workplace: the factory. The absence of the father took its toll on the children's sense of self and on the family's overall security. A vast amount of 19th- and 20th-century poetry expressed a longing for the lost father, a longing exacerbated by the two world wars. The second-wave economy stripped the nuclear family of its traditional functions. What was left were fragile psychological bonds easily snapped.

The third-wave forces have not yet found their voice in terms of family and schooling, but I believe that the families and schools that give voice to them will dominate the future.

THE RETURN OF A CENTRAL FAMILY

So here at the dawn of the 21th century, we sit in our raw vulnerability, in the opening throes of a sweeping economic transformation marked by extraordinary technology, rapid change, and an almost obsessive/compulsive drive for innovations. Indicative of the scope of change in this third wave—the information age—some people estimate that the knowledge base in any discipline will be changing every 3 months by the year 2025.

One impact of the third wave is that it has demassified society and created unprecedented diversity (waves of individuals who prize their differences). In short, the third-wave economy, as the Tofflers write, "restores many of the lost functions that once made the home central to society."

Here are some examples.

◆ An estimated 30 million Americans now do some part of their work at home, using computers, faxes, and other third-wave technologies. This shift in workplace preference creates dramatic potential for a more interdependent family.

◆ Several of my friends are choosing to homeschool their kids, and it will not be long before computers-cum-television educational courses hit the household. Already, people can earn degrees taking courses on college-affiliated PBS stations. In a short time, all our children can have the best teachers in the world at their disposal—right from their homes.

◆ My family is very involved in learning about traditional as well as alternative medical resources. We can now check our blood pressures, do pregnancy testing, place a heart monitor on the phone to have our heart checked at home—all tests once dependent on going to the doctor's office or the hospital.

◆ My best friend's wife recently chose to leave the hospital and die at home. Families more and more are scrutinizing nursing homes and deciding to nurture their elders at home. Most people want to die at home.

New Rules for Parenting

This return to more centralized third-wave family existences demands new ways of interaction; in particular, new ways of communicating between adult and child. We have come a long way in learning to treat children with dignity and respect. Blind obedience was the core of our family morality in the past, but blind obedience is an obedience without content. I was taught to obey any adult simply because they were an adult. We now know that such a form of moral teaching sets a child up for child molesters as well as future Hitlers, Stalins, and Jim

Joneses. Maria Montessori wrote, "No slave was ever so much the property of his master as the child is of his parent. . . . Never were the rights of man ever so disregarded as in the care of a child." Montessori saw the oppression of the child as the most universal social problem.

The psycho-historian Lloyd de Mause stated the problem clearly: We can create a better future generation by changing the way we parent our children. He wrote, "The history of childhood in fact determines which element in all the rest of history will be transmitted and which will be changed."

It is hard for us to realize that child rearing was a nightmare in the past. Infanticide was not a crime in antiquity. Every river, dung heap, and cesspool was littered with dead infants. The historian Polybius blamed the depopulation of Greece on the killing of legitimate children. These practices continued well into the Middle Ages. In 1527, infanticide was confined to the killing of illegitimate babies, but one priest admitted that "the latrines resound with the cries of children who have been plunged down into them."

Fortunately, as our collective consciousness has expanded, we have come to realize that a child has the same human rights as an adult.

I see the rights of children expanding in the future. I believe there will be more lawsuits by guardians of battered children and laws regarding a child's rights to choose to stay with their adopted or foster parents in cases where biological parents suddenly want to reclaim "their" child.

It is also clear that our young children and early adolescents still need solid structure and firm guidance. Setting boundaries and teaching children empathy and self-control are obligations of parenthood. But there needs to be a democratic process in the forming of the rules of guidance. Parents need to listen to their children and have real dialogue in understanding each child's uniqueness and point of view. Once decided upon, though, boundaries need to be enforced.

There is a move to involve whole neighborhoods in town hall meetings in order to agree on a set of boundaries for the children in the neighborhood. This is difficult because of religious and ethnic diversity, but it has been tried in several places with stunning success. We are starting to believe that it not only takes a village to raise children, it also takes a charter.

Serving as a form of extended village, I see the Internet as a great resource for parents. Chat groups allow the exchange of experiences and practical information on child rearing. Parents need not feel so alone when they encounter problems with one or all of their children.

Most of us tend to parent the way we were parented. We often do or say things to our children that, because they were done to us, we vowed we would never do or say. But we are learning that there are a variety of innovative ways to deal with children. We can tap into this collective wisdom through third-wave technology.

New Definitions of Family

The demassification of the third-wave economy—this new pursuit and acceptance of individual uniqueness—implies that we will embrace more open-ended definitions of family and family function in the future. Certain practices that have been labeled as morally bad, for example, may indeed play a positive role in the future.

For example, people who have been married many times could be looked upon merely as people whose interest span is short and who like variety. Why not have limited marriage contracts from 1 to 5 years? There could be legally sanctioned childless or open marriages where people agree to their own kinds of sexual contracts. The success of such marriages has not been stellar in the past, but who can say that certain couples cannot succeed at them?

There may be a valid place for group or communal marriages. Marriage today is a legalized relationship between a male and a female adult that entitles each of them to property and a certain guarantee against exploitation. Why does it have to be limited to one man and one woman? Communal marriages need not be focused on interchanging sexual partners. The communes of the 1960s failed pretty miserably at such experimentation.

Many families endure unnecessary loneliness because of their smallness. Single-parent families (usually headed by one adult female) prohibit the mother (or father) from experiencing herself as a fully functioning individual. Parents with an only child limit their child's social experience. The fulfillment of selfhood is difficult in a single-parent family. It is out of this awareness that many people are experimenting with supporting one another and creating different types of family cooperatives. I think we will see more of this experimentation in the coming years.

Once it is understood that our current divorce rate estimate of 50 percent is not an annual rate but rather calculated in 40-year periods, and that in the past marriages were terminated long before that average by the death of one partner, we will realize that divorce is not the heinous thing we often accuse it of being. Indeed, divorce, at times, may be a desirable social necessity. Historian Lawrence Stone suggested that divorce has become "a functional substitute for death" in the modern world. Stephanie Coontz wrote, "At the end of the 1970s, the rise in divorce rates seemed to overtake the fall in death rates, but the slight decline in divorce rates since then means that a couple marrying today is more likely to celebrate a fortieth wedding anniversary than were couples around the turn of the century."

There has also developed an acute awareness of the impact of divorce on children. As a result, children of divorced parents are receiving new forms of social support and are being offered more opportunities to express their grief than thought necessary before.

Many of the experimental families we are seeing now are not new. If we read the historical literature on family, we will see that variations of many of our current experiments were tried from time to time in the past.

My belief is that gay and lesbian marriages will become a fact in the 21st century. They will slowly be given the legal rights they deserve. Almost anyone who has engaged in or understands real biblical scholarship scorns the fundamentalist, literalistic belief that God has expressed reprobation about gay and lesbian people. Most theologians and compassionate people believe that gays and lesbians are part of God's plan, part of the diversity of creation. As the evidence continues to grow and is fully established, many church leaders will hang their heads in shame.

HOPE FOR AN UNDEFINABLE FUTURE

When you are pioneering a new civilization, old institutions inevitably will crash. This means living with uncertainty. It means expecting disequilibrium and upset, and it means no one has the full and final truth about where we are going—or even where we should go. The Tofflers wrote, "Toleration for error, ambiguity and above all diversity backed by a sense of humor and proportion are survival necessities as we pack our kit for the amazing trip into the next millennia."

My hope is that we will choose to bear the discomfort of uncertainty and have the courage to bear ambiguity and adversity.

Perhaps then we will see the end of people relating through force, blind obedience, dictatorship, and violence. I doubt that it will be a nuclear war that destroys us. It will more likely be our refusal to accept the great opportunity to create a deep democracy, one in which we trust one another, love the stranger, and have compassion for those who are weak and in need of our care. The French novelist Paul Claudel summed up the future of the family for me. He wrote: "There is no one of my brethren we can do without. In the heart of the meanest miser, the most squalid prostitute, the most miserable drunkard, there is an immortal soul with holy aspirations, which deprived of daylight, worship in the night. . . . We need them all in our praise of God."

★★★

John Bradshaw is one of America's foremost experts on family relationships. His PBS series *Bradshaw On: The Family* won widespread acclaim, and several of his books have been best-sellers, including *Healing the Shame That Binds You, Creating Love, Family Secrets,* and *Homecoming.*

RELATIONSHIPS

Daphne Rose Kingma

Imagine a world in which love is lived as love itself, in which men and women in relationships focus on love more and on their relationships less. Would relationships as we know them vanish like the mastodons? Sink out of sight like the wounded Titanic? No, they would rise to the high occasion and re-form themselves. However love wanted them to look, they would look like; however long love wanted them to last, they would continue.

Love has been our dream of union, and relationships the medium for our exploration of the mysteries and magnificence of union. We have been falling in love for centuries, and our falling in love, particularly in this last century, has expressed itself in what we have fondly come to call our relationships. We have held our relationships as precious to our hearts, pearls of great price; so precious, indeed, that we have often seen a relationship as an absolute, that rarefied condition of being to which we could look for complete emotional and spiritual fulfillment. The reason we have been so audacious as to do this is that our relationships, more than anything else we undertake in this life, have always been the container for what we know of as love.

While sages have wisdom and the enlightened have the capacity to experience all worlds, for most of us, the experience of union—indeed of the magnificent energy of love—is what comes to us in our relationships. We fall in love; we experience the ecstasy of romance.

These feelings of romance intoxicate us; and we want to capture those feelings, to contain that energy in the box or chalice or crystal vase of a relationship. Although a relationship can take many forms—dating, being a couple, living together—the strong loving feelings of romance in our culture are generally geared to the destination called marriage. We want to come home to each other, to have a place and a way to be with our beloved, to share a domestic life, daily habits, social rituals, community.

What often happens, however, is that the social habits of a relationship—the maintaining of its structure and the duties of domestic functions—take over. Love, the ecstatic energy, dissipates; relationship, the structure, remains.

Now, though, we are being invited to turn a spiritual somersault: To have love itself be the form and our relationships the content; to have our relationships develop in such a way that they are really more and more about love. I believe that we are being invited by Love itself to have our relationships become more and more about love—the energy of love, the power of love, the meltdown of love, the passion and compassion, union and communion of great love. Instead of being about wanting and having, in the material sense; or about solving and resolving personal life history and emotional issues, in the psychological sense; or about securing the survival of the species, as they were in the past; or even about maintaining the social structure or propping up the personal ego, our relationships are being egged on by this vast mysterious force called Love to be first of all and as much as possible about love.

Love is the energy of life itself. It is the place we occupy, the gift we offer when we know no distance, feel no differences, have no axes to grind. Love is light. Love is energy. Love is life. It is the ecstatic, energetic essence of our being, infinitely translatable into millions of idioms of human social experience and relationship epiphanies. It is a higher level of experience, a concerto of exalted moments in which we recognize our perfect connection with one another, embrace our differences, bask in the similarities, come home to the common ground, are woven together by the common thread.

In ordinary human life, love has attributes and behaves in certain ways. It is patient and gracious and kind. It is not narcissistic. It is willing to go through things and willing to see things through, one person on behalf of another. It has the power to endure. Faith is spiritual genius, and hope an uplifting of the human spirit, but love is greater than either of these; only love will go with us after our human sojourn is over.

I believe that, just as in an M. C. Escher print, where the background is continually becoming the foreground, we are all moving from the state in which the forms of our relationships are primary to the place where our greatest commitment is to the magnitude of the love that they are able to contain. Love itself is becoming the form and the many splendored epiphanies of human relationships; it will be like stars, distinct points of light in that great vast shimmering galaxy of light that is the energy of love. Love is our destination, and the myriad possible relationship variations are how we will get there.

My friend Nell, who endured in a single year the death of the three men closest to her, spoke of her experience watching her best friend, Tom, die of AIDS. "It was devastating, of course, to watch him die, but the closer he got to death, the more we all got into the Big Love. All the arguments we'd always had about how he should be cared for, and even the lifelong terrible grievances I myself had always had with him, all began to fade out. Everyone who came into his hospital room started melting; by the time he died, all our differences had vanished. We all loved one another—nothing else mattered anymore."

Why do we wait until somebody's dying to allow ourselves this oneness, this ecstatic experience? The future is inviting us to have the Big Love now, and to have it through the medium of our relationships. But how will we have it? What will it look like when we are actually living it in relationships? And what, if anything, do we need to do in order to get it?

First, we need to long for love. This is not an emotional yearning, but a spiritual undertaking. Our souls must long for love. Just as the lovestruck teenager lies in her bedroom painting her toenails with iridescent blue polish, desperately waiting for the phone to ring, or the 58-year-old man, devastated by the end of his 30-year marriage, agonizes over what he believes to be his failure and longs for the love that will restore him to well-being, so must we all—the whole humankind of lovers—long for, dream of, and yearn to experience love itself, this higher octave of union. We must want to be where love is, we must want to feel it where we are, and we must want to be nowhere else.

Second, we must recognize that whether we like it or not, whether we want to go there or not, we're already on our way. A meltdown is happening. People are loving more in spite of themselves. The walls between us and love are falling down. It's getting harder and harder to keep armed guards at the boundaries of our hearts: to disown our ex-spouses and lovers, to nurse our old miseries and grudges. God—spell that L-o-v-e—won't let us do it anymore. The love we've been looking for is also beating down the bushes in search of us.

Our relationships are already changing in ways that, willy-nilly, allow more love to seep in. Marriage—now at least half of the time merely the prelude to divorce—is spawning commingled families. People are learning to love more in spite of themselves, to include in the circle called family others who before would have been strangers or outcasts to them. In a world where the traditional family once consisted of two parents and four children, it now just as often consists of four parents and two or more children—the serially married mother and father and their bouquet of children. It would seem that our relationships themselves are in a state of dissolution, and yet in all this falling apartness we have stumbled on new capacities for love. We have a particular relationship and move on. We divorce and forgive. We marry someone else and continue to love the person we loved before, though differently. A man I know speaks of how all his ex-wife's adorable attributes were what enticed him to marry her in the first place, were the very qualities that eventually drove him crazy, and are now, since they've been divorced, the things about her he delights in again.

Love, we see, is not a fixed point—it's a journey, a continuum. The changes we see in the world of our relationships are leading somewhere, and not just to cavalier moral sloppiness but perhaps, and surprisingly, to something beautiful. To something even more real. To more opportunities to experience, as itself, this magnificent thing called love.

We will come to this Big Love just as we make any other change, one little tiny step at a time, until all those millions of tiptoes turn into an explosion of transformation. But, for the time being, we will approach it and it will approach us through the many exquisite life and relationship experiences that tell us Love is truly present. Sometime, somewhere, we all have already had an ecstatic experience of love: that flash of pure communion in a sexual encounter, music that momentarily unraveled our souls from our bodies, beauty that literally took our breath away. In such moments, our souls are cracked open and love pours in. This is this feeling, this is the experience, this is the rarefied state of being that we are looking for in relationships.

This ascension to love requires that we embrace the feminine, step into the receptive surrendering mode, and allow love to affect us, to change the way we think and how we operate. This implies a great challenge for men, asks that they be willing to surrender—their egos, their insistence on structure, on the power of the mind and the impulse to aggression, so that gradually their hearts can open and more and more love can have its way with them. This transformation is already under way and will continue. As our relationships are transfigured, men, rather than holding the line at the DMZ of our old forms of relationships, will mosey into the garden of new possibilities, not to conquer or take control of the transition, not even to protect and defend, but to be able to be loved, to be healed themselves, to be transformed by the power of love.

In order to accommodate this new Big Love, the shapes of our relationships will change. Rather than having a single lifelong relationship, most of us will naturally have a number of intimate connections, either simultaneously or in succession. We will welcome each connection when it arrives, cherish it while it flourishes, and surrender it with grace when it has ended.

Marriage as a form of relationship will not be extinguished, in spite of statistics that seem to predict its extinction, but neither will all relationships look as much like marriage as they used to. Marriage, the theme, will have its multiple variations. So it is that a man may pledge his sexual fidelity and economic resources to the woman he calls his wife, yet have an intimate spiritual connection with one or more other women with whom he shares a life's work, a spiritual practice, or a profound emotional connection. A married—or unmarried—couple may choose a third partner to be a sexual and/or emotional consort to their primary relationship. A woman may never marry but have a series of life-changing relationships with a number of men. Or she may change her heterosexual orientation in midlife and share the remaining years of her intimate life with only women. A couple will look like whatever people design it to be, and couples—male and female, male and male, or female and female—will be conjoined for as long as love calls them into their particular configuration of connection.

Marriage in its generic form will remain, but, like the organs of perception that actually serve to limit the range of our perceptions, these marriages may continue to serve a social function but comfortably limit the amount of ecstatic energy that can be contained in them. There will also be new and illumined forms of marriage, with sacred vows and a commitment to explore the limits of conscious partnership, whether through deep psychological work, spiritual practice, or tantric sexuality.

Because of economic circumstances and the growing need for true emotional connection, friendship and community will become increasingly viable and clearly identifiable forms of relationship. For a whole variety of reasons, many people will choose a single, nonsexual friendship as their lifelong relationship of choice. Others will conduct their entire relationship lives by phone or on the Internet rather than in physical proximity. Monogamy won't be the defining characteristic of a relationship; Love will be. Whatever the form, love will outshine the form, while the form itself will still maintain its unique integrity.

The Internet is dissolving boundaries right and left. We click our way into the hearts and souls of utter strangers. This is the myth for where we are going. The path is unclear, it is literally invisible; and yet our hearts are being moved, our souls split open. Love is taking us on a journey to itself, and when we get there we will find us, the infinite singular self that is each of us and all of us at once. Together, in union, we will arrive at the timeless place, the place without tears or unfinished business. We will abide there without effort in the landscape of utter and absolute peace and see in the infinite mirror that we are all reflecting one another to ourselves.

Every time that we dissolve the box by stepping outside of our fears and courageously loving, we expand the field of love. Every time that we open-heartedly welcome the friend of a friend; each time a woman adopts her husband's children from a former marriage and embraces them as her own; each time a man can welcome his new wife's ex-husband as a brother and honor him for the love that he gave her in his time, the chalice is filled to overflowing.

Imagine a world in which love is lived as Love itself, where love is the form and the content of relationships. This is what the future holds; this is the world we will live in. Our relationships will be wild new flowers blooming in a luminous garden.

★★★

Daphne Rose Kingma has worked as a psychotherapist and relationships expert for the past 25 years. She is the author of several books on love and relationships, including *The Nine Types of Lovers*, *True Love*, *Coming Apart*, and *The Future of Love*.

SEX

David Deida

S ex provides most men and women with both intense pleasure and heart-wrenching pain. Pleasure, because sex allows a deep dissolution of boundaries, opening your body and heart to be filled with love and energetic delight. Pain, because as your boundaries open, your heart is exposed, and few people know how to give their love as a vulnerable gift—which is the only way to offer yourself sexually that doesn't create suffering.

Many men in America today—the so-called evolved men, the new-age men—are heart wimps. They have grown beyond the macho rigidity of their fathers but have yet to grow through their fear, to face their deaths fully, and to discover the purpose of their lives. They are hesitant and ambiguous. They can't feel the depths of their consciousness and don't know where they are going, so they can't *take* their lovers, sexually or spiritually. Most women today feel "untaken" by their men, unravished to God by their men's relentless, forceful, and exquisitely sensitive loving.

Many women in America today, the independent women who have learned to love themselves rather than look for love elsewhere, are deeply unfulfilled. Their bodies are angular with a mission adopted to cover and hide yearning hearts. Distrustful of men's love—having experienced betrayal or simply inadequate men who are unable to open their women's hearts and bodies to God through deep sex and committed daily loving—many modern women are afraid to sur-

225

render, open, and trust love to live through them. Because they are unable to open fully, divine love cannot enter them, claim them, take their hearts to God and lift their bodies as offerings of devotion. And so they settle for good food, nice homes, and relationships that leave them wanting more, wanting deeper, weeping inside, acting self-reliant on the outside.

Modern American culture has moved from macho men to sensitive men, from submissive housewives to career women. And though nobody wants to go backward to old sex roles, nobody is God-blissfully happy either. Something is still missing. The heart's deepest desire remains unfulfilled. Today's more balanced men and women are still dissatisfied, and thus another step is beginning to take place, beyond old-fashioned, narrowly defined limits and also beyond modern financial, social, and political equality.

American sexuality is in a transition phase. A dissatisfying arrangement of false characters populates the cultural cutting edge: women who have betrayed their own hearts' desire by protecting themselves in tense-body forts of independence, and men who have lost touch with the clarity of consciousness that cuts through every moment to reveal their hearts' deepest truths. Relationships are safe, respectful, and often boring.

Sex between so-called spiritually evolved men and women often seems like a session between therapists, each partner discussing needs and feelings in a civilized fashion, waiting for permission to bodily yield as expressions of their greatest impulse: to offer themselves so fully that they are gone in the giving. And even when sex is infinitely loving, what happens after great sex? How can a habitually heart-protected woman and a man who is afraid to murder her open in love's obliteration sustain love's bliss throughout the day?

The next stage of sexual awakening is beyond biological urge and emotional need. If you are ready for this new stage, you have grown beyond the narcissism of self-centered me-pleasuring: "I'll do to you whatever you want as long as you love me." "Okay. Do to me what I want and I'll love you."

You also have grown beyond the safety and fairness of us-centered we-sharing: "Let's create a beautiful life together. You give me pleasure the way I want it, and I'll give you pleasure the way you want it, and we'll never violate each other's boundaries."

Furthermore—and perhaps most crucially—you are ready for authentic spiritual sexuality only when you have grown beyond the new-age separatist safety net: "You are responsible for your own happiness and I am responsible for mine. Although we can do our best to help each other, in the end, we are each responsible for ourselves."

The next stage of sexual loving, which grows beyond dysfunctional abuse and victimhood as well as beyond self-responsibility, requires bliss-forceful heart surrender despite all boundaries and fear, feeling so widely and giving so openly that you are alive as all beings. When you have grown this open, you recognize that you are utterly responsible for the one-bodied form of the divine as well as the two-bodied form, no boundaries allowed or enabled. The openness of unsafe, heart-ravishing, two-bodied divine love is not for everybody but requires a deeper understanding of sex and a readiness to open as wide as the entire moment, inside and outside your skin.

Even now, as you read this, "sex" is alive as all, including you. If you go deep within, you will find nothingness: an unchanging empty witness of all, the one who is reading these words, the same one who read words when you were 10 years old, the same one you always are, behind every thought, feeling, emotion, sensation, and perception. That is the masculine divine.

Everything else, everything that is now dancing as change inside and outside your body—your emotions; the lights you see; the sounds you hear; your thoughts coming and going; the seasons cycling hot and cold; all bodies being born, living, and dying; everything and everyone that you can experience—is the feminine divine.

The ever-divine moment is the union of He-emptiness and She-fullness, the sexual play between unchanging consciousness and ever-dancing light. That is why bodily sex is so painful and pleasurable: unless you are able to open without boundaries and merge fully, sustaining love's openness as full-blown conscious light alive in two-bodied form, you will experience an occasional fleeting grace of immeasurable bliss surrounded by many moments of knowing *this isn't it.*

Most moments—sexual or otherwise—are not recognized, felt, and lived as love's bliss appearing through many bodies. She-fullness is not allowed to dance open as love's all-giving life-light, and He-emptiness is not allowed to fearlessly penetrate and lovingly pervade Her bright showing. Ravishment is disallowed. He holds back. She dims down. You kiss your lover on the cheek, settle for occasional peaks of bliss surrounded by years of something missing. Few moments are allowed their magnificent display of light yielding open as love, perfectly, without residue or regret.

Instead, the masculine divine is kept sheathed in false layers of hesitancy. Today's man has learned to let his lover talk on and on, even when he is bored witless, even when he would rather enter his lover's heart with the same boundary-annihilating penetration of consciousness, pervading the moment, open, full of love, and gone now. And now. Meanwhile, she waits to be felt by him through and through, she waits to be seen, really seen, and adored as the light and love she is.

"Take me," she silently yearns, unfulfilled, unravished, aching inside to be claimed by a man of utter integrity. "I want to take you," he squeamishly desires, squelching his passionate depth beneath tons of false pursuits.

The next sexual step is a spiritual one. He recognizes who he is and offers himself as God's unchanging and all-pervading presence: "I am consciousness, and you are mine, you love-wild bitch."

She relaxes her body open, actively receiving his true claim, displaying her deepest heart as God's love-light, unafraid to cut off the head of any false wimpiness that enters the depths of her heart: "I am light. Take me, if you dare."

She is alive, as all-alive as anger, joy, sadness; bliss-opening as every form of love; dancing as every shine of light. He is feeling her deeply, feeling through her as deep as the moment goes, opening as her body and emotions, invited by her heart's radiant yearning to surrender, together opening as One, as God, as the He-She that is.

Or not. She can focus on her career. He can relax in Bali with his girlfriends. And then, sooner or later, she and he will die.

To die without coinciding with this moment's blissful openness—at first in rare moments and, with practice, in all moments—is to die uncomplete, unfinished. Like lousy sex, a residue of dissatisfaction lingers, which, strangely enough, makes you want to try again and again, until the trying itself is too meaninglessly painful and you relinquish your boundaries of safe striving. Finally, you exhaust the illusion of self-responsibility and are open to be lived as the heart's surrender. You open to be lived by God, to be lived open as love. And this is the basis for every moment of your life, including sex.

America has often been at the forefront of sexual exploration and political innovation. The next sexual step is a spiritual commitment to making love for the sake of God, which requires that He is willing to fully claim Her open and She is willing to fully shine Him open, as love, as One Heart appearing through two-bodied merger. This moment, as it is, right now is already ravishing—or you are hiding behind boundaries of safety.

Either your consciousness is already fully offered as unrelenting presence, ravishing all forms open to God, or you are holding back your masculine gift. Either your body is already surrendered open, as an active invitation to be claimed by love's force—breathing as the bliss of love, rippling with pleasure, undulating with pain, raging as anger's passion, showing your open heart as all love-light—or you are hiding your feminine gift.

Sensitive men and independent women are a necessary transition step. But in 50 years, perhaps, these images will be humorous enough to forget: a man, unsure of his deepest purpose, lost in temporary projects, pretending to be interested in spirituality as long as he can still hold back his absolute commitment—especially from his woman, who, not trusting his ambiguous love, tries to love herself, direct her own life, and postpone the heart-crushing knowledge that she is growing older and has never been claimed for real.

The choice is yours right now: Are you opening to feel all bodies, offering your vulnerable, indestructible love through every moment with every breath, even when you are hurt, or are you still protecting your deepest heart, waiting?

★★★

David Deida teaches and writes about sexuality, women's spirituality, and the men's movement. He is a founding member of the Institute of Integral Psychology and has taught and conducted research at the University of California, San Diego, School of Medicine; the University of California, Santa Cruz; San Jose State University; Lexington Institute in Boston; and École Polytechnique in Paris, France. He is the author of several best-selling books, including *The Way of the Superior Man* and *Intimate Communion: Awakening Your Sexual Essence.*

FEMINISM

bell hooks

Imagine a world where everyone understood intimately that we enter paradise right here on Earth—not somewhere else, not in the heavens, not in a world beyond death, but right here and right now. Imagine a world where children are told from the moment they are born that the first paradise they will know, that the palace of bliss that they have been given, is their own bodies. And that with and through the body, they can know the divine.

Imagine if this were the narrative foundation of all sexual awakening.

I learned some bit of this as a child. Religion taught me that Adam and Eve were one in the Garden, dwelling in a paradise of earthly delight. But this perfect vision of bliss quickly became blurred when I began to understand that Eve had done something bad enough to make God take paradise away. Using childhood wisdom, I instinctively held on to the parts of the story that made the best sense to me: the part that proclaimed the essential goodness of the body, the part that said paradise is our true home. From childhood on into womanhood, I held to the belief that together, women and men, dwelling in oneness, could know bliss and reestablish paradise.

Clearly, domination in any form rends and separates us and takes us away from paradise. As a feminist theorist, I have been consistently troubled by origin stories that suggest that male domination, embodied in violence, is the first primal connection between male and female to shape our sexual dynamics and our emotional bonds. Of course, there is more than evidence of life among archaic folk to challenge this narrative. I am troubled that males and females cling to these negative stories as a way of framing male-female bonds when there are foundational narratives we can choose that not only evoke a moment of origin when women and men work together for mutual human survival, but that offer us a vision of oneness that does not deny difference but transcends it.

Too much of feminist politics is grounded in negative thinking about maleness and masculinity. More often than not, this thinking deflects attention away from the visionary feminist theory that projects an origin story in which male and female are wedded by bonds of inescapable mutuality, bonds that are assaulted and severed by patterns of domination of which patriarchy is central. In visionary feminist thought, males and females share *equal* accountability for our sustained investment in patriarchal domination, and therefore men are never seen as "the" enemy. Not only are we caught in the grip of patriarchy *together*, it is our destiny as males and females to work together to restore our original state of connection, rooted in mutuality and devotion to cultivating human well-being.

Until feminist politics stop insisting that men are the enemy, we cannot join on the path leading us toward a blissful gender future. That path lies before us. And we reach it by reclaiming our bodies, our gendered beings as the place where we enter paradise.

More than any other factor, our recognition of the ever-present reality of death—the dying of young and old—will lead to the future revolution that will bring us back to the basic understanding of our bodies as the place where we enter paradise. In this revolution, we will again learn that sexuality rooted in love and connection is the place were we can know endless bliss as well as have a sense of belonging to ourselves and the Earth that heals all fear of abandonment.

I once thought that enlightened sexual politics would be the path leading us back to the body. But we see that it is so difficult to inspire and seduce women and men to claim that space. Even though sexual politics have been altered by the feminist movement, gaining women greater equality with men on almost every level in our society, this equality in the realms of work and civic life has not lessened the war between the sexes. It has intensified it. So much reformist feminist thinking and action pitted women against men and goaded women to change by consistently, insistently, in overt and covert ways, claiming that men were the enemy, simply reversing the sexist assumption that women were the enemies of men.

Even as a child, I understood that in the story of Adam and Eve, the bad thing Eve had supposedly done was to open the door to intensified pleasure by uniting bliss with awareness. Eve made knowledge a site of passion. And that pitted her against man/human and god/man, who wanted to keep access to knowledge a secret. As long as society continues to envision our gender origin story as one where women are the enemies who cast men out of paradise, and as long as women seek to reverse this origin story by suggesting that the first moment of gender contact is war—male against female—we cannot positively change sexual dynamics.

Let us imagine together an origin story for the future in which we begin with the essential truth that males and females enter paradise in a context of mutuality; that while we realize that biology both *marks* and *makes* distinctions, these distinctions also serve to intensify our wonder; that divine spirit embodied in our flesh is simply marvelous; that our differences are there to remind us everyday that there is joy in mystery (those differences—the world of the unknown and unfamiliar—cultivate and heighten in us a spirit of wonder, intensify our pleasure, and call us to new heights of play). Imagine how our sexual dynamics change when we think of gender difference as a heavenly site of play where we can toy with one another in myriad ways.

In such a world, the ideal sexual dynamic is one rooted in the understanding that interdependent connection is the key to life; that the practice of mutuality is the way the heart makes love visible in everyday action. When females and males see our reason for being on Earth as enhancing life, as giving and receiving love, we no longer accept any notion that we are essentially at war, either among ourselves or against the Earth. We are essentially in a state of wonder about ourselves and gender.

We truly communicate when we acknowledge the wonder, the unknowing, the need to learn one another. When we do not acknowledge that, we become beholden to fixed notions of gender, of what it is to be male or female, man or woman; and that creates a wall of refusal that blocks our reaching for one another in wonder.

And again, more than anything, it is as males and females are carried away from life toward and into death that many of us begin to let go, for the very first time, of fixed sexist notions of gender identity or who we must be. We see this shift most in aging men who, though they have been wedded to patriarchal thinking for the majority of their living days, suddenly find that in the nearness of death, in the recognition that they will not escape dying, they have gained the strength to resist old notions of masculinity. With age, they no longer believe that to express the longing for connection is weakness or that the tender expression of deep emotional feeling and need makes one less of a man. At this point, many males let go of their fear of the female for the first time.

This is why so many of us as children had our first insight into true love emerge in our relations to grandfathers. Imagine a future world where grandfathers become the primary spokespersons, leading us away from patriarchy into the bliss of feminist-based gender mutuality. For that is the paradise for which we yearn.

Imagine a world where everyone comes to see the feminist movement as inviting us *all* to end sexist exploitation and oppression. I treasure this definition of feminism because it does not imply that men are the enemy. Rather, it reminds us that females and males are both agents of sexist thinking and practice, and that if we want to change sexism, everyone has to change, not just men.

Imagine a world where females and males are ever aware that our time on this Earth is so brief that we must spend it in a spirit of celebration, expressing a joy in living by choosing life. And in choosing life, we choose love. In such a world, boys and girls are taught, from birth on, a vision of love rooted in mutual communication between the sexes. In this world, such communication will be effortless because the will to connect, to be compassionate and forgiving, will be ever constant. In this world, there still will be conflict, but the sexes will learn—again, from birth on—constructive ways to cope with conflict.

The path of passion is emotionally complex. Within our spaces of erotic longing, whether heterosexual, bisexual, or homosexual, there will always remain the desire to consume the other. Yet it is knowing how to transform the *will to dominate* into the *will to connect* that will enable us to embrace our gender difference.

The ideal sexual dynamic is rooted always in mutuality. Our yearnings and our inclinations will differ, but our commitment to creating bliss will remain constant. In the future, by teaching girls and boys and reeducating women and men to have faith in mutual-gendered affirmation of life, we set the stage for a liberating sexual dynamic, for the practice of love.

In the future, we will not need the sorrow of loss or dying to remind us that our bodies long to connect and express life, for we will teach one another how to love. Schools of love will be created, so that even before children acquire other forms of book learning, even before they learn to read or write, they will be schooled in the art of loving. And they will be taught to see the sexual-bliss fulfillment of love's promise.

We will begin that teaching with the body, in remembrance we take eat, we taste and see. And as males and females, we will live fully, telling our story that here in these bodies is the door to paradise, telling each other and the new world that we are together making, that paradise is our home and love our true destiny.

★★★

Writer, feminist theorist, and cultural critic bell hooks has been identified by *Utne Reader* as among the top 100 visionaries working to transform society. She is the author of more than 19 books, most recently *All about Love: New Visions.*

CHILDREN

John Gray

The children of the year 2050 will be better understood and, as a whole, better loved and nurtured than the children of previous generations. I say this with some certainty because we are already well along the evolutionary path toward its realization.

In the closing decades of the last millennium, there was a noticeable shift in how we communicated with children and how we welcomed their communication into our adult world. Concepts like "Children should be seen, not heard" fell out of favor. Adults began to praise one another for their ability to communicate with children. The standard of successful parenting no longer was having a quiet, well-behaved child that lived in a world that was distinctly separate from the parents' life. Instead, we began to appreciate a family life that functioned as one integrated unit. Interactivity between parent and child became the accepted behavioral model. A parent that could draw out their child's hopes or concerns, and therefore communicate more effectively, became the parent that others admired and praised.

But perhaps the most significant behavioral shift in parenting style has been the general acceptance that fear-based parenting is not the most effective way of raising respectful and cooperative children. In its place has emerged what I would call positive parenting. This cultural shift, like all evolutionary changes, did not occur in a few years. In fact, it was a transition that clearly required decades. The process began to take hold in the 1950s with the parents of the baby boomers.

The popular debate of the time is captured in the admonishment from older generations that if you spare the rod you will spoil the child. Of course, in times of stress, the children of fear-based parenting returned to the parenting model that they witnessed as children, and indeed, they didn't always spare the rod. In this way, the concept of fear-based parenting was instilled in their children. That recurring cycle will take nearly a century to break down.

But I believe that by 2050, positive parenting will secure its place in our society as the accepted method for effectively motivating children to reach their full potential as whole and healthy adults.

A Global Shift in Consciousness

Prior to the 20th century, an introspective exploration of our inner feelings, desires, and needs was not important in the daily lives of all but a tiny segment of society. The issue for the masses was survival and security. You see that demonstrated dramatically in the shifting behavior of what I have described as the traditional Mars-Venus dynamic. In 1900, a woman looking at a man as a life partner placed her greatest value on his ability to provide safety and security for her and their future family. But in 2000, the most desirable value in a mate was his or her ability to bring romantic compatibility. The bride and groom's question that they asked of themselves was simply: Is this a partner that will bring me a chance to experience love that will last a lifetime?

The world changes, and what we expect of one another changes as well. When security and safety were no longer the paramount issues, when the art of survival no longer dominated our daily thought, the roles of men and women changed too. The attributes of love, compassion, cooperation, and forgiveness are no longer lofty concepts limited to philosophers and spiritual leaders. In previous centuries, societies were commonly suppressed, controlled, and manipulated by strong, punishing dictators. This type of rule is no longer welcomed, and dictators are an endangered species. In the world of 2050, dictatorship will be a thing of the past in matters of state as well as in our private lives.

Accordingly, children will know what is unfair and abusive behavior and will not tolerate it. We will have to communicate proactively and positively or we will quickly lose our influence over them.

When parents yell at children, it just numbs their ability to hear. The world of 2050 will revolve around the art of communication, and effective communication skills are most effectively learned when children listen to their parents and parents listen to their children.

PROVIDING FILTERS TO THE WORLD

In the dawn of the information age, we passed along to our children without great thought whatever came into our home, first in print, then via radio, television, the Internet, and broadband digital streaming. What we began to understand and better appreciate at the beginning of the 21st century, however, is a phenomenon that could simply be described as "violence in, violence out." Media without filters or adult communication bringing balance to topical material is a type of abandonment of parental responsibility. This was not a problem commonly faced by previous generations, but in the late 20th century it compounded the problems of fear-based parenting.

After the riots in Los Angeles in 1989, different groups of children were shown videotapes of the violence for 3 minutes. Afterward, they played in a room where there were violent toys and nonviolent toys. When told that the violence on TV was just actors pretending to be violent, the children didn't play with the violent toys but played with more neutral or nurturing toys. When told that the violence on TV was real, almost all the children played with violent toys. Aggression dramatically increased.

In the first decades of the new millennium, this understanding will become more widely held. Too many movies or too much television, even without violence and acts of cruelty, can overstimulate children. Children under the age of 14 learn primarily by imitation.

What they see is what they do. Parents leaving their children in front of a television and walking away are inviting problems if there is no communication with the child about the programming seen and no balance of other activities provided.

When children become overstimulated by the aggression displayed in their society—be it in the media or in their own homes—they become hyperactive. This invariably leads to low self-esteem. Only by recognizing the damaging effects of an unchecked flow of information—particularly that which is violent in nature—can we begin as a society to correct this behavior.

THE RISE OF POSITIVE PARENTING

As we gained the common knowledge that abusive adults were invariably abused children, we recognized that this cycle of violence began innocently enough with fear-based parenting and evolved with the rising, unchecked influence of a violent society. With a global shift in the collective consciousness universally, the mode of positive parenting opens us all to a world of new possibilities.

In my view of our future, the new order of respect and openness begins when we take on the role of being better parents by accepting the challenge to change and mustering the courage to leave old beliefs behind. Think of the change in our global village when the adults of 2050 have been raised by parents who sought to listen and understand their children as opposed to being feared by them. The love and understanding that was given to them will be further enhanced and passed on to their children. Rather than a world where negative emotions are handed down generation to generation, positive behavior becomes the standard. This fundamental change in our family life can bring astounding changes in society as a whole.

We are in the process of learning that we cannot have a peaceful and prosperous world until each and every one of us is respected for who and what we are. This does not just mean respecting different races and cultures, but also that gender prejudice and age bias are no longer acceptable. A 90-year-old and a 9-year-old are entitled to our respect and attention for their own unique needs and abilities.

We come from a world that has marginalized the value of many human beings; we are heading to a world that celebrates all people. We will all be the better for that.

FIVE POSITIVE MESSAGES

Positive parenting begins with five simple messages that allow us to raise cooperative, confident, and compassionate children.

- ◆ *It's okay to be different.* Every child is born unique and special. Children may be very different from what parents expect them to be. Each one has his or her own special gifts and will face unique challenges. As parents, our job is not just to tolerate differences but to embrace them. The absence of this positive message suggests a negative one: Something is wrong with my child; he or she needs to be fixed rather than nurtured. In reality, children need a clear message that they are okay and that differences are fine and to be expected.

- ◆ *It's okay to make mistakes.* Besides being unique and different, every child comes into this world with his or her own bundle of issues and problems. In spite of our expectations, the simple truth is that all children, like all adults, make mistakes. To expect our children not to make mistakes sets a standard that they can never live up to. When parents expect perfection, children can only feel inadequate and powerless to live up to their parents' standards.

- ◆ *It's okay to express negative emotions.* All children experience negative emotions in reaction to life's challenges and restrictions. Negative emotions are a natural and important part of a child's development. Through the process of experiencing their emotions, children learn to adjust their expectations and accept some of life's limits. As parents, it is not our goal to shut them off from their negative emotions but rather to listen with empathy. The goal is to provide opportunities for children to learn appropriate ways to express their negative emotions. In the past, the common parenting approach was to control children by conditioning them to suppress their feelings. Shaming or punishing children for being upset subdues their passion and breaks their will.

◆ *It's okay to want more.* When children don't know what they want, they become vulnerable to the wants and wishes of others. They lose the opportunity to discover and develop who they are and, instead, become what others want them to be. In the absence of knowing what they want, they assume the wants of others and disconnect from their own power, passion, and direction. Too often, children get the message that they are wrong, selfish, or spoiled for wanting more or for getting upset when they don't get what they want. In the past, the message we gave to our children was to be happy with very little, and in most cases that is exactly what they got in life. Their wants were ignored and overlooked not only as children but as adults as well. However, it's okay for children to want more. In fact, it can help them develop a stronger sense of who they are and what they are here to do in this world.

◆ *It's okay to say no (but Mom and Dad are the bosses).* The basis of positive parenting is to instill in each child a sense of individuality and freedom. Letting children say no opens the door for them to express feelings and to discover what they want and then negotiate for that. By no means does this suggest that you will always do what the child wants. Instead, parents take the time to hear and consider the resistance. Positive parenting allows the child to express him- or herself openly, and this in itself often makes a child more cooperative.

To apply these five messages of positive parenting, we first have to understand the right conditions that allow them to work their best. It is not enough just to stop punishing our children; we must apply new skills to create cooperation, motivation, and control. Our role is to provide a safe and nurturing environment so that each child can develop and express his or her full potential.

PARENTING SKILLS OF THE FUTURE

The transition between the past and the future is occurring right at this moment. By 2050, a new set of parenting skills will have completely replaced the traditional ones that became outdated in the modern era. We are faced with nothing less than the challenge of reinventing parenting.

The children of today and the near future are more in touch with their feelings and therefore more self-aware. With this shift in awareness, the needs of these children have changed as well. New skills are required of parents to help meet these changing needs. The goal of these new skills is to motivate children with love as opposed to punishment, humiliation, or the loss of love.

For example, one of these new skills is to learn to ask your child to do something, not order or demand. This gets to the question of how we should communicate with our children in a way that creates a willingness to listen and respond to our requests. An endless string of commands is not effective—a child's daily life can be filled with hundreds of orders. But commands can easily be turned into requests. Rather than demanding, "Go brush your teeth," simply ask, "Would you please brush your teeth before going to bed?" Persistence and patience are key to this approach. In a short time, the child will respond positively to the change in the parent's tone.

There are other, equally subtle ways to create big changes in parental communication style. For example, a negative message is "Your room is a mess again." A positive message is "Would you please clean up your room?" But in making this shift, don't make the mistake of providing explanations. Remember that Mom and Dad are still boss. You can make a request in a positive, nondemanding tone without providing an explanation. When you begin to explain why the room should be neat, the teeth brushed, and so on, you justify your request and give up your power. The child ultimately is confused. One of the shifts that has to occur for positive parenting skills to take root is the understanding that a positive parent is not a pleading parent. When the child does not hear your positive request, you make it again—not with an explanation but simply by repetition. Giving up explanations goes a long way toward encouraging cooperation.

The shift to positive parenting will involve revising all of our parenting skills so that we can minimize resistance, improve communication, increase motivation, assert leadership, and maintain control. Time-outs, for example, will not disappear, but they will be used far more effectively as a time for children to regain their own sense of control. A brief time-out gives a child the chance to confront his emotions and to process his own feelings about the offending behavior. Physical punishment sets up a cycle in which the child as an adult will seek to punish himself rather than consider his actions and the emotions that they raise.

The simple truth is that all children have a basic desire to please their parents. The skills of positive parenting are primarily focused on recognizing that desire and giving every child the structure to thrive in a supportive environment.

Realistically, we have little hope of creating the future that we want without evolving in our most essential act of communication—that between adult and child: parent to offspring, teacher to student, coach to player. Every chance that we have to speak to our children is our opportunity to touch the future. Acting faithfully with that careful consideration in mind, the year 2050 will find us living in a far better world than the world of today.

★★★

John Gray, Ph.D., is a family counselor and psychologist who has written several international best-sellers, including *Men Are from Mars, Women Are from Venus, Mars and Venus in Love*, and *How to Get What You Want and Want What You Have*. His most recent book is titled *Children Are from Heaven*.

DIVORCE

Debbie Ford

Divorce is one of the darkest times in a person's life. For many of those who go through it, divorce is the turning point, the end, the pain that shuts out love and hope forever.

An epidemic that began in the late 1960s, divorce now permeates our society, breaking up homes and leaving many children and adults as wounded as if they had lived through a violent war. Divorce is a time when love dies. Instead of being a holy event where we acknowledge all the gifts that our partnerships have brought, most of us bury our loss in hate, anger, blame, and bitterness.

Anyone who has been through a divorce will tell you that it rocks the very foundation of our beings. Most of us got married to complete ourselves and to live happily ever after. We grow up longing to create the family of our dreams, and most of us strive to do it better than our parents did it. But with divorce, we are left face-to-face with shattered dreams and a deep sense that we have failed. Unable to deal directly with the pain brought on by our separations, we distract ourselves by blaming our partners for the collapse of our marriages. Many of us spend countless hours taking inventory of our partners' defects and wrongdoings, and some of us spend the rest of our lives trying to retaliate against the ones who have broken our dreams.

Our negative feelings—our anger, sadness, frustration, loneliness, fear, rage, and guilt—are stuffed within our consciousness. Left unhealed, these unresolved emotions fester inside us, camouflaging themselves as anxiety, depression, obsession, addiction, and other self-defeating behaviors. In order to heal, we must learn to delve into these dark emotions and face our pain head-on. Hiding, denying, and suppressing are the defenses we use to avoid dealing with our pain and loss. But these methods are the culprits that keep us tied to the past and rob us of a future filled with possibility. Unless we choose to heal and grow, our alternatives are bleak.

Using a divorce as a catalyst for healing causes you to step into a new reality where you become responsible, empowered, and a creator of your own future. Allowing your divorce to use *you* leaves you a victim of life and keeps you stuck in the pain of your past. You can choose to use your divorce, or you can let your divorce use you. Until you find the gift of any situation, it will continue to use you.

When we view our confusion, pain, and sadness through God's eyes, we can see that such feelings have been catalysts for great discovery. It is during times of crisis—and divorce is surely one of those times—that we have the opportunity to explore our inner worlds and become intimate with our most extraordinary selves. Pain is the force that compels us to break free from our limited perceptions about ourselves. The pain of divorce serves as a spiritual wake-up call, a spotlight that illumines the places within us that are crying to be healed. Our anguish is not our enemy but our teacher, a beloved friend that seeks to lead us into unexplored territories. We must ask better questions of ourselves—not, Why did this happen to me? but, How can I use this to grow? Divorce in the new millennium, while certainly not pain-free, will be seen as an opportunity for spiritual transformation.

THE SPIRITUAL DIVORCE

A spiritual divorce is one in which we use our divorce to improve our lives; our experience becomes one of gain rather than loss. A spiritual divorce is a divorce used to bring us back into the presence of our divinity and heal the split between our egos and our souls. When you use your divorce to become a more loving, conscious human being, you have truly had a spiritual experience and a liberation of your soul. While the new vision for divorce cannot take away the pain triggered

246

by separating from a spouse, it creates the possibility for us to use divorce as a catalyst for healing and growth.

The first step toward making divorce a spiritual experience is having a shift in perception. Marcel Proust said, "The real voyage of discovery consists not in seeking new landscapes, but in having new eyes." New eyes allow us to see our ex and all the events that led up to our divorce as guides leading us to the exact place we are supposed to be. With these eyes, we understand that it is in times of great distress that we become open and receptive to new ideas.

We must come to see our partners as teachers, friends, and guides who are there to support us in manifesting our full potential. When we come up against a roadblock like the end of our marriage, most of us will think that something is wrong or that we have failed. But this hurdle is actually a clue, telling us that there is a better direction for us to take. In the new millennium, we will come to understand that to have the life we desire, we will have to let go of the life we are living.

In the 21st century, we will perceive our intimate relationships as great opportunities for self-discovery and spiritual growth. In order to use our relationships as a tool for our personal evolution, we must step inside a reality that says: Life is a school to the wise man and an enemy to the fool. If we choose to be the wise man or woman, we will learn from our mistakes and gain strength from our shortcomings. We will take the time to study and contemplate the events that led up to our current situation, and to heal the pain of our past. Every experience—whether we judge it as being "good" or "bad"—presents us with an opportunity to graduate to a higher level of consciousness. Each person, circumstance, and event that we encounter holds a key that can unlock the door to our deeper wisdom.

Divorce helps us break free from the confines of our limited thinking and beckons us to explore new thoughts, beliefs, and possibilities. In the 21st century, when the spiritual divorce will prevail, we will discover that life is not always about living happily ever after, but about learning and evolving into the highest expression of ourselves that we can achieve. Our difficulties launch us into new states of consciousness where we are inspired to step out of the reality of our smallest thoughts and step into the limitless freedom of our biggest dreams. All living things must grow or they die. Divorce is the tool for growth that helps us fulfill our collective mission here on Earth: to grow and evolve, to shed the old in order to embrace the new.

A GLIMPSE INTO THE FUTURE

Consider the following scenario of a spiritual divorce. Imagine that the end of your relationship is near. Although you and your partner are very likely feeling sad and disheartened, you commit yourselves to having your separation be a sacred and holy experience. Knowing that this is an emotionally volatile time, you seek out the company of supportive, loving, conscious friends who will assist you in using this time of transition for your highest good. You make the conscious choice not to gossip, verbally attack your partner, or seek validation of how wronged you have been. Instead, you try your best to embrace this time as one of healing and resolution. Although this is not how you wanted your marriage to end, you accept that your divorce has not occurred by accident and that there are no coincidences. You trust that the decision to dissolve your marriage is in the highest good for all involved. You breathe deep and relax in the comfort that your relationship with your spouse is not ending but merely changing forms.

Driven by the pain of your present circumstances, you commit this time to deepening your relationship with yourself and the Divine. You immerse yourself in meditation and prayer, and trust that your divorce is part of a divine design, one that is furthering your own unique evolution. You are keenly aware that there is no change without loss, and no growth without change. So, willingly, you surrender into the sea of emotional turbulence, knowing that your pain is helping to give birth to a new and higher version of yourself. Gradually, you begin to trust that the universe has a greater plan for your life, and your hardened defenses are replaced by loving compassion.

As an emotionally responsible adult, you recognize yourself as the co-creator of your marriage and your divorce. You understand that in order to heal, you must accept responsibility for your circumstances and your feelings. You begin the difficult but rewarding task of looking for the lessons that your partner came to teach you, knowing that every painful experience serves a vital purpose for your growth. You make a list of all the insights that you gained and all the gifts that you received as a result of having this person in your life. Even though a voice inside your head may be screaming, There's nothing good about this! My partner never gave me a thing! you march on, determined to find the gold in the dark.

With these wedding gifts in hand, you experience a shift in perception that opens you up to new realities. Inside this new reality, you see your life and your ex through a heart of gratitude. You feel authentic appreciation for the times that you've shared together and the dreams that you made come true. You give thanks for all the ways that your partner has helped you to grow and for all the experiences your marriage made possible. And if you've been lucky enough to be blessed with a family, you honor the spirit of your children by respecting the love that created them. When you receive the blessings of your union, you have access to the compassion, gratitude, and forgiveness that lies in each of our hearts. And with an open heart, you acknowledge the essential role that your partner has played in awakening you to your own magnificence.

THE SEVEN LAWS

In order to make this new future possible, we must be willing to let our separations be guided by a new set of principles. We gain access to this higher possibility when we understand these basic universal laws of spiritual divorce. These laws will guide us through the process of healing, returning us to a place that is filled with wisdom, knowledge, and a deep compassion for the human experience.

These seven spiritual laws are designed to help you break through your fears, dissolve your pain, and understand the "why" of your situation. When these laws are integrated and practiced, they will give you the freedom to create the life you have always dreamed of.

The Law of Acceptance

Everything is as it should be. This is the first and possibly the most important spiritual law. Nothing occurs by accident and there are no coincidences. We are always evolving, whether we are aware of it or not. Our lives are divinely designed for each one of us to get exactly what we need to support our own unique evolutionary process.

The Law of Surrender

When we stop resisting and surrender to the situation exactly as it is, things begin to change. Resistance is the number one culprit in denying us our right to heal. We resist out of the fear that if we let go, if we surrender, our lives will go out of control or we will be faced with circumstances that we can't handle. When we are willing to look at our situation and admit that we don't know how to fix it, we are ready to get the help we need.

The Law of Divine Guidance

God will do for you what you cannot do for yourself. When you get out of your own way and let go of your defenses, you become humble. Humility is the doorway through which the Divine can walk into your life. Without humility, we believe we can do it ourselves. Without humility, our false sense of pride, or ego, prohibits us from seeing the entire situation with clear eyes. Our egos remain in charge until we step outside our righteous belief that we are independent and separate beings. As long as this myth is intact, we keep the door closed to our higher wisdom.

The Law of Responsibility

With divine guidance, we can look at exactly how we participated and co-created our divorce drama. We can begin to take responsibility for our entire situation and make peace with our past. We can see how we have chosen the perfect partner to teach us the perfect lessons. Once we have asked God to come into our lives and guide us, we begin to heal.

The Law of Choice

Having taken responsibility, we can choose new interpretations that empower us. We become responsible, and the designers of our new realities. We can separate from our partners by taking back the aspects of ourselves that we've projected onto our mates. We can distinguish what our self-defeating behaviors have been and learn how to act instead of react in difficult situations.

The Law of Forgiveness

After we have taken back the aspects of ourselves that we have projected onto our mates, we will be able to ask God to forgive us. Doing this allows us to let go of our judgments and beliefs about what is right and what is wrong and find compassion for our entire self. Compassion unfolds when we are in the presence of the perfection of the universe, when we can experience ourselves in another. It comes with the great understanding of the difficulties and ambiguity of being a human being. Compassion is God's grace for those who ask. Once we have received compassion for ourselves, we will be able to find compassion and forgiveness for our mates.

The Law of Creation

Experiencing the freedom of forgiveness opens up the gates to new realities. Forgiveness breaks all the cords that keep us tied to the past. It allows us to experience an innocent heart filled with love and an excitement for life. This is the time to create a new future, one grounded in your divine truth.

MARRIAGE 101

Education is paramount if we are going to change the way our relationships end. We can no longer assume that our relationships will last forever, so we must be better prepared to deal with endings and loss, to move forward instead of backward. We must understand the nature of intimate relationships and learn how to take better care of ourselves while sharing our lives with those we love. We can't drive a car without going to school; we can't get a good job without an education; so why would we be able to be married without first attending Marriage 101? This would be a basic course in how to support your spouse—to communicate and create a healthy, functioning, empowering relationship—and how to deal with change and loss.

This basic course in marriage and divorce would be a reality check for those hoping to stay in the blissful premarital state of love. It would teach people the skills of transition for when the illusion of love changes or when sexual desire lessens. It would impart great wisdom from those who have succeeded in happy, vibrant marriages and from those whose marriages have ended. Marriage 101 would teach us how to empathize and validate our partners' experiences, how to listen in a way that leaves our partners empowered. This premarriage course would show us how our withheld anger can destroy our family units and leave our children with emotional wounds that will last a lifetime.

The curriculum would look at the many choices we would be faced with if our marriage should end, and it should explore the possibilities of life after marriage. Everyone would learn how to deal with divorce before they ever took the vow of marriage so that they could be prepared for the storm, even if it never comes.

Marriage is difficult and requires hard work. Many people struggle miserably with it. But if we were taught at school about human relations, emotional wholeness, and the ups and downs of life, we would be better prepared for what we all will face during marriage. With proper education, each of us who stepped into the institution of marriage would go in with a greater chance to win. We would understand the trials and tribulations as well as the joys and the triumphs. We would have the basic problem-solving skills that are needed to sustain loving, forgiving, and nurturing relationships and be better prepared to take care of ourselves mentally, spiritually, financially, and emotionally if the end ever came.

Our institution of marriage must shift if we are to have spiritual divorces. The marriage of the future will be a spiritual contract between two people based on mutual support, love, respect, and honor of the highest aspects of each other's spirit. Marriage will be seen as a place to grow, change, and evolve into the person we always desired to be. It will be a communion held together not by the imprisoning belief that we will be together forever, until death do us part, but by the mutual agreement that we will stay together as spiritual warriors until we have completed our lessons together. Our partnerships will be based on the knowledge that there is an abundance of love available to each one of us, and that if the love we have together is no longer serving us, there is a greater possibility that awaits us both.

AGENTS OF HEALING

My friend John McShane, a renowned divorce attorney, has described divorce not as a legal problem or even a relationship problem but, at its most fundamental level, as a spiritual problem. This insight has inspired him to lead a nationwide movement toward what he calls collaborative divorces. In the 21st century, lawyers like McShane will be seen as agents of healing. Although they will provide legal remedies, their main focus will be as spiritual guides, supporting families in the restructuring process. Nurturing and supportive, such lawyers will look out for the psychological, spiritual, and financial well-being of the entire family. The attorneys of the future will put together multidisciplinary teams that will include social workers, child psychologists, and financial planners to help couples at every juncture. Most important, they will see themselves not as arbitrators, mediators, or adversaries but as negotiators of peace and positive change for all the parties involved. No longer will the goal be to obtain what is the most favorable result for the client; rather, these agents of healing will address the broader vision of what is best for the whole family.

The divorce lawyer will help design a future for the once-united family that balances the needs of all. As team captains, lawyers will help create unity where there was once separation, harmony where there was once discord. These agents of healing will strive to understand the psychology of both marriage and divorce and provide a cooperative and harmonious environment for those seeking resolution. A divorce victory in the 21st century will be one where everyone wins. A successful legal victory would leave everyone with greater self-knowledge and a profound appreciation for themselves and their partners.

Divorce in the new millenium will change from crisis to opportunity, from conclusion to beginning, from disaster to spiritual awakening. Divorce will no longer be viewed as a negative event; rather, it will be embraced as a sacred time of renewal and reassessment, a time when we have the chance to meet ourselves anew. A spiritual divorce is an invitation to shift gears and launch our unfulfilled dreams. It's a time to reflect, learn, and change the direction of our lives. It is a time to transform our sadness into joy, our pain into pleasure, and our anger into compassion. The 21st century will give birth to the possibility that every divorce will bring emotional healing and spiritual transformation. As a society, we will make a conscious choice to use divorce as a catalyst to make peace with our past and to reconnect with our divine nature.

Imagine a world where endings and change are celebrated. Where separation and loss are transformed into freedom and full self-expression. Imagine a world where divorce is a collaboration of healing, a sacred event where we learn to see ourselves in the reflection of another. Imagine a world where children come first. This is ours to have, and it is easily within our reach. In fact, it can begin now, two people at a time.

★★★

Debbie Ford is a faculty member at the Chopra Center for Well Being in La Jolla, California. She is the author of *The Dark Side of the Light Chasers: Reclaiming Your Power, Creativity, Brilliance, and Dreams.*

AGING

Gay Gaer Luce

Thanks to the miracles of medical science, we are soon going to experience a significant extension of human life span and, with it, far greater numbers of healthy, educated old people in our society. This comes at a paradoxical time. Up until now, respect for the wisdom of the elders has been largely pragmatic, especially in indigenous populations where elders have provided the library of the cultures' knowledge. But today, in technological countries such as ours, respect has faded into bare tolerance, and we have demanded that older people act, look, and talk young. Our lack of respect for the elderly reflects the meagerness of our respect for life itself, as we choose in its stead affluence and the demands of a marketplace-driven world.

As America grows old, this view is bound to change radically. There comes a time when the drama and rewards of the marketplace no longer outweigh the values of love, honesty, and relaxation. Aging as we have known it—disability, loss of mental capacity, diminished energy—will not be the experience of newly arrived elders in 20 years. If our productive economy continues, we will live in a society of healthy elders with great longevity. We will be entering a golden age as we move from health to wisdom and even enlightenment.

What would happen if you could be healthy for 150 more years? When I imagine the spaciousness of such a long life, I am dazzled by the possibility of living out all the hidden facets of my personality: my unused talents, my suppressed yearnings to see the world, my desire to offer service, my wish to test my strengths and fears and talents, my search for knowledge and love. Endless possibilities.

But then the voice of my ego begins to wilt, and these desires dwindle. Instead, my soul speaks. What it calls out for is not out there in the material world. My soul cries for its birthright experience of its inherent light and oneness with all there is. It calls out for spiritual enlightenment. Is this soul-demand part of the evolutionary trend that is creeping up on us with the mass aging of our society?

ENVISIONING THE NEW LIFE SPAN

Five hundred years ago, survival was assured only to a small elite. In fact, the average human life span was around 18 years until the 19th century. People didn't age; they died. Then, in the past century, breakthroughs in health care began eliminating many of the diseases that killed us young. If Americans rarely reached the age of 65 a hundred years ago, today 33 million of us are 65 and older.

Although our media and culture are still focused on youth, the United States is becoming a middle-aged country. Our elderly people have received—through radio, television, the Internet, and travel—the equivalent of 10 times more life experience than their parents. Yet, with all of our riches, we now face the economic and social challenge of caring for an older population in ill health and without the resources that our generation will have. These needy ones are our family, and we cannot ignore them any more than we can cut off our right hands. But the advances coming from technology and, particularly, genetic research suggest that if we show some social savvy, we may be able to repair much of the damage caused by earlier poverty and ill health.

With the expectation of greater longevity, we won't follow the traditional linear life plan: migrating through 12 to 18 years of education, then working for 30 years, and then retiring with the expectation of leisure while knowing that we are no longer welcome in the workforce. What if we could intersperse education, work, and leisure repeatedly throughout our life spans?

I think we will. In decades to come, tens of millions of outspoken, long-lived men and women will redefine the purpose and arrangement of work in our lives. We can already see the popularity of sabbaticals, phased retirement programs, flextime, job banks, and retraining programs geared to new careers for older workers. We see only the tip of the iceberg now as elders like Ross Perot make an impact in politics and an unexpectedly young Gloria Steinem says, "This is what 65 is like!"

Breakthroughs in longevity are creating a *gerontocracy*, a population of elders. The largest generation in American history, the baby boomers, will soon be elders. We need to revise our clichéd picture of the United States as young and family-centered, as the census reveals that we are older and that nuclear families make up only about 25 percent of the population. We also need to release our images of aging: withdrawal, physical deterioration, and irrelevance to society. We inherited these from grandparents and parents, embellished by threats from the medical profession of Alzheimer's and life-sapping diseases.

But cumulative progress in biological research and research on the aging mechanism in every cell may soon give us the option of living to not only 100 but 200 and beyond. Stem cell and telomerase research could allow us to grow new organ tissues, replacing damaged and diseased cells and extending the life of cells, perhaps indefinitely. Some people speculate that we will be living to 150 or even 250.

Old people today, even those disabled or ill-educated, have a new instrument for communication: the Internet. Blue Shield and other large institutions are offering computer training for the elderly because this is a means by which even the most frail can participate in life. In many institutions today, people talk with their families regularly and see them, share pictures, and interact via e-mail. The interaction is becoming easier, and telephone, video, and other services are becoming very inexpensive. With just a little means, the elderly person who has a desire to know about the world at large need only click on the computer to encounter possibilities too vast to mention. The finest education in the world will soon be available to people at home, and disabled people will no longer be at a disadvantage, as they attend the great universities through Internet classes and acquire the breadth and skill training they need to participate in an ever more ramified world. Automatic exclusion because of age is ludicrous in the domain of virtual commerce, where the pertinence of talent or wisdom is becoming the sole criterion for acceptance.

In the United States, people over 50 already control 70 percent of personal financial assets. There is a trend toward wealth consolidation among the elderly that will only increase with the aging of the so-called baby boomers. Accordingly, the consumer market will shift to please adults who are 40 and older. Healthy, educated older people who can use the Internet to participate in the dialogue of the world probably will not use their money in the same way as the more isolated folks of the past. The existence of organizations such as the AARP and the widespread concern among elders over the cost and quality of medicine suggests that they may choose instead to be the benefactors of some deep social changes.

Retirement today is more than Sun World, gated communities, and luxury travel. It is more than Elderhostel and hobbies, new relationships, and new forms of service. It is more than our grandchildren and the bonds of accruing family. It is more than computer participation in economics, science, government, and education. Although we will doubtless be exploring space and the many material realms in ways that are not yet imagined, as well as microrealms that our instrumentation is just beginning to postulate, none of these will take us to the outside limits. For what we seek is not static or material. As we humanly contribute to the evolving "Divine Show," we know of only one way to perceive life. We must have an experience. Having outworn other roads to the singular truth that haunts our souls, I believe that we will use our extended elder years to cultivate spiritual actualization—even if not consciously.

In the 1970s, a group of us created an experiment we called Senior Actualization and Growth Explorations, or SAGE. At the time, it was a pioneer program to bring the tools and spiritual practices of the human potential movement to elders who were left out, deemed unable to change, and socially discarded because of their age. At the time, most of the community around us—including our immediate families, gerontologists, and other relevant professionals—doubted that these people could still lead vital lives, adopt a spiritual practice, and radically improve their well-being. The project was considered improbable. Then it happened, and its success was stunning.

Today, SAGE is history. We have since seen many innovations to benefit an aging population, like the Longevity Institute, with programs of exercise and nutrition (primarily reduced caloric intake) to produce youthful vitality and physique in people well into their seventies. We have met 91-year-olds who ran the Boston Marathon and participated in Elderhostel, traveling and teaching all over the world. Affluent and educated people in the United States are living more healthfully and longer—and yet most are far from enlightened. Is there a life span at which accumulated wisdom shifts into realization?

THE PATH TO REALIZATION

With the additional years with which medical science will grace us, there will be more opportunities for the elderly to contribute to society and to extend education into spiritual training. In ancient times, for instance, leaders of society were educated in mystery schools that combined the subject matter of traditional high-level education—Harvard, MIT, agriculture and architecture schools, art and metaphysical schools—with a spiritual boot camp that ensured the sterling character of the trainees. Participants were initiated so they could be connected with their divine natures and thus use their healing and intuitive powers. Ancient mystery schools were secret and elite.

In the past 20 years there has been a surfacing of modern versions of the mystery school. My teaching experience in one of these schools suggests that middle-aged and older people are gravitating to them, hungry for both experience and spiritual training. They are seeking in a gutsy and uninhibited manner that is a quantum leap from our SAGE experiment of the 1970s. Numinous changes in these people make them models of an inspiring old age.

Even though spiritual values and wisdom are given lip service rather than widely valued, society is about to get a jolt when it feels the effect of a large population of enlightened elders. Thirty-three million people over age 50 is a large potential voting block. As more of this older population becomes Internet-sophisticated, spiritually re-fined, and aware of itself as a political block, the result will be an in-crease in our society's respect for them.

If we simply live long enough, we come face-to-face with the paradox of our egos. With extended life spans, we will have enough time and vitality to indulge almost every imagining our minds can concoct. We can live multiple tracks, experiencing some strands of our personalities while composting and sheltering others until they seem ready for exposure. In this unplanned fashion, souls seared by lifetimes of material and emotional teachings will be left clear to see without the cultural dark glasses we have been taught to wear.

We will be too long on Earth to embrace our old character de-ficiencies, like characters in a sitcom, pretending to be what we are not or grasping and competing for material accumulations. We will outlive the naïveté that allowed us to believe cultural promises about the way life should be. Upon reaching age 120, the strident clamor of passionate selfishness simply may not be worth the effort. So long as we believe that there is some prize somewhere else, we can pursue multitudes of romances, families, professions, changes of living stan-dards, travels, careers, friendships, hobbies, philosophies.

Eventually, the sheer accumulation of experience will begin to wear out our demands. The nature of the prize will change. The in-evitable next step, I believe, will be a default process of spiritual real-ization. Rogues and wastrels, over time, can become saints. We may not set out to embody goodness, but with the years, goodness be-comes of us. We can back ourselves into wisdom, becoming eccen-tric and deep in spite of ourselves, filled with appreciation for the preciousness of being, simply because this is the structure of existence.

In a country that is predominantly aged, government will be run by a proportion of elderly men and women who are no longer dom-inated by the need for power and recognition. Not to say that old people have no passions, but prolonged familiarity with one's own passions can lead to being unenslaved.

We will see what happens as people turn soul-deep. As in child-hood, we recall vast and uncountable insights and intimations of intangible magnificence, a remembrance of life perceived from essence. It seems sweeter than our present social norms, allowing us once more to have innocent aspirations to become the peerless people that mystery schools strove to produce: valorous and true, capable of deep compassion, of supreme beauty, of intuitive genius.

A Life Reassessed

Only a few articulate writers in middle and great age have expressed the subtle ways in which the lens of vision changes with the years. As I have lived longer, I have been seeing the earlier treasures, dramas, and goals of my life as part of a learning curve—neither intrinsically wonderful nor bad. Each year, I look back, and the turning of the glass reflects actions that were thought praiseworthy but actually caused harm, and things I judged harshly simply indicated my narrow-mindedness at the time.

In short, as I grow older and hopefully wiser, the meaning of life rests on my willingness to see that no outside goals were intrinsically important. There was no prize, after all. What is important to me is freeing myself from my conditioning, which is like a mummy wrap to unwind; a long life can become an endless concatenation of professions, travels, and relationships all bound by the same limiting point of view. The merry-go-round of personal likes and dislikes finally loses power. Eventually, I want to come Home. Home to the soul. Home to my miraculous nature, to my vast and precious essence.

As the natural human psyche yearns for spaciousness, the quality of our day-to-day lives again becomes important to us. Only when our lives matter will we genuinely care for the rest of life on Earth. But so long as we stay on the fast track, we will continue to generate a kind of carelessness—a karma to regret. The fast track is leading to a crisis of meaning among the privileged and a crisis of survival among the poor. It is about to displace indigenous elderly in countries like Indonesia where global technology is just beginning to make profound changes in space, participation, and family. The fact that we can be instantly anywhere, see anyone, and be cared for from a distance means that we will encounter human needs that are independent of culture. To live in such a world, we will need greater ability to communicate innermost desires and subtleties of observation and feeling.

Most of us were not taught how to communicate our moods, reactions, expectations, and needs in a clear and nonviolent manner. Until we can express ourselves, we lack the primary tools of relationship. Very decrepit people in nursing homes can now communicate and converse with family members by e-mail—a reassuring collapse of distance. But lack of expressive skill often prevents the satisfaction of shared intimacy.

The depth of personal satisfaction we receive from a family visit also comes from hugs and energetic exchanges that don't demand digital skill. As we rely more and more on a digital medium like the Internet, we will need to be able to translate our feelings into the medium. The ability to have nonlocal energy exchanges means that spiritual connection can happen on the Internet, just as it happens in distant healing. One of my mystery school groups has experienced resonance through a chat room, and I have been astounded to feel how profound the mutual resonance becomes even though we are very different individuals spread around the United States and concentrating for only a few moments. Conscious use of subtle energy could become a deep well for using the Internet to enhance healing and inspiration. Indeed, silent moments of deep resonance on the Web may surreptitiously contribute to the spread of compassion. This is another way in which a seed population of elderly, realized people could begin to lift the vibrancy of the world.

The poet Delmore Schwartz said that "Life is the school in which we learn" and "Time is the fire in which we burn." When we have been burned clean, we will have no other possibility than to live from essence and in harmony with universal law.

★★★

Gay Gaer Luce is the founder and has been the leader for the past 16 years of the Nine Gates Mystery School, which teaches individuals how to more effectively tap into their personal energy and spirituality. In the 1970s, Luce founded SAGE, a program for growth and spiritual community among the elderly. She is an internationally known science writer and the author of five books, including *Body Time* and *Longer Life, More Joy*.

IN GOD
WE TRUST

AN AMERICAN PRAYER

Michael Lerner

We awaken to a new day. We open our eyes on the unimaginable beauty of the world around us. As dreams recede, we resolve to maintain our connection with the unlimited layers of complexity through which we were swimming as we slept, even as we arrive at our current level of consciousness.

We move to morning exercises. Some of us stay inside our homes; others take to the streets, which are filled with people similarly engaged in tuning and attending to their bodies. We are aware now of our bodies—complex systems of openings and closings, secreting and pumping, of consciousness and feeling. How amazing our bodies are! We thank the universe and take a moment to appreciate and fully recognize the miracles that are going on within us.

The eyes that bring us visual stimuli, the ears that make it possible to hear, the nose and mouth that bring us taste and sensual pleasures and the capacity to talk and sing—thank you. We acknowledge our lungs, which have been working for us night and day, transforming air into useful oxygen and pushing out CO_2 to nourish the plants and trees. We no longer poison our lungs as people did only half a century ago, when every breath brought in environmental hazards and many lungs succumbed to cancer.

Thank you, lungs. And thank you, heart. We envision the

complex system that circulates our blood, delivering food and oxygen to every cell while removing waste materials. Thank you, blood system! And thank you, stomach and genitals, which participate in the processes of food absorption and the elimination of what we don't need. Thank you for the many joys of sexual pleasure and sensual ecstasies that we've enjoyed. We envision our entire nervous systems and our brains, and we recognize their unbelievable complexity.

Again, filled with joy, we accept the ways in which human beings are ongoing miracles. We take time each day to stop what we are doing and revisit this place of deep marvel. Thank you, God, and thank you, universe, for making us this embodiment of wonder.

Once, a half-century ago, our cities were filled with automobiles. Now that we've developed a beautifully maintained mass transit system, mostly underground, the streets are given over to bike lanes and devices that help those who need assistance going from their homes to the nearest transit entrances. Some former thoroughfares are reserved for jogging, but many have been filled with flowers and trees.

Everywhere we look, people are praying, singing, or, in those areas designated for quiet, meditating. Some people call on the prayers of traditional religious communities, while others have created their own. On certain city streets, poets assemble each morning to offer their latest compositions. Some elicit raucous laughter or inspire playfulness; others lament moments of failed connections; still others share their visions of the next stops in the development of consciousness.

We value our poets and musicians, our artists and our gardeners, our writers of short stories and novels, and all those who are involved in bringing beauty into our physical and emotional lives. Such people are employed by the commonwealth to write and paint and sculpt and create, so that when we take breaks from our own work, we can be enriched and inspired. Some write or paint about the good old days, when no one paid attention to their work and they were scorned and struggling outsiders (and some do their best to retain that position, denouncing all that is happening around them). But most have been able to retain their critical perspectives even though people appreciate their work and honor their creativity. The society as a whole ensures that they are able to enjoy the blessing of material well-being that has become the common legacy of the human race now that we have reoriented economic production and dramatically scaled down consumption.

We go to work with a feeling of excitement and joy. Work has been reconstituted so that we only do those things that are absolutely necessary to provide a joyous and comfortable life for one another. With unnecessary production a thing of the past, and with all humans voluntarily reducing their levels of consumption so that they can live lives of graceful simplicity, the total workload has been reduced to 5 hours a day. Work has been spread over 7 hours each day, however, to ensure an adequate amount of time for exercise, prayer, meditation, artistic expression, or simply playing with one another. There's a midday break that's long enough to allow coworkers to organize intramural sports or to watch videos, surf the Web, or attend lectures or political meetings. Public spaces have been shaped to make all of these activities possible in every neighborhood.

Work still has elements of drudgery, but we're comforted by the knowledge that what we are doing is for the well-being of everyone. We also know that all of the good things we enjoy in our own lives come from everyone else similarly committing their time and energy.

We begin each workday by reviewing what our particular employer is seeking to accomplish and how this objective relates to the larger goal of sustaining the planet. If we believe that our managers have lost touch with our mission or are no longer serving a higher, spiritual purpose, we can request a meeting of all employees to discuss these issues. Many workplaces have been reconstituted by workers who felt such a need, so we know that raising these issues will not bring us disdain but rather respect and appreciation. Supervisors are elected by the workers, and they can be recalled and replaced should they lose their sensitivity to workers' needs.

We know that one of the goals of work is to foster an environment in which our own spiritual capacities become manifest. We are not judged or punished for small failures, and we support one another so that we may all "go for" our highest level of fulfillment. There are enough workers engaged in each vital task to ensure that the critical work gets done with time to spare for paying attention to one another. We've all seen videos of the old days, when workers frantically produced newer and more consumer goods and competed for money and power. Happily, those days are over. Today, we know that the process is more important than the product, that there will be enough food and electricity and community services for everyone, and that the most vital thing we can create together is spiritual centeredness and balance.

Some of us may choose to start each workday with a few moments of silence to restore our inner balance. Others may begin with a song or with warm embraces for coworkers. What all of us have agreed to do is to stay attuned to our highest visions, even as we attend to the details of our work.

When we break for prayer, play, meditation, or to surf the Web or attend a meeting or cultural event, we momentarily reconnect with our center and then to the Unity of all Being. We allow ourselves to experience our connectedness to others—not only to humans but to all other life forms and to the universe as a whole. We walk outside and once again experience the magnificence of the ordered cycles of creation. We include ourselves and one another in the miracles that we experience. We see the face of the Divine in one another, and so feel surrounded by God's presence. We feel close to the ground of being, and we are filled with joy and humility at the grandeur of creation, including the grandeur of all that we, momentary manifestations of the Spirit of God, have been able to create.

We are particularly joyful for the cosmic multiplicity that confronts us wherever we turn. There is no one "right way" to do anything. People continually delight one another by incorporating their own ethnic, religious, spiritual, and cultural heritages into everyday activities. The old animosities and prejudices have been vanquished, and our city streets are awash in a multicultural festival of sights and sounds.

Yet, no matter how exciting it is to be alive in this society, we know that our spiritual centers need to be in balance. The first step in that process is to quiet our minds, which readily race to take in all that delights us. We do this by regularly engaging in a few minutes of meditation.

Meditation trains us to recognize and accept our various states of mind. We sit quietly, noticing how our minds wander, and then gently focus on something specific—often on our breathing, but sometimes on a particularly evocative phrase or mantra.

The more we succeed in quieting the mind, the more receptive it is to the Unity of All Being, and the less frenetic we become. We know that we can be misled by momentary excitement, so we sit and allow ourselves to relax, to experience fully the interconnectedness of everything. We are not seeking a society in which excitement has been eliminated, only one in which we can continually recenter ourselves so that our actions are congruent with our highest visions.

Although we've succeeded in restructuring society to provide for ecological sanity and spiritual growth, we still have the ongoing task of overcoming our egos and the tendency to put ourselves and our needs at the center of the universe. Naturally, the ego imagines that it can control everything around us, so part of our spiritual work each day is to identify the many ways in which we are not in control. We review our lives and acknowledge that much of what has happened to us has been a matter of circumstance and not of our own choosing or shaping. We contemplate our coming deaths and accept that we are merely momentary manifestations of the divine energy of the universe. In doing so, we strengthen our capacity to take control of those aspects of our lives that we can and should control: loving others, serving others, and living each moment to the fullest.

In fact, it is when we are most in touch with our limitations and have quieted our minds and momentarily restrained our egos that we can begin to comprehend one of the deep truths that fill the consciousness of every being: We are enough, and there is enough. We don't have to do anything special to be wonderful manifestations of the Divine—we already are. Yet this thought does not incite us to inactivity. The more we realize that we are enough, the more fully we can experience the joys of creativity and the pleasures of serving one another through socially useful activities. Knowing this truth allows us to drop all frenetic activity aimed at self-enhancement and to focus on the real task at hand. No longer crippled by doubts about self-worth and the value of our activities, we return to our work after the meditative break feeling blessed to have the opportunity to be useful.

There are inevitably moments, both at work and in our personal lives, when we will make mistakes, say things that are inappropriate and potentially hurtful to others, step on sensitivities that we did not know were there, or revert to ways of treating one another that came from the legacy of human cruelty and pain that has not yet fully been extinguished. So, each day we make time to engage in acts of repentance and atonement for not being able to share our love with those around us.

We return from work filled with joyful energy and excited to see friends, family, and loved ones. Our central spiritual practice after work is to give love to all whom we encounter. We know that there is no shortage of love, and that the more we give to others, the more we will have to give. We are no longer engaged, as previous generations were, in calculations about how much to give and what reward we should receive. We do not focus on whether any particular person has given back to us as much as we have given to him. Rather, we feel bathed in love because people are pouring it out into the world. We give for the pure joy of giving to others, and we receive that love in return.

The love that we receive from others is only one manifestation of the loving energy that pervades the universe. We know that we are the beneficiaries of a legacy that has been pouring through each generation for tens of thousands of years, a legacy rooted in God's love for us that led to our creation as beings capable of experiencing and sharing that love. So, as families and communities gather to share their meals, many of us choose to dedicate 15 to 20 minutes first to its grandeur and goodness. There are those who celebrate in other ways, and no attempt is made to put those people down. We respect the solitude of others, insist on their privacy and their right to forgo participation, recognizing that each can find his or her own way to God, including ways that deny God or reject spiritual language.

As day turns to night, we are filled with humility at our small place in this vast universe. We envision our planet, the Earth, moving slowly around the Sun, which is a million times bigger. We see our Sun as one of millions of stars and our galaxy as one of the 50 billion galaxies that scientists tell us fill this universe. We know that we will soon be dead and another generation will come after us to look up at this same sky, experience the same awe. But this is our moment. Surrounded by those whom we love, we join in song and dance to celebrate the many joys of being alive.

★★★

Michael Lerner is the editor of *Tikkun*, a magazine focused on spiritual healing and societal transformation. He is the author of *Spirit Matters, Jewish Renewal*, and *The Politics of Meaning*, among other books. Awarded a MacArthur Fellowship for his work in public health in the 1970s and 1980s, he currently serves as the rabbi of Beyt Tikkun synagogue in San Francisco.

THE SOUL

Deepak Chopra

One of the most striking phenomena at the dawn of the 21st century is the great yearning to reconnect with the soul that millions of people are expressing. People talk about their souls much more than they used to, and books extolling the care of the soul have become amazingly popular. I say "amazingly" because the 20th century did everything it could to crush the soul. The human soul could be the first item on anyone's endangered species list, for what is more soul-killing than the 20th century's invention of concentration camps, world war, mass refugees, genocide, and totalitarianism?

What all these soul-killers have in common is that they deny the sacredness of human life. The soul, whatever it may be, is our speck of the sacred. The current fascination with the soul therefore marks a swing away from horror and dehumanization. People want to believe that the soul is real.

My vision is that in the new millennium, our longing to know that we have souls will actually be fulfilled. In the 21st century, the soul could be reborn.

Of course, if your soul is immortal, it doesn't need to be reborn. In the ancient Vedas of India, it is said that there is a part of yourself that does not believe in death and therefore cannot die. What cannot die also cannot be born. To prove the existence of the soul, we would have to prove that inside you is a speck of spirit that was never born and can never die. It is this proof that I mean when I refer to the rebirth of the soul.

The first birth of the soul, its first appearance in human awareness, was religious. In the religious view, our souls came from God and will return to God after death. Although some religions do not adhere to this simple outlook, most faiths ask us to believe that we are more than mortal flesh and blood. If you are religious, you harbor a profound conviction that your soul connects you to God, and the struggle of the soul—whether it is cast down and troubled or joyous and raised in triumph—is the life of spirit in traditions of both the East and the West.

Yet religion did not manage to make the soul stick. If it had, we would never have heard the terrible words "Auschwitz," "H-bomb," "ethnic cleansing," "terrorism," and all those other signifiers of violence that depends on mass ignorance of the soul.

In the 21st century, the second birth of the soul will stick. I say this with some confidence because for almost 100 years we have been staring directly at the proof of the soul. It has been as plain as love, truth, and beauty—to name other invisible things of which we are certain. Yet proof of the soul comes from a strange place, a place that not only has no religion in it, but seems to contradict religion.

Quantum physics, the greatest intellectual triumph of the 20th century, has made the spiritual worldview completely believable. Albert Einstein and his brilliant cohorts saw beyond the horizon of time and space; they went into the invisible domain where the soul must also exist. In going there, however, they did not pack religious words in their suitcases. Instead of *God* and *soul*, they packed words such as *quark*, *neutrino*, *relativity*, and *wormhole*. These words mean little to ordinary people, even to this day, and the fact that they refer to the soul's territory comes as a revelation. Only a handful of physicists have realized (as Einstein did) that a theory of the cosmos must inevitably be a theory of how God's mind works. Both aim at the ultimate source of reality.

To make the soul stick, the obscurity of quantum theory has to become clear and simple enough that people will say, "Ah, so that's what my soul is." Religion did not accomplish this, because although religion certainly entered our living rooms, the best that most people can say, after a couple of millennia of dogma, is, "Maybe I have a soul. Who knows?" This isn't good enough to inspire a radical change in human nature from violence to peace, from alienation to love. As the devastatingly honest French writer Simone Weil has said, "In what concerns divine things, belief is not appropriate. Only certainty will do. Anything less than certainty is unworthy of God." The same is true of the soul.

The soul is that part of consciousness that exists beyond body and mind. Time and space are the glass through which we view the soul. Causation is the mechanics through which the soul acts in the world. Surprisingly, the soul behaves very much like the subatomic world that physicists explore. There are some startling similarities.

- In the quantum world, there are no material things, only possibility waves. In other words, a quantum event can potentially occur in two places at the same time. The same is true of consciousness: You can converse with me and worry about your mother's health at the same time.
- In the quantum world, two subatomic particles, even though they may be at separate ends of the universe, can be in communication with each other, correlating their activities even though they don't exchange signals. This is called nonlocal, acausal relationship. Your consciousness operates in a similar way. When you start to think, you activate different parts of your brain, which in microscopic terms are the equivalent of millions of miles apart. All these different parts are in communication with one another. Their activities are correlated, even though there are no electrical or other signals being exchanged between them. Your consciousness orchestrates quantum mechanical nonlocal, acausal interrelatedness through mere intention.

◆ In the quantum realm, there is a phenomenon known as the quantum leap. A particle can move from one location to another without traveling through the space in between. Similarly, your consciousness can in one moment be in New York and the next moment in New Delhi without having to go through Europe in between.

◆ The Heisenberg uncertainty principle operates in the quantum world. You can't know both the position and the momentum of a particle at the same time. Similarly, your consciousness can be focused either on the content of thought or on the stream of consciousness but not both at the same time.

◆ Before a subatomic particle appears from the infinite void, it exists as a potential in that infinite void. So too, your thoughts, before you have them, exist only as possibility. They reside in your soul, which, like the quantum void, has no location in space and time.

What we are learning from these insights is that even though your soul is without dimension and beyond space and time, it is real—just as real as the quantum reality that gives birth to the whole material universe. Your soul gives birth to your mind and body. In the Bhagavad Gita, Lord Krishna says of the soul, "Water cannot wet it, wind cannot dry it, fire cannot burn it, weapons cannot shatter it, because it is ancient, unborn, and never dies."

The real you—your soul—is the potential that creates all your reality, including your physical body and mind. Your wholeness lies in the invisible but pregnant possibilities that your life unfolds. One life can express only a tiny fraction of the richness that your soul keeps in its treasure trove of infinity.

The five parallels between quantum mechanics and the soul could be infinitely expanded, because quantum theory is incredibly ambitious. It aims at nothing less than TOE, the physicist's shorthand for a theory of everything. My concern is just the soul, which plays little part in physics and yet—I think we would all agree—certainly cannot be left out of a theory of everything.

These five parallels describe the kind of thing your soul is.

- ◆ Your soul is universal—it is not located in any one place.
- ◆ Your soul relates to you without any connectors that you can see, touch, or hear.
- ◆ Your soul gives rise to new and creative impulses, seemingly out of the blue.
- ◆ Your soul's status in the everyday world is uncertain, yet you can be certain of it by setting aside everyday rules.
- ◆ Your soul is the potential for everything in your reality, the possibility that your mind turns into actuality.

If I had all the space in the world, I could connect these spiritual assertions to facts about the quantum world, facts that science uses to make particle accelerators and even the transistors in your bedside clock. In this limited space, however, we can highlight only the most important conclusion, which is this: *At every moment, your soul is turning virtual reality—the invisible realm beyond time and space—into your slice of material reality.* This process is the entire basis of life; without it, nothing could exist.

The quantum pioneers took an astounding leap when they said that everything visible has roots in the invisible, that all things in time spring from the timeless, and that all certainties are actually mysteries, when you come right down to it. If religion had proved the same facts about the soul, we would know that our souls exist as surely as Einstein knew that the speed of light was an absolute number, beyond which nothing in the cosmos can reach.

Like the universe, you are both relative and absolute. The relative part is made up of everything you think, do, desire, will, and perform. The absolute part is the potential to do all those things. In a coma, you lose the ability to connect relative and absolute, despite the fact that nothing material about you changes much. Going to sleep at night, you erase your personality, your memories, and your likes and dislikes. Yet when you wake up the next morning—or when you come out of a coma—you are there, reborn in an instant, complete with your sense of identity. That you were not erased during the night (the way a computer's random-access memory is erased when you turn it off) is because part of you rests in your soul, untouched by space/time events.

In the 21st century, more and more people will realize that the soul is a switching station between space/time and the virtual realm—or between Earth and Heaven, as religious believers may put it. It is easy to accept that a mountain can be broken down into tiny atoms, and it is not much harder to accept that atoms are made of vibrating energy. But quantum physics teaches us that energy can be broken down into nothing. A cubic centimeter of empty space, the pure void of cold blackness, contains more virtual energy than a blazing star. If you can grasp this abrupt leap from something to nothing, from solid to intangible, from energy to potential, from action to possibility, you have grasped your soul.

The cosmos is a vast, churning machine for turning one level of reality into another, and so are you. The most creative act anyone can perform, far in excess of anything achieved by Leonardo da Vinci, is the act of creating reality. This is done from the soul level as follows:

◆ Eternity is sliced up into bits of time.
◆ The void is compacted into bits of matter.
◆ Creation is incubated in the womb of possibility.
◆ Memory gives birth to new perceptions.
◆ The cosmic I becomes the individual I.
◆ Nonlocal events are organized to fit together.
◆ Intelligence unfolds.
◆ God's mind knows itself.
◆ Grace (the loving intent of God) orders all events.

All the great spiritual masters wanted us to see ourselves in this light, as the universal self coming into the world to experience the human self. You are the whole point of the cosmic dance. The entire universe has conspired to bring about this very second in your existence. Why should you believe that you are a paltry creature who is born and dies, when every atom since the big bang testifies to your real status? The human self should rejoice every day that it has a soul, not because the soul gets you to Heaven, but because you are already there—and here at the same time. This quantum paradox is made beautiful in our own lives, where ecstasy is possible in the midst of so much fog and confusion.

The soul isn't a luxury, but a necessity. A necessity implies that we already know our souls, and yet we don't. Let me show how we can bring this necessity to life. In a room with a large grandfather clock, you are reading a book. You notice that you have been so absorbed in your book that you have not heard the clock ticking. Certainly, the sound was there. Vibrations were set up in the air, these vibrations reached the ear, and the ear sent the appropriate signals to the brain. Yet even with these mechanics in place, you did not hear the clock. The reason is that your mind was not engaged with it. The physical world, with all its activity, is not enough to register in your consciousness. It is not present without the mind, even when every step all the way to the brain is present.

The mind itself, however, is still not enough. Your mind can be distracted, its powers wax and wane, and in sleep, the mind doesn't even operate. It takes the soul to awaken the mind and give it direction.

When the soul sends its signals to you, there is a cascade of consciousness. This is like a waterfall made of light. At the top is the soul, which shines by itself and comprehends all that you are. Its intention is communicated down to the mind, the mind awakens the brain, through which it interprets the signals from the ear, and the ear receives the raw data of the physical world, which is just meaningless vibration. The same is true of all five senses. This cascade tells us how reality is created by the soul. The soul is the maker of reality, subjective and objective.

In quantum terms, we would say that the invisible subatomic void vibrates, sending energy waves that become organized into particles, the particles into matter, and matter into the complex structures of the brain. Finally, these structures close the circle by registering signals from the five senses as reality.

The two processes—the cascade of consciousness and the quantum mechanics of perception—are exactly the same. Thus, you are a particular form of your soul, as this world is a particular form of the all-embracing quantum realm.

I foresee that once enough people get over their nagging doubts about whether human life is sacred, they will leap to the conclusion that the only sane way to live is from the level of the soul. And as more of us get in touch with our souls, we will also recognize that our souls occupy three domains of existence simultaneously: the personal domain, the collective domain, and the universal domain. Getting in touch with our souls will begin a process in which we learn that we are inextricably woven into the patterns of intelligence that structure not only our collective society, but the whole cosmos.

What, then, of America? I see America taking a leadership role in restoring what ancient traditions called dharma. Dharma is the unique relationship that we have with one another and with the larger web of life, the ecosystem, the biosphere that nurtures and contains us. As a result of discovering our souls, we will begin to heal our extended body—Mother Earth. And we will ensure not only her survival, but also her health and well-being, her grandeur, and her beauty.

It seems that nature—the cosmos, the Earth—is becoming self-conscious through us, through the human nervous system. This is a great privilege, and as human beings we have the responsibility to ensure that there is balance in the ecosystem and the biosphere.

In Vedanta, the ancient Indian system of philosophy, it is said that when a society loses its karma, evil becomes manifest. It is difficult for people to understand just how closely natural catastrophes, holocausts, or the reign of tyrants can be related to loss of karma. But the turbulence of our minds and of our consciousness disturbs the information and energy fields of the larger ecosystem of which we are a part.

Normally, there's an exquisite balance maintained between the forces of entropy and decay on one hand, and the forces of evolution and creativity on the other hand. When our collective choices disturb that balance, disease results—whether that disease is in our individual bodies, in the collective body that we call society, or in the extended body that we call nature. It is in this way that our loss of soul in the past century has led to such evil.

Our collective choices are crucial in maintaining a balance that prevents the birth of evil. As we discover our souls and become intimate with the three domains of existence—the personal, the collective, and the universal—we will experience true compassion, love, and healing. Ultimately, this is the only solution: love, not as a mere sentiment, but as the ultimate truth at the heart of creation, the truth that we are all the same spirit in different disguises.

How must we act as individuals to help achieve this harmony? There are four ways:

◆ *The way of action:* We each do what we feel we must to uphold the karma in action. Upholding the karma means making choices that nurture the larger web of life. It means having an inner attitude that what we are doing comes from God and belongs to God, that every movement we make is a divine movement that is part of the eternal. This is what it means to act from the soul level. It is a level where we can be engaged and detached at the same time. From this place, we can uproot evil, not out of a sense of self-righteous morality or anger, but because it's the right thing to do. In this way, we become cosmic warriors.

◆ *The way of love:* We make love the determining factor in every choice we make.

◆ *The way of spiritual discipline:* We get in touch with our souls through spiritual disciplines such as meditation and prayer. As the poet Alfred, Lord Tennyson, said, more things are wrought by prayer than this world dreams of.

◆ *The way of scientific understanding:* We come to understand that our souls are the only reality and that everything else is impermanent. It is in that everpresent witnessing awareness of soul that the whole cosmos arises and disappears. So, by knowing our souls, we can know everything.

How can we spread these lessons? There is only one way. This knowledge has to become part of the curriculum for teaching our children. We teach them everything about the world, but nothing about themselves.

We must teach them a spirituality that transcends traditional religious thought. We must teach them that when you relate to any other person, your assumption must be, "You and I co-create this world, we both intend the best for it, our substance is the same, and so is our status in the universal eye." This isn't wishful thinking, but pure, stark, quantum truths.

Someone of deep religious conviction may object that I have left out love and God from this curriculum. I left out both on purpose, because once you realize how quickly love turns to hate, once you regard the bloody wars fought in the name of God, your allegiance shifts. You feel that the old religious truths are not enough to bind a new world.

That doesn't mean that you should discard them. The concepts of love and God are precious, but they need to be reborn, just as the soul does. Love should be the impulse of the soul, received from the universe and given to others universally. God should be the One and All, a reality that cannot be divided into fractious faiths.

I heard a man on television talking in worshipful tones about a media idol—it could have been any golden, youthful celebrity—and someone commented, "But you know you're just talking about an image. In reality there is only an ordinary person with a job he hates and a ton of insecurity, like the rest of us."

"So what?" the man retorted. "If the only alternative is reality, then reality offends me."

This striking response applies tenfold to the soul. Compared to our vision of a transcendent self who knows all, understands all, loves all, and forgives all, who wants drab reality? Why risk turning God into yet another of life's big disappointments? The great thing would be to find that reality matched the vision. It takes courage to ask to meet God face-to-face, but the rewards would be infinitely satisfying.

What if the whole world is topsy-turvy? Instead of God being a vast, imaginary projection, he could be the only thing that is real. So-called miracles might be normal. Certainly our hearts yearn for them, and their shining promise lifts the heart as nothing else can. Quantum theory is not a place to turn to for love. But it tells us that there is an unknown realm that is our source, and it hints that this unknown place is infinite, intelligent, capable of organizing the entire universe, full of possibilities, without end.

The unknown is God in one inescapable regard: It is the only place where you can truly know the fate of your soul. In the 21st century, everyday events will take care of themselves and human nature will roll along a course well-charted by philosophy and psychology. Only the unknown can change this course, and the unknown is inside ourselves. Revere this place. When you can embrace it fully, the supreme miracle—a world that can finally live in peace and love— must occur.

★★★

Acknowledged as one of the world's greatest leaders in the field of mind-body medicine, Deepak Chopra, M.D., is the founder and head of the Chopra Center for Well Being and is known worldwide for his teachings and writings on health and the soul. He was the chief of staff at Boston Regional Medical Center and taught at several prominent medical schools before embarking on a quest in the 1980s to expand our healing approaches through the integration of the best of Western medicine with natural healing and spiritual traditions. He is the author of 25 books and more than 100 audio, video, and CD-ROM titles. His newest book is *How to Know God: The Soul's Journey into the Mystery of Mysteries*.

INTUITION

James Redfield

I believe we all know, at the deepest level of intuition, that the human world is changing. The shift has been slow and gradual, but the polling data accumulated over the last decade is unmistakable. We are becoming more spiritual. A Gallup Poll from November 1999 contains an amazing finding: Between 1994 and 1998, the number of people reporting that spiritual growth was a very important part of their lives increased from 59 to 84 percent, and all indications suggest that this trend is continuing.

The use of the word *growth* in the poll and the positive reaction it elicited may, in fact, shed light on precisely how we are changing. If in the past our spirituality has been defined more by a system of belief, now our sense of the spiritual seems to be moving deeper—toward actual experiences of spirituality. For thousands of years, mystics of every religious tradition have described experiences that go far beyond an intellectual understanding, that give us a sense of being expanded and evolved; in short, experiences that provide a sense of spiritual growth. I believe that we are now searching for and discovering these experiences as never before.

Moreover, I believe that this shift toward a deeper spirituality, although quiet now, will turn out to be one of the most dramatic in history. In effect, it will usher in what can only be called a new spiritual worldview that will ultimately transcend the old Newtonian/Cartesian view of life that has ruled the West, and increasingly the East, for so long. For 500 years or more, this scientific ethos has reduced the universe to its base material components and irrationally sought to push away any hint of the miraculous or spiritual mystery from our everyday lives. In this old reality, humans were thought to have evolved accidentally, or to have been pushed into existence by a distant force, and now are left alone to forge out a living with their wills against a dead and impartial natural world. Of course, our years of materialism no doubt have been part of a necessary evolution. Faced with a chaotic medieval culture of corrupt churches, charlatans, and salvation-for-sale, our emphasis on rationalism was important. We established the scientific method as a way to build a consensus about the world around us. But there were problems from the beginning.

In an uneasy truce with the church, science focused first on the simplest and most concrete phenomenon: the outer, physical universe. Because the need was mainly to make the world orderly for technology and commerce, science tended to stop there and to assign all inner psychic or religious phenomena to the realm of the fanciful. In this way, science suffered from and created in the masses the illusion that the universe was ordinary and devoid of miracle and mystery. That's why over the entire 20th century, the investigation of deeper spiritual experience was avoided by any scientist who wanted to be accepted by the mainstream. They were not willing to confront what I like to call the dilemma of skepticism: the fact that while a doubtful attitude is essential to logically exploring our surroundings (we don't want to jump to conclusions or adopt theories prematurely), some phenomena of life (states of awareness, extrasensory perception, etc.) are not detectable unless skepticism is suspended, at least temporarily.

Yet we can see now that the old worldview couldn't last. At some point, the blinders had to come off. Physics woke up first, totally undermining, with the work of quantum mechanics, the whole idea that we live in a commonplace world of solid matter. Atoms, once thought of as material building blocks, are now known to be composed of mysterious vibrating patterns of energy that demonstrate unbelievable characteristics, such as moving backward and forward in time, communicating across large spaces without a known medium, and spontaneously rising from and disappearing into the nothingness of the quantum void beneath them. Just as mysterious is the rising new consensus, since Einstein, about the universe. We now know it to be a place where time speeds up and slows down, where black holes possibly link multiple dimensions and parallel universes, and where time travel seems possible.

Psychology has added to the new picture, creating a fuller understanding of the transpersonal spiritual experiences available to all human beings and giving us new evidence of the intriguing powers lying latent in our own minds—including telepathy, clairvoyance, and precognition. New studies on intention and prayer are finally convincing us that our mental outlooks and attitudes move out from our minds and actually affect the state of our health (and that of others), the quality of our relationships, and even our individual destinies. Within this context, add the writings of the mystics themselves (all telling us that we can discover direct perceptual evidence that there is a spiritual dimension working in our lives), which have enjoyed unprecedented attention and discussion for more than three decades, and the scene is set for dramatic cultural change.

This is what began to happen in a mass way in the mid–20th century, and it is slowly continuing now. The mystery of life came gushing back into consciousness and we began to see human existence in a new way.

DEFINING OUR NEW WORLDVIEW

As the new millennium gets under way, I believe enough of this new viewpoint is coming together to begin to describe it cogently and to bring it more completely into our everyday awareness. All we have to do is imagine and reflect on how our experience and perception is already changing. Rather than Newton's mechanical, uncaring universe, what we see when we look out our windows now is a world that is alive, interconnected, and reflecting an intelligence beyond anything the old worldview understood.

Mountains, wild streams and rivers, the world of trees and other plants, the mysterious behavior of animals in the wild—these no longer seem commonplace or explained away by dismissive terms such as *automatic response* or *instinct*. We can feel that everything around us has an impact that goes well beyond the material or biological. We are somehow being sustained by the energy and beauty of nature at the spiritual level as well. Those who have walked the energy hills of Sedona, Arizona, or any high desert mesa or virgin forest know exactly what I'm referring to. We are boosted, empowered, and the effect can be felt and built upon.

Such newfound mystery imbues the human world as well. When we look out of our windows at the clamor of human work and activity, we now see a new mystery in the people we meet, in the conversations we have, and in the sudden manifestation of opportunity in our lives. We know that the universe around us reflects back to us a strange sort of guidance that we have grown to call synchronicity. Coined by the Swiss psychologist Carl Jung, this popular term refers to the occurrence of "meaningful coincidence," events that seem to be so timely and moving that we know them to be beyond mere chance. They feel destined. Jung argued that synchronicity is a vital operating principal in the universe, as real as the orbits of the planets or the laws of physics, and is a directing intelligence that pushes humans toward psychological and spiritual growth.

By now, we've all experienced such synchronicities. Human biographies are replete with such events and always have been. The chance meeting of a stranger brings us information that takes our careers in a new direction. We wake up in the morning, thinking about an old friend, and decide to call, hearing the familiar "I was just thinking of you" or "I have something important to tell you" coming from the person on the other end of the line. And suddenly, our lives change.

For most of us, these important coincidences represent the evidence that the mystics were talking about. We suddenly know that a divine intelligence is involved with our lives, that the working of the world is mysteriously pushing each of us toward some best destiny. The recognition of this fact always brings the same reaction: We want more of this magic flow. We want these guiding synchronicities to come more often and to be clearer in their meaning.

In this new worldview of ours, I believe we are becoming ever more centered on what we must do next. We must push even further, knock on the door with more intention, open up more fully to the mystery surrounding our lives. We must open up to a greater, spiritual side of ourselves that all the mystics declare is waiting.

A Sense of Higher Self

We know this experience can occur via many pathways—prayer, meditation, pilgrimages to sacred sites, dance and the movement arts, even transpersonal "zone" moments during sports activities. But regardless of our entry into this perception, the mystical experience is remarkably similar for each of us. We suddenly feel expanded and transformed from within. We feel lighter on our feet, as though a new energy fills us and lifts us up. Colors and shapes in our environment begin to stand out with greater presence and almost overwhelming beauty. As we look, spellbound, the world around us comes alive, and we immediately feel as though we are an integral part of the grand design behind the universe. The sensation fills us with an overwhelming sense of love and well-being. Most dramatically, our old sense of self—who we think we are as an individual—expands into a larger, higher self that feels wiser and more capable. Intuitions rush in that not only give us clarity about what we should be doing with our lives in the present, but provide a vision of what we could do in the future that would inspire us beyond anything imaginable, provided we stay on the path.

Not that this powerful experience lasts forever. We know that it does not. At some point, we find ourselves suddenly back in a world that seems too ordinary. But the inner opening of awareness has been experienced and suddenly the mysterious coincidences make more sense. We know that the flow of synchronicity is there to lead us ever closer to the maintenance of this higher-self awareness and toward the step-by-step actualization of what can only be called our path of destiny, a best life course and contribution to the world that feels like a mission.

We also notice that the flow of mysterious coincidences begin to have a certain structure. Synchronicity usually begins with an intuition, which, more precisely, is a thought that comes to our minds to do or say something. It might be an intuition to go by the bookstore or to start a conversation with a stranger. And while our egos often question the practicality or timing of our intuition, we know now that if we courageously follow our thought and go to the bookstore or risk that chance conversation, we often discover a book that leaps out at us from across the room or find ourselves in a timely discussion that mysteriously leads to an important project or advance. The role of intuition is to move us into the right place for mysterious events to unfold.

In this way, by staying in touch with our higher intuition, synchronicity begins to increase in our lives, provided that we follow one other rule. I believe our new worldview now confirms that we must always look for only positive interpretations of the events surrounding our lives. Nothing brings us down faster and stops the flow more suddenly than turning negative about our circumstances. Obviously, this is difficult, because very challenging, often traumatic events happen to everyone. People grow ill. Projects fail. We have long runs of so-called bad luck. But I believe that we have learned that in every event lies a silver lining.

Often, in order to continue to grow and progress toward our life purpose, we must come face-to-face with our own worst traits. Synchronicity brings them back into our focus until we get the message. The message may be to overcome a fear, become aware of our over-controlling, change some way we react to other people, or shift the direction of our projects. Whatever the case, a silver lining always exists, and we know that if we always find it, we can stay positive and the synchronistic flow will move us through any period of challenge into one of unbridled success.

A New Interpersonal Ethic

There is something else we know about the process of synchronicity: Most of the meaningful coincidences that occur in our lives arrive through interactions with other people. Our experience confirms that. Depending on the posture that we take toward others, we can either increase the probability that a synchronistic message will be conveyed or hamper it.

Here's what I mean. If we stay in the higher-self perspective with another and remain alert to the spiritual mystery of the moment, we can help the other move into a higher awareness as well. We can do this merely by the focus of our eyes. If we focus on and look for the higher self in the expression on the other's face and speak to this part of the other person, regardless of the content of the conversation, then something magic often begins to take place. Sometimes the other person is lifted into a higher connectiveness and awareness just by talking to us. He or she begins to feel more inwardly secure and suddenly in touch with inner intuition. Timely ideas come in, and often we are told something that moves our own lives forward. For our effort of consciously uplifting, we get back a synchronistic moment.

This new ethic of looking for the best in others is one of the most striking elements of our new worldview because it is so clearly different from the old way. In Newton's uncaring universe, one feels alone and insecure, and in spite of certain rules of politeness, others are often regarded as competition, obstacles, or devices to be used as we struggle forward in a never-ending search for power and security. In this mindset, humans are constantly trying to manipulate, control, and one-up one another with a vast array of psychological strategies and in so doing miss the true synchronistic occasion of their meeting in the first place. We can see that competition has led to all the conflict we see in the human world, but it is not a result of inherent human nature. In fact, the opposite is true.

We can see now that humans have been constantly striving all through history to transcend violence and to achieve the higher spiritual awareness contained in the worldview now emerging. The long road of human progress has been taking us not just toward a better state of material civilization, but step-by-step toward what will ultimately become a completely spiritual culture on this planet. We can see that all of human history has been a struggle of discovery and progress, completed mainly by heroic individuals who were half-consciously following the same synchronistic process that we are becoming fully aware of today. Every milestone, every great movement has been accomplished by individuals struggling to follow vague hunches and mysterious signs to make things better within the context of their times. Amazingly, the worldview that is arising today may be the first to contain an awareness of the historical/spiritual process itself and to set it up as a context for daily life.

WHERE ARE WE GOING?

What will happen as more people begin to fully adopt the new worldview that we have been discussing? How will our world change as the 21st century unfolds?

I believe that our highest intuition provides the answer. As we become more intuitive, more sensitive to our own best path of accomplishment, human progress will speed up in relative terms and we will move more quickly toward the spiritually ideal at every level.

Here's how it will happen. First, increasingly more people will move synchronistically toward their best domain of inspired work and creativity; in other words, toward that area of human life in which synchronicity is leading them to make a contribution. This inflow of inspired workers will force every part of human society, every existing institution, into a phase of introspection wherein they will begin to become conscious of their true role of service to society in general.

Look at a few examples. In the area of our legal institutions— law, justice, etc.—we currently find a system that is still half corrupt and oriented toward vested self-interest. Lawyers take cases to court that could be settled privately, or chase ambulances in order to create legal disputes where none existed before, just to create more expense and thus income for themselves. Yet, slowly, more reputable attorneys are moving the profession toward arbitration, settlement, finding true win-win situations that are fair and equitable, because this is the only way one can be a lawyer and still stay in a higher-self, intuitively directed awareness. Eventually, only those who realize that they have a gift, a talent, for resolving conflict and preventing it in the first place will want to become attorneys.

Heath care is another example. In a hundred years, physicians will be appalled at the behavior in their field today. Too often, physicians find themselves caught up in a circle of self-interest between themselves and the pharmaceutical industry, where "magic bullets" are sought as easy solutions for modern diseases that are largely related to lifestyle. Hence, we have physicians who try to maximize profits by seeing too many patients, leaving little time to stay abreast of the latest research on disease, and who react to their patients' desire for an easy fix by dispensing pills. The main source of information for both the doctor and the public in this scenario is the pharmaceutical salesman who shows up at the door or advertises on television. Yet this state of affairs is beginning to change. The image of the physician as all-knowing is thankfully fading. The American Medical Association's own research is showing the staggering number of deaths, more than a hundred thousand a year in hospitals alone, that are occurring because of legal-drug reactions or misuse. The public is finding out just how dangerous and invasive most drug therapy is—and we would have known earlier had hospitals, according to the researchers, not been actively covering up these deaths by misrepresenting the situation.

Such revelations are helping to hasten reform. As more intuitive people enter the field, medicine is moving toward a search for the true causes of disease: an individual mixture of genetic predisposition, lifestyle, and dietary and environmental factors. The toxicity of modern processed foods will be finally disclosed. (It already has been, actually, but because most doctors don't want to change their own diets, nobody gets the word.) And the true gift and talent of those meant to work in medicine-related fields will become more conscious. Those who are guided to help us heal and stay healthy are those who have an intuitive ability to assess our attitudes, resentments, reaction to foods, and secret fears and to help us come up with a true longevity plan.

In a similar fashion, the influx of intuitively and synchronistically led individuals will reform every other domain of human life toward its ideal state of functioning. Education, one of the most important institutions, will shift, as teachers using intuition, example, alternative teaching aids, and experiential modules transform this area of life from one that deals in abstraction and seldom explores the true talents of the student into one that is oriented toward facilitating spiritual growth, synchronistic perception, and the role of the student's inner dream. Science will take its role more seriously and develop ever more creative ways to explore the world, especially our inner experience. Certainly ecological science will shift toward an exploration of the psychological and spiritual benefits of keeping the natural world, most especially wilderness, healthy and vibrant. In the end, the battle to save the environment will be won not at the level of intellectual understanding but at the level of spiritual perception.

This goes for every other idealistic mission active in the world. We want to rid the planet of poverty, hatred, overpopulation, tyrannical governments, and its pockets of violence. To do so, we can't uplift at the level of logic alone, teaching people to follow a road of self-interest to acquire a better life. Rather, we have to stay in a place of higher-self awareness, remembering our interpersonal ethic, and thus share with and uplift people in need toward both a logical course of action and an enhanced synchronistic perception, instructing them in how to take advantage of every intuition, every mysterious opportunity. What is being added here, again, as each institution moves toward its ideal functioning, is an amplification of an evolution that has always operated behind the scenes. We're just making the whole spiritual process of human evolution more conscious. In this process, each person will voice his or her deepest intuition and vision to everyone else in a kind of ideal democratic interaction, one that will eventually transform politics as well.

TRUTH IN POLITICS

Currently in the United States we have an immensely embarrassing political system where the two major parties try to out-maneuver and one-up each other in the arena of public opinion. In the last few national elections, this tendency has increased to the point of absurdity in a kind of distortion politics, where Madison Avenue firms are hired to make the other side look bad by any means necessary. Supposedly, Democrats want only to tax people and spend the surplus, setting up giant bureaucracies and eroding personal freedoms with their do-gooder projects; Republicans want to hand over the country to a venal corporate culture in which most citizens are helpless pawns as the world's resources and environments are demolished in the limitless pursuit of greed. Neither view is really true.

This amplification of distortion and growing lack of regard for the truth is no doubt setting up the system for an overhaul, and in light of our discussion, I believe we can already see what will happen. As politics is pushed toward its more ideal functioning, one main truth will emerge: that the political parties came about because they allowed our nation to evolve through a kind of practical political dialectic.

The Democrats represent the push for change, the voicing of what is wrong with the country and what needs to be fixed. But the party has a weakness. Its drive to fix things entails trying to get people to behave differently or actually legislating that they do so. Democrats currently want to control public education more completely, pass more gun regulation, enlarge Medicare. The Republican party, on the other hand, focuses on the protection of individual freedoms. They constantly ask why more regulation is necessary. Why can't there be a tax cut? But they drag their feet whenever a proposal to fix things is offered. Their weakness is that, too often, they're against everything.

Obviously, for our nation to progress and handle new problems, both orientations are necessary. We need some people to be constantly pushing to make things better, and we need others to watch that individual liberties are not unduly limited. The key is that the dialogue be truthful so the public can participate in the decision to push ahead or pull back at any given time. As more people engage in politics from a higher, intuitive level, the first thing our intuition will sniff out is who is telling us the truth and who is not. Distortion is already turning so many of the voters off that the practice will eventually fall of its own weight and we will begin, in fact, to demand the opposite in the behavior of our politicians. We will elevate the great liberal and conservative debate to a new, more spiritual dimension, as both sides vie for the public's support by telling their version of the truth with the greatest authenticity. Imagine it—politics becoming more spiritual. It will happen because we intend it to be so.

USING THE POWER OF INTENTION

There is one final aspect of our new worldview, one that is perhaps the most challenging and important if we are going to participate fully in bringing about the reforms we intuit. Imagining is one thing— using our intention to actively help bring about this new world is something else. We are rethinking and mastering this power within us that has always been called intention and prayer. In the old worldview, Descartes established a fine division between our minds and the outer world; we could think about things around us, name them, use them, but our minds could not directly affect the natural world—they were separate. Yet the mystics have always suggested otherwise. They warned that attitudes matter, that faith and expectation and prayer is a force that does, in fact, have influence. As noted earlier, scientists have turned their attention to studying this power with careful experiments, and the findings have been nothing short of remarkable. This research has been documented now in great detail by popularizers such as Larry Dossey, M.D., and the information is beginning to change the way we view the power of our minds.

In one famous study, a cardiologist, Dr. Randolph Byrd, divided selected heart patients into two groups, then recruited volunteers to pray for one group and not the other. The findings were spectacular. The group that was prayed for had overwhelmingly fewer requirements for medication, fewer surgeries, fewer deaths—they did better in every way. This study has now been replicated many times. In related research, individuals have retarded the growth of bacteria in laboratory conditions, increased the growth of nerve cells, and altered the results of a machine designed to produce random sets of numbers, all by using visualization, prayer, or focused intention.

From these and numerous other studies, as well as from the mystical literature, our new understanding and experience of prayer seems to be coming together in the following way. Prayer and intention definitely have an effect. But prayer from a higher-self connection works better, especially if it is done with a faithful visualization, a clear affirmation that it will indeed work. When we truly expect results, prayer has greater power. But of course, this fact has ominous implications that we all must take to heart, because if it is true that affirmative prayer has the greatest effect, then it follows that any affirmation is in some sense a prayer—even if the expectation we hold is less than positive.

For instance, think of a tyrant or terrorist that makes the world news, someone who has committed terrible acts. If we think of him as evil, as a person capable of diabolical deeds, and we affirm this idea of him in our beliefs about the world, we are then sending a wave of prayer that acts to keep him in that mindset. We are in effect praying for him to be that way. Conversely, if we hold a firm belief that this individual, as horrible as his behavior is, is capable of rising into a higher-self awareness like every other human being, and if we affirm that image, then we are in effect helping to move him in the direction of positive growth and increased attention to conscience.

Such a new understanding of intention and prayer applies to the everyday criticisms we make about one another, or about ourselves for that matter. If we secretly think we are incapable of handling some challenge, for instance, or that we can never experience the same degree of higher awareness as the mystics, then that is the prayer effect we are creating around us. But again, thankfully, the opposite is also true. If we affirm daily that our lives can be filled with the mysterious flow of destiny, and that the world around us can continue to progress toward the ideal, then this is the field, the prayer effect, that we are sending into the world with our minds.

BEING BOLD

When will this new worldview emerge completely, to be the prevailing reality in human culture? I believe the answer depends on how seriously we practice this new outlook, and how bold we are. At this point, it is not enough to look out of our windows and see a new world, or even to have experienced it at times. The materialistic view nags and pulls at us to slip back into the old, habitually stressed out, manipulative way of life. We have to remind ourselves each morning to find our higher-self awareness and to set a prayer field that goes out the door ahead of us and expects, visualizes, faithfully projects that we and others stay in this higher place.

And we must proclaim what is happening to those who cross our path. The emergence of this new worldview is occurring mainly through a kind of person-to-person contagion between people, where one person sees others operating from a higher self-perception, notices the higher energy level, the sense of well-being, the perception of synchronicity, and realizes that this is a more fully functioning approach to life that must be explored.

Our conversation with such a person is very important. Often it begins with very skeptical inquiries. How do we know that synchronicity is real? Is the higher-self experience an illusion? If in the past we tended to shrink back from such questions, I think now we are beginning to answer truthfully and boldly. No, there isn't yet scientific agreement on these perceptions, but there is evidence. It is the evidence of one's own experience. These perceptions can be discovered and proven on one's own.

If the person remains skeptical, then we can just wink and smile and tell him not to worry. Sooner or later, the awareness will find him. It's guaranteed, it's certain, it's inevitable. . . . It's the purpose of existence itself.

★★★

James Redfield is the author of the international best-sellers *The Celestine Prophecy* and *The Tenth Insight*. His newest book is *The Secret of Shambhala*, a spiritual adventure exploring the power of prayer, intention, and human destiny.

RELIGION

Thomas Moore

The past 100 years in America has been a high-speed ride into the future. Everyone talks about how quickly life is changing. But creeping along beneath the surface of our hyperactive inventiveness is a slow-moving but steady story about the nature of things, about the meaning of life, and about purpose. We imagine ourselves to be evolving, and especially to be sophisticating ourselves out of the dark ages of superstition and faulty science. We mark our progress and project our future largely according to the machines we make and the factual discoveries we total up. Information, research, evidence, reliability—these are the measures of our intellectual life. Like our Enlightenment ancestors, we don't trust the reality of a thing unless we can kick it and measure it. We hope for a perfected world that we will fully understand and control, and we hope for a perfected human being who will live long (if not forever), comfortably, and conveniently.

My field is religion, where professionals speak easily of the myths that underlie our cultural values and styles. Here, "myth" doesn't mean falsehood; it refers to the narrative that gives us an imagination of self and life, allowing us to live meaningfully and purposefully. A life-defining myth is not usually conscious to the people who are living it. Like all peoples, we take our myth literally. We assume that our myth is mere fact, and our explanations for things the simple truth. We don't usually reflect deeply enough to understand that the world we see all around us is highly filtered by the myth in which we believe.

The modern American myth has many dimensions, but for short we could call it secularism. Inspired by this myth, we separate religion from everyday life. Our doctors are not priests and our artists not in the service of ritual, as they might be in India, for example. We trust research, empirical methods, experiment, and measurement. Even psychology, a field whose name refers to the soul—psyche—uses the methods of science. Emotionally, we favor the ego; we like self-control and personal growth and self-esteem. Other cultures might place a high value on states of mind far from consciousness, but we mistrust such excursions and are quite concerned—some would say obsessed—with controlling "mind-altering" experiences.

But at the end of the 20th century, a remarkable thing happened. People of all kinds became attracted to spirituality. On the surface, this would seem to run counter to the prevailing myth. And yet people are meditating, eating differently, forming new churches and communities, and looking to Indian gurus and Sufi poets for inspiration. Rumi is reportedly the best-selling poet in America.

For many, religion is definitely out while spirituality is in. Many members of the new movement say they're tired of religious institutions. When queried about this, they respond less with criticism of the institutions than with the desire to have meaningful *personal* experiences. In some new churches, personal spiritual empowerment goes hand in hand with lessons in health, fitness, success, and emotional stability.

My impression is that there is a lot of spiritual improvisation going on. Based on my limited exposure, some of our new spiritual leaders seem to have influence because of their charisma or their ability to know exactly what people are hungering for. Others have a solid education in theology and are addressing the real concerns of people from a religious point of view, but one that is free of much of the historical baggage of the traditional churches.

But I wonder if this latest spiritual renewal—America has had many in its history—is a passing reaction to a period of secularism or a foretelling of a radical shift in the myth we live by. Because of the sentimentality, personalism, and lack of grounding in many of the new spiritualities, it may seem that they are not serious enough to herald a new era. Still, there is no doubt that the world is changing quickly and deeply. You don't invent huge passenger jets and a World Wide Web without a significant impact on the way we perceive ourselves. So perhaps our new appeal to the spirit runs deep.

Many people today are waking up to themselves. Many tell me that they had been going along, living the American myth, when one day they realized that it wasn't enough. They felt a hunger for more, a yearning for something that could really challenge and inspire them. A large number of people tell the story of how they decided rather abruptly to quit the corporate world or leave a job and career that wasn't doing anything for them personally.

When people work too hard for rewards that are only material, two things may happen: They wake up to the realization that they want more out of life, or they find themselves plagued by alcoholism or some other addiction, divorce, or depression. These are the common complaints of our time.

Still, I wonder if the current spiritual unease will amount to a significant shift. Many of the men and women I talk to who are enthusiastic about some new spiritual movement still seem deeply unsettled. It's as if their top halves have been rescued by the appeal of an inspiring new teacher or system but their lower halves remain in turmoil. They may move frequently from one teaching to another, or their new spiritual views may be more emotional than thoughtful. They are in a vulnerable condition and are susceptible to teachings that may not be well grounded.

The new spirituality, like the mainstream churches, can be cut off from the culture at large. For many, the new spirituality is a form of self-care and the narcissism in it is inescapable. With some exceptions, the new groups don't seem to be seriously concerned about social issues, and they don't have a strong voice in national and international affairs. The emphasis seems to be on personal spiritual development, which is not a negative factor unless it is in fact self-absorbed. But when the emphasis is on the community of like-minded seekers instead of on the community of the nation or the world, one suspects narcissism, which would be a token of the movement's inherent weakness.

Both mainstream religion and the new spirituality can proceed without challenging the myth of secularism. Mainstream religion usually doesn't insist on a radically alternative worldview; instead it tries to inject conscience, values, and vestigial forms of worship into a fully secular life. As long as it is content to be marginal in this way, it colludes with secularism. And as long as the new spirituality remains focused on the individual, it too—for all its novelty and widespread appeal—will help keep the myth of the secular in place. People can live double lives: fully involved in their secular jobs and lifestyles and fully involved in a separate world of spiritual meanings and practices.

If I am correct about the current situation, it signals a long period of confusion about the spiritual life and possibly a long delay before a really significant religious change can occur. But to be clear about what I mean by a significant shift in the myth we live by, it might be helpful to look more deeply at the meaning of religion and spirituality.

A New Definition of Religion

Many people today assume that the word *religion* refers to an institution—an organization weighed down by outmoded authoritarianism and irrelevant traditions. With this definition, they can argue against religion quite easily. But their idea of religion is a straw man, a caricature, or a bad personal experience generalized into an indictment of religion as a whole. Religion is also the Song of Songs, the Buddhist sutras, the Zen arts, the great cathedrals, the thousands of beautiful and powerful rituals, Gregorian chant and Hindu ragas, the great mosques, the Navajo sand paintings, the writings of Thomas Merton, Abraham Heschel, and, yes, Rumi.

Religion is full of wisdom, beauty, and inspiration. Spirituality doesn't have to be invented; it has been flourishing for thousands of years. Can any modern spiritual creation equal the cathedral of Chartres, the great Buddha statues of the East, or the solar altar at New Grange in Ireland? The great mystical writers from many traditions from all over the world have been writing for eons about the spiritual life, and monks and nuns of many traditions have long worked out the details of living in spiritual community.

Probably because I am a Catholic and because my field is religion, I have great respect for these traditions and for their rituals and mysteries. Because I was a monk myself, completely dedicated to the spiritual life, it has never entered my mind to separate spirituality from religion. I, too, have serious problems with the institutions and their authoritarianism. But spirituality is not the whole picture.

Let me suggest a definition of religion I think might satisfy our desire for personal spiritual experience and yet appropriately go beyond it. *Religion is an attitude of reverence and a method of connecting to the mysteries that we find in our world and in ourselves.* No definition would be adequate, but I want to insert some key ideas into our thoughts about religion. I think one of the problems in our day is that we think of religion in terms of our personal experiences, the highly visible and often defensive churches that claim religion for themselves, or hollow institutions.

I've chosen the words in my definition carefully. The word *reverence* refers to awe and honor. Its root refers to watchfulness. Religion is a way of regarding the world and everything in it. Basically, to be religious is to be capable of awe and respect, two qualities that usually disappear when secularism begins to dominate.

I refer to religion also as a method. This is an ancient idea found in many traditions: that religion shows us how to be reverent. What worries me most about a spiritual movement that separates itself from religious traditions is that its methods will be personal and ephemeral. We have much to learn from traditions about sacrifice, ritual, prayer, atonement, healing, and many other basic elements in the spiritual life.

In my definition, I use the word *connecting* because one meaning of the Latin *re-ligare* (from which the word *religion* is derived) is "to connect." Re-ligion is like a ligature. Religion allows us to be in touch with the great mysteries of our lives: illness, birth, death, love, failure, creativity, meaning. The fully secular person is disconnected in this way and therefore might feel lost and aimless. When psychotherapy is understood as a secular activity, it might not reach far enough into the religious issues of meaning and values. We need religion in this broadest sense just to get along and not feel disconnected.

Secularism considers mystery a problem to be solved. It is the enemy. Whereas religion is in the business of mystery and does everything it can to preserve mystery. Mystery is not a problem; it is a rich, unfathomable aspect of human life that requires contemplation. It is best addressed symbolically and ritually. Religion places us in constructive relation to the mysteries and allows us to deepen as persons through our initiation in them.

My question, then, is this: In the next decades and perhaps centuries, will we extricate ourselves from the materially productive but self-destructive myth of secularism, in which religion and life are divided? Will we enter a new era where the two will be united in a way never seen before? Is it possible that this new rush of spirituality will be sufficient to goad us into a new way of life? In my view, anything short of this radical shift is old-time religion conspiring with old-time secularism.

Re-Organized Religion

In the future, will we need religious institutions? We certainly don't need the medieval authoritarianism and hierarchies we still find in place today. In my view, we can benefit from the wisdom, the beauty, and the ritual of literature, poetry, and other arts. These could be sufficient in a people interested in shaping their own spiritual lives. We might understand that the emphasis on authority is one fantasy among many by which religion can be given form. But it isn't necessary. The religious world will not fall part if the authoritarian structures disappear. We simply have come to equate religion with authority and perhaps haven't thought radically enough about alternatives.

An *ecclesia*, which we usually translate as "church," is basically a gathering of people. We could trust people to gather in ways in which the talents of various members could provide the ritual, the theology, and the social and ethical guidance that are part of religion. I, for one, see no point in starting over. We have much to learn from the many traditions, but it isn't necessary to literalize that learning in rigid hierarchies of power. Leadership and expertise are one thing, power is something else.

If we were to find our way into a new myth where religion and spirituality are not marginalized, I would expect a new and central role for theology. Up to this point, theology has usually been practiced as the study of a particular tradition or as how the teachings and values of a tradition are applied to ordinary life. In the new era, theology could simply be the study of the invisibles, the mysteries that form the deepest layer of our many situations.

In the new era, politics would not be a purely secular enterprise; its sacred roots would be evident. Theologians could explore the deep issues in politics that escape the attention and expertise of the social and behavioral sciences. Is a president only an organizational manager, or is he or she a hierarch in the civil religion of the nation? The government of a nation always has religious undertones, even if they are not explicit.

A family has its own spirituality, and theologians could study the mythology of family, family rituals, and so on, as religion scholars do today. Would the religion scholar and the theologian be the same person? Perhaps the theologian could keep the more traditional role of speaking for the practicing community, while the religion scholar speaks from the academy. Without expertise in the mysteries that underlie every aspect of individual and cultural life, we are left with purely secular approaches, which are valuable but insufficient.

Peace on our streets and in the world is not going to come about by rational means. We have tried everything at that level. What is needed is a point of view sufficiently deep and complicated to appreciate the mysterious motives, desires, and frustrations that lead to violence and conflict—not psychological reasons, but reasons of being, of the very nature of things.

The religious organizations might survive, but only if they undergo radical change and offer leadership instead of authority, example rather than dogma, and holiness rather than correctness. But even then, the emphasis would be not on membership but on wisdom and service. The role of the priest is to offer sacrifice, to care for the temple, and to represent the people. The rabbi and Zen master are teachers. The medicine man is a healer. All of these roles could be maintained by the newly organized religions without any emphasis on dogma or moral edicts.

Having been a psychotherapist for 25 years, I expect that in the future we will realize that psychology has shown its limits and that some kind of nondenominational religious counseling is appropriate. Religion and healing go together, because illness of many kinds is the expression of life's meaning lost or gone awry. In the future, I think, medicine will abandon its mechanistic point of view and will finally explore specific ways in which the events of a life or the ways of a society make for illness. Then the spiritual staff of a hospital will have a primary role in the care and healing of patients. One hopes that a hospital will become what the name implies, a guest house for the sick, and not remain merely a place of machinery and technical expertise for fixing broken bodies.

THE COMMUNITY OF TRADITIONS

Attitudes toward the many different religious and spiritual traditions have been a problem for hundreds of years. Rather than enter this steamy discussion in literal terms, I'd rather consider the psychology of membership. What are our fantasies in being members of spiritual organizations or communities? What kind of emotions are involved? What are the deeper issues in the antagonisms between various groups?

It's obvious that religion touches deep and sensitive emotions in most people. It's always a risk to discuss religious views with someone.

The emotionalism is understandable in that religion has to do with beliefs, worldview, and values that give us existential security. At birth, we were not given an owner's manual. It isn't easy to establish a coherent and meaningful life. It helps to accept many of the assumptions of the society, but there comes a point when we are each alone in the face of meaning and values. Religion and spirituality dare to give us guidelines in this, the most important and yet least grounded task— the making of a coherent and meaningful life.

And so we quickly become defensive at the slightest challenge to the belief system that gives us our security. We might keep this simple idea in mind when we talk to any other person about the spiritual life. Each of us requires extraordinary respect for the path we have either chosen or inherited, and we owe the same respect to others. The only way for religion to progress in the coming decades is for it to become sophisticated enough to deal with this basic insecurity and its corresponding defensiveness. Today, some writers refer to our situation as one of religious diversity. If we don't learn to enjoy this diversity, it's difficult to foresee religion maturing as the society changes.

When I look into the future optimistically, I see a growing appreciation for religious diversity and a diminishing of defensiveness. I think it's a mistake to deal with the issue by assuming that all religious traditions are in essence the same. They are different, and only in the most abstract theology can they be seen to express the same thing. Besides, the value of religious diversity lies precisely in the richness of different beliefs and approaches to making life holy.

For a deepening and maturing of the religious attitude, each person has to deal with this fundamental issue. Each has to arrive at the point where one can accomplish a simple emotional and intellectual task: to remain loyal to one's own spiritual views and path and at the same time develop profound respect for the viewpoint and method of every other person and group. This doesn't mean that we agree with one another, but rather that we respect alternative points of view. It also doesn't mean that we can't criticize and warn against certain belief systems. We've seen instances in which large groups have become charmed by a leader and led to mass suicide. We should be able to distinguish a belief system from an obsession, although this is a very subtle business.

Abandoning old antagonisms can lead to a positive embrace of religious differences. My own case is a good example. I was raised in an Irish-American Catholic family, and for at least 15 years I was taught to keep my distance from anything non-Catholic. But fortunately, in later life I had the opportunity to study several other religious traditions, and I feel so enriched by my encounters with these alternative beliefs that I can't express my appreciation adequately. I have learned important lessons from Buddhism, Hindu traditions, paganisms, all sorts of Christian groups, Native American beliefs, Judaism, Islam, and several smaller traditions. My Catholicism is more valuable than ever to me, but it has been transformed by my exposure to other systems. In my estimation, it has been strengthened and deepened.

Today, I frequently find myself standing in the pulpit of a church I know little about or before a religious group quite foreign to my background, and yet I still feel at home. We are all doing our best to make sense of this life with an attitude of respect for one another's approach. We can then learn much from one another without feeling threatened.

Coming to appreciate religious diversity is largely an emotional issue, and we don't usually talk about the spiritual emotions and spiritual passions. We take belief too literally and argue points of view without addressing the underlying feelings. I see no separation between maturing as a person who can be tolerant of other political and philosophical points of view and maturing as a spiritual person.

The future of religion may hang on the direction education takes in our brave new world. Will we find ways to teach cultural diversity and mutual appreciation (I want to go beyond tolerance), or will we remain on our present course and put our trust in machines, information, and training, leaving the great issues of meaning to be improvised by an ill-equipped citizenry?

RELIGION AND SECULARITY

One key development I would hope for in the religious situation to come is a reconciliation of the sacred and the secular. This would entail finding our way out of the defining myth of secularism—not just by getting away from it, but by fulfilling it, turning secularism into secularity. In the current arrangement, we separate the spiritual from the secular in many ways. Of course, most spiritual people try to live out their spirituality in the context of ordinary living, but that is not really a blending of the two. For all our churches and spiritual communities, we still carry on our daily lives in the context of secularism.

We are quite properly worried about the relationship between church and state. If our vigilance fails even momentarily, we could lose our freedoms in this area, as is demonstrated in many parts of the world. But our current solution has the negative effect of maintaining secularism as a way of life. It's my conviction that our secular disciplines and institutions are not capable of dealing with our social problems. They don't reach deep enough and they fail to address questions of meaning and value. They can only handle social manipulation, when it is the soul of the culture that is in trouble.

As many writers have pointed out, our poets and artists keep alive connections between ordinary living and the ultimate issues. But in a secularistic society, the arts lie at the margins and don't have a central impact. The churches seem content to remain on the sidelines as well. They don't seem to have the vision to challenge secularism at its heart and with equal intelligence. Even the environmental movement seems motivated more by practical concerns than by an appreciation for the inherent sacredness of nature. We use these words frequently enough, but we don't take them as seriously as we could.

At this point in the discussion, I suddenly remember my worry and pessimism about the future of religion. All the exits seem to be blocked. The religious institutions are giving way to secularism. The new spirituality is self-absorbed. The arts either remain marginalized or give in to the secularism. Academia has surrendered completely and has cut off all discussion with the rest of the world except to enjoy secularistic patronage. Governments and business have largely given up all values except for control and profit. Is there a window open anywhere through which some new life might come?

But then I remember two things. First, I recall the deep hunger people feel today for a rich spiritual existence. A sure feeling of need can always be the beginning of a shift in the narrative by which we live. Second, I recall the last writings of the sensitive theologian Dietrich Bonhoeffer, who was hanged by the Nazis for his participation in a plot against Hitler. He makes these points: We are now a society come of age. Our achievements are important and deserve our participation. With regard to religion, we have to practice it at the very point where we are strong as a people, not out of our neediness alone. About God, we need to recognize the paradox that we have to live as though God were not a factor, but live that way in the presence of God.

His views remind me of much older ideas about God being hidden or even withdrawn—*deus absconditus* and *deus otiosus*. We have to be as pure in our beliefs as possible, avoiding the temptation to fabricate a God tailor-made for our own comfort. According to mystical theologies, God has to be beyond naming and beyond understanding. If we can live in this world with faith and an active spiritual sensibility, we do not need naive expressions of that belief. In this way, religion matures and becomes less divided from secularity.

If we can perceive that every aspect of daily life has immeasurable depth and potential, that it is inherently sacred, then our secularism, which is an exaggerated and defensive denial of the spiritual, could turn into secularity. We could be religious in our secularity, and in that way the gap between the sacred and the profane would be bridged. This requires an extremely sophisticated notion of spirituality and insight into the profundity of secular life. On the other hand, as a Zen master might say, it requires no sophistication at all, only a life free of attachment to ideology.

If we could shift from the fantasy of religion as an organization or a denomination to seeing religion first of all as an attitude and a way of life, we might be able to acknowledge the sacredness of all aspects of life, which is simply the other side of the coin of enjoying life's secularity. As I read Bonhoeffer, his ideal is a life fully sacred and fully secular.

Such a life would be lived quite differently from the style we're used to. Our belief would not be an intellectual piece of turf that we choose jealously and then feel compelled to defend. Belief and faith would be essentially trust in the life that is given. The rituals of civil life would take on considerably more importance because we would recognize the deep calling in politics and the sacredness of community life. Cultural analysis would include the spiritual and the theological so that in all areas of life, without exception, we would appreciate the role of the mysteries and the validity of religious forms.

We are far from this kind of sensibility, but I don't see how the hunger for spirit can be satisfied without such a radical shift in our mythology. For a long time now we have found security in collective ways of thinking spiritually and submitting ourselves to teachers and systems and traditions. But there is a more solid security available, one more suited to a society come of age, where science and religion stop battling over interpretations of facts and experience. We could discover the kind of security that comes when our questions are wide open, when we give up huddling in factional belief systems, and when we trust and respect one another enough to recognize our common humanity in our search for meaning.

I believe that in a new myth of culture, where secularism would finally be transcended, the religious traditions and spiritual teachings of the world would come to fruition, freed of their unnecessary authoritarianism and factionalism. They would be our rich and trustworthy guides to a vibrant spiritual life lived in the context of a world we could embrace and love. As it is, religious factionalism distracts us from life's beauty and nature's need for us.

This new myth is not entirely new. It is being lived by individuals, but it hasn't yet come close to the critical mass needed to make a shift in the old paradigm. As much as many people today try to live their small lives with a new sensibility, the mass media, governments, and business continue to live by another code, which day by day seems increasingly anachronistic. We seem to be on the cusp between myths, with many individuals displaying the beauty of a new way while others are stuck in old-fashioned narcissistic, competitive ways of being.

Personally, I don't see how business can continue to make idols of profit and money. Isn't it obvious that other values of community, family, creativity, and equality make for a better life for everyone? Isn't it clear to governments that their job is to contribute to the tranquility of life needed by citizens for their own fulfillment and creativity? Power-mongering, violent solutions to problems, demonization of enemies—these are all products of the secularist myth. National self-interest is outmoded as a value, and yet it continues to be paraded as a principle of international relations.

These secular issues have everything to do with religion of the future, because in the future we will not divide issues of everyday life from spiritual concerns. The division is artificial and destructive. The pursuit of peace is a religious issue, as is every other concern of secular living. The deepening of the spiritual life and the liberation of religion from factionalism are of great importance to secular living, because that significant liberation will give secularity the foundation it needs to serve human beings, who are essentially both secular and spiritual.

As individuals, we can move toward a new myth of culture by refusing to separate into competing spiritual groups, by drawing as much inspiration and knowledge as we can from the religious and philosophical traditions, and by living our secular lives with generosity and vision. We move into a new myth one by one, and in the long run, the imaginative and courageous efforts of a single individual make it all happen.

I expect to be a Catholic all my life. I hope that I can embrace the monastic spirit I learned as a young man even more intelligently as I get older. Yet I hope to learn continually from every possible spiritual tradition in the world, deepening my Catholicism and my humanity at the same time. As I become more religious, I expect to be that much more involved in the secular world, coming to it full of vision and a deep, open pursuit of values. I hope to be liberated more and more from my sectarianism and my limited sense of meaning. I have much to learn from everyone I meet who is also openly approaching the mysteries that make us human and allow us to live together in a world that needs our participation.

I don't want anyone telling me for my own good what I should think or how I should live, but I need models of holiness and fresh ideas about the nature of things. I will continue to take as spiritual guides the poets and writers who are clearly open to an authentic muse. I will continue to read and study the literature and art of the world's religions. And I will pray that this world finds the peace it requires, because then I will know that the myth will have shifted. Secularity will have been freed from its symptom of secularism, and religion from its symptom of factionalism. I expect secular life to become humane only when religion, too, has come of age.

★★★

Thomas Moore is an internationally renowned theologian who writes and lectures frequently on psychology, mythology, religion, and the arts. A former Catholic monk of 12 years and a psychotherapist for more than 20 years, he has authored several best-selling books, including *Care of the Soul: A Guide for Cultivating Depth and Sacredness in Everyday Life*, *Soul Mates: Honoring the Mysteries of Love and Relationship*, and *The Soul of Sex: Cultivating Life as an Act of Love*.

LIFE

Neale Donald Walsch

Total transformation.

That's what I see for life in America by the middle of this century.

Total transformation of our political system, total transformation of our socioeconomic structure, total transformation of our personal relationships, and total transformation of our relationship with the sublime and powerful energy of the universe that some of us call God.

Now, I know that this is easy to say and perhaps even expected in a book such as this, but let me tell you why I believe that it is actually going to happen.

I don't think there is any way we can stop it.

Not that we would want to, but if we did want to, I'm not sure that we could.

The systems and the infrastructures have already been put into place to support such a transformation—and, indeed, to render it virtually inevitable. Chief among these is the marriage between cosmology and technology that I have observed over the past decade. Cosmology (the way we look at things; the conceptual constructions of our society) and technology (the way we functionalize what we are looking at) have met at the crossroads of human experience and become one. Our technology is our cosmology. Our cosmology is our technology.

This marriage has already given birth to a new state of being that can now only grow in the years ahead, playing a larger and larger role in the way we experience life on our planet. I call this new characteristic of our society instaparency.

Instant. That is the first word that comes to my mind when I think about what life will be like in America 50 years from now. Life will be instant. Instant awareness. Instant communication. Instant decisions. Everything instant.

The second word I think of is *transparent.* Life will be transparent. Transparent social interchange, transparent financial and business dealings, transparent political processes. Everything transparent.

Instaparency is being produced by a technology that has reduced to nanoseconds the time span between our exposure to new ideas, and by a cosmology that has pushed hidden social agendas, under-the-table business dealings, and back-room politics outside the mainstream of contemporary thought regarding appropriate human interaction. Where once they were de rigueur, now they are at the very least passé and, in fact, unacceptable.

Everyone in the future will be able to instantly know everything. Just about anything we wish to know will be available to us at the push of a button. How much does the boss earn? What were my firm's financials last month? Has my new boyfriend ever been married before? Is he married now? What is the military budget of the government of any country, and where are its military resources deployed?

Anything. We'll be able to find out just about anything. And very little will happen in the world that will not be communicated to us. Immediately. We'll know what's happening in the four corners of the world and in the farthest outposts of civilization, both here and off the planet.

This quality of instaparency will bring us together as nothing has ever done in the history of the human race. That is because it will cause us to be aware of the commonality of our experience, and it will give us the tools with which to respond in common to that experience with all the power that only unified action involving millions can create.

No longer, for instance, will maniacal despots in the governments of tiny countries (or of large ones, for that matter) be able to rob and steal, jail and kill, and call it an internal matter. The world community will know—as it does today—of every action, every decision, every repression; but, more important, it will be able to *bring instant social, political, and economic pressure to bear in that situation.*

We will not have to wait for a deeply politicized world organization to do something. Citizens of the world could announce an immediate economic boycott, kill the tourist trade within seconds, dramatically lower stock prices within that country's business sector in one trading day, boycott any and all products coming out of that country and, in short, cause its leaders to rapidly rethink their decisions.

Within our own country, elections will be held and joint decisions will be made on important matters within minutes, by instant electronic plebiscites.

All of this instantness will produce the beginnings of a new (and perhaps our last great) spiritual evolution: the movement to Oneness as an experience rather than as merely a concept. Our experience will be one of true unity because *we will all come to know the same thing at the same time.*

In the past, what has separated us from one another—spiritually, philosophically, politically, economically, socially—has been nothing more than time and space. The distance between people (and groups of people, which we call families, neighborhoods, states, and nations), and the time it has taken for all people to know the same thing, has produced varied responses and reactions to essentially the same circumstances. It has also allowed those who would seek to control those circumstances the tools (mainly, the tool of ignorance) with which to do so.

In the future, time and space will no longer produce a distance between people. We will all be able to know whatever it is that we want to know as soon as we wish to know it; and we will even be able to physically be just about anywhere we want to be within a few hours (ultimately, within a few moments), thus erasing the traditional separations of time and space and their traditionally separating influences.

As mentioned, the spiritual fallout of this phenomenon will be immense and enormously meaningful. Instaparency will eventuate a huge shift in collective consciousness. Seeing themselves and experiencing themselves as One will motivate people to use Oneness as the central theme of a worldwide spiritual movement. Individual religions, just as individual cultures, will still flourish, but we will have understood at last that these individualizations of life's expression need not become competitions nor fall into an imagined hierarchy of superiority. We will decide that differences need not mean divisions, and we will celebrate our diversity, not denounce it.

Our instant combined experience will produce new and collective political action. We truly *will* be the United States of America. Awareness will jump sky-high. Ignorance is the roadblock to awareness, and apathy, its enemy. Both will be impossible at the level of critical mass precisely because our mass consciousness will continue to be so vitally and continually engaged.

Newness and openness will be other hallmarks of tomorrow.

During the 1800s, it was possible for a person to hold on to an idea, a concept, or a thought about things throughout an entire lifetime. Traditions ruled. Opinions held firm. The pace of information was so slow that evidence that might contradict a prevailing thought took forever to spread wide enough to make an immediate difference.

In the 1900s, the time between forming an opinion and possibly changing it was reduced dramatically as the century proceeded, with few people able to move through one entire lifetime without facing evidence that could challenge their most firmly held beliefs. I remember my grandmother watching the first manned landing on the moon. She was quite elderly at the time, and as she witnessed this televised event, she could not hold the information in her personal data bank. There was no place in her belief system in which to store it. She insisted that the program must be a drama, an Orson Wells–like fantasy.

In this—the beginning of this 21st—century, the average person is lucky to get through 10 years without confronting new discoveries, new inventions, or new developments that seriously challenge every assumption held in the mind about life. The unwrapping of the mystery previously shrouding the human genome is but one startling and brilliant example. This decoding miracle will likely change many people's firmly held beliefs about life and "how it is." It will challenge the human race, in the years just ahead, at every level. It will have economic, political, social, and religious or spiritual fallout beyond anything that we can today even begin to imagine. And it is but one of an endless number of such discoveries occurring with increasing speed and becoming known by everyone instantly.

By the middle of this new century, that time span between forming an idea and possibly having to change it could be reduced from 10 years to 10 months, 10 days, or 10 minutes.

We will all have to be very light on our feet.

I see this as very good, not bad. The speed of life will invite us to "be here now," as Ram Dass would say. It will challenge us to live in the moment, at every level. It will cause us to be more responsible in creating our own realities and less dependent on what someone else has told us is right or true.

Again, the implications in the area of religion and spirituality alone are staggering. Concepts of God and our philosophical constructions around life could be somewhat shaken by instant news of the discovery of life on yet another planet every 14 months, to use just one example (and to say nothing of the possible arrival on this planet of one of those life forms).

That is why I see, as I have said, a spiritual renaissance of gargantuan proportions between now and the year 2050. I believe that we will be invited by events to rethink our every idea about who we are and how we relate to one another.

Not only will our spirituality and our politics be impacted and changed forever by instaparency, so too will our economics and our whole social order, including the most critical ways in which we now interact with one another. I believe that our interdependence will become increasingly clear and obvious and that this will create a vastly different kind of world. A world in which killing one another as a means of resolving our disputes will no longer be acceptable. A world in which doing virtually nothing while 400 children a day die of hunger will be wholly unsupportable. A world in which kindness and compassion and fair sharing of our most precious resources will be our natural and immediate choice. A world in which we will, at last, stop our insane competitions for bigger, better, more, and redefine our ideas about success, about how it is to be alive, and about what it means to share membership in the human community.

We will create what spiritual leader and author Rabbi Michael Lerner calls "a new bottom line in America," a movement away from power and wealth as the focus of our endeavors (as well as the prime indicators of their success) to a sense of awe and wonder at the universe and life itself and a new valuing of caring and compassion in the human encounter.

Success in the future will, in fact, have so little to do with the accumulation of money and material objects that we will have to find a new way to grant status to members of society. Status will be accorded to those who have been conspicuous in their service of humankind, by whatever means best reflects an individual's talents and interests.

I believe that civilized societies—and I certainly believe that America will be among them—will have put into place by the middle of the 21st century a means by which the dignity of every individual will be honored, with basic survival needs guaranteed. The struggle for minimal levels of food, clothing, and shelter will be over.

This will be accomplished without the imposition of a single tax or governmental levy. In fact, I believe that in the future, *taxes will be totally abolished,* to be replaced by voluntary tithing of 10 percent to a central fund used to finance all social programs.

The incentive for the voluntary tithe will be quite simple: instant transparency. Each month, there will be widely publicized, in all electronic newspapers and on television on a specific channel, a list of all the people who have refused to tithe or who have tithed significantly beneath the 10 percent level. Simple public awareness of who is contributing to the welfare of the whole and who is not will be sufficient.

Everything will be financed by this money, from traffic signals to road pavings to schools to assistance for those less fortunate. The entire social infrastructure will be financed voluntarily, as people see clearly and differently their roles in the creation of humanity's collective experience. No one will have to convince anyone to do this. Sharing for the common good will be natural. *Not* sharing will be what is uncommon.

The publicized list of undercontributors and noncontributors will be very small, since in the year 2050 it will be unthinkable for an individual not to willingly choose to provide from his or her blessings for the general good of the entire community.

With everyone's basic needs met and with our sense of competition with one another muted, there will be no further need for massive military machines to be maintained by the states of the world, any more than there is today for the states in our union to maintain them. Funds now used for such worldwide military activities—at present levels, many trillions of dollars—will be reallocated to educational and social programs aimed at ending poverty and unequal economic opportunity, which are the real causes of war.

In this new scheme of things, there may be those who would worry that human beings will lose their motivation to succeed or, for that matter, to even bother working at anything at all. Previously we had survival as our main motivation, and then greed. But with survival guaranteed, what could cause us to want to do anything? And with greed unwelcome and very out of style in a society whose members see themselves as One, what could cause someone to want to get ahead?

I suggest that a new motivation will be found, replacing the need to survive as well as the drive for bigger, better, more. This new motivation will arise out of our change of mind about what to honor.

In 2050, we will no longer choose to honor individual survival at the expense of group survival, nor will we chose to honor having that which is bigger, better, more. What society will honor is that which more directly *supports life*.

Life will become the value, and the quality of that life, for ourselves and others. We will understand at this new point in our cultural development that that which does not support a quality life for all does not support a quality life for any. We will step away from the fiction that if I am doing well, how well you are doing doesn't matter. We will also understand that stress-inducing activities required for us to gather bigger, better, and more things are not life supporting for ourselves or others.

In the New World of Tomorrow, the highest honor will go to those who provide the highest service to humanity. The Human Family will be deeply aware of its single identity; the suffering of one will be experienced as the suffering of all; and the joy of all will be the objective of all. No one will be on the outside, looking in; no person or group will be excluded; nor will any segment of the population be marginalized or ignored.

I do not believe that this New World that I envision will be a Utopia. It will not be a problem-free society, nor one without challenges. What will be different is that we will have begun in earnest to face and to solve our problems together. We will see them as *our* problems, not as *their* problems. Our ideas of every man for himself and to the victor go the spoils and survival of the fittest will have been abandoned at last, after thousands of years in our Cultural Story. We will agree that the fittest among us are not fit at all until all among us are fit. And we will come to this new agreement out of our new awareness of our unified identity.

What it will take for this all to happen is very clear to me. We must begin now to end the divisiveness that has characterized our societal interactions through all the thousands of years that have brought us to this present day. We must preach a new gospel: the gospel of Oneness and of the End to Better.

By the End to Better, I mean a discontinuation of the idea of superiority that has plagued humankind forever. Already, insta-parency is causing us to acknowledge that we are all rowing the same boat, that we are in this together, that our challenges as a species are far better faced collectively than individually. To put this knowledge to work, I believe we must abandon at last our thought that one of us—one group, one race, one gender, one faith, one political party, one economic system, one nation or culture—is somehow better than another.

The human race—and, indeed, all of life—is a manifestation of the One Thing That Is, and a thing cannot be superior to Itself. Our present idea that there is someone else to whom we can feel superior is being shattered by our growing awareness that there is no one and nothing else out there but different expressions and other manifesta-tions of Us.

Our job is to turn this awareness into social change. Then we will have turned the corner toward our Newer World. Yet what could produce such change? Is it even possible to create social transforma-tion? How can we cause huge institutions—governments, corpora-tions, colleges—to embrace and accept these new ideas and values?

In the end, the only thing that will instigate long-term change in our behavior is long-term change in the human heart. The good news is that this part of the process we can begin today: first, by changing what is in our hearts, and next, by causing others to change what is in theirs.

The magical aspect of this process is that the second objective is achieved through achievement of the first. For when we change our hearts, the alteration in our own behavior causes change in the hearts and behaviors of others. We become walking messengers. Indeed, *we are the message we seek to send*. It is a message to the world about itself.

This is a new way of thinking about life and our role in it. It is precisely this new way that will produce the New World that I have here described.

It was the late Robert Kennedy who once urged all Americans to "seek a newer world." I urge the same thing today. If we ever, as a nation, moved to the highest thought that we have about ourselves, we could re-create our collective reality in this country overnight.

Kennedy also said, "Of those to whom much is given, much is asked." I agree. We have been given so much in this country. If the world truly is to change, I believe it is the most fortunate among us who must take responsibility for modeling the changes we seek to induce.

Finally, it was Robert Kennedy who, paraphrasing George Bernard Shaw, said in his last political campaign, just before he was assassinated, "There are those who see the world as it is, and ask why. And there are those who dream of things that never were, and ask why not."

What it will take for us to bring about the tomorrow of our highest dreams is to ask the question, Why not? Why not a country in which spiritual values take precedence over the values of power, greed, and wealth? Why not a life in which awe and wonder replace bigger, better, and more as the prime experience? Why not a world in which no one is considered "less than" and everyone truly has equal opportunity?

The magical question—Why not?—and its answer can be put into practical action by creating a new kind of politics where Oneness and the unity of all life rests at the core of every program, platform, and proposal. A new kind of economics where caring for the Earth and compassion for its people drive every choice and decision. A new kind of education where awareness, honesty, and responsibility become the core values, not bigger, better, more. A new kind of spirituality where no one's God and no one's way of getting to God is touted as the One Way, the Only Way, the Better Way, but simply as *a* way.

Such creations are now underway. These efforts are observable everywhere in our society. All we have to do is support them. And what could cause us to do that? Perhaps simply capturing the vision.

That's what's going on now. The vision is being articulated and captured. Thanks to the beginnings of instaparency, it is now being placed before more people, and faster, than ever before. We are rapidly reaching critical mass. Soon, the vision for a Newer World will be expressed in form because people all over America and around the world are choosing to imagine the world as it could be. They are saying, as we all are saying in this book, just . . . *imagine.*

★★★

Neale Donald Walsch is the author of the international best-selling book series *Conversations with God*. He and his wife, Nancy, are founders of ReCreation, a nonprofit foundation for personal growth and spiritual understanding. He is also the cofounder, with Marianne Williamson, of the Global Renaissance Alliance.

THE NEW CIVITAS

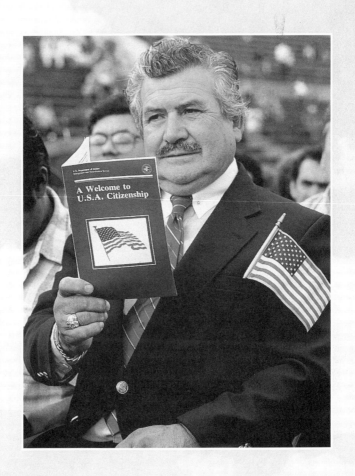

CITIZENSHIP

Paul Rogat Loeb

When I was a child in the 1950s, I envisioned the future in terms of technologies and objects. Flying cars, Dick Tracy two-way wrist radios, Disneyland houses of tomorrow. Technologies have obviously transformed our lives and will continue to do so. But when I imagine the world that I want to help create, I think less of technical artifacts, however consequential, than of the webs of cultural, economic, and political arrangements that will determine whether our inventive and transformative genius becomes a blessing or a blight. I think of the qualities and choices necessary to shape a more humane world.

We've made some major democratic advances during the past half-century. Legal segregation no longer rules the American South. Women are far less economically marginalized. Gays have come out of the closet. America's military interventions are now often challenged. We've begun to think about the environment.

Yet the gaps between rich and poor are wider than ever. It damages us all that the United States leads the advanced industrial world in rates of homelessness, child poverty, lack of health care, infant mortality, and nearly every other index of desperation among the voiceless and vulnerable. For all the environmental talk, we continue to despoil the Earth. Large numbers of Americans feel disconnected and powerless. How do we create a more humane world during the next 50 years?

We can begin with some deep-rooted wisdom about mutual

respect. Two thousand years ago, Rabbi Hillel explained, "What is hateful to you, do not to your fellow man. That is the entire Law; all the rest is commentary." Yet we've still not lived up to Hillel's words. We've still not created a world in which everyone has access to food, housing, and medical care; in which no one beats, shoots, evicts, tortures, or otherwise degrades their fellow human beings; and in which individuals can express what they believe without fear. Most of these values were enshrined just after World War II in the United Nations' International Bill of Human Rights, signed by all the major nations on Earth. But it will take more than formal pronouncements and more than individual acts of decency and civility to make these rights global realities.

A good society would create a sense of economic security for all—so that, in the words of singer Bruce Cockburn, "nobody has to scrape for honey at the bottom of the comb." Virginia Ramirez, a San Antonio woman with an eighth-grade education, testified before the U.S. Congress and Senate that she sees human dignity embodied in how we treat our children. "I'd like to see a world where every child has the same opportunity," she said. "I see children suffer from hunger, sickness, cold, and lack of education. Or they're abused, humiliated, or whatever. That's the hardest thing to take, to see children suffer. To me, there would be justice if every child in this world got treated well. I don't know if that's ever going to happen. Maybe it won't. But for me, that would be perfect justice."

A good society gives ordinary citizens opportunities to shape a common future. "What we're trying to do," says longtime community organizer Ernie Cortes, "is to draw people out of their private pain, out of their cynicism and passivity, and get them connected with other people in collective action." In this sense, the very act of taking responsibility for our communities embodies the vision we seek. It makes democracy more than a vague slogan masking manipulation and greed, but rather a living process by which all citizens participate in the creation and governance of society. It makes the public arena the property of everyone.

330

In America now, too many of us treat the choices by which we decide our common future as the territory of others. We feel that we don't know enough to act on issues that concern us, and that our actions will make no difference, our voices will never be heard. This creates a self-fulfilling prophecy. The more we withdraw from civic life, the more we leave immensely consequential decisions to a politics driven by greed, short-sightedness, and expediency. Conversely, the more we take on the difficult problems of our time, the more we can tap common power, creativity, and strength.

In 50 years, I hope that our culture will have learned to encourage citizen involvement rather than delegating our most urgent common concerns to distant and unaccountable experts or to the small number of socially involved individuals whom we think are more noble and saintly than we. Most Americans think that Rosa Parks started her activism that famous day on the Montgomery, Alabama, bus and have not even a notion that it began a dozen years before that, when Parks became active in a local NAACP chapter. Our current myths suggest that change happens when individuals act on their own, in isolation, for mysterious reasons. The real history teaches lessons of common action, of perseverance, of working together for change.

Imagine if we taught how ordinary citizens have changed the world, again and again, even against entrenched resistance. Young women and men just coming of age would learn the stories of citizen efforts like the abolitionist, women's suffrage, populist, union, civil rights, and environmental movements—how ordinary people have learned to act despite their flaws, hesitations, and failings; learned to persevere, even under the most difficult of circumstances; learned to keep on until they prevailed. Historical examples can teach how seemingly impossible efforts can create powerful change. They give a sense of possibility that counters cultural cynicism. They allow those coming of age to think not only about addressing small, immediate issues, but also their deeper roots. They teach the arts and skills of democracy—how to reach out to our fellow citizens, organize them for change, and make our common voice heard.

Civic conversation needs to continue well after citizens leave school. In the Scandinavian countries, study circles encourage citizens to take on the most difficult common issues, coming together to reflect and to act. Participants even get tax credits for participating. We too could institutionalize these approaches and make our schools, libraries, churches, and temples centers for reflection and discussion. Whatever our desired society of 50 years to come, civic participation must be at the heart of it.

A good society would help each of us fulfill the full bloom of our uniqueness, what Jungian therapist James Hillman calls the acorn of our character. It would honor our individual gifts and encourage our particular callings. It would give all its inhabitants the economic, emotional, and spiritual support needed to follow their dreams. Unjust societies, in contrast, starve hopes, aspirations, and possibilities. They stunt lives and potentials.

Because we realize ourselves fully only through interaction with others, a good society would foster community in all its forms. It would nurture rich and vibrant places to live where we are surrounded by friends and acquaintances, feel a sense of belonging, look out for one another's children. Such communities once existed in our small towns and urban neighborhoods. The longing that most of us have for places where intimate connections are commonplace speaks to the depth of our social needs—our reliance on the company of other human beings to feel at home in the world. We need to rebuild a world of face-to-face exchange, of communities where we are known, of places that are not interchangeable.

Wherever we reside, we'll realize neither our individual nor our communal selves if we're totally consumed by our work. That points to another feature of a good society: We should be able to make a liveable wage without sacrificing our psychological, spiritual, and sometimes even physical well-being by giving over our entire lives to our jobs. The saying on the bumper sticker THE LABOR MOVEMENT: THE FOLKS WHO BROUGHT YOU THE WEEKEND is more than a joke. For generations, citizens struggled to shorten the hours they worked; indeed, democracy is impossible when employers control our every waking minute. But the time that we spend related to our jobs has been steadily increasing for the past several decades, even though American industrial productivity has more than tripled since 1948. A good society would allow citizens time to think and reflect, to be with their families and friends, to engage themselves in their communities. It would foster a culture that allows us to slow down the pace of global change, challenge the idolatry of mindless consumption, and wield our awesome technological capabilities with enough humility to respect the dignity of the Earth.

Aristotle once said that a barbaric culture consumes all of its resources for the present, whereas a civilized culture preserves them for later generations. Many of our society's most destructive present actions yield consequences whose gravest implications aren't immediately apparent. That's true of our casual destruction of the planet. It's true of our writing off entire communities of young men and women who will grow into adulthood bereft of hope and skills. It's true when we say, in one of the richest countries in the world, that we can't afford to address our most pressing common problems.

The alternative, as environmentalist David Brower said, is to act so that "the new child or the new fawn or the new baby seal pup that's born a thousand years from now . . . opens its eyes on a beautiful, livable planet." Latina activist Virginia Ramirez touched on this in explaining why it's important to persist: "Maybe the things we're working on today won't bring about changes for years. But it's just as important that we do them."

Working for the future requires a vision of accountability by which we hold individuals and institutions responsible for the impact of their choices, linking even seemingly disconnected actions and consequences. Congressman Ron Dellums once said that we know the state of a nation's soul by looking at its budgets. In Dwight Eisenhower's classic words, "Every gun that is made, every warship launched, every rocket fired, signifies in a final sense a theft from those who hunger and are not fed—those who are cold and not clothed."

I've seen this statement on so many posters, banners, T-shirts, and signs over the years that by now I barely notice it. At present, we spend $300 billion a year on what we call defense—as much in real dollars as during the heart of the Cold War and a figure that, when added to costs still being paid from past wars and weapons buildups, accounts for nearly half of all current discretionary federal spending. Shifting from this direction would ease the endless cycles of threat and counterthreat, retribution and vengeance, into which we put so much of our energy, passion, and creativity preparing to annihilate our fellow human beings.

A good society would be clear about the human toll of our choices, asking who benefits and who pays. When a nurse I know was conducting physical exams of inmates in Seattle's local county jail, she discovered that a huge percentage had chronic ear infections. That prompted her to think about the implications of young kids with untreated earaches: They can't concentrate in school because it's hard to hear what the teacher is saying. This makes them feel angry and edgy. Soon they drop out, start stealing to survive, and end up in jail. My friend wondered how many of these young men might have followed a different path had their families had access to decent medical treatment.

In 50 years, we should have long since exhausted our excuses about providing health care for all of our children, ensuring that they attend adequate schools, making sure that they have roofs over their heads. We will have stopped building prisons and returned to building youth employment programs, so that we can nurture those who fall between the cracks. We will have made a priority of protecting our environment, the world our children and their children will inherit. "We can clone animals," pointed out David Lewis, who spent 17 years in the California prison system before founding a pioneering drug rehab center. "We can send rockets into space. But we can't give young people anything better to believe in than worshipping the god of money. We can't make drug treatment programs available to everybody who wants and needs them. I would like to see that same kind of effort applied to saving people's lives."

David's point hits home to me. Enough resources exist in America to meet our public needs. If we learn to consume sustainably, our inventive spirit should serve us well in the future. But we must reform the policies and institutions that allow our society, in the words of economist John Kenneth Galbraith, to be dominated by "private affluence and public squalor." Budget numbers seem abstract until we realize that they represent the common resources of our society—resources that could support better schools, efficient mass transit, low-income housing, community-investment corporations, inspiring arts programs, universal health care, or a serious effort to repair the environment. The most successful attempts to heal our society's ills and promote human dignity are often local grassroots efforts; imagine their impact if we gave them enough resources to do their work as well and as powerfully as possible instead of forcing them to scramble constantly for crumbs.

To borrow a phrase from the ecologists, imagine if we developed a full-cost accounting of all our political and economic choices, so that we realized what we're losing by our shortsightedness: When kids don't get treated for earaches, many end up in jail; when watersheds are devastated on speculators' whims, salmon runs dwindle; when the wealthiest get an endless succession of tax breaks, children go hungry; when corporations lay off employees, speed up production, and reduce benefits, families disintegrate and communities erode. We need to think about all of the deferred, denied, and unintended consequences that ripple out over time, including opportunities lost and potentials unrealized. Only by being honest about the consequences of our choices can we move forward.

★★★

Paul Rogat Loeb, an associate scholar at Seattle's Center for Ethical Leadership, comments on social involvement for the *New York Times*, the *Washington Post*, the *Los Angeles Times*, *Utne Reader*, *Mother Jones*, *New Age Journal*, CNN, NPR, C-SPAN, and elsewhere. His most recent book is *Soul of a Citizen: Living with Conviction in a Cynical Time*. His previous titles include *Nuclear Culture*, *Hope in Hard Times*, and *Generation at the Crossroads*.

LAW

Peter Gabel

The most profound definition of justice is Martin Luther King's: "Love correcting that which revolts against Love." Its power comes from its affirmation that we are first of all *connected*, that as individuals we are but unique incarnations of a spiritual force that unites us, and that justice is the making manifest of that love by correcting, through the inherent ethical call that this love makes upon every one of us and all of us, the spiritual distortions that revolt against love and seek to deny it.

It was to this inherent ethical understanding—emanating from the very essence of our social existence, pulling upon the conscience of the oppressor as much as giving courage to the oppressed—that King always addressed himself. Injustice is as self-evident to us as the presence of justice—even the Nazi cannot stop killing for fear of becoming aware of what he knows—and it is the necessity of love that both enables us to tell justice from injustice and calls upon us to move from the one to the other.

Law ought to be the temporal embodiment of our effort as a real, historical community to move from one to the other. Law is not a body of rules or any other such thing-like entity but rather a *culture of justice* whose ethical legitimacy depends upon how deeply and sincerely it enables us to carry out the work of justice, of love correcting that which revolts against love. Thus conceived, legal culture ought to be a spiritual practice through which the community calls upon love's evolving wisdom to heal the spiritual distortions that continue to alienate us from love itself as the realization of our social being. Like the mountain climber who *first* throws his pick up to the top of the mountain, making sure that the pick is anchored so as to maximize the tension in his rope, and who *then* seeks to pull himself upward by intuitively gauging the rightness of every step in relation to his ultimate and transcendent end, law must maintain its connection to justice by following an ethical intuition anchoring the present to the future, an intuition of what we are in our being but are not yet in reality.

America's legal culture at the turn of the millennium has temporarily lost this connection to justice because its great historical accomplishment—the affirmation of the freedom of the individual and the protection of the individual from officially sanctioned group coercion—has been misunderstood to require the denial of the spiritual bond that unites the individual to the other and, through love, fulfills the individual in his or her social existence.

As a result, alongside the accomplishments of constitutional democracy and the Bill of Rights, which liberated the individual from the officially sanctioned religious and political oppression of previous historical periods, we have created a society of disconnected monads, spiritually isolated and starved for love and recognition. This collective spiritual starvation has progressed to the point of posing a threat to the very existence of the planet. The denial of the universal need for loving connection has spawned a pathological, paranoiac scramble to exploit everything outside oneself—other people and the natural world—in order to "save" oneself.

This spiritual starvation has also failed to secure the liberty of the individual in whose name the denial of our spiritual bond was legislated. Today, as "free individuals," we live most of our lives in a completely unnecessary spiritual prison, each of us longing for the same liberation that only we can provide one another, each of us denying that this longing exists within ourselves because of the doubt that we have that it would or could be reciprocated by the other.

Since this is the *Imagine* project, let us begin by acknowledging that it is we, and not merely Eleanor Rigby, who are all the lonely people, withdrawn into our heads and peering out at a world whose collective gaze we have come to fear and whose love, whose reciprocating acceptance and affirming recognition, is at the same time our only spiritual salvation.

Of course, the law is not exclusively to blame for this, but it does have a special responsibility because it legitimizes our predicament in the name of justice. Law cannot exist without claiming to be just; it would be superfluous to elevate what are merely orders backed by the threat of violence to some higher cultural status. But when law loses its true spiritual connection to justice, it becomes "legitimation," a justification of the status quo that lacks the ethical legitimacy that only moral anchorage in true justice, Martin Luther King's justice, can provide. Law as legitimation exploits the longing for justice by using the claim of justice to legitimate an alienated society that the community, deep in its core, experiences as spiritually and ethically illegitimate.

Thus, however much we are tempted to blame the present ecological and spiritual crisis on the global capitalist marketplace, for example, we must realize that this marketplace is held in place, so to speak, by a legal culture that through a vast network of "rights" allows the community of souls that form that marketplace to believe that what it is doing is right and even required by justice itself.

If the prevailing culture of justice declares that individual liberty *means* there exists no spiritual force uniting us to one another and to the sacredness of the natural world and the wider universe, then the universal longings of the soul are in contradiction with the community's public declaration—through the official political and legal institutions that define the community's very public existence—of the ethical basis of community membership. To put it simply, absent the support of a spiritual/cultural/political movement, the isolated soul cannot but believe that its longing for a loving and spiritually connected society is "wrong" and that the ethics of the marketplace is both "right" and a condition of social membership.

Thus the prevailing legal culture, which we begin to internalize even before the explicit conditioning of seventh- and eight-grade civics class, plays a unique and powerful role not only in sustaining what is, but in keeping our spiritual longings and our spiritual knowledge a collective and even unconscious secret (unconscious because these longings are suppressed within a circle of collective denial that each of us has been conditioned to participate in).

Since what we are to imagine, in a moment, is precisely the legal/spiritual revolution that will dissolve these invisible walls that separate us, we must first enumerate the elements of our existing legal culture that contribute to this state of affairs and that must be revolutionized. All of these elements reflect the central mistaken conviction that the protection of individual liberty requires the denial of, rather than the affirmation of, the spiritual bond that unites us. Here are the most important ones:

1. Our legal culture declares that disputes are to be resolved through an adversary system that defines differences as antagonistic clashes of conflicting interests; that fosters hostility, mutual deprecation, and lying; and that rejects any moral objective that might inform the process beyond the parties' own self-interested goals. Protection of the "rights of the individual" is thought to require that each side treat the other with skepticism and mistrust, to demean the other's position while exaggerating the virtue of your own, to use cross-examination to undermine the testimony of even those you believe to be truthful, and to conceal any information that might be harmful to your side unless your opponent extracts it from you under penalty of perjury (only in rare circumstances is voluntary disclosure legally required).

This adversary process assumes that justice is best served by the use of evidentiary rules that limit what the judge and jury may hear to the proof of empirically verifiable facts. Any evidence regarding the spiritual and social *meaning* of the dispute or of the social and ethical context that might bring out this meaning is inadmissible because it is regarded as "merely subjective," a matter of opinion that cannot be determined to be true or untrue and therefore can only unfairly prejudice the objectivity of the proceeding. The assumption is that the vindication of "individual rights" is the basis of law's claim to justice, and that objectivity in pursuit of that end is best assured by having an impartial third party (sometimes a judge, sometimes a jury) evaluate each side of the case after the other has had full opportunity to destroy it.

2. Once the "facts" are thus determined, the basic rules of substantive law that are used to resolve disputes—embodied in, for example, the law of contracts, torts, corporations, and property—assume that people are essentially unconnected monads whose principal desire is to pursue their own material self-interest in the competitive marketplace, and whose principal social concern is limited to protecting their persons and property against unwanted interference by others. Even the Constitution, often thought to be among the world's great documents in securing social justice, provides no recognition of the human longing for community, for social connection, for the authenticity of mutual recognition, for the creation of a society that fosters our awareness of the sacredness of life itself and of the natural world. Instead, the main text of the Constitution provides only the formal structure to secure a democracy of strangers—an unconnected collection of individuals protected against their neighbors by the secret ballot and against abuses by the government itself through the "checks and balances" secured by the separation of powers. Similarly, the Bill of Rights does not aspire to *connect* us to one another but to protect us against one another, against the community's interfering with our right as isolated individuals to speak, to assemble (if as disconnected monads we can find anyone to assemble with), to be secure in our homes (those supposed havens in a heartless world), and even to keep others from taking away our guns—the preoccupation with which is a contemporary example of a highly visible appeal to the Bill of Rights (in this case, the Second Amendment) that reveals how clearly its protections equate individual freedom with fear of the other rather than connection with and love for the other.

3. In their training and in the disciplinary and ethical rules that govern the legal profession, lawyers are encouraged and even to some extent required to ignore ethical considerations beyond the narrow self-interest of the client. Because our legal culture lacks a spiritual and moral direction, or more precisely because it denies the legitimacy of embracing such a direction in order to defend an isolated conception of individual liberty, the role of the lawyer is simply to advocate for the legitimacy of whatever the client wants or does (so long as it is not a crime). Legal education is almost exclusively directed toward teaching students the analytical techniques of rule manipulation. The best students are those who can demonstrate their capacity to argue for any side, irrespective of moral consequences; no part of a law student's education is directed toward instilling in the student the obligation or the capability to promote the creation of a more loving, more spiritually whole society. And once in practice, the lawyer's professional "duty of zealous representation" virtually requires the lawyer not to allow his or her own "private" ethical concerns to interfere with the zealous pursuit of the client's ends, irrespective of the impact of these ends on others, on the society as a whole, or on the environment.

Because the individualistic, materialist, and adversarial character of this legal culture is "binding" on the consciousness of society—because its assumptions about who human beings are and how we ought to relate to one another are also the Law—we cannot overcome the spiritual alienation that is at the heart of our own and the world's suffering without a fundamental transformation of this culture. And because the great social movements of the 20th century did not grasp this, they foundered when they entered the legal arena. The labor movement, the civil rights movement, and the women's movement, for example, were fundamentally spiritual movements aspiring to a new kind of connection that would realize our common humanity—even the word *movement* denotes the spiritual emergence of just such a vitalizing connection. But once these movements began to translate these spiritual aspirations into a demand for legal rights, their very victories became a cause of the defeat of these aspirations. Absorbed into the law's individualistic and materialist framework, the labor movement's aspiration to a classless society based on solidarity and universal brotherhood became the right to bargain for higher wages and safer working conditions; the civil rights movement's aspiration to love across our racial differences became the right of "the individual" not to be discriminated against on the basis of race in order to protect his or her liberty to pursue "equality of opportunity" in the marketplace; the aspiration of the women's movement to replace a world of power, hierarchy, and heartless rationality with a communal, intuitively grounded fabric of care became the right not to have one's liberty to pursue material success in the marketplace impeded by gender. No matter how important these liberal victories were, they required looking in a mirror that made these movements' spiritual bond and their spiritual aspirations for a fundamental social transformation invisible.

Yet for a complex of reasons—the most important of which are probably the failure of the very success of the liberal global marketplace to create a meaningful, much less sustainable, existence, and the failure of the movements for social transformation to be able to sustain themselves through either the liberal or the materialist-socialist framework—a new flower has begun to sprout across the face of the world. This flower is the worldwide spiritual/ecological movement that is finally helping the necessity of love to *recognize itself* as the spiritual force that unites us. And to bring this recognition to fruition, to enable this flower to grow in spite of the centuries of alienation and mistrust and "misrecognition" that have preceded its birth into awareness, we must create a new legal culture . . . and are already beginning to do so.

LOVE CORRECTING

A legal culture that can begin to realize Dr. King's great description of justice is one in which the community's response to conflict of every kind—civil and criminal, to use the current categories—begins with a moral awareness of the love, the sense of compassionate and caring social connection, that is to be restored through the legal process. This requires that law's primary focus no longer be judgment directed toward divided individuals, but the healing of wounds to the connection that is to be restored.

This in turn requires that the three principal elements of the individualistic and materialist legal culture undergo the following transformation.

The End of the Adversary System

The adversary system should be abolished and replaced by processes that encourage empathy, compassion, and mutual understanding. Each human and ecological problem that requires community resolution should proceed by locating the presentation of all facts within a context of *social meaning* that reveals their ethical significance. Within this transformed framework, the courtroom would be the public space devoted to healing the spiritual wounds of alienation by allowing the community to hear these wounds in their full human dimension instead of restricting what constitutes evidence to intentionally despiritualized facts. For example, imagine the effect of a single public hearing of a case of racial oppression in such a setting. Imagine if the community and the perpetrator listened with a legally sanctioned compassion to the suffering of the victim, and then with equal compassion to the desperate allegiance of the perpetrator to whatever distorted vision of racial superiority and false communal identity led him or her to inflict humiliation and pain on another (for listening with compassion does not mean sparing the offender of moral responsibility). And imagine the healing effect on the wider culture of watching such spiritual truths revealed on television—in contrast, say, to the alienating effect of watching the manipulations of the O. J. Simpson trial. The effect of a single such act of collective witnessing would have an immense impact by giving communal recognition, through a public legal process, to the pain of separation that pervades all of our lives and produces our worst distortions.

If you find it difficult to imagine how we could arrive at such a transformed vision of law's purpose and process, consider the rapid spread of the restorative justice movement in criminal law in America today. All across the country (but especially in Austin, Milwaukee, and Minneapolis), concerned lawyers, religious leaders, and community members are seeking to heal the community wounds caused by crime by creating safe contexts for victims to confront those who have hurt them with the full expression of the pain they have suffered, by allowing the perpetrators to come face-to-face with *the reality of the Other* that such a confrontation permits, and by sometimes eliciting sincere apologies and the sincere forgiveness that is the only true way to repair the spiritual harm of violence.

Of course, these restorative justice processes also require the offender to provide appropriate and meaningful restitution to the victim where possible—such as requiring, in one case, two teenagers who had defiled a Des Moines synagogue with swastikas to remove the offending symbols, perform other community service, and study Jewish history in addition to coming to understand, through face-to-face encounters with Holocaust survivors who were members of the synagogue, the enormity of the suffering associated with the swastika.

But the essential point of restorative justice is responding to crime in a manner consonant with love correcting that which revolts against love, with understanding crime as a wound to love that is itself almost always caused by such a wound that preceded the criminal act.

The power of this re-imagining of the healing power of law has been nowhere better revealed than in the work of South Africa's Truth and Reconciliation Commission under the leadership of Bishop Desmond Tutu. That commission has sought to avoid the vengeance that almost inevitably accompanies revolutions against a legacy of oppression by seeking, on behalf of the black majority, to forgive the white minority for the crimes of apartheid so long as the offenders acknowledged the truth of what they had done. With all its limitations based on the immense political complications accompanying the TRC's work (hearing and televising a review of some 22,000 cases, often involving extreme violence), the TRC is one of the greatest experiments in human history in a spiritual approach to healing social conflict. Imagine if we began now to take the next millennium to build our entire legal culture on the TRC's premise, announced in the title of Bishop Tutu's recent book, *No Future Without Forgiveness*.

Aspiring to Ideals, Not Complying with Rules

The basis for resolving disputes in civil cases should greatly diminish the role of rules in favor of wisdom guided by ethical and spiritual ideals. And just as the restorative justice movement has sought to foster the healing of the effects of violence on individuals and communities in criminal cases, the process of resolving civil disputes should draw upon the healing-centered focus of today's transformative mediation movement to assist in the realization of these spiritual and ethical ideals.

The importance of this shift can be best understood by grasping the changes in legal culture that will have to occur for David Korten's visionary conception of a postcorporate, sustainable economy to actually come into being. Korten's visionary alternative to globalization calls for the creation of "mindful markets" that will be based on such ethical values as true mutuality and cooperation, respect for the meaningfulness of one another's labor, the production of material goods that satisfy real human needs in a manner that respects the sacredness of the Earth, and respect by economic actors of the integrity of one another's local cultures. But the only way to bring about such an economic transformation is to build a parallel legal culture that gradually helps to develop acceptance of these values as expressive of a *just* economy, and to fill out the practical meaning of these ideal values through the resolution of individual cases over time—through a spiritual/ethical equivalent of our present individualist/materialist common law.

What this new legal culture requires is not a new set of abstract rules to be applied neutrally and logically to strangers who want to remain strangers, but a legal process that emphasizes empathic listening and the elicitation of the social meaning of an economic exchange in order to gradually overcome the legacy of capitalist self-interest that presupposes disconnection between the parties. The purpose of the legal proceeding must be to bring into being a *connection* expressive of Korten's vision of an ethical and sustainable economic culture. If a dispute develops between a buyer of coffee in the United States and a supplier from Central America, the legal resolution of the dispute should perhaps begin with a period of meditation and a sharing of food and music, followed by a telling of respective stories and a period of questioning (not "cross-examination") aimed at resolving the dispute in accordance with the aspiration to a spiritual and ethical ideal. The aspiration to respect the inherent worth and meaningfulness of one another's labor cannot be realized by a verbal statement of this ideal in the form of a rule to which alienated actors must conform their conduct, but by a process that realizes that this aspiration is an ideal "in front of us" that must be nurtured into existence through empathy, education, and reciprocal sensitivity.

Accompanying the replacement of rules with ideals in substantive law must be the development of spiritual remedies for the resolution of differences. In today's legal culture, the measure of all things is money. Consistent with the law's emphasis on material self-interest and the profit motive as the driving force of humankind, the legal remedy prescribed for almost every injury, whether economic (such as breach of contract) or noneconomic (such as sexual harassment) is money damages to be transferred from one disconnected stranger to another. In the civil area as in the criminal area, remedies aimed at creating social connection must emphasize acknowledgment of wrongdoing and the elicitation of genuinely voluntary apology and forgiveness. Of course, some and perhaps many cases will require some material restitution for material loss unjustly suffered by one party, but even here the aim wherever possible should be the promotion of future material assistance freely given, rather than just the payment of money.

Finally, while I have here emphasized re-imagining the relationship between a new legal culture and a new economic culture, the same re-imagining should occur in the noneconomic sphere of a reconceived civil society that aspires to connect us rather than separate us. To take but the most obvious example, the present rule of American tort law that there is no duty to attempt to rescue someone in distress—for example, someone drowning in front of you in a swimming pool—should be replaced by the ideal expectation that we will do all we can to rescue one another from isolation, fear, and danger, whether someone is drowning or someone is homeless. That we today associate this expectation as making sense only in relation to intimate family members is but a result of our conditioning that transforms those outside the tiny circle of blood relations into mere strangers, mere vessels of anonymity to whom we are not essentially related.

Lawyers as Healers

The role of lawyers must be equally reconceived as a calling rather than a trade. Instead of lawyers understanding themselves as neutral legitimators of their clients' individual self-interest, lawyers must reconceive of themselves as healers—that is, as spiritual actors whose aim is to reconcile the goals of their clients with the creation of a loving world. No longer should the ethics of the profession encourage the criminal defense lawyer to seek the acquittal of those whom the lawyer knows has committed violent acts, or, for example, encourage the lawyer for a lumber company to help his or her client destroy old-growth redwoods with impunity. Instead, lawyers should be trained from the first day in law school to engage every human situation with which they are confronted so as to create a better, more spiritually connected world. Rule manipulation and the cultivation of cleverness should give way, through the study not of "cases" but of ethically compelling and challenging situations, to empathic engagement with both one's clients' deepest hopes and the reconciliation of those hopes with the law's substantive ethical ideals. The purpose of the profession as a whole, therefore, should be the deepening of the collective moral consciousness of the community as a whole, as the community—finally facing the inevitability of the destruction of its own species if it cannot overcome the fear of the Other that has come to dominate its existence—approaches Martin Luther King's simple and universally desired moral truth.

Whether this vision sounds hopelessly utopian to you or fully realizable and even necessary—whether you believe such a profoundly connected vision of law and legal culture cannot be accomplished without unacceptable threats to individual freedom, or whether instead you believe such a vision of legally recognized spiritual connection is essential to the fulfillment of individual liberation—depends upon whether you really can embrace Martin Luther King's affirmation that loving connection made manifest in the world will be but the realization of who we already are. I can embrace this. And with Dr. King and John Lennon in my mind's eye, I know I'm not the only one.

★★★

Peter Gabel is president of New College of California and associate editor of *Tikkun* magazine. His new book is *The Bank Teller and Other Essays on the Politics of Meaning.*

THE ECONOMY

Hazel Henderson

April 17, 2050
Dear Hazel:

I write this letter in your memory. Even though I am approaching 60, I still miss having my grandmother here with me. I will never forget our long telephone discussions about the future. Though I was just a child, I knew about the work you did—trying to wake people up—and it made me proud. Especially that you had your own Web site. I was worried about animals going extinct, so I made you promise to take me on some of your trips—to China, India, Brazil, and other exotic places. And when you did, it helped me see our precious blue planet and understand the problems we humans faced at the turn of the century. You always used to say, "We humans can learn! Why, we only use about 10 percent of our brains!"

You'll be happy to know that we *did* learn.

As you know, the 20th century, the bloodiest in human history, left the human family with some unfinished business. Despite the veil of prosperity in America at the start of the new millennium, visionary people were able to see clearly the potential problems and sketch out an agenda of change.

You and many other futurists, scholars, and activists were warning us of the dangers of terrorism, small-arms trading, and local conflicts; the explosive gap between rich and poor; the spreading of new and old infectious diseases; the economic consequences of drug trafficking, money laundering, and speculation in the global currency markets. In addition, there was the threat of global environmental deterioration—spreading deserts, climate change, loss of species and biodiversity—due to primitive industrial technologies driving narrowly measured economic growth.

The problems went deeper. As you wrote so frequently, our extraordinary array of technological tools was both life threatening and life enhancing. These new tools ranged from nuclear, chemical, and biological weapons and bioengineering to jets, satellites, computers, the Internet, and the new tools of mass communication. *All* of these technologies, unassessed and unregulated, became global by the turn of the 21st century.

It was also becoming clear that the resource-rich developing countries, exploited under colonialism, were falling far behind the economic and social gains of the developed countries. Change was inevitable.

As you used to point out, all these threats to humanity's future were beyond the reach of any one country; national politics were just too divisive to create meaningful global changes. We needed a much larger, planetary context for all of our decision making—from personal and local to national, international, and global.

We have achieved this. Today, the world thinks in a more worldly way. Technological and social innovations are better aligned with global values, goals, and policies. These now promote human development, social justice, health, and well-managed economies within ecologically sustainable parameters. And these values are enshrined in global treaties, codes of corporate conduct, and civic principles that have created the better lives we enjoy now in 2050.

There are lots of examples. In 2001, the so-called G-7 industrial nations agreed to write off the unrepayable debt of heavily indebted countries, mostly in Africa. Many of these countries had been bypassed by the Industrial Age but began to flourish under the Solar Age. Information technologies enabled them to leapfrog the earlier, wasteful industrial models and avoid the huge infrastructure costs of highways and electric grids.

You would be happy to know that your proposal with Alan Kay from 1995 for a United Nations Security Insurance Agency was finally implemented. By 2010, 40 smaller U.N. member nations had joined the insurance pool. Their premiums now fund a properly trained contingent of peacekeepers and a grassroots network of local civic volunteer organizations that offer conflict resolution through truth-and-reconciliation hearings. This standing humanitarian force had first been requested by the U.N. secretary general in the late 1990s; it took just 10 years to reach fruition.

As a result of the success of the insurance initiative, several small Central American countries were able to shift their military strategies toward disbanding their armies and buying peacekeeping insurance policies. They redeployed their military budgets away from old U.S. F-16s and poured them instead into retraining soldiers; the windfall also benefited education, health, and infrastructure, and helped build homegrown economies linked via communications.

One more example of a smarter world order that would please you: The United Nations Security Council was expanded to include India, Brazil, and South Africa as permanent members, and the veto was abolished.

Part of this shift toward a worldcentric mindset was the result of the rise of women in leadership roles. Today, women own or manage 50 percent of the businesses and nonprofit organizations, and they hold a similar share of seats in parliaments, local governments, and judicial bodies. This has been achieved despite much patriarchal opposition, as your friend Riane Eisler predicted in *The Chalice and the Blade*. Helping it to occur was the emergence of universal availability of education, health care, and family planning.

Media has also played a role in creating a more worldly sensibility. The world court of public opinion on TV, radio, and the Internet has grown enormously, providing instant feedback, judgments, and sanctions on any overaggressive leader. As you know, the International Criminal Court, supported in the Rome Agreement of 1999, was at last ratified by the United States and the few other holdout countries in 2005. Today, Interpol swiftly arrests political tyrants and brings them to publicly televised trials. Thanks to multiaccess media, the Information Age has morphed into an Age of Truth where any corporate, institutional, or government malfeasance is instantly reported on the Internet.

NEW ENERGY SOURCES

Today, in 2050, our planet is ecologically rehabilitating. Its climate is stabilizing and its ozone shield is almost restored. Motivation to change our ways was stimulated by the tragic floods caused by megahurricanes and typhoons in 2031 and 2032. Ironically, it was the insurance companies that insisted on these laws to limit carbon emissions.

Much rangeland is reforested, because most people shifted gradually to healthier, vegetarian diets. Biodynamic agriculture replaced industrial, fossil-fueled megafarming in the early part of our century. This, along with the worldwide return to organic food and fiber production, restored soil fertility.

As for our cities, they have grown by in-filling wasted urban brownfields and parking lots. It took until 2025, but mass public transit finally replaced many freeways and unclogged downtown streets. Small, lightweight, zero-emission "hyper-cars" now tool between cities, powered by hydrogen fuel cells. By 2010, oil and gas had been replaced in the global economy by hydrogen, which flows in converted pipelines, as you predicted it would back in 1981.

You wouldn't be surprised that I went into an Internet-based energy bartering venture after our second trip to China. The enterprise became profitable in 2023, and its IPO did well on the Shanghai stock exchange. My wife and I enjoy Shanghai, now with clear skies, and we fish back in the Huang Po and Suzhou Rivers. The Shanghai municipal government's environmental bond issue of 1999 was spent well—on state-of-the-art green technologies.

The need for energy has been halved worldwide, even in industrial areas. The widespread use of communications, computers, TV, and the Internet made this possible, together with vastly increased energy efficiency and ecological design principles. The shift began in earnest in 2001, when OPEC announced that it would no longer feed the world's oil addiction but shift to cleaner natural gas. Oil became too valuable to burn; instead it was kept for making plastics and higher-value uses. This kicked the solar and renewable energy sectors into high gear. High gas prices in 2000 and 2001 accelerated the development of fuel-efficient cars, at last sending the internal combustion engine to the Smithsonian where it belonged. OPEC countries became major investors in the hydrogen economy and solar power.

By 2010, on-site, cheap solar power started lighting village homes and schoolhouses in OPEC countries as well as from Mongolia and Vietnam to Africa and the remote towns of Russia, Australia, and the Americas. Off-grid electricity powered Internet access, together with Palm Pilots. Millions of villagers started small communications businesses as Internet service providers, following the example of the Bangladeshi women partners in the Grameen Phone company. Shortwave, human-powered, windup radios, cell phones, and pagers became virtually free.

THE NEW GOVERNMENT

You'd be pleased, too, how governments have become more effective watchdogs for people and the globe. Some of the things that you envisioned, such as taxing currency speculators, arms traders, and polluters, are now part of international law. These taxes, as well as fines for abusing our global commons, were first collected by national governments to replace the taxes lost to speculators and island tax havens. After the financial crash of 2010, nations signed agreements and securities laws, like a global version of the old U.S. Securities and Exchange Commission. Tax evasion was outlawed, and many of these islands instead created thriving economies based on high-tech, web-bartering businesses and ecotourist attractions.

National budgets for education, health, social services, and ecological restoration gradually increased relative to military weapons procurement, as more women and their male supporters lobbied and organized for such new priorities. As you know, the 1990s post–Cold

War rethink of what constituted a country's sovereignty and national security continued well into 2010, despite the success of the U.N.'s military insurance program. Ultimately, these paradigm shifts in public debate and policy led to a redefinition of threats, particularly those posed by the 20th century's proliferation of weapons of mass destruction. Such weapons came to be seen as too dangerous to manufacture, stockpile, or transport, let alone use. Indeed, major sectors of our early 21st century economy were based on cleaning up nuclear stockpiles, radioactive waste facilities, and other toxic sites.

By 2010, this rethink of true human security slowly began to shift government budgets toward longer-term outcomes. Today, policymakers focus on prevention, futures research, technology assessment, scientific research, and new multidisciplinary statistics measuring overall quality of life to steer their decision making. As a result, decisions are more forward-looking and less political. Last year, for example, the U.S. Department of Defense and Peacekeeping allocated 50 percent of its budget to diplomacy and peace-related work.

Because of these changes, many of our brightest students now choose to embark on careers in global problem solving and public service. You would be happy to know that your great granddaughter, named for you, is a rising international public-interest lawyer.

And thanks to the Internet and other enhanced information tools, the democratic process is flourishing. Today we have electronic town meetings, referenda, and public-interest polling on major issues. The curse of money no longer taints elections now that all media, even in the United States (the last holdout), apportion free airtime to all candidates as a license requirement. The public—we all own the airwaves—finally reasserted their right of access to media. This took a long struggle with media owners over violent, degrading, distorting, and mind-numbing programming. But we succeeded.

THE NEW ECONOMY

All of the changes I've described have caused corporations and our concepts of value to change drastically.

This is best seen in how the field of accounting has evolved. Accounting (as well as economic analysis) has expanded to include multidimensional valuations of knowledge, software, human and social capital, and ecological assets. Likewise, social and environmental costs of all public and private policies and decision making are now deducted to allow full-cost pricing and accurate national indicators. This shift caused the accounting and statistics sectors to boom, as we learned that we needed to measure what we treasure and monitor unhealthy trends.

Information has become the modern currency. The change began around the turn of the century, when distorted money-flows and cronyism in credit-creation created inequities that led to the rise of barter—negotiated, naturally, via the Internet and involving participants both local and global. The International Monetary Fund was abolished, you remember, in 2005, after another meltdown of the old money system. The World Bank's lending was then focused on education and health delivery in partnership with civic society. All information on the activities of such international agencies—as well as those at national and local levels—was posted daily on their Web sites by 2004.

Back then, corporations, most of which had become global by the late 20th century, managed to escape national taxes and regulation. But after the famous Microsoft decision of the U.S. courts in 2000, antitrust laws were extended globally via international agreements. Corporate chartering also came under internationalized laws. Companies could no longer incorporate in tax havens, which allowed the old scams of less-than-full disclosure, insider-trading, and annual reports that concealed the social and environmental costs incurred by their business operations.

After the defeat of the notorious Multilateral Agreement on Investment and the decline of the World Trade Organization after the "Battle of Seattle" in 1999, corporations were rechartered to optimize the interests of all stakeholders: investors, consumers, employees, local communities, and the environment. Charters had to be re-earned every 5 years. Many companies chose employee stock ownership, as you promoted. After all, employees are more motivated as shareholders in the enterprise. Besides, knowledge has at last become recognized as a basic factor of production—along with natural resources and social capital. Capitalism had changed accordingly, as employees carried a company's intellectual capital in their heads and could walk out at any time.

Even by the year 2000, inventors in many thousand of garages and small start-ups had created the new economies of information, electronic trading, exchange and barter, preventive health care, education, and services. Millions of formerly disabled people were absorbed into jobs with the enabling technologies of computerized interfaces. By 2009, biotech companies had perfected artificial eyes, muscles, and other organs. All of these were supported by technologies of the post-fossil-fuel, solar-based economies of today's Solar Age.

Not all of these 21st-century technologies were developed in response to traditional money-based price signals. Indeed, most of these start-ups in solar and renewable energy, biotech, the Internet, and human services were unprofitable. They required billions in frontloaded capital by visionary investors and venture capitalists who believed that the world's economies and societies could be redesigned to work for 100 percent of humanity. In risk-taking cultures like the United States, we saw millions of day traders buy these stocks by borrowing, as in the gold rush era. Millions were made and lost—as in all periods of rapid technological change. Many voluntary nonprofit groups, some of them leaders in environmental and human rights, spurred on the visionary entrepreneurs and investors. Together they led the great transition to the knowledge-rich, ecologically based, sustainable economies that emerged by 2025.

These pioneers operated in the nonmoney half of all societies, where visions, ideas, entrepreneurialism, and faith in the future come before profit. They championed the real needs that the traditional price system did not detect or serve. These pioneers of the unpaid, cooperative, voluntary sectors—your "love economy"—organized at local, state, and national levels. They served people directly, educating the public, politicians, and government officials, using all of the new public-access media and the Web. They reshaped academic curricula and helped enshrine into laws the enhanced rights, public investments, and social innovations we now enjoy.

The economy slowly dematerialized as the use of energy and materials became superefficient. Companies, pushed by laws at the turn of the century, soon reaped profits in reclaiming their cars, computers, and other products for reconditioning and resale. More people turned away from consumer goods to self-development and services in the human potential movement and the love economy. For millions, their time had become more valuable than goods or money.

These economic changes occurred first in industrial societies, with a myriad of new businesses emerging to fulfill important social needs, delivering home-based services, health care, fitness, and care for the disabled and elderly as well as a variety of essential maintenance activities. These private businesses also offered community education, social services, drug counseling, youth rehabilitation, recycling, garbage composting, thrift stores, barter clubs, local-contract organic food, and solar and renewable energy companies. The old Gross National Product based on goods and money transactions began tanking in 2003 in Europe and North America. Millions of citizens simply no longer found the time spent shopping as satisfying as family and community activities. We all rejoiced with you when the new Quality-of-Life Indicators (such as those you pioneered and produced with the Calvert Group of mutual funds in 2000) began to soar!

Today, in 2050, these activities are all multi-billion-dollar sectors that provide around 50 percent of our jobs and livelihoods—just as weapons contracting and other heavy industries did at the end of the last century.

All of us have benefited from the changes. By 2010, the sustainability boom had led to virtually zero unemployment. Prison populations in the United States fell from two million in 2000 to one million in 2010 as the health, education, and caring sectors grew and poverty decreased. The curse of racism in the United States diminished too, in a media-rich, multicultural, interdependent world. Your friend, Reverend Jesse Jackson, was right. It is cheaper to educate all of our young people at Harvard than to send them to prison.

Thinking globally was the first step toward creating the policies and private changes that we needed to make. They led to the world of 2050, of which we are proud today. Things are not perfect, of course. Life would be boring!

But it also took a rebirth of spirituality. Over the past 50 years, our understanding of human psychology and spirituality has begun to match our knowledge of the material world. We have learned that in times of accelerating change, visioning exercises are necessary and pragmatic and can yield practical results. You would be happy to know that visioning a world of peace, equity, cooperation, and ecological sustainability is taught in all of our schools. Parenting is honored, and loving relationships are taught and showcased in our media.

It has been a pleasure to reconnect spiritually with you on my birthday via this letter, dear Grandma Hazel. We continue to share our visions and intentions in the great quantum hologram of our cosmos. When I decide to discarnate, probably early in the 22nd century, it will be a joy to join you in the infinite abundance of the cosmos.

Your loving grandson,
Brendan A. Cassidy

★★★

World-renowned futurist and economist Hazel Henderson is the author of *Beyond Globalization: Shaping a Sustainable Global Economy* (1999), *Building a Win-Win World: Life Beyond Global Economic Warfare* (1996), and *Paradigms in Progress: Life Beyond Economics* (1991).

GOVERNMENT

Dennis Kucinich

As the chambers and passageways of the Great Pyramid are said to have encrypted the past and predicted the future, the majesty of the U.S. Capitol—its chambers and passageways, its paintings and pronouncements—is similarly evocative of the past, present, and future of America's government.

As I sit inside the chamber of the U.S. House of Representatives as a member of the 106th Congress and try to imagine the best this government can be a half-century from now, I am moved by the beauty of the People's House. A giant eagle soars above, etched in glass against a huge canopy, its wings spread over the assembled Congress. I noticed it instantly when I first walked onto the floor as an elected member. The eagle is quick, daring, possessed of exceptional vision. It is symbolic of our national spirit, which, when it soars, is awesome to behold. Secure in the eagle's beak is a prophetic banner inscribed with our nation's original motto: E PLURIBUS UNUM. "Out of many, one." I think of my own journey as one of 435 members of the House representing 50 states. Here, I and those who chose me establish the merger of "We the People of the United States." The unity that the banner forever proclaims above the heads of the members of Congress speaks not to the fixed idea of flat history but to our interconnectedness—how the choices that each one of us makes are choices for all of us; that the idea of unity precedes us, is present before us, and calls to us from a distant future. The very first sentence of the Declaration of

Independence, in performing the act of dissolving "the political bands which have connected" people with one another, confirms the underlying power of cohesiveness. The consciousness of interconnectedness, together with the principle of freedom, was the thought that birthed a nation.

"We the People" is also prologue. The constitutive is intuitive. The awareness that America exists as the thoughts, words, and deeds of each and every one of us can empower us to begin to create today the nation that we want for ourselves and for our children 50 years from now.

Each time we vote, each day we address the House, members of Congress face the Speaker's rostrum, above which, carved in marble, is the national motto adopted by Congress in 1956: IN GOD WE TRUST. This act of faith is stunning in a nation whose Constitution celebrates not only freedom of religion but the separation of Church and State in the First Amendment. Separation of Church and State is an ethic that encourages the unity of all Americans, whether Christian, Jew, Muslim, Buddhist, other faith, or nonfaith. It is, after all, the House of all the people. A paradox occurs: It is clear that the founders never intended to separate the government from spiritual values. Otherwise, what of the summary appeal to the protection of Divine Providence in the Declaration itself? A tour of the Capitol reveals the spiritual heritage of the United States, with images of angels, divine light, and entreaties for holy intervention abounding in paintings, sculpture, and inscription, all describing a nation walking a lit path toward something intangible, just beyond the five senses. How else to explain, in the very center of the Capitol, in the canopy of the dome above the Rotunda, Constantino Brumidi's fresco *The Apotheosis of Washington*? Rising above a rainbow, looking down from starry heavens, our first president is flanked by winged beings in a joyous masterpiece of the transfiguring power of democracy. I've often come to the Rotunda in the early mornings, approaching it as I may a grand cathedral, to seek solitude for reflection.

At the beginning of every day, Congress is called to solemn attention with a prayer—a focused, concentrated meditation, a call for higher consciousness to help us carry forward the people's business. Congress as a repository of faith might strike some as brilliant hyperbole. But as representatives of the people, we are truly called by faith and *to* faith. Faith in our constituents, faith in ourselves, faith in our nation, faith in something that transcends our condition, some higher awareness that we can reach for, some understanding that comes from spirit when we ask for it. That we ultimately get what we pray for is a truism. What shall our prayers be for the government of the United States of tomorrow? Can you imagine the power of unity of prayer and purpose? Some religions teach that faith is empowered through good works. What if in the next 30 years we pray and work for Union, Justice, Liberty, Tolerance, and Peace, those foundational spiritual principles memorialized at the base of the Speaker's platform that faces the assembled Congress? What if we pray and work for a more perfect union 50 years hence?

In the Capitol, you can sense a certain spirit permeating the air, and you can imagine the possibilities of the people's government to inspire, to create new forms. The Capitol is infused with the energies of everyone who ever served here; of every member of Congress, every senator, every president. The energy and the intentions of not only officeholders but of all Americans are charged in this alabaster city. People can feel the history of the Capitol. They can feel the portent as well. This sense of discovery gives loft to our highest aspirations for ourselves and our nation. It confirms our sense of achievement. It informs our sense of the physical beauty of the structure of thought of our constitutional democracy and the principles that shaped it. Imagine the possibilities of tapping into the higher consciousness of the Spirit of America.

But just as our nation's great heart can almost be heard to sing, comes a jolt—and one is returned to a dense, painful reality: Washington, D.C., 2000, is hyper-paced, fearful, and confused. Instead of debate that leads to a new synthesis expressing an underlying unity, we are trapped in dichotomous thinking that devolves into the incoherence of right versus left, Democrat versus Republican, rich versus poor, male versus female, young versus old, black versus white. The same discontinuity that occurred when our nation divided North from South is accelerated in the separation of people from the very government that is the work of their own hands.

Government is a manifestation of the impulse of the human community to organize for social and economic purposes. The attack on government is essentially an attack upon ourselves and our aspirations of what we are to become as a people. The attack on the institution of democratic government is in and of itself antidemocratic. It is a theft of the anchor points or philosophical coordinates of a free society. It would disestablish the American community and replace it with the tyranny of monolithic rule, whether by concentrated wealth or corporate control. As conscience becomes subordinate to commerce, we become alienated from our inalienable rights. Lost in an alien nation, people do not trust the government and the government does not trust the people. A dialectic of fear sets in. Institutional decay and public apathy follow. Self government deteriorates as people feel that neither their voice nor their vote matters. Government then loses its legitimacy, and Lincoln's prayer for an imperishable "government of the people, by the people and for the people" is not heard, lost in the deafening roar of the cash registers of interest groups who view democratic principles as an impediment to doing business, notwithstanding human needs.

Capitol Hill today is abuzz with busy people. We run, under the watchful eyes of a large security force, past the metal detectors, from meeting to meeting, tethered to our cell phones and our pagers, in a time famine, starving for an extra moment, rushing headlong as to the Mad Hatter's tea party, just a step ahead of an avalanche of details. The pace of Congress is not a human pace, and one gets the feeling of the rehearsed, automatic activity of a supernumerary who is not permitted to know the main plot. As we hurry from vote to vote, the most frequently asked question members ask on the floor of the House is: "What are we voting on?" No time to say hello or good-bye—we are already late for our next meeting. We are bombarded with information that will be absolutely meaningless 50 years from now, sapping us of the time we need to do things that *will* matter 50 years from now.

It is urgent that we require of ourselves a more human pace, a slower, more natural rhythm of human interaction that provides for something more than a superficial presence in relationship to ourselves, our loved ones, and our nation; to take time to think about the America of tomorrow and our place in it, that we may again make great plans. We have to transport our consciousness of America into the future and imagine that which cannot be imagined; we must re-create, summon new forms from the unknown, and draw forth new structures that spring from higher awareness, a greater understanding of ourselves, our nation, and the world. A spiritual dedication and practice of transcendence to create new alternatives can awaken our highest aspirations, can invoke a sense of great purpose, can energize our spiritual capabilities and lead to our own transformation and to the transformation of our nation. How much power has the human heart!

Remember a child's belief in the power of magic, of wizards, of shape shifting. That towering instinct toward transformation is nascent in the human heart. Once joined to the soul's purpose, that instinct lets the human spirit take flight to explore the stars in the heavens within and above us, and we take our place within Washington's apotheosis. It is that instinct that led the Founders to create beyond existing structures of 18th-century thought and fling far into the future a United States built upon hallowed Liberty, Justice, Equality—principles that give America the ability to adapt to an undreamed of future. While we recognize that the Founders participated in a world of exceptional cruelty, with its dependence on the abominable institution of slavery, its disregard of the essential role of women as cocreators, and its appropriation of the land and lives of its Native American sons and daughters, we can still retrieve the highest sentiments of the time. At the same time, we must include the lowest sentiments of our historical experience. The path to the future is now, through truth, reconciliation, and transformation.

Can you hear the reveille of the American Spirit? It calls us forth to remember where we came from as a nation, to reclaim our spiritual heritage and the finest human potential that radiates from it.

On my way to vote, I complete my climb up the stairs of the House of Representatives and pass through doors on which three-dimensional iron figures reveal another reality of our national identity: war. The heavy metal passageway that leads to the floor of the House is a gallery in high relief of grim reminders from the American Revolutionary War, of the clash of arms and the sacrifice of lives to ensure America's survival as a nation. This very House was burned by the British in 1814. On some evenings, a faint, acrid smell (something burnt?!), its origin unknown, haunts the air near the upper entrance to the House.

The Capitol, and all of America, is a panorama of battlefield tributes, exacting such a powerful claim on our national psyche that even in peacetime, even after the demise of the Soviet Union and with it the end of the Cold War, our nation still spends more than $300 billion a year to warranty our preparedness for future fighting. Ghosts gather, blood spirits hover, and our fears float freely when our country's resources are to be allocated.

The searing truth is that in the 20th century, more than 100 million members of the human community, most of them civilian noncombatants, perished in wars. At the dawn of the 21st century, violence seems to be an overarching theme in the world, encompassing personal, group, national, and international conflict. It now extends to the production of nuclear, biological, and chemical weapons of mass destruction for use on land and sea, in air and outer space. Real and anticipated conflict is accepted, even glorified, as intrinsic to the human condition, with few questions about whether the structures of thought, word, and deed that we have inherited are relevant to the maintenance, growth, and survival of our entire civilization.

Our national policy dialogue is infected with war metaphors: the war on poverty, the war on drugs, the war on illiteracy, the war on this or that. Our children are immersed in video war games. Our sports are rife with war talk. Our media often glorify war. How did we as a society develop such an ardor for arms? Our Founders, while providing for the Common Defense, did not envision America as a land of conquistadores. President Franklin Delano Roosevelt, at the beginning of World War II, encouraged steadfastness among the American people: "We have nothing to fear but fear itself." As the war wound down, FDR aspired to ending the beginning of all wars: "Today we are faced with the pre-eminent fact that, if civilization is to survive, we must cultivate the science of human relationships—the ability of all peoples, of all kinds, to live together and work together in the same world, at peace."

As we stand on the threshold of a new millennium, it is time to free ourselves, to jettison our illusions and fears and transform age-old challenges with new thinking. We can conceive of peace as not simply the absence of violence but the active presence of the capacity for a higher evolution of human awareness, of respect, trust, and integrity. Of peace, wherein we all may tap the infinite capabilities of humanity to transform consciousness and conditions that impel or compel violence at a personal, group, or national level toward creating understanding, compassion, and love. We can bring forth new understandings where peace, not war, becomes inevitable. Can we move from wars to end all wars to peace to end all war?

As our fears ossify thought, so our hopes can excite new thinking toward the construction of a new social reality for the new century, to create a new architecture for human relationships and transport its structure directly to our system of government. America can, in the first half of this century, create a cabinet-level Department of Peace. The mission would be to make nonviolence the central organizing principle in our society, advancing human relations in domestic as well as foreign policy. It takes an act of Congress and an act of faith in our transformative capacities to evolve to a condition where violence and war become archaic.

One possessed of a sober understanding of politics and government could fairly challenge such a concept as impractical and hopelessly idealistic since, in the view of some, war is the very invention of politics and government. We look to government to repair the nation, yet our challenges at their core are not necessarily those on which government trains its focus. Our greatest challenges are spiritual at their source: a misunderstanding of power, the heavy burden of unrelieved materialism, fear of death. If all that government does is address symptoms, we will always be dissatisfied with the government. Government itself must be moved to a higher level of thought, to a quickened cognizance of its generative role as a convenor of consciousness for the country. Our Founders understood that the material foundations of an enduring democracy rest upon immaterial principles. They knew that our journey here on Earth is to carry spiritual principles into the material world, and in spiritualizing the material, our thoughts, words, and deeds are made holy, and we are elevated with them.

"We must cultivate the science of human relationships," said the noble FDR shortly before he passed away. You are wondering what a Department of Peace might look like. A proposal is being crafted at this very moment, with the help of thousands of people across America, to create a Department of Peace whose domestic application would be to develop policies that address human aggression, domestic violence, spousal abuse, child abuse, and mistreatment of the elderly. It could work to create new policies directed at drug and alcohol abuse. It would lead to a reevaluation of the causes of crime. It could give us a new chance to review failed approaches to punishment that have resulted in more than two million Americans being confined. It should enable the rescue of human lives and the liberation of our society from self-imprisonment. It could analyze present policies, employ field-tested programs, and craft new approaches for dealing with violence in our society: school violence, gang or racial violence, violence against gays and lesbians, and clashes between police and community.

In its international work, the Department of Peace would deal with issues of human security, whether that security is threatened by geographic, religious, ethnic, or class conflicts. It would face the economic threats to human security, from inequities resulting from trade, unequal distribution of wealth, or scarcity of natural resources. It could foster a new consciousness of peace in our society, just as our national consciousness is informed by other structures in the government. It can be done. It starts with our own commitment to peace, to nonviolence in our own lives. The hymn entreats us: "Let there be peace on Earth and let it begin with me."

There is an intricate, synergistic relationship that exists between the people and their government. The idea of self-government implies that the self and the government are interrelated. We live in the nation and the nation lives in us. In understanding the reciprocity between ourselves and the government, we come to understand the power that we have to move our government, as we have the power to move our own lives. This is not an abstraction. This is an application of the spiritual principles that the Founders and their successors brought to us. We call upon them, as secular saints, for inspiration to help us become more than we are as a nation.

We call upon Washington to reconfirm our nation. We call upon Jefferson to enlighten us. We call upon Lincoln to heal our divisions. We call upon Theodore Roosevelt to embolden us. We call upon Franklin Roosevelt to encourage us. And we call upon the Founding Mothers and their successors to temper us, to nurture us, to make us gentle, and to seek peace as a light within. We ask forgiveness as we call upon our slave ancestors, who built this country from their stolen labor and ruined families. We seek atonement as we ask them for the courage to overcome and to continue the upward quest toward the emancipation of each and every human being. We call upon our Native American ancestors to help us reestablish our relationship with the Great Spirits of the Earth—the water, the sky, the wind—to give us the wisdom to heal the land to which we all belong. We seek reconciliation with our American Indian brothers and sisters through restoration of their dignity and full opportunity. We can call and they will answer, because time is an illusion and in matters of spirit and energy, the past, the present, and the future are one.

Each of us can lead in this effort to renew America, and to enable this nation to take its rightful place as a nation among nations, a "shining city on a hill" whose light gleams not only from the Capitol Dome against the darkest night, but whose light shines from within its people. We can become as presidents of our own lives by harkening to the words of "America the Beautiful," confirming "thy goal in self-control" to understand the interrelationship between the unfolding of democratic principles in our own lives and the upholding of democratic principles in the life of our nation, to consider that personhood and nationhood is a craft of the spirit. It is how we treat everyone. It is how we speak to one another. It is in affirming the humanity of anyone we may view as an enemy, whether across the street or over the seas, that we assert our own humanity.

None of us will go forward unless we all go forward together, united as Americans—we the people, continuing the work of forming a more perfect union, under the watchful eye of the Spirit of America.

★★★

Dennis Kucinich, a Democrat, serves in the U.S. House of Representatives, representing the 10th district of Ohio. Among his congressional assignments is serving on the Committee on Government Reform. Kucinich's political career began in the late 1960s when he was elected to the Cleveland City Council. In 1977, at the age of 31, he became mayor of Cleveland. After serving one term, Kucinich went on to become a teacher, writer, consultant, and commentator. He returned to politics in 1994.

POLITICAL PARTIES

Robert Roth

It is the first Tuesday of November 2050. Voting day. We Americans are casting our ballots electronically—in homes, hospitals, colleges, businesses, rest homes, hotels, airports, everywhere—and yet it's a national holiday, so everyone can consider their choice carefully, so everyone can vote.

It's been a short campaign season: 12 weeks. Five candidates vie for president. We know what the candidates stand for, who their running mates will be, who will serve in their cabinets. We know enough about their personal lives to know that they are honest, honorable women and men who genuinely seek to lead. We know all this because information about them abounds—widely disseminated, equally available to all. Campaigns are issue driven. Long gone are the days of soft money and political action committees that ripped out the heart and soul of our representative democracy. In its place are publicly funded campaigns.

All political parties qualify for the ballot on equal terms. When we register to vote, we simply check off the box for the political party of our choice on the registration form. Taking a cue from fair-minded laws passed at the turn of the century in several progressive states, any political party that registers $\frac{1}{20}$ of 1 percent of a state's voters automatically earns a spot on the ballot. Because we now use the system of proportional representation, candidates don't really have to run against an opponent; they run on their own platforms, their own records. If the candidates for a party get 5 percent of the vote, they gain 5 percent of the seats in Congress.

It all seems so simple, so obvious, such common sense. And it is. How we got here is a another story. And understanding the path helps us cherish—and preserve—our hard-earned democratic gains.

The old adage is true: "All politics is local." It's also true that "All political transformation is personal." How we got to where we are today can best be told through the lives and experiences of millions of people who lived through the turn of the century and who helped to forge our new politics. What follows is my story. It is not unique. It is just one voice. But it is a voice from those wonderful, tumultuous, sacred times.

What a difference 50 years makes. Really, only the most delusional or most utopian thinker—or one who was in on the ground floor when the "spirituality and politics" movement first caught fire at the dawn of the new millennium—could possibly have envisioned the transformation of our political process that we enjoy (and I emphasize that word *enjoy*) midway through the 21st century.

Gone are the terrible days of money-driven politics; of slanderous campaign ads; of the gnawing sense of impotence that our votes truly did not count, that our voices were not heard.

Instead, people vote. And votes count—they actually shape public policy. We have now what most democracies (except America) had at the end of the 20th century, only better: a fair-minded system of proportional representation. Honorable candidates run for office and are able to remain honorable, untainted as they are by special interest influence. Hot-button issues of the political reform movements of 50 years ago, such as spending limits, term limits, and ballot access limits, are a distant memory. Today, many political parties flourish, fueled not by contentious debate but rather by a healthy spirit of political diversity and consensus building. Our elections are now, as James Madison hoped they would be nearly 300 years ago, "a national conversation." Our politics are a collective means to arrive at a common good.

Am I kidding? Not a chance. At least that's what I would have said, in more graphic language, 50 years ago. And for good reason. After all, I was one among so many who demonstrated on Telegraph Avenue back in the 1960s at the University of California, Berkeley, and again who pushed so hard against the two-party corporate monolith in the 1990s in Washington, D.C. Despite my legendary optimism, at the time I couldn't see the extent of the progress, couldn't see how it would all come out in the end.

Yet it is quite clear that the seeds for our current political renaissance were sown in those months and years around the turn of the millennium. Our new politics emerged out of the rubble of a bloated two-party political system that imploded on itself. It was a time when we took back our politics. When voter turnout had sunk to the lowest in U.S. history—and less than 1 out of 10 college students were bothering to drag themselves to the polls. What happened to fill the vacuum? Did the two main parties wise up and reconfigure themselves to meet the desires of the people? Nope. Didn't happen. Instead, alternate "third party" movements caught fire, capturing the hearts and souls of the young and the disenfranchised, altering forever our political landscape. It was also a time when citizens did an end-run around legislators intoxicated by special interest money, writing their own reform-minded legislation and passing it into law before any government committee could table the discussion.

Those were the millennial days. But in truth, the seeds for political transformation were being sown decades before the year 2000, as millions of people were waking up, as if from lifetimes-long slumber, to see a clearer picture of life—of the interconnectedness of all things, of the essential wholeness of life, of spirituality as the driving force behind all things human and divine. Seeds were being sown for a political renewal unimaginable to the casual observer of the day, as the invisible but very real content of spirituality arose in our lives and transformed everything about the way we lived, including the way we healed our sick, grew our food, fueled our cities, educated our young, and resolved our conflicts in our homes, communities, and world. When that rising tide of spirituality finally reached our politics, then life changed fully and wholly for all of us.

I pause here to apologize for my zealotry. But you see, I am what my friends used to call a political junkie. I have been that way my whole life. In fact, I was born into a family of political junkies. I grew up in Northern California with three adults in my life: Mom, Dad, and a man named Adlai Stevenson. (A few of you *must* remember Adlai. He was a Democratic senator from Illinois who ran twice for president and lost handily to Dwight Eisenhower.) I was raised to revere politics. As a Reformed Jew, going to synagogue was a good thing, an option, but as an Orthodox Liberal, *caring* about politics, participating in the *process*, that was sacrosanct. Then suddenly President Kennedy got killed, and then Martin Luther King Jr. That was devastating. But what really blew me away was Bobby Kennedy's assassination. I was a high school senior then, working hard for him. I saw him speak in San Francisco a few days before I saw him killed on television that night in Los Angeles. I think it took me 25 years to get over that one. I had this innocent, open heart, and *bam!* I got it smashed.

I wasn't alone, of course. It blew most of my friends away. It knocked me out of politics for a good long while. I went to Berkeley in October 1968. I remember it like it was yesterday. I was drawn by my genetic makeup to the honest principles of radical politics, but repulsed by the divisiveness, the violence, the insatiable quest for power.

I started looking elsewhere for making a change, for making a difference. I started meditating and I loved it. I taught meditation to inmates on death row at San Quentin Prison and to executives and factory workers at General Motors. I even wrote a book about my experiences. I got interested in developing higher states of consciousness and lost my connection to big-party politics. Gradually, gradually, I pretty much stopped taking sides, stopped caring, stopped voting. And I wasn't alone. We all did.

That is when I remember that politics got weird. Politicians from the two main parties more and more started sounding the same. Oh, yes, there were differences on a few key issues like gun control and abortion. But on other big-ticket items, such as health care, fighting crime, energy, and foreign policy, I was hard pressed to find anything substantive to distinguish the two.

Of course, there were millions and billions of dollars floating around the campaigns of both parties. While we were sleeping (or meditating), lobbyists for huge corporations were wide awake, funding their favorite candidates, writing their own laws and pushing them through Congress—basically taking control of the government. And, amazingly, we let them! We didn't believe that what was happening in Washington, D.C., made much of a difference anyway.

Then we learned that it did. When we wanted to know if the foods we were eating had been genetically engineered, the government said that we didn't need to know—and wouldn't tell us! When we wanted money to rebuild the decaying infrastructure of thousands of public schools, the government said no, there was no money to be found. We never heard any serious discussion about redirecting billions of dollars to education that had been allocated to building costly weapons the Pentagon did not even want!

In the midst of our own deep inner peace, cultivated by years of personal work, we got fed up. We did. We got active again. And then things really started to change. We joined nonprofit groups, pressuring and lobbying and coercing and voting out elected leaders who answered to special interests and not the people's interests. It proved to be so much work, though. There were so many causes, and too much resistance from corporate lobbies who outspent us 100 to 1, 1,000 to 1, 1,000,000 to 1.

We didn't give up. We kept at it. Then some of us had a thought, a simple, quiet, abstract, almost annoying little thought: Let's get political. We ignored it and pushed it out and drowned it out and diluted it with other thoughts about the filth of politics and the irrelevance of politics and the irreverence of politics. But the thought wouldn't go away—at least for some of us, whose calling it was to be involved in politics.

We migrated toward third-party politics and worked with Ralph Nader of the Green Party and John Hagelin of the Natural Law, presidential candidates whose personal ethics and social vision we shared and admired. We worked with countless wise and dedicated seekers of public office on the local level. We faced head-on the mean-spirited, mind-numbing, energy-depleting laws put into place by political powers designed to keep out the contrarian voice from the national dialogue. We collected millions of signatures to get our candidates on the ballot while the Republicans and Democratic organizers sat back and collected none. We were locked out of taxpayer-funded debates, so we held our own—or turned to the Internet to get our word out. We received a huge boost from the two main parties, who continued to say things and get caught doing things that drove millions and millions of thoughtful people to think out of the box, to think that maybe the two main parties did not have a monopoly on the best solutions to our problems and that maybe, just maybe, other political parties might give voters a reason to vote.

Looking back, third parties (oh, how I detested that phrase, but today we have several strong parties, so no matter) accomplished a lot in those heady, transitional days. They mobilized people, injected a new dialogue into the political debate, and gave people a reason to care and a reason to vote.

Powerful new organizations emerged for people who did not have partisan politics in their blood—organizations that provided an effective forum for a new political activism that married spiritual growth with social involvement, a precursor of what we have today. For example, Marianne Williamson's Global Renaissance Alliance showed millions of people that the same mechanisms that we use to transform our inner lives must be put to use to transform our world.

But what really opened the door wide for an influx of new ideas and the onset of our new politics was an obscure little process called ballot initiatives. Ballot what? you might have asked, even back then. It turns out that ballot initiatives were a huge loophole in the regulations, and a major crack in the armor of the political status quo. They were an opening that no one saw coming but that helped to change everything.

Here is what happened. Frustrated with politicians who repeatedly ignored widespread public sentiment for something as commonsense as campaign finance reform, citizens in every state and in every community circumvented the politicians. They took advantage of their constitutional right to place on the ballot legislation they crafted themselves. Overcoming unimaginable resistance from politicians and special interests, unsung democratic reformers won approval for foundational laws that changed our politics for good. They passed laws that provided public funding of election campaigns and leveled the playing field for all legitimate political parties to gain access to the ballot. They even reworked our electoral methods, opening the way for a fairer form of government-proportional representation.

When you are swimming in a vast ocean of change, trying with all your might to stay afloat, you never know which moves that you make will turn out to be significant and which will not. But now, with the benefit of hindsight, the cornerstones of our new politics are clear.

In 1999, citizens in Maine used a ballot initiative to pass a campaign finance law—long dismissed by the state legislators despite overwhelming public support—appropriately called the Clean Money Reform Act. This law gave candidates an opportunity to receive public funds for running their campaigns. (To qualify, they had to demonstrate a modest but fair ability to raise a few hundred contributions of $5 each.) The alternative was to continue to use soft money, PACs, and so on. The grassroots initiative was fought in the courts before it appeared on the ballot. It was fought again in the courts after the initiative won the vote, and in the process it captured widespread public support to create a new atmosphere of candidate accountability in the state. The Maine initiative was promptly copied in several other states and served as a catalyst for the overhauling of our campaign finance laws into what we have today—public financing for all election campaigns.

The ballot initiative process also worked its magic on ballot access laws, overturning, for example, a terrible law that had been on the books in Florida since the 1920s that had effectively banned all political candidates other than Republicans or Democrats from running for office. Think I am exaggerating? Consider this: In 1998, if you wanted to run for statewide office on the ballot in Florida as a Republican or Democrat, you would need to collect zero signatures. If you were an Independent, Green, Reform, Natural Law, or Libertarian candidate, however, you would be forced, by law, to collect 250,000 valid petition signatures. Is that a lot? Yes, when you consider that the number of signatures is more than you would need if you wanted to run at the time for *head of state* in all the countries in Europe, New Zealand, Australia, and Canada combined. The Florida legislature refused to change that law for more than 75 years. But in 1998, citizens qualified a ballot initiative that completely eliminated that outrageous requirement. Of course, the law was met with fierce resistance by Republicans and Democrats as well as the National Rifle Association and the National Organization for Women. Nonetheless, Revision 11 won by a whopping 2-to-1 margin in the popular vote.

Finally, who would have thought that a ballot initiative campaign launched in 1998 by a handful of citizens in Alaska would be the catalyst for the kind of sweeping electoral reform that we have across the country today? I am speaking about the ballot initiative that was to make proportional representation the law in the state in 2002. "PR," as it is more commonly called, was the system in place in most every democracy in the world by the end of the 20th century. Unlike the winner-take-all approach that defined the U.S. democracy until a few decades ago, proportional representation gives voters direct representation in Congress based upon the total percentage of votes each political party receives in the election. Controversial, even radical at the time, it was an approach favored by a people weary and frustrated with a system that had yielded them nothing even though their candidates had attracted sizable numbers of votes.

Isn't it interesting that so much of our political system today grew out of the formative grassroots movements at the turn of the millennium? Who knew at the time that such small, bootstrap efforts would produce something so grand and noble as we have today? I certainly didn't see it coming—not to this extent, not on this scale.

I often reminisce about how different it is today compared to what it was like when I was 20 years old, or even 50. Then, politics was so contentious, so criminal. Today we have none of that. Then, the two extreme political poles—left and right, liberal and conservative—drove a wedge between neighbors, clouded issues, dominated debates. Today there is none of that. It turned out, for example, that the solution to the health care crisis that had polarized liberals and conservatives at the dawn of the new millennium did not come out of an agreement over who would pay for whose illness. Instead, the solution featured proven strategies to *prevent* illness and make people healthier. A foundational change in our entire health care system pursued prevention with at least the same vigor as the old system had focused on disease care. Prevention saved money—that kept the conservatives happy—and prevention kept more people healthy, making liberals happy.

As I've mentioned, today our campaign seasons are short. A few weeks. There are several political parties on the ballot. Every party collects the same number of petition signatures to enter the political arena. No candidate or party feels compelled to seduce money from anywhere. The First Amendment still guarantees freedom of speech—and everyone, in principle, can give to any candidate they choose.

Nonetheless, no candidate opts to take that money. We taxpayers are happy to give a small token of our incomes to support the political process.

It's true that we now take for granted the political world in which we live. How could it have been otherwise? A better question is, How did it change? It changed because we changed. We woke up to the interconnectedness of all things. In our families, in our churches, temples, synagogues, and mosques, in our schools and in our businesses, on our farms, even in the way we conduct our foreign policy, we have come to live one of the greatest scientific and spiritual truths of all time: We are all one. We are united at our source. That unity, which has always pervaded us, which has been sung by the wise throughout the ages and glimpsed by scientists in this modern age, that great, grand, awe-inspiring unity has come to be lived in our daily lives. Without such a powerful inner transformation, there could have been no transformation in our politics. But with such a change, politics could be nothing else than what it is today—a process of consensus building, a celebration of where we have been and where we are headed as a community, as a nation, and as a world.

Politics in 2050 is a chance for those among us who wish to serve, to serve. It is a chance to gather the best ideas, the best thinkers, and to allow the ablest among us to lead—and for us to follow, if we so choose, willingly and with great gratitude and alertness.

With this living reality, our politics could be nothing other than a mirror of who we are, an outer reflection of the higher consciousness of our own individual lives.

★★★

Robert Roth is the author of the political best-seller *A Reason to Vote*. He is a founding member of the Fair Elections Commission, a nonprofit, nonpartisan organization dedicated to election law reform and campaign finance reform. He is also the director of communications for the Natural Law party, America's fastest-growing grassroots political party.

THE PRESIDENCY

Barbara Marx Hubbard

It's the night of the presidential inauguration, 2009. We are in the White House with the new presidential team that has just transformed the political system of the United States.

The president is having a good time. Her beautiful red velvet gown shimmers in the candlelight while her long dark hair frames her intelligent face in casual splendor. Her vice president is standing behind her, recounting their amazing victory. It is a moment of reminiscence and celebration.

Something radical has just happened, despite the predictions of the pundits and the mass media. The presidential team has been swept into victory by an 11th-hour popular uprising. They developed a campaign so powerful at the grassroots level that they are being called the founding mothers and fathers of the next stage of democracy. They were the first team who could begin to appeal to the higher needs of an incipient majority for unity, compassion, and a comprehensive approach to the environmental crisis. They are basking in the glow of a truly great achievement.

Just as the experts had been astonished when the Berlin Wall came down in 1990, so now the pundits sit in stunned amazement at the White House celebration, speechless for once in the face of the vast social uprising that came forth during this campaign. Here are but a few highlights of what happened. The full history has yet to be written.

MAKING THE DECISION

In 2006, in the privacy of her heart, after deep contemplation and prayer, a woman made a critical decision. Eve Fuller (a fictional name) was a mother, an author, and a student of evolution, history, and social/spiritual change. She knew we were a global system at the edge of chaos. A small perturbation could transform the whole system, for good or for bad. Since it was a whole-system crisis, what was needed was a whole-system response. The American people needed a realistic vision of positive options for the future; not single examples of hope, caring, and success against the tide of despair, but innovations and breakthroughs that were interconnected and that together represented the natural evolutionary trend—the organizing intelligence of nature itself toward a more cooperative and life-enhancing world.

Eve's ideas had been shaped by Abraham Maslow's humanistic psychology that each of us has intrinsic growth needs for higher values and chosen, meaningful work; by Pierre Teilhard de Chardin's idea that God is at work in the process of evolution, leading to ever more complex systems with ever greater consciousness and freedom; and Buckminster Fuller's awareness that we have the resources, technology, and know-how to make this system work for everyone without damage to the environment.

Eve's profound indignation at the suffering of billions of people was combined with a passionate love of science, quantum physics, the space program, and the evolutionary significance of high technology as, potentially, an expansion of human consciousness and freedom. She saw that these new powers were preparing the way for our species to evolve from its self-centered, planet-bound, scarcity-ridden condition to its whole-centered, spirit-centered, literally universal phase.

She felt that the secular and the spiritual are fused in the deep human impulse to create and express the potential within each of us. She knew that everyone has a vital creative calling that is needed for the fulfillment of the person and the whole community. It seemed impossible in the competitive, commercial world to create a society in which people could express their life purposes in meaningful work,

THE PRESIDENCY • *Barbara Marx Hubbard*

since most of us are now trapped in jobs or roles that inhibit self-expression and deaden our souls. Yet Eve saw that this will become possible—indeed, natural—at the next stage of socioeconomic development, when people are reassembled in human-scale communities and the Knowledge Society/Solar Age matures.

This was the real opportunity that was brought for the first time on Earth to masses of people by an affluent and free society. Material goals, once achieved, do not fulfill the human spirit. They are not the end; they are the beginning of the next phase of human development. Eve envisioned a presidential campaign that could ride upon the crest of desire to self-actualize through meaningful life purpose.

CREATING LEADERSHIP

Once she had made her decision in the privacy of her heart, Eve's first step was to call her friends to help identify the best leaders in each key field, practical visionaries who had already manifested success in their work and who were well networked with others in their fields. She sought to form a transition team that would incorporate new paradigm thinkers and activists with establishment baby boom leaders who—as a result of entering their sixties, moved by inner spiritual awakenings, their children grown and their careers secure—were looking again toward the future. This coalition between establishment types and new paradigm leaders would be difficult to create. However, she felt that it would be possible due to the fact that the nation was at peace, China had developed a more democratic system and was no longer perceived as a threat, and everywhere people realized that the environmental crisis was the number one threat on Earth.

By 2006, moreover, there was enough consensus on new public policy and conflict prevention that she believed that more establishment types would be ready to learn from the new paradigm leaders. People like William Ford of Ford Motor Company, retired general Colin Powell, and former secretary of the treasury Larry Summers were already transitional leaders from the establishment.

The paradigm leaders were people like Dee Dickinson in education, who had put together the New Horizons for Learning Web site for innovations in mind/body/spirit education and was already reaching hundreds of thousands of teachers; Hazel Henderson in eco-economic and social policy; Paul Hawken and Amory and Hunter Lovins in environment and energy; former Republican congress-woman Claudine Schneider in spiritually motivated political action; Larry Dossey, Andrew Weil, and Deepak Chopra in alternative, in-tegrative, and complementary health and healing; Jean Houston in human potential; Lester Brown, Robert Kennedy Jr., and Thom Hartmann in environment; Marshall Rosenberg in compassionate communication and conflict resolution; Scott Peck in community building; citizen diplomat Rama Vernon and Joe Montville, formerly of the State Department, in conflict prevention and citizen diplomacy; Eleanor LeCain, Gordon Davidson, and Corinne McLaughlin in best practices; Peter Senge, Margaret Wheatley, and Dee Hock in organi-zational development; Neale Donald Walsch, best-selling author of *Conversations with God*, and Barbara Field Bernstein, master of orga-nization, in spirituality and religion; and many others.

Eve also contacted John Hagelin, quantum physicist and founder of the Natural Law party, which had been creating the largest third-party effort in U.S. history, collecting the millions of petition signa-tures required to be on the ballot in all 50 states, running thousands of candidates for local, state, and federal offices. For many years, he had asked people to "take ownership of the party." She knew that this party was founded by people who practice Transcendental Meditation and believe that the development of our full mental and emotional po-tential is the key to social change, and that over the years the party had expanded to embrace all forms of practical spirituality, seeking out so-cial innovations and solutions that would work in all fields.

She also asked Don Beck, author of *Spiral Dynamics*, who had charted the memetic codes that guide the behavior of different cul-tures and who had helped overcome apartheid in South Africa, to help them construct a new memetic code based on life-enhancing policies and social innovations in every field. (A meme is a self-replicating idea that guides the development of a culture, just as a gene informs the building of a body.)

Her list made, Eve invited these leaders to meet as the guests of a church where she had once spoken. Its motto was "Resolve to Evolve—The Only Solution Is Our Evolution." In the sanctuary of the church, she stood and bowed her head in silence. It was a sacred moment.

Eve lifted her head and said, "I propose that we form a presidential team to transform the American presidency and to set the pattern for the transformation of our society.

"This team is to be initiated by people like ourselves who are willing to spend enough time to learn what one another knows, to discover the synergies between our various initiatives, and to work together to develop an Evolutionary Agenda—the real, practical options for a positive future. Although we can reach into the past for the wisdom we have lost, we cannot go back. We can only move forward.

"The Agenda will seek to realize Abraham Maslow's hierarchy of needs applied to society: basic needs for food, security, shelter, self-esteem; growth needs for self-rewarding work of intrinsic value; and transcendent needs to be part of a larger whole and to go beyond the limitations imposed upon us by self-centered consciousness and a constricted view of our full personal, social, and technological potential. Our task is, at this stage, to link evolutionary, futuristic innovations that work with the best of existing environmental and social policies—to pull the whole system forward.

"Instead of playing adversarial politics, we will develop a 'politics of the whole.' We will form a Citizens' Coalition. Our motto will be 'Don't attack, attract.' The process of the campaign is the key, not only the policies, important as they are. Representative individualistic democracy has reached a limit. We need a more cooperative, participatory, synergistic democracy, a 'synocracy,' to fulfill the next phase of the American Revolution.

"We will invite people, regardless of party or ideology, to gather in large town meetings in the round, representing the community as a whole system. People will be invited to enter the sector of their choice—health, education, environment, economics, arts and media, and so on—to express their visions, their goals, their needs, and their personal desire to create in that field. We will facilitate them to seek common goals, match needs and resources, and find teammates to realize their vocations and projects. We will ask them about what they know is really working.

"I propose that we work with the Natural Law party, which is on the ballot in every district of the country. John Hagelin has already formed a national coalition of third parties, including the Greens and the Reform party, along with mainstream Republicans, Democrats, and those who do not vote because they do not believe it will make a difference."

She nodded in appreciation to John, who for almost two decades had dedicated himself to building this new political base. A look of relief and joy crossed his features. He bowed his head.

"We need only one more catalytic act to shift the tide of American politics," Eve concluded.

Her speech was met by silence. Finally, one of the listeners arose, a highly successful academic and author. "My dear," he said, "you have stated the case. You have set the goal. I have been waiting all my life for the chance to do this. I'm in!" One by one, all the guests, who had been well-selected, stepped forward and committed themselves to the great work ahead.

PREPARING THE MESSAGE

The team spent the next few months on the Internet and in occasional meetings, sharing their visions, their personal intuitions as to what is emergent and working, and how the various projects and programs interconnect as parts of a living system that is based on the scientific reality of underlying unity from which all of nature's evolutionary laws can be derived.

They acted as if they were already members of the cabinet of the United States that actually guides the nation. They solidified the vision, bringing the future into the present. They decided that they would offer themselves as a team, to dispel the fallacy that any one person knows how to save the world. They saw an essential role of government to be to empower, coordinate, and inspire the work and creativity of the people and grassroots organizations already working effectively on a small scale.

Eve was their presidential candidate. The first man to offer his support at the meeting, Dr. Alan Jones, was selected to be the vice presidential candidate. Three teams were set up: one for policy, another for participation and synergy, and a third for social innovations.

They then began the fascinating work of reaching out to projects that had already been working to change a whole system, like Mimi Silbert's Delancy Street Foundation in San Francisco, where ex-convicts and former drug addicts learn entrepreneurship and rarely return to prison; like microcredit loans for the very poor, which were begun in Bangladesh and are now spreading around the world; and like Deborah Myers's South Central School in Harlem, where 90 percent of the students go on to college.

They started to flesh out the Evolutionary Agenda based on these initiatives, which were already creating new possibilities.

Working with Eleanor LeCain, they developed an Internet site called the Peace Room to scan for, map, connect, and communicate the best innovations and practices in every field, to allow people who want to get involved to know what is working, who can be their mentors, and how to find their teammates right where they live. They declared that the Peace Rooms on Earth would one day be more sophisticated than the war rooms of the world.

The team connected all relevant hot links and leaders of networks of positive change in every field, devising the most exciting set of options for the American people that had ever been put together—a new American pragmatism, irresistibly attractive, practical yet visionary.

It was the first campaign for, of, and by what social analyst Paul Ray called "the cultural creatives," people whose values were already changing toward planetary consciousness, gender balance, sustainability, human rights, compassion, partnership, personal responsibility, social justice, nondenominational spirituality. At the end of the 20th century, they were an estimated 44 million strong, or one-fifth of the American population. Their numbers had since swelled, and they formed an incipient majority.

Eve believed that the campaign could gain immediate financial support from some of the founders of the high-tech era, those who had personal spiritual experience combined with the vision of resource-efficient economic growth and the intention to prevent further environmental destruction. She was grateful that the campaign finance laws had been changed and there was now full public sponsorship, including free media, and no soft money for the presidential race. The campaign was launched on CNN worldwide. (Eve was a good friend of Ted Turner's. He agreed boldly to give the campaign worldwide coverage.) The event was designed with the flair of a NASA space launch. The whole team was on the set, standing together.

Eve stood forward and said, "This is an announcement of the Campaign for a Positive Future. I am running with this team for the presidency of the United States of America. If you elect me, here are the people who will serve you with me. Our purpose is to provide to you, to every person in this country, the opportunity to participate in creating the world you choose.

"We will come to every region of the United States to meet you face-to-face and find out from you what is already working. We will invite you to gather in large town meetings in the round, to share with one another and with us what you want to create, what your needs are, and what resources you are willing to give.

"Our Peace Room on the Internet will map and track break-throughs from one part of the country to the next. We will ask that old military bases be used as situation rooms. Many retired military and corporate executives are offering to help design and monitor the vital signs of problems and solutions, of creativity and new possibilities in the United States. We are inviting our friends and neighbors in every country in the world to do the same. The Peace Room is open to the planet. In our first 4 years, we will have a full picture of the emerging world. This campaign is a call to bring together the greatest force for positive change that the world has ever seen."

A large wheel representing all sectors of society was visibly and graphically displayed on television. Innovators and projects already working were flashed on the screen and shown to be connected as vital parts of the whole system. Many of the social pioneers were gathered in the television studio, dramatically sharing their vision and practical solutions. Innovators came in by satellite to demonstrate the actions that were already working to educate, to clean the environment, to develop nonpolluting energy, to heal, to resolve conflict, and so on. The vice presidential candidate, followed by members of the proposed cabinet, stood forward and spoke, pointing to demonstrations to back up policies and initiatives.

Eve concluded her talk. "We can ensure that every new automobile gets 100 miles to the gallon, according to William Ford, our proposed energy secretary and former head of Ford Motors. We can save the world's rain forests, coral reefs, and oceans by shifting 2 percent of the defense budget to such goals without endangering national security, a plan to be implemented by Colin Powell, our proposed secretary of defense. We can focus on low-cost disease prevention rather than continue to waste money on high-cost cures, a new direction that can save $100 billion in the nation's medical bills, according to studies conducted by Andrew Weil and Dean Ornish, our nominated advisors to the Department of Health and Human Services.

"Come and join us in creating a positive future for yourself, your children, and your communities."

THE MOMENTUM OF CHANGE

The event was a spectacular success. It topped the ratings for that night, causing panic in the other campaigns. It no longer seemed cool to make your announcement all alone and pretend that you knew what to do. The other candidates began to seek out initiatives that were working. In fact, it became the new one-upmanship in American politics. Instead of fighting against one another, political candidates in the Democratic and Republican parties tried to gain attention by finding the most exciting innovations.

But Eve and the Citizens' Coalition were way ahead of the others. They were already networked to the vast civil society. The social-potential movement came alive. Musicians drew crowds to the town meetings in the round, which became combinations of revival meetings, country fairs, and Chautauquas.

Politicians of all kinds wanted to speak at the events. No one dared be left out. Teams of therapists and counselors assisted citizens who had been marginalized. They formed a Council of High Priority Needs and coached people who had been rejected to enter the process of change. Organizational Development consultants helped design and facilitate the synergistic meetings.

CNN covered the events live. Town meetings in the round spread like wildfire at the grassroots level. The meetings were like self-replicating cells of a new social life, working on the "3 P's": policy, projects, and process. They spread to other countries. In China, a mass movement appeared, attracting people to an effort to build a freely co-operative process to take them beyond the social failures of greed, pollution, and unemployment brought on by the early stage of capitalism. The meetings proclaimed the era of cooperation and creativity. The Communist party did not know whether they were to be feared or propagated.

Wherever town meetings occurred, permanent Positive Future Centers sprang up, serving as hubs for like-minded citizens to gather, support one another, pray together, and work to rebuild their communities. The candidates asked all centers, at every meeting, to visualize the victory of the Campaign for a Positive Future as already accomplished, to affirm that the people had won, that the team had been elected, and that Positive Future Centers were self-organizing throughout the world. Thousands of separate centers began every meeting with envisioning, praying for, and affirming the victory. The larger mass meditations for peace all predicated the campaign's victory.

The power of prayer was directly applied to healing social disease and promoting wellness throughout the land. The secular and the spiritual joined in one breath and one purpose, animating the people involved with a new spirit of hope and even happiness. Instead of rallying for a war effort or natural disaster, people were excited about coming together to create. Eve coined the saying, "Vocational arousal is sweeping the nation."

The team discovered that a community in Santa Barbara, California, had already pioneered tools and templates for any community to form a "more perfect union" where every person was called upon to make a contribution and where all levels of government and citizen groups were coordinating themselves for long-range, holistic environmental and social goals. The Santa Barbara cooperative worked around the clock, training facilitators from all over the country.

Although extreme right-wing conservatives were dismayed, and at first attempted to discredit the team, they were eventually disarmed because the programs and processes were in fact new ways to realize their goals of less government control and more responsibility at the local level. The team also attracted Libertarians, liberal baby boomers, disaffected voters from both main parties, and, above all, the young. This was their campaign, and they would win it! The momentum was irresistible.

There was a three-way race—as had happened years before for the governorship in Minnesota—between Eve and the team, a Democrat, and a Republican. The Citizens' Coalition won. In one profound moment, the United States returned—after a too-long hiatus—to being a beacon for the next stage of human freedom, a partner to people everywhere on Earth.

★★★

Barbara Marx Hubbard is a futurist and lecturer who has authored four books, most recently *Conscious Evolution: Awakening the Power of Our Social Potential*. Hubbard was placed in nomination for the vice presidency of the United States on the Democratic ticket in 1984, where she received more than 200 delegates' signatures to propose to the Convention a Peace Room in the office of the vice president. She is president of the Foundation for Conscious Evolution in Santa Barbara, California.

ACTIVISM

Sam Daley-Harris

WE AREN'T PASSENGERS ON SPACESHIP EARTH, WE'RE THE CREW. WE
AREN'T RESIDENTS ON THIS PLANET, WE'RE CITIZENS. THE DIFFERENCE
IN BOTH CASES IS RESPONSIBILITY.

—*Apollo astronaut Rusty Schweickart*

I believe that a friend of mine had it right when he said that one of our principal jobs in life is to leave the campsite cleaner than we found it. Imagine what America would look like if each and every American were seriously engaged in his or her own act of cleaning the campsite. Some might take on healing our fragile environment, and others might take on ending hunger and homelessness. Still others might focus on transforming our schools, especially for those who are most often left behind. I really believe that if every American embraced this idea, there wouldn't be enough problems to go around.

So why don't we? Why does it seem that there are too many problems to tackle and that one individual can't make a difference? Is it that we don't know much about the problems we face and the opportunities that exist to solve them?

I grappled with these questions more than 20 years ago when I first got involved in ending world hunger. I had lived in Miami all of my life. I was 31 years old, had studied music, taught high school, and played percussion instruments in the Miami Philharmonic for a dozen years. None of these are major credentials for a budding career as an activist. To make matters worse, I felt absolutely hopeless about solving any global problem. So what were the steps that took me from hopelessness to action?

In 1977, I went to a presentation on the Hunger Project. Up until that point, I hadn't thought about world hunger much, but when I did, I was quite sure that hunger was inevitable, mostly because there were no solutions. It had to be that way, because if there were solutions, they certainly would have been implemented. But at the presentation it became clear that there was no mystery about growing food, becoming literate, and gaining access to clean water, better health, and nutrition. When I looked at it honestly, I discovered that I was not actually hopeless about the perceived lack of solutions. No, what I felt hopeless about was human nature! People just couldn't be counted on to do the things that could be done to end hunger. I also realized that there was one human nature that I did have control over—my own.

This was an epiphany for me, and it forced me to confront my whole relationship with commitment. Up until that point, for me, commitment had a kind of "I will if you will" ring to it. "I'll recycle if you will," I might think. "Oh, you won't? Then I won't either." But at that moment, commitment began to shift from an "I will if you will" to an "I will whether you will or not."

The hopelessness I carried was not unique to me. We all have our own versions of it. And we must face the sluggish, sticky ugliness of the hopelessness we carry around if we are to make any headway. So start with Step 1: Get in touch with your commitment to serve, your commitment to leave the campsite cleaner than you found it. You might do this by remembering a time when you were moved by some simple act of kindness, from one person to another or from one person to many others. You might think about a time when you were moved by one person's courage, perhaps a person of limited means or limited power having the courage to take a stand.

Then go to Step 2: Face a problem that concerns you, preferably something about which you could feel passionate—something that lights you up. If nothing comes up at first, that's probably an indication of deep resignation about addressing local, national, or global problems. Don't worry, you are exactly where you should be. Give it some time and thought.

That will immediately lead you to Step 3: Face the hopelessness you feel about the problem. Maybe you were very active in the past but have given up in some way. Your inaction or limited action on the problem is probably a symptom of your hopelessness.

Step 4: Look for solutions. This step requires a little research. What is the best thinking on the problem? What ideas or interventions could make a real difference if people got behind them?

Try this one on. UNICEF, the United Nations Children's Fund, states that each day, 30,500 children die from largely preventable malnutrition and disease. Yes, that's 30,500 children dying every day, and yes, from largely preventable malnutrition and disease (such as malnutrition coupled with measles or malnutrition coupled with pneumonia). I know, it's very hard to let something like this in. Recently, I had a glimpse of what it might mean.

A few weeks before beginning this essay, Washington, D.C., the city where I live, was hit by a snowstorm that was followed days later by an ice storm. While carrying my 22-month-old son, Micah, I stepped off the curb and slipped, and both of us fell to the icy pavement. He was unhurt, but he could have suffered a severe, even fatal, injury. In the days following that fall, every time that I let myself consider the worst-case scenario, waves of grief swept over me. I know that the 30,500 sets of parents who will lose their children today feel a far deeper grief than I felt at just the thought of losing my beautiful son.

What would it cost to save most of these lives? Maybe a few cents' worth of measles vaccine, maybe a dollar's worth of antibiotics. These figures make the following statement by retired Oregon senator Mark Hatfield even more prophetic. Speaking in 1984, at the height of the nuclear freeze movement, Senator Hatfield said, "We stand by as children starve by the millions because we lack the will to eliminate hunger. Yet we have found the will to develop missiles capable of flying over the polar cap and landing within a few hundred feet of their target. This is not innovation. It is a profound distortion of humanity's purpose on earth."

Think about it. We live in a country in which the will to develop missiles is much stronger than the will to save millions of children each year. That's something worth getting passionate about. And isn't that one of the major reasons we are here, to find and correct profound distortions of humanity's purpose on Earth?

This inevitably leads you to Step 5: See the warrior inside of you, the person of courage that maybe you've never really expressed. You'll need to connect with your courage because you'll face constant pressure from yourself, friends, and the culture to not get involved or to give up when things get hard.

Here is another way to look at the kind of courage I'm talking about. For the last few years, I have been director of the Microcredit Summit Campaign. It is an effort to reach, by the year 2005, 100 million of the world's poorest families, especially the women of those families, with credit for self-employment and other financial and business services. I have a small, young staff. Whenever I do an interview with a prospective staff member, I let them know what I am looking for in an employee. The first thing I say is that I am looking for someone who is committed to expressing his or her greatness. "What does that mean to you," I ask, "and when have you expressed your greatness?" It is fascinating to see how people react to that question and hear how they respond.

For me, expressing your greatness is doing something that you can't see yourself doing. It's going beyond your perceived limits. There is an anonymous quote that begins to touch the place about which I'm talking. "Be outrageous. It's the only place that isn't crowded."

So you've 1) gotten in touch with your commitment to serve, 2) faced a problem that concerns you, 3) faced the hopelessness you feel about the problem, 4) looked for solutions, and 5) connected with your courage. That logically leads you to Step 6: Find others to work with, both locally and, if it's a national or international problem, with an institution and people that are working at that level. In other words, don't do it alone. If you try to do it alone, you'll never make it.

I moved through these six steps and started a journey that I could never have predicted. In 1978, I began speaking to high school classes about world hunger. Between 1978 and 1979, I spoke to 7,000 high school students. In preparation for my first presentation, I read statements from Jimmy Carter's Commission on Hunger and from the National Academy of Sciences Food and Nutrition Study calling for the "political will" to end hunger. At that point, I wasn't sure what political will was, but I knew it might start with a basic awareness of who represented us in Washington. So I asked that first high school class to tell me the name of their representative in Congress. I was shocked to learn that only 4 out of 28 knew the answer. So I asked the next class, and none of the students knew. Do you have any idea how many of the 7,000 students knew their U.S. representative's name? Two hundred.

I started RESULTS, a citizens' lobbying organization dedicated to creating the political will to end hunger, as a result of this gap between the studies calling for the political will to end hunger and my experience with these 7,000 students. When things got difficult, the experience with these 7,000 students served as part of my foundation, part of my grounding. It gave me a direct sense of what needed to be done. We had to find a way to generate political will. We had to teach the skills of democracy and acquaint people with their government, starting at the most basic level.

That was in 1980. Due largely to RESULTS' leadership, U.S. government funding for UNICEF and the Child Survival Fund (a foreign-assistance program focused on basic health measures like child vaccinations) has grown from $42 million per year in 1984 to about $455 million a year in 2000. Child death rates have declined from 41,000 a day in 1986 to 30,500 today, saving some three million young lives each year. This is real progress, but the child death rates are still scandalously high.

Michael Rubinstein, a RESULTS volunteer leader in Maryland, tells of his first RESULTS International Conference in 1986 and provides a glimpse into how this shift in priority and funding occurred. He describes a Congressional staff panel on increasing the Child Survival Fund from $25 million to $75 million.

"The Hill staffers told us we shouldn't ask for more money," Michael remembered. "We were lucky, they told us, if we got a slight increase. If we asked for the full $50-million increase, we would just alienate members of Congress.

"The message that the Hill staffers shared with us had no impact whatsoever," Michael continued. "The 300 RESULTS partners in the room listened carefully, asked questions, were polite and respectful—even enthusiastic. But they were completely unmoved by the discouragement. Nothing was going to stand in the way of our vision. Children were dying and they needed vaccines. The politics were irrelevant. I have seen too many starry-eyed, pie-in-the-sky dreamers. But this was different. Behind the vision was a hard-nosed practicality."

Michael saw the hard-nosed practicality when one of the RESULTS staff asked him to call the local television affiliates to try to get a viewer commentary. "I said, 'Gulp,'" Michael recalled. "I was familiar with the idea. I remembered an episode of *All in the Family* in which Archie did a viewer commentary opposing gun control. It had never occurred to me that I could do such a thing. The idea terrified me. It took me about 3 days to screw up the courage before I called the three stations. Amazingly, the NBC affiliate accepted my script."

Michael faced his next challenge, looking presentable. "At the time," Michael recalled, "I was never much into looking good. I was young and never took myself very seriously. I looked into my closet and found a navy blue blazer that had been lent to me by an acquaintance in college. He had never come back to pick it up. I noticed that I had a pair of blue pants that matched the color perfectly. I now had a suit. I had just gotten a haircut for the occasion, cutting my 'Jewish Afro' really short. I put on a necktie, a very rare occurrence for me, and made myself look as good as I could.

"I went to the station at the appropriate time," Michael continued, "sat down in the chair, my throat dry, looked into the camera, and said, with all the passion I could muster, that the deaths of 3.5 million children each year due to vaccine-preventable diseases is a holocaust of staggering proportions.

"Then they flashed my completed viewer editorial up on the television monitor. I saw my name and my town on the screen, below a face I didn't recognize. There was this respectable young man, a community spokesman, up there on the screen, speaking in strong terms about an important issue of the day. I had never seen myself in that light before, and I have never been the same since."

As Michael's television editorial was airing, the last of 90 newspaper editorials in support of increasing the Child Survival Fund was published. Congress got the message and agreed to the full $50-million increase. What did the additional $50 million mean? In 1986, UNICEF estimated that it cost $5 to fully immunize a child, from manufacture of the vaccines to injection. As a result of this $50-million increase, 10 million children would be immunized, saving, by UNICEF's conservative estimate, 125,000 young lives. Fourteen years later, U.S. government funding is more than five times greater, helping to save millions of lives annually.

This progress occurred because of actions like Michael's. His story is about who we are as problem solvers—people who overcome their hopelessness and act as spiritual warriors committed to service. It is an example of what America could be in the 21st century: a nation that cares not only for itself but for all of humanity.

Some of you might ask: Aren't our elected officials the ones to take responsibility for the state of our planet and its people? I think Apollo astronaut Rusty Schweickart answered this question best when he said, "We aren't passengers on spaceship Earth, we're the crew."

But most of us see ourselves as passengers, not as crew, in the mission of stewarding the health of this planet and its people. At about the time that Michael was doing his television editorial, a number of us began to get up out of our passenger seats, walk to the cockpit, and realize . . . there was nobody up there.

Those cockpit seats are *our* seats. This essay is about the migration to the cockpit of ordinary citizens. I have tried to show how some of us have started and how the rest of us can follow.

My journey took me and others into civic and political action. That may not be your path; it might be hands-on work instead. But don't let the rage that most people feel about government and politics keep you from working in that arena if you feel pulled there. I think that Israeli diplomat Abba Eban touched upon our deep discouragement with politics when he said, "Governments can be counted on to do the right thing, but only after they have exhausted all other possibilities."

What Michael Rubinstein and his colleagues were doing was making sure governments did the right thing without wasting so much time.

Be true to yourself. Get involved. Listen to your thoughts and feelings. If you feel a need to pull back, decide whether it's because it's hard or because it doesn't feel true. Listen to the latter, not the former. Remember the words of futurist Buckminster Fuller, who said, "The things to do are the things that need doing, that you see need to be done, and that no one else seems to see need to be done."

Then answer this question: Isn't it time to find your way of leaving the campsite cleaner than you found it?

★★★

Sam Daley-Harris is the founder of RESULTS, a nonpartisan citizens' lobbying group that fights hunger, poverty, and death due to preventable disease. He is the author of *Reclaiming Our Democracy: Healing the Break Between People and Government.* Currently, he directs the Microcredit Summit Campaign.

THE FUTURE

Margaret J. Wheatley

I am on Lake Powell in the southwest United States, drifting along the borders of Utah and Arizona, thinking about America's next 50 years. I am floating in deep redrock canyons that are several hundred millions of years old. Whenever I look up from my computer, I see awesome slickrock wantonly displaying its entire evolutionary history. These rocks are here today because the beaches of ancient seas were compressed into sedimentary rock that formed into thousands of layers that were then uplifted by massive earth upheavals to form these towering red mountains, which were then carved into canyons by relentless rivers only 10 million years ago. I tell you this just to keep things in perspective.

Lake Powell highlights more than evolutionary time—it was created by human imagination wedded to unwavering arrogance. In the 1950s, American engineers proceeded to dam up several canyons and rivers in order to produce electricity, create reservoirs, and develop recreational areas. Lake Powell was created by flooding Glen Canyon; next on the list to be dammed was the Grand Canyon (!). We were spared that incomprehensible act because of public outrage at the loss of Glen Canyon.

Lake Powell is a dramatic testament to the troubling American impulse to use our technology and daring to coerce nature to our own purposes, our belief that the planet is here for whatever use we can make of it. And while the redrocks of Powell speak to the planet's history of creative forces, they also alert us to the ahistoric moment we occupy now. For the first time, the consequences of our acts affect the entire planet, all peoples and all beings. As I imagine what the next 50 years might bring, I know that we either will have learned to be responsible planetary stewards of our human creativity, or will have wreaked unimaginable havoc on our only home.

We have never been at this point before. Human imagination has given us powers unlike anything in the past. Our immediate challenge is to deal with the consequences of human imagination, and to use this special gift of the human species on behalf of all life. (But whatever happens to us, the rocks will continue their cycle of emergence and disintegration.)

Human imagination thrives in the United States; we entice everyone to our shores with its magic. As a nation, we have given the world many things, but our keen defense of individual freedom has allowed imagination to soar and to explore the limitless sky of human creativity. Nowhere else have I experienced the boundless sense of possibility that is so easily available in Americans. We are the most optimistic nation on Earth, and people risk everything to get here so that they might breathe in this great space of possibility.

During the next 50 years, we need to keep making this gift of human imagination available to the world. But our particular challenge as a nation is to use our creativity to embrace and support every living thing, not just a few of us. We will need to both raise and resolve these questions: How will we use our gift of human imagination? Who do we need to be?

Lake Powell is not my only companion as I think about these questions. I am spending the week on a 54-foot houseboat with 13 boys between the ages of 15 and 20. Lest you doubt my sanity or survivability, know that I learned a long time ago that my teenage sons move as a clan, comfortable and happy only when surrounded by friends. This vacation was planned for the clan, not our family, and I am having a wonderful time on this houseboat in this redrock landscape, tuning in to life as seen by strong, creative, young American men.

The future depends on our young men and young women. In 50 years, they will be 65 to 70 years old. I expect they will not even know what "retirement" means; that concept will have long disappeared by then. This America I am trying to imagine is really theirs to create. What they do in the next five decades will be the determinant. The world they will have created by then will be the world their grandchildren inherit.

As soon as I realize that I am surrounded on this houseboat by one of the generations responsible for the future, I put aside my notes and ask if we can talk. Some are already gathered in the cabin and I ask them to tell me what they imagine for the future. When they are 65, what do they hope the world will be? Within minutes of beginning this conversation, other boys flock in, and soon all 13 teenagers are gathered around. For the next hour, I just listen to them, honored that they want to be in this conversation with me. I revel in how intent they are, how no one drifts out of the room, how much they love being asked their views on something this big and important, how most of them have very strong views about the future, how they're in this conversation with one another, not just me.

This is what I hear them say: They want less hate. They fear for the planet. They want robots to do dull work. They want schools to stop being so awful. They expect pure (electronic) democracy by then. They want to stop violence. They want to stop being desensitized by the media to violence, suffering, warfare. They want families, and they want to be loving, supportive parents. They want to stop taking America for granted.

I ask them, What do you hope for? They reply: I want to know I've given my best, no matter what. I want a lot less negativity. I want the Second Coming of Christ. I want to know that I have encouraged another human being. I want children. I'm afraid to have children. I want something to happen that will unite us as humans—maybe this will happen if we make contact with extraterrestrials. I want to end the greed of corporations. I want to teach my family good values. I believe one person can make a difference, like Gandhi did. I don't think one person can do anything. I want us to stop being hypocrites and take responsibility for our own behavior.

Who are these children, these 13 beings camped in a houseboat among ancient redrocks looking into the future they will help create? They are wonderfully American: Among them is one South African immigrant, one first-generation American with parents from Argentina and the Cherokee and Chickasaw nations, many of northern and southern European descent, one with Choctaw nation ancestors, and one descendant of U.S. general and president Ulysses S. Grant. President Grant's descendant has had a very difficult life and is in foster care; many of the others, including my two sons, are children of divorce. Socioeconomic status ranges from struggling to making ends meet to easy affluence.

And they are representative of America in other ways. We all agree that we are living the American paradox. We know that the things we do are destructive to the planet or use too many of the world's resources, and yet we can't stop living the life we live. We want to help the environment, but every day of this vacation, we're burning up 30 gallons of carbon-based fuels to play on our Jet Skis. We want a world that works for all, but we willingly consume far too much of the world's resources, as evident by our daily three bags of garbage. We know that the Earth is running out of critical resources such as water, but we ourselves run out of water on the boat because we don't appropriately monitor our usage. We want everyone in this world to enjoy a better life, but we can't stop ourselves from living the good life, which we know is destructive to others.

One other thing I notice about them, not only in this conversation, is the quality of their relationships. Instead of the anticipated contesting, competing, and generally expected macho behavior, I observe consistent levels of support and concern. When one young man freezes on a cliff, paralyzed by vertigo, three others work with him patiently and lovingly to help him down. Vertigo strikes a second time on another hike, and again I witness an intense desire to help him. These incidents are never brought up, never thrown in his face.

They don't even notice how different they are from earlier generations, when competition kept us separate from one another. At night, they sit on the roof of the boat and write music together. There's no sense of individual ownership. One person develops a musical theme, others chime in with their instruments, and the banter back and forth is playful, excited, complementary to one another.

They love to create together—I watch them composing together, coaching and teaching each other, admiring one another's talents. I admire their talents also. One is a genius at creating Web sites; several are musicians; two are writers; four of them play high school football and are strong athletes. All in all, they are funny, talented, and astonishingly convivial—with me, one another, and any adults who will pause to talk with them.

I am also surprised by their sensitivity to human psychology. They seem to know what's going on at deeper levels, and they use this awareness to explain one another's motivations—why any one is doing what he's doing. When any two start arguing or get angry at each other, there are others who step forward to help them work it out. I'm amazed at how well they process things—listening to all sides, figuring out ways to move into new behaviors, creating compromises. They are far more skilled than many adults I know.

Most of these children are embodiments of American optimism: They believe in themselves, one another, and the future. But they do not seem to act from the same fierce nationalism that has plagued many earlier generations, including mine. Their hearts are more wide open. The world they know is much smaller than the one I grew up in. They are connected to children all over the world through a global culture of music, movies, and sports. Many of us have (quite rightly) decried the loss of local cultures and the Americanization of the planet, but when I observe how easily my sons talk with teens they meet in Brazil or Zimbabwe or Europe, I realize that something good is happening as well. They don't have the concept of "foreigner." Their world isn't filled with strangers—they can instantly talk about a musician or a movie and have an energetic conversation where cultural differences dissolve. They live in a world that feels connected, not Americanized. It is impossible to motivate them by calling for traditional patriotism.

In the 50 years these children have to create something new, they can't create anything but a networked, boundaryless world. My generation has tossed this idea around, but these kids live it. Even when they develop into tight groups, cliques, and gangs, they know that there's a big world out there as close as their CD player, TV, or computer screen.

So are my boat companions a "normal" group of teen-agers, those to whom I have entrusted America's and the planet's future? I hope so. I think these kids are quite typical, and I feel extraordinarily privileged to have lived with them so intimately for 6 days. Here is what I want to say to them.

Thank you for letting me see you. Thank you for being people that it's fun to be with, to think with, to dream with. Thank you above all for not taking at face value what my generation has believed and tried so hard to teach you. We would have you believe that the world is ruled by competition, that only the strong survive, that you must look out always and only for yourself, that to survive in this world you must practice deceit, greed, selfishness, and violence. We haven't taught you about honor, sustainability, community, or compassion. We've failed to show you how to be wise stewards of the Earth, how to care for one another, how to resolve conflicts peacefully, how to enjoy others' creativity as well as your own.

Yet, miraculously, you are learning these things! These more humane capacities have captured your attention, more than our incessant messages to the contrary. Maybe you're reacting to watching your parents' compulsive pursuit of self-interest and individualism. Maybe you're expressing the fundamental need of humans to be together. (As a species, we humans have struggled to live together more than we have fought to be apart.)

I am excited that you seem to be figuring it out for yourselves. I only want to encourage you in the direction you're already moving. If you pay attention to certain strengths that you already have, then I believe the future we talked about is truly possible.

Here is one strength that I see: You know how to enjoy one another's gifts. You don't feel diminished by one another's talents. You take delight if one of you is a great guitarist, one writes terrific songs, one doesn't like music but loves computers, one plays sports, one plays computer games. You don't need to be alike. You seem to know that your diverse talents are your collective strength. I love how you revel in your diversity—this is something that other generations never figured out. If you keep reveling in how individual uniqueness adds to your collective ability, you will have moved past one of the most troubling issues of this time, when there are more than 60 wars going on in only 230 nations. Maybe you will be the ones to help all humans take the leap toward greater human diversity.

Another strength: You need one another. I believe that we adults have inadvertently helped you here—we have ignored you, denied you, seen you as a problem. You learned to stay together because other generations couldn't or wouldn't invite you to join them. You learned to support one another when older people withdrew from you. (Outside of Columbine High School, you huddled in one another's arms, guiding yourselves into sudden adulthood in a world where violence was random but did make sense.)

I believe that you understand more about the terrors of separation than I do—you experience so much violence, so much stereotyping, so much exclusion, that you must know feeling separate does terrible things to the human spirit. I hope you can carry that awareness with you into adulthood—I hope you are the ones that hold onto one another and refuse to move into the competitive space of feeling better than, feeling different from, feeling holier than. To succeed where all we others have failed, you will have to hold on to your present sense of outrage over exclusion, and turn that anger into compassion. You will have to keep your hearts open rather than contract them. You will have to help rather than judge the kids all around you who choose to protect themselves by forming exclusionary groups. I hope you remember, as you said on the boat, that you can't solve violence with more violence.

Another strength: You love creating and you claim that freedom. You do not tolerate nearly as much confinement or as many rules and repressive structures as I and your parents did. You walk away from disrespectful employers, boring work, uninteresting activities. As parents, we have been quick to criticize you—we fear that you have no work ethic, no standards, no values. But you make me hopeful, because your refusal to conform and comply might save you from being diminished. I see you standing up for who you are. I see you reclaiming the freedom and respect that every human spirit requires if it is to flourish. If you are successful here, you will have claimed a future where many more people feel welcome to offer their unique creative gifts.

Here is something I'm not sure you know. These three strengths must work together. Things go terribly wrong when only one is emphasized. Many generations and civilizations have failed because they supported only one of these essential aspects of human nature. In America, we have fought to develop and sustain individual freedom, and we have ended up with a litigious society where everyone knows their "rights," but few know how to be in community. Many indigenous cultures honor the diversity of individual gifts but hold those gifts as belonging to the community. Individuals are not free to express themselves as they might want; they are there to serve the community, not themselves. Many societies know the human need to be together, but they build up their collective by separating themselves, drawing hard barriers between themselves and others. This is the world you grew up in, a world populated by enemies and strangers, where ethnic wars, genocides, and border conflicts predominate.

And now it's your turn to experiment with the mystery of human society. What will be its next form? You may be the ones who learn how to weave these three strengths together: a swirling spiral of our unique gifts, our desire for community, and our need for individual freedom. If you figure this out, we will move forward as a planetary community where people experience what it means to be fully human. I believe that this is the next evolutionary leap of our species—how to take our diversity, our personal freedom, and our creativity and use it to create a planetary community where all life can flourish. No generation before you has figured this out, but we've chronicled our experiences and they are there to help you.

These three human strengths are not particular to Americans—they are common human longings—but because you are maturing in America, you have the gift of freedom and the opportunity to explore them, to observe them, and to learn from others. In that way, you are unique, and if you succeed, you will be creating a new world for all, not just for Americans. And I know you already know that.

In 50 years, maybe you'll be back on Lake Powell, being with the redrocks. If the lake is still here functioning as a healthy ecosystem, that will be the first sign that you have succeeded. And if you are still friends who want to be together, that will be the sign that you have truly succeeded.

You may be the ones. I pray that you are.

★★★

Margaret J. Wheatley writes, teaches, and speaks about new practices and ideas for organizing in chaotic times. She is president of the Berkana Institute, a charitable global foundation, and was an organizational consultant for many years as well as a professor of management in two graduate programs. Her work appears in two award-winning books, *Leadership and the New Science* and *A Simpler Way* (coauthored with Myron Kellner-Rogers).

About the Photography

Joseph Sohm

My profession is my passion. Since the early 1980s, I've been photographing all things American: big cities, small towns, lush landscapes, and the people of all colors who comprise our nation. The tools of my trade are the required cameras, film, tripod, a rental car with unlimited mileage, and an airline ticket to Anywhere, U.S.A.

Mostly, I shoot America on a good day. The photographs I took for this book required bright sunny days, deep blue skies, and ideally, white puffy clouds. If the sun came out, I would shoot all day. Summer shooting results in 16-hour days. I wake up 45 minutes before sunrise to capture the "pink moment" and quit 30 minutes after the final, fading sunset glow. In between, I drive 200 to 300 miles, scout locations for future tripod holes, send film to labs, and clean my lenses.

I am often asked, Where did you find that picture? My response is, I don't find pictures. They find me. When I'm deciding what to shoot, many elements must magically align themselves in a unique arrangement: the quality of light, time of day, main subject matter and background, choice of lens and film, and, most important, where I decide to stand. That fifteenth-of-a-second exposure can be preceded by hours of forethought. If I approach an image mentally, the options are staggering. If I work intuitively, the image unfolds organically. As Michael Jordan has said about shooting baskets, "I wait for the shots to come to me."

My most important tool in this process is an understanding of where we come from. As a former American history teacher, I believe that history is the pathway to the future. If I listen to America with all of my senses and not just my eyes, I hear American voices past and present speaking to me.

While shooting Monticello, I became fascinated with Thomas Jefferson's vision of the American empire stretching from sea to shining sea. Jefferson acted on his dream by presiding over the Louisiana Purchase in 1803. In 1804, he commissioned Meriwether Lewis to explore the vast frontier separating the Mississippi River from the Pacific Ocean. Lewis became President Jefferson's eyes, and the Lewis and Clark expedition became the greatest American adventure prior to Neil Armstrong's walk on the moon.

As I was setting up my tripod to shoot Jefferson's futuristic 18th-century home, I realized that Jefferson had to rely on Lewis's written description of the American landscape. If only Lewis had had a camera! Fortunately, I do. With Jefferson in spirit and my cameras in hand, I have crisscrossed America in search of the towns, events, and landscapes that define who we are as a nation and a people. Spanning 20 years, I have witnessed firsthand what Thomas Jefferson could only imagine. Sometimes with maps, often with none, I mostly listen to America for my guidance on where to go and what to shoot. The guidance always comes.

★★★

Joseph Sohm's photographs of America are seen regularly in such publications as *National Geographic*, *Newsweek*, *Time* magazine, the *New York Times*, and the *Los Angeles Times* as well as in advertising for companies including IBM, Ford, AOL, Microsoft, Sony, Kodak, Merrill Lynch, Apple Computer, and Chrysler. His photographs have been exhibited in various American embassies by the U.S. Department of State, at New York's Neikrug Gallery, and at the Ira Robert Gallery in Los Angeles. He was President Clinton's campaign photographer for the Democratic National Committee and conceived of, photographed, and coproduced the official MTV presidential inaugural video *Portrait of Change*. For information on his work, visit VisionsofAmerica.com.

412

About the
Global Renaissance Alliance

All author proceeds from the sale of *Imagine* will go to the Global Renaissance Alliance, a nonprofit, citizen-based network of spiritual activists. Our mission is to make a stand in our local and national communities for the role of spiritual principle in solving the problems of the world.

We feel that a holistic political conversation—one honoring the powers of mind and spirit to help heal the world—is emerging throughout the global community. The Global Renaissance Alliance embodies its vision through small gatherings of citizens called Citizen Circles. Meeting in living rooms, at churches, around campfires, or anywhere else, we are joined with others of like mind in meditating for world peace; speaking from our hearts about our wishes for a better world; and working together to make it so. Within the Citizen Circle, we commit to cultivating an intimate fabric of deep community, and through our individual and joint efforts to create real change in ourselves and the world around us. Dedicated to the divine love in ourselves and in one another, we seek to extend the principles of forgiveness, atonement, reverence for life, faith, service, and compassion into the political and social dynamic of our times.

To learn more about our work, to start a Citizen Circle in your community, or to join others in existing circles, contact us at:

The Global Renaissance Alliance
P.O. Box 3259
Centerline, MI 48015 U.S.A.
General information: (541) 890-4716
Office: (810) 754-8105
Fax: (810) 754-8106
Web site: www.renaissancealliance.org
E-mail: info@renaissancealliance.org

To continue exploring the topics in this book, order the *Imagine* newsletter and visit the *Imagine* section of the GRA Web site. There you will find follow-up pieces to these essays, links to organizations involving our contributors and their work, actions you can take to apply the ideas presented here, and discussion boards where you can exchange your ideas with others.